MASTERPLOTS
FIFTEEN-VOLUME
COMBINED EDITION

Volume Three
Char-Deat

Masterplots

DIGESTS OF WORLD LITERATURE

FIFTEEN-VOLUME COMBINED EDITION

VOLUME THREE
CHAR-DEAT

Edited by FRANK N. MAGILL   Story Editor DAYTON KOHLER

CURTIS BOOKS
A division of
The Curtis Publishing Company
Philadelphia • New York

CHARLES DEMAILLY

Type of work: Novel
Authors: Edmond (1822-1896) and Jules (1830-1870) de Goncourt
Type of plot: Naturalism
Time of plot: Mid-nineteenth century
Locale: Paris
First published: 1860

Principal characters:
CHARLES DEMAILLY, a young author
MARTHE MANCE, an actress whom he marries
NACHETTE, a journalist and critic
COUTURAT, another journalist
REMONVILLE, Charles' friend, a writer
CHAVANNES, Charles' boyhood friend

Critique:

Charles Demailly, originally published as Les Hommes de Lettres, is among the early works of the Goncourt brothers, whose novels were of great importance in the development of naturalism. Their joined effort to convey contemporary life in all its details is shown here in a realistic dissection of the world of letters, and their interest in the secrets behind man's behavior and in the undiscovered or overrefined aspects of both personality and society led them to depict the impact of this world on a hypersensitive young writer. The course of the story is interwoven with discussions from many points of view on art and literature.

The Story:

A new kind of literary world came into being in Paris during the mid-nineteenth century. This world was that of the journals, the little newspapers which thrived on gossip and superficial aesthetic criticism by creating, or catering to, the shifting fads of the fashionable world yet debasing tastes through a concentration on personality, modishness, and sensationalism.

Two young men among the writers for Scandal, one of these journals, were thoroughly immersed in their world. Nachette, a belligerent, clever man who had fled his father's bad name in his home province, enjoyed the power, which he felt the journals possessed, to create or ruin a reputation. Couturat, hiding behind a mask of innocence and gaiety, was a thorough opportunist. Also among the group was Charles Demailly, who disliked these dilettantes and their trivial gossiping but seemed unable to do anything more than observe them ironically as he accompanied them to cafés, salons, and balls.

Charles, after many illnesses as a child, had grown up a nervous and acutely sensitive young man. The heightened perceptivity of all his senses extended to an unusual awareness of emotional nuances in those around him. This oversensitivity, however, kept him from finding satisfaction in real life. His search for perfection always met his uncanny ability to perceive imperfection- pleasure for him paled at the slightest false note. Even in writing, his real refuge, his hypersensitivity was a handicap, for his meticulously keen observation and attention to detail almost precluded true depth and greatness.

A letter from an old friend, Chavannes, urged Charles to visit him in the country and settle down to serious writing. Although Charles declined the invitation, he did shut himself up to work on his novel. At last his book, La Bourgeoisie, was finished but his late friends of Scandal, irritated because he had deserted them and jealous of his potential success, decided to harm him. Scarcely bothering to read the book, they ignored its attempt to convey psychological reality. Instead, they used the title as an excuse to generalize wittily on it as an inept social document. Full of anguish at this criticism, Charles wandered about the streets until he met Boisroger, a poet who cared nothing for the fripperies of society. Seeing the worth of the novel, he introduced Charles to a circle of men who were truly artists in various fields. Charles, happy among these vivid, intelligent people, admired greatly their individualism and their informed opinions on art and literature.

Charles' uncle died, leaving him feeling bereft. A discussion of the nature of love led some of his friends to assert that the artist cannot be a true husband or lover; other men seek in love what the artist finds only in creation.

These two factors may have predisposed Charles to fall in love himself as a protest against the loneliness which his friends felt inevitable. At the theater he saw a charming young ingénue, Marthe, and fell violently in love with her. At last he met her at a masquerade ball; three months later they were married.

For a time they created a blissful world in which only they existed. Marthe entranced Charles with her affection and endearing, childlike ways. Charles worked secretly on a play whose heroine captured Marthe's coquettish innocence. Finding his hidden work, Marthe was enraptured by it because the role was so well suited to her. Charles, delighted by her appreciation, failed to look beneath the surface and assumed, in his idealization of her, that she was actually the character he had created.

After Marthe had read an article by the now fashionable Nachette, criticizing Charles' work, she suggested that he find a collaborator to help him with the play. Realizing that she cared only for his reputation and its effect on her own, and not for his work, Charles began to see her as she really was: an insensitive chatterbox, full of false sentiment and other people's ideas. Marthe, too, had tired of her sweet role. Now she tried another, the woman who despises her husband for the love he bears her, who delights in violent changes of mood and becomes wholly self-absorbed.

His distress at his disillusionment and Marthe's behavior made Charles ill, and the couple went to stay at a provincial spa so that he might recover. Charles rejoiced in the placid beauty of the country. Marthe, bored, posed as the martyred wife. Refusing to leave, she showed her pique in subtle ways. Her banality and insincerity further tortured Charles; but the growing knowledge that she no longer loved him was even worse, for it threatened to destroy what remained of the image he had created.

At a country fête they met the group from *Scandal*, and the visitors returned to dine with them. Nachette, however, stayed on for a week. Shortly afterward a mock play in which a sweet ingénue was held prisoner by a neurasthenic appeared in *Scandal*. Charles was hurt, not by the silly play but by knowing that Marthe had deliberately created the impression on which it was based.

Charles grew well enough to return to Paris. There, however, events combined to break him down again. He first discovered that his wife had borrowed money, ostensibly because he was a madman who never gave her any. In retaliation for his indignation at her falsehoods, she announced that she was leaving her role in his play, which had gone into rehearsal. At length, trying to create a scene, she told him that she loved Nachette. When he refused to give her the opportunity for histrionics, she walked out.

Next day she returned, stricken with remorse, and almost succeeded in captivating Charles again by her winsome affection. For two weeks she behaved as if they were again on their honeymoon. Then she asked to have her role back. When Charles refused, saying truthfully that it was too late for any change before the opening night, she broke into a furious tirade, saying that she had never loved him and that she had spread stories to dishonor him. Overcome with anguish, Charles wept. When she laughed at his tears, he ran into the street. At last he acquired enough self-control to return and order her out of the house.

When Marthe left, however, she took the letters Charles had once written to her while gaily parodying some of his friends in the inner circle of artists into which he had been welcomed. Really innocuous, when lifted out of context and changed slightly they looked like malicious attempts to scoff at his friends. Marthe, unable to bear the thought that her husband's play might be a success without her, believed that if these influential gentlemen were offended, they might somehow contribute to its ruin.

Spitefully, she gave the letters to Nachette, who was engaged in a silent struggle with Couturat for control of *Scandal*. Nachette recognized their sensational value but told Marthe to leave him: she could do him no good and her ingenuous charms were wearing thin. Couturat, the opportunist, won the paper, however, and saw in the letters, set up on the front page, an excuse to fire Nachette and to establish himself as a good fellow. He sent one copy of the front page to Charles and burned the rest.

Charles' friend Chavannes brought news that Charles had suffered an attack on seeing the journal. At length Charles himself, wraith-like but calm, appeared to hear Couturat's supposedly profound apologies. To Charles, the knowledge that Marthe had been behind the attempt to ruin him was intolerable. Loathing Paris, the theater, life itself, he refused to allow the performance of his play and withdrew to another part of the city. There only his old nurse cared for him as he sank into apathy and madness. Feeling his reason slipping away, he tried to write, but could only scrawl his own name over and over.

Charles was taken to an asylum where steady treatment brought him gradually to himself. When he was at last well enough to go outside, he rejoiced at a new life opening up. He felt able to attend a small theater, but when he saw his wife on the stage—for Marthe had descended to playing in second-rate theaters—madness overcame him once more. After months of violence, he became calm again, but with the calmness of an idiot or a beast. So he lived, little more than a heap of flesh, to the end of his days.

CHARLES O'MALLEY

Type of work: Novel
Author: Charles Lever (1806-1872)
Type of plot: Picaresque romance
Time of plot: 1808-1812
Locale: Ireland and Europe
First published: 1841

Principal characters:
CHARLES O'MALLEY, an Irish dragoon
GODFREY O'MALLEY, his uncle
WILLIAM CONSIDINE, a family friend
CAPTAIN HAMMERSLEY, O'Malley's rival
GENERAL DASHWOOD
LUCY DASHWOOD, his daughter

Critique:

Charles O'Malley, the Irish Dragoon is a light novel in the Irish romantic style. It has little plot and slight structure. The value of the book lies in its great fund of stories and anecdotes of Irish prowess and cunning and in a highly romanticized picture of the Napoleonic wars. To the Irish dragoon, war is a gay and adventurous affair much like a combination fox hunt and banquet. The novel ranks high among works written simply to delight the reader.

The Story:

At seventeen Charles O'Malley was tall and broad-shouldered, deadly with a gun and sure in the saddle. He possessed in abundance the qualities of generosity and honor expected of Godfrey O'Malley's nephew. Godfrey, of O'Malley Castle, Galway, was still a good man on a horse and quick to pass the bottle. In his ruined old castle hard by the river Shannon, he held the staunch affections of his tenants.

Old Godfrey was standing for election to the Irish Parliament. Unable to leave home during the election campaign, he sent Charles to the home of a distant cousin named Blake to ask his support in the coming election. But Blake belonged to the opposition, and although Charles did his best to win help for his uncle, he hardly knew how to handle the situation.

Part of the trouble was Lucy Dashwood. She and her father were visiting Blake while the general tried to buy some good Galway property. Charles was jealous of the general's aide, Captain Hammersley, who was attentive to Lucy. At a fox hunt Charles led the way at first, but Hammersley kept up with him. Charles' horse fell backward in jumping a wall. With cool daring Charles kept on and took a ditch bordered by a stone rampart. Hammersley, not to be outdone, took the ditch too, but fell heavily. Charles was first at the kill, but both he and Hammersley had to spend several days in bed.

One night at dinner one of the guests spoke insultingly of Godfrey O'Malley, and Charles threw a wine glass in his face. Billy Considine, who had been in more duels than any other Irishman in Galway, arranged the affair as Charles' second. Charles left his man for dead on the field. Luckily the man recovered, and Charles escaped serious consequences for his rashness.

Charles went to Dublin to study law. There chance led him to share rooms with Frank Webber. College life became for Charles a series of dinners, brawls and escapades, all under the leadership of Frank.

While in Dublin, Charles saw Lucy again, but she was distant to him. Hammersley was now a favored suitor. Charles became increasingly attracted to military life, the more so since he seemed unfitted for study. Perhaps Lucy would approve his suit if he became a dashing dragoon. Godfrey arranged for a commission through General Dashwood, and Charles became an ensign.

His first duty was in Portugal. Napoleon had invaded the peninsula, and England was sending aid to her Portuguese and Spanish allies. In Lisbon Charles' superb horsemanship saved Donna Inez from injury. His friendship with Donna Inez was progressing satisfactorily when he learned that Inez was an intimate of Lucy Dashwood.

A his own request Charles was sent to the front. There he soon distinguished himself by bravery in battle and was promoted to a lieutenancy.

Lucy had given him letters for Hammersley. When Charles delivered them, Hammersley turned pale and insulted him. Only the good offices of Captain Powers prevented a duel.

Charles saw action at Talavera and Ciudad Roderigo. In one engagement he sneaked under cover of darkness to the French trenches, and by moving the engineers' measuring tape he caused the French to dig their trenches right under the British guns. Wherever Charles went, his man Michael Free looked out for his master, polished his buttons, stole food for him, and made love to all the girls.

After Charles received his captaincy, news came from home that the O'Malley estates were in a bad way. The rents were falling off, mortgages were coming due, and Godfrey's gout had crippled him. Charles went home on leave, arriving in Galway shortly after his uncle's death. There was little money for the many debts, and the estate would require close management. Because a last letter from his uncle had asked him to stay in Galway, Charles decided to sell his commission and retire to civil life.

Billy Considine, who acted as his adviser, told him a distressing story. General Dashwood had sent an agent to Galway to buy property. Thinking of Dashwood as an English interloper, God-frey had written him a harsh letter of warning to stay out of Ireland. In spite of his gout, Godfrey had offered to go to England to do battle with the general. Billy himself had sent a direct challenge to Dashwood. The general had answered in mild tone, and the two hot-headed Irishmen felt their honor had been vindicated. But Charles heard the story with a heavy heart. Lucy seemed lost to him forever. For two years Charles led a secluded life, scarcely quitting his farm.

Charles and Michael, his servant, were in Dublin on the day news came of Napoleon's return from Elba, and Charles decided to go back into the army. He and Michael went to London. There he was appointed to his old rank on the general staff.

Charles arrived in Brussels just before Waterloo. The Belgian city was crowded. General Dashwood and Lucy were there, as were Donna Inez and her father. Charles was safe in one quarter, however, for Captain Powers and Inez were to be married. One day in a park Lucy sat down alone to await her father. Hammersley came to her and asked hoarsely if he could ever hope for her hand. Although not meaning to eavesdrop, Charles heard Lucy dismiss Hammersley. Charles saw Lucy again at the ball, but she seemed as distant and cool as ever.

Charles became a special courier, and in the discharge of his duties he was captured by the French and thrown into prison. To his amazement his cellmate was General Dashwood, condemned to die for having used spies against the French. St. Croix, a French officer whom Charles had befriended in Spain, offered to help him escape. Unselfishly Charles let General Dashwood go in his place. Napoleon himself summoned Charles to an audience, and throughout the battle of Waterloo he saw the action from the French lines. He was watching his chances, however, and when the French troops were scattered he made his way back to the English lines.

After Charles' heroic action in saving her father from execution, Lucy could not longer refuse him. Charles and Lucy went back to Galway to stay, and the Irish tenantry bared their heads in welcome to the new mistress of O'Malley Castle.

THE CHARTERHOUSE OF PARMA

Type of work: Novel
Author: Stendhal (Marie-Henri Beyle, 1783-1842)
Type of plot: Historical romance
Time of plot: Early nineteenth century
Locale: Italy
First published: 1839

Principal characters:
FABRIZIO DEL DONGO, a young adventurer
GINA PIETRANERA, his aunt
COUNT MOSCA, Gina's lover
MARIETTA, an actress
CLELIA CONTI, Fabrizio's mistress

Critique:

The Charterhouse of Parma is one of the earlier examples of French romantic prose. The scene is the principality of Parma in Italy, and the long, involved plot takes the reader through many adventures, light-hearted and tragic, from Waterloo to Bologna. The story, a historical romance, contains also the elements of social comedy and more serious reflections on the futility of life. The novel has a sustained dramatic interest which contributes much to its recognition as a classic of French romanticism.

The Story:

Early in the nineteenth century Fabrizio, son of the Marchese del Dongo, grew up at his father's magnificent villa at Grianta on Lake Como. His father was a miserly fanatic who hated Napoleon and the French, his mother a long-suffering creature cowed by her domineering husband. In his boyhood Fabrizio was happiest when he could leave Grianta and go to visit his mother's widowed sister, Gina Pietranera, at her home in Milan. Gina looked upon her handsome nephew very much as a son.

When he was nearly seventeen, Fabrizio determined to join Napoleon. Both his aunt and his mother were shocked but the boy stood firm. Fabrizio's father was too stingy to allow his womenfolk to give Fabrizio any money for his journey, but Gina sewed some small diamonds in his coat. Under a false passport Fabrizio made his way to Paris as

a seller of astrological instruments.

Following one of Napoleon's battalions out of Paris, Fabrizio was arrested and thrown into jail as a spy. His enthusiastic admiration for the emperor and his bad French were against him. Released from jail by the kind-hearted wife of the turnkey, Fabrizio pressed on, anxious to get into the fighting. Mounted on a horse he bought from a good-natured camp follower, he rode by accident into a group of hussars around Marshall Ney at the battle of Waterloo. When a general's horse was shot, the hussars lifted Fabrizio from the saddle and the general commandeered his mount. Afoot, Fabrizio fell in with a band of French infantrymen and in the retreat from Waterloo killed a Prussian officer. Happy at being a real soldier, he threw down his gun and ran away.

Meanwhile, at home, Gina had succumbed to the pleadings of Count Mosca, prime minister of Parma. They made a happy arrangement. Old Duke Sanseverina wanted a diplomatic post very badly. In return for Mosca's favor in giving him the post, he agreed to marry Gina and set her up as the Duchess of Sanseverina. Then the duke left the country for good, and Mosca became Gina's accepted lover. It was a good thing for Fabrizio that his aunt had some influence. When he returned to Grianta, the gendarmes came to arrest him on a false passport charge. He was taken to Milan in his aunt's carriage. On the way the party passed an older man and his younger daughter, also arrested but condemned to walk. Graciously Gina and Fabrizio took General Conti and his daughter Clelia into the carriage with them. At Milan Fabrizio's difficulties were easily settled.

Gina was growing very fond of Fabrizio, who was a handsome youth, and she took him with her to Parma to advance his fortune. There, upon the advice of Mosca, it was decided to send the young man to Naples to study for three years at the theological seminary. When he came back, he would be given an appointment at court.

At the end of his studies Fabrizio was a suave, worldly young monsignor, not yet committed to a life of piety in spite of his appointment as alternate for the archbishop. At the theater one night the young cleric saw a graceful young actress named Marietta Valsera. His attention soon aroused the anger of a rascal called Giletti, Marietta's protector.

Fearing the consequences of this indiscretion, Mosca sent Fabrizio to the country for a while to supervise some archeological diggings. While looking over the spot, Fabrizio borrowed a shotgun and walked down the road to look for rabbits. At that moment a carriage drove by, with Marietta and Giletti inside. Thinking that Fabrizio intended to take Marietta, Giletti leaped from the carriage and rushed at Fabrizio with his dagger. In the fight, Fabrizio killed Giletti. The alarmed Marietta took Fabrizio with her to Bologna. There his aunt's emissaries supplied him with ample funds, and Fabrizio settled down to enjoy his lovely Marietta.

News of the affair reached Parma. Political opponents of Mosca found an opportunity to strike at him through Gina, and they influenced the prince to try the fugitive for murder. Fabrizio was tried in his absence and condemned to death or imprisonment as a galleyslave.

Fabrizio soon tired of his Marietta. Attracted by a young singer named Fausta, he followed her to Parma. There he was recognized and imprisoned. In spite of his influence, Mosca could do little for Gina's nephew. But Fabrizio was happy in jail, for Clelia, the daughter of his jailer, was the girl to whom Fabrizio had offered a ride years before. By means of alphabet cards the two were soon holding long conversations.

Outside Gina laid her plans for Fabrizio's escape. With the help of a poet named Ferrante, she arranged to have ropes smuggled to her nephew. Clelia herself was to carry them in. Fabrizio escaped from the tower and fled to Piedmont. At Parma, according to Gina's instructions, Ferrante poisoned the prince who had condemned Fabrizio to imprisonment. In the resulting confusion Gina and Fabrizio returned to Parma, now governed by the new prince. Pardoned, he was named coadjutor by the archbishop. Later he became archbishop and attracted great crowds with his preaching. In the meantime Clelia had married a rich marchese. One day, moved by curiosity, she came to hear Fabrizio preach. Her love finally led her to take him for a lover. Every night he came to her house. After their child was born, Fabrizio took the baby to his own house and Clelia visited her small son there. But Fabrizio was to be happy only a short time. The infant died and Clelia did not long survive her child. Saddened by her death, Fabrizio gave up his office and retired to the Charterhouse of Parma, a monastery on the river Po, where quiet meditation filled his days.

A CHASTE MAID IN CHEAPSIDE

Type of work: Drama
Author: Thomas Middleton (1580-1627)
Type of plot: Farce
Time of plot: Early seventeenth century
Locale: London
First presented: 1611

Principal characters:
SIR WALTER WHOREHOUND, a man about town
YELLOWHAMMER, a goldsmith
MOLL, his daughter
ALLWIT, a complacent cuckold
MISTRESS ALLWIT, his wife
TOUCHWOOD (SENIOR), a man rich only in progeny
TOUCHWOOD (JUNIOR), his younger brother

Critique:

A Chaste Maid in Cheapside, the only play now extant known to have been acted at the Swan Theatre, belongs to that lively series of farcical comedies which Middleton produced between 1604 and 1612. Bawdy, skillful, and wholly laughter-provoking, it is notable for its exceptional freedom and audacity, even if not for its chastity. Its story interweaves most adroitly the affairs of several households, and it travels at a fast pace through wildly comic situations to a satisfactory conclusion. Despite the lightness of its subject matter, however, the drama is given some ballast by its incidental comment on contemporary manners and customs. In one hilarious sequence, Middleton sees to it that detested police informers are made ridiculous; in another, a realistic christening party provides certain pious Puritan ladies with an excuse for imbibing wine with a zeal over and beyond the demands of mere politeness.

The Story:

In the London shop of Yellowhammer, the goldsmith, a family discussion was taking place, a sharp, even quarrelsome exchange. Maudlin, the goldsmith's wife, was finding fault with Moll, her daughter. Moll, opposed to the distasteful marriage into which her parents were trying to inveigle her, was not attracted to the elderly libertine, Sir Walter Whore-

hound, whose suit the parents had encouraged. Nevertheless, her final consent was being taken for granted by her mother, who railed against Moll for her lack of enthusiasm for the match. So anxious were the Yellowhammers to achieve that connection with Sir Walter that they proposed to cement the family alliance in still another way. As a bride for their son Tim, a bemused student at Cambridge, they had approved Sir Walter's supposed niece, reportedly a Welsh heiress owning nineteen mountains. Actually, the Welshwoman was Sir Walter's mistress, whom he was conveniently preparing to discard as a preliminary to his marriage to Moll.

As the Yellowhammers argued, Sir Walter entered their shop, accompanied by his "niece." From all except Moll, the newcomers received a warm welcome. In the festivities which followed, the younger Touchwood made a casual entrance and, under the very nose of her father, slipped a note to Moll. To the latter, Touchwood posed as a customer, in the shop for the purpose of ordering a wedding ring. He said that he had forgotten the correct size, but he was sure that it would be satisfactory if it would fit the finger of the goldsmith's daughter.

In another household, that of Allwit and his wife, Sir Walter was also held in high esteem, but for very different reasons. Allwit, the nominal master of the household without being its breadwinner, was an arrant but satisfied cuckold whose wife had been Sir Walter's mistress for many years and the mother of Sir Walter's six children. At the time, in fact, she was expecting the imminent birth of a seventh. Allwit, anxiously awaiting Sir Walter's arrival and complacently reviewing the advantages of his singular situation, gloated over the fact that Sir Walter maintained the house, kept it stocked with food, begot Allwit's brood for him, and even—by being jealous of Mistress Allwit—relieved the husband of that irksome prerogative. The only cloud on the Allwit horizon was the possibility that Sir Walter might eventually grow restive and drift into marriage with someone younger and more attractive. Allwit had spiked such disastrous prospects before by making judicious hints to those rich widows and landed virgins who had found favor with Sir Walter. He intended to do the same again before parting with such a prize as his treasured benefactor.

Elsewhere in London, the older of the Touchwood brothers was persuading his disconsolate but understanding wife that they must separate from each other for a while. Touchwood Senior's infallible gift for acquiring paternity had brought their domestic establishment to the verge of financial ruin, and there seemed no other way to slow down the steady increase in the size of his family. This matter settled, Touchwood Senior—a generous man—prepared to help his younger brother, who had requested aid in securing a marriage license.

At the same time, Touchwood Senior was, unknown to him, the subject of conversation between Sir Oliver and Lady Kix, a childless couple who bewailed the fate that kept them without heirs, thereby diverting income and property that should be theirs into the coffers of Sir Walter Whorehound. To achieve parenthood, they had tried numberless remedies in vain, in the meantime endlessly debating the blame for their childless state. Their hope had been quickened when their maid recommended the services of Touchwood Senior, who reportedly worked wonders with a fabulously effective, though quite expensive, type of water.

Mistress Allwit gave birth to a fine girl and in preparation for the christening Allwit and Sir Walter collaborated in the choice of godparents. To allay suspicion, Sir Walter appointed himself, along with his fiancée, Moll; Allwit selected Touchwood Junior. At the christening, the latter was able to exchange a few hurried words with Moll, commenting with satisfaction on the fact that the goldsmith had completed work on the wedding ring.

A short time later Touchwood Junior and Moll met secretly to be married. Their plans were thwarted, however, when Yellowhammer and Sir Walter burst in and took Moll away. The goldsmith promised, henceforth, to keep his daughter under lock and key until her marriage to Sir Walter could be accomplished. Meanwhile, Touchwood Senior, motivated by the prospect of both revenge and profit, agreed to turn the tables on Sir Walter by bringing parenthood to Sir Oliver and his lady. Sir Oliver was induced to drink a dubious liquid and then was sent to ride horseback for five hours. In his absence, Touchwood acquainted Lady Kix with the measures connected with her part of the treatment.

Allwit, disturbed to hear of Sir Walter's wedding plans, told Yellowhammer some colorful details of Sir Walter's behavior. Although the goldsmith professed dismay at the disclosure, after Allwit's departure he reaffirmed his intention to give his daughter to Sir Walter. Moll, however, had once more proved resourceful enough to escape her father's house, only to be brought back dripping wet and dragged by the hair by her angry mother, who had overtaken the runaway after a chase along the river. Angry, Yellowhammer decided to forestall any additional attempts of the kind by setting the next day for Moll's marriage. Desperate at the thought of losing his sweetheart, Touchwood Junior forced Sir Walter into a duel in which they were both wounded.

Sir Walter, distraught, was carried to Allwit's house. His reception there, however, did not follow the usual pattern of unquestioning welcome. Bad news came thick and fast: one moment he heard the rumor that he was guilty of the death of Touchwood Junior; the next, his spirits sank at the news that Sir Oliver Kix's wife was finally pregnant. Allwit, sensing the turn in his benefactor's fortunes, decided to get rid of Sir Walter, even in his wounded condition. When he blusteringly threatened the old libertine with the law, Sir Walter woefully directed his servants to take him away. Left alone, Allwit and Mistress Allwit congratulated themselves on the profits they had gained from Sir Walter's past generosity.

Moll, ill from exposure and grief, received a letter purportedly containing a dying message from her lover. Swooning, she was carried out by Touchwood Senior and the servants of the Yellowhammers. Conscience-stricken, the goldsmith and his wife berated themselves for causing her death.

Later, in church, the coffins of Touchwood Junior and Moll were placed by separate doors. To the surprise of the mourners assembled, however, the supposed corpses rose from their coffins and revealed the lovers as alive and well. The goldsmith and his wife at last conceded defeat and agreed to the marriage of Touchwood Junior and Moll. Since his son Tim had just married the Welshwoman, Yellowhammer consoled himself with the fact that one wedding feast could serve for the marriage of both his son and his daughter.

CHÉRI

Type of work: Novel
Author: Sidonie Gabrielle Claudine Colette (1873-1954)
Type of plot: Psychological realism
Time of plot: c. 1910
Locale: Paris
First published: 1920

Principal characters:
LÉONIE VALLON, called Léa de Lonval
FRED PELOUX, called Chéri
MME. PELOUX, Chéri's mother
EDMÉE, the girl Chéri married
MARIE-LAURE, Edmée's mother

Critique:

Chéri is probably the most perfect example of Colette's exploration of the human heart through the five senses. The emotional truth with which she is concerned is complemented by her disciplined intellect, and a balance is maintained throughout the book between Léa's shrewd personal vision and the wholeheartedness with which she abandons herself, with Chéri, to sensual delight. Colette holds her unique place in French literature in part through the central matrix of sensuous perception in her work. In highly individual language which is both lyrical and precise, she wittily and dispassionately measures the cost of man-woman relationships. Amoral, but never irresponsible in outlook, Colette was at the time of her death the foremost woman novelist in France.

The Story:

In the pink boudoir of Léa, a still lovely courtesan, Chéri, her handsome young lover, demanded her valuable pearls to play with. She discouraged his mood, fearing that the removal of her pearls might cause him to notice that her neck was showing the wrinkles of age. Chéri cursed his luncheon engagement with his mother. Léa gently and teasingly helped him in his erratic dressing. Although he became lazily aroused at her touch, she managed to send him away.

Alone, Léa dressed with efficient care, choosing a white-brimmed hat for her visit to Mme. Peloux. She ate a good lunch before joining Chéri at his mother's house. There she found Mme. Peloux loud-voiced, gossipy and inquisitive; but years of familiarity, and later Chéri, had cemented their relationship. There also were Marie-Laure, an elegant woman of forty, and her quiet daughter Edmée, whose looks nearly equaled her mother's. They left as soon as Léa arrived and the degree to which mother and son then relaxed disgusted Léa. Despite his careless manners Chérie still looked to her like a young god.

She remembered him as a very beautiful and lonely child who had soon developed his mother's miserliness and her keen business sense. In his late adolescence Léa had taken him away to Normandy to feed him well and also to remove him from his dissipated life in Paris. Her offer to do so had been accepted with a kiss which had inflamed them both.

In Normandy they had become lovers. Chéri was devoted to Léa for her passion and solicitude, and she to him for his youth, ardor, and faunlike freedom. At that point Léa would still have been willing to abandon him because of the inconvenience he caused her; he was, in succession, taciturn and demonstrative, tender and spiteful. But after they returned to Paris Chéri still wanted Léa, and he became her established lover. He had remained with her for six years.

When Chéri returned to Léa after the luncheon party, he told her that he was to marry Edmée. Since Léa had always known a marriage would be eventually arranged for Chéri, she did not outwardly react to this news. Chéri declared that his wife would influence him little and that she already adored him. Wounded by Léa's apparent lack of emotion, he declared that he would like her to hide herself in Normandy and grieve. He desperately wanted to be her last lover.

In the few weeks before Chéri's marriage he and Léa were very gay, though at times she was appalled at his heartlessness toward his future bride and realized that by pampering him she had maintained in him the immaturity of a child. When Chéri chattered about his honeymoon, Léa reminded him that she would not be there. Chéri turned white and gave her great happiness by announcing ambiguously that for him she would always be there.

While visiting Mme. Peloux during the honeymoon, Léa was suddenly overwhelmed by an ill-defined grief. Thinking that she was ill, she returned home and went to bed. When she realized that she was for the first time really suffering from the loss of a great love, she fled from Paris and stayed away for a year.

Chéri and Edmée lived with Mme. Peloux at Neuilly until their own house was finished. Chéri, also miserable, questioned his mother about Léa's uninformative parting note. No one knew where she had gone. Sometimes he fought viciously with his young wife, who loved him and bored him. Again, he would become obsessed with plans for their house and give many and contradictory orders for exotic decorations.

Edmée became so unhappy that at last she resorted to looking for love letters in Chéri's desk. When she accused him of

loving only Léa and wept unrestrainedly, Chéri was unmoved but clinically interested; Léa had never cried. Edmée deeply offended Chéri when she suggested that their own love-making was not really love. Chéri explained that no man could tolerate such remarks. Their quarrels finally forced Edmée to suggest a divorce. Chéri calmly rejected the suggestion because he knew that Edmée loved him and because divorce offered no real solution to his problem.

Chéri next went to Léa's house, but her servants had no news of her. In deep despair he dined away from home for the first time. He stayed in Paris, living a miserable and silent life with a young man who had frequently lived on his money before. He recovered the strength to act when at last the lamps in Léa's house were again lighted. Then, without seeing Léa, he bought jewels for his wife and returned home.

Léa did not wholly regret her exile, but she was distressed to discover how much the year had aged her. Only her eyes remained as lovely as before. Although a visit from Mme. Peloux restored her spirit, she was hurt by the news she received of Chéri, and she realized that she was not free of her love for him. While out walking, she twice saw young men who she was convinced were Chéri. Knowing that she was not yet strong enough to meet him unexpectedly, she returned home. She changed her street clothes for a peach-colored robe and paced about her room while trying to face the fact that she was alone.

About midnight Chéri arrived, sullen and disheveled, and declared that he had returned to her. She quarreled with him for a time but at last was so completely disarmed by his pleas that she kept him there. For the first time, that night, they declared to each other that they were in love.

In the morning Léa, unknowingly watched by Chéri, made wild plans for their departure together. She looked old to Chéri and he felt exhausted. Unable to draw him into her plans, she bitterly abused Edmée. He stopped her by insisting that she was not being the fine and lovely woman he had known. She told him gently that their fate had been to love and then part. Chéri, although he knew how he had hurt Léa, was unable to follow any course but return to his family. Léa begged him not to make Edmée miserable and told Chéri how she loved him. Having thus successfully sent him away, Léa last saw Chéri breathing in the air of the courtyard as if it were something that he could savor and taste.

THE CHERRY ORCHARD

Type of work: Drama
Author: Anton Chekhov (1860-1904)
Type of plot: Impressionistic realism
Time of plot: Early twentieth century
Locale: An estate in Russia
First presented: 1904

Principal characters:
MADAME RANEVSKAYA, a landowner
ANYA, her daughter
VARYA, her adopted daughter
GAEV, her brother
YASHA, a valet
DUNYASHA, a maid
FIERS, an old footman
LOPAKHIN, a merchant
CHARLOTTA, a governess
PISCHIN, a landowner
TROFIMOV, a student

Critique:

The Cherry Orchard is Chekhov's best-known play. In this work his characters are not tragic in the usual sense of the word because they are incapable of any great heroic action. But for what they are he sees them clearly and sees them whole, in their frustrations, jealousies, and loves. In addition to his subtle characterizations, he has caught in Madame Ranevskaya's household a picture of the end of an era, the passing of the semi-feudal existence of Russian landowners on their country estates.

The Story:

When Madame Ranevskaya's little son, Grischa, was drowned only a year after the death of her husband, her grief was so overwhelming that she was forced to go to Paris in order to forget, and she remained away for five years. The Easter before her return to her estate in Russia, she sent for her seventeen-year-old daughter Anya to join her. To pay the expenses of her trip and that of her daughter, Madame Ranevskaya had been forced to sell her villa at Mentone, and she had nothing left. She returned home to find that her whole estate, including a cherry orchard, so famous that it was mentioned in the Encyclopedia, was to be sold at auction to pay her debts. Madame Ranevskaya was heartbroken, but her old friend Lopakhin, a merchant whose father had once been a serf on her ancestral estate, proposed a way out. He said that if the cherry orchard were cut down and the land divided into lots for rental to summer cottagers, she would be able to realize an income of at least twenty-five thousand roubles a year.

Madame Ranevskaya could not endure the thought that her childhood home with all its memories should be subjected to such a fate, and all the members of her family agreed with her. Her brother Gaev, who had remained behind to manage the estate, was convinced that there must be some other way out, but none of his ideas seemed feasible at the moment. It would be fine, he thought, if they all came in for a legacy, or if Anya could be wed to a rich man, or if their wealthy aunt could be persuaded to come to their aid. But the aunt did not entirely approve of Madame Ranevskaya, who, she felt, had married beneath her.

The thought that Gaev himself might do something never occurred to him; he went on playing billiards and munching candy as he had done all his life. Others who made up the household had similar futile dreams. Varya, an adopted daughter, hoped that God might do something about the situation. Pischin, a neighboring landowner, who had been saved financially when the railroad bought a part of his property, advised a policy of waiting for something to turn up.

Lopakhin, who had struggled hard to attain his present position, was frankly puzzled at the family's stubborn attitude. He had no illusions about himself; in fact, he realized that, compared with these smooth-tongued and well-mannered aristocrats, he was still only a peasant. He had tried to improve himself intellectually, but he fell asleep over the books with which he was supposed to be familiar.

As he gazed at the old cherry orchard in the moonlight, the cherry orchard which seemed so beautiful to Madame Ranevskaya, he could not help thinking of his peasant ancestors, to whom every tree must have been a symbol of oppression. Trofimov, who had been little Grischa's tutor, and who was more expressive than Lopakhin, tried to express this thought to Anya, with whom he was in love.

The cherry orchard was put up at auction. That evening Madame Ranevskaya gave a ball in the old house, an act in keeping with the unrealistic attitude of her class in general. Even her aged servant, Fiers, supported her in this view by his loyalty to her and her brother. Lopakhin arrived at the party with the news that he had bought the estate for ninety thousand roubles above the mortgage. When he announced that he intended to cut down the orchard, Madame Ranevskaya began to weep. She planned to return to Paris.

Others were equally affected by the sale of the cherry orchard. Gaev, on the basis of the transaction with Lopakhin, was offered a position in the bank at six thousand roubles a year, a position he would not keep because of his laziness. Madame Ranevskaya's servant, Yasha, was delighted over the sale because the trip to Paris would mean for him an escape from the boredom of Russian life. But for Dunyasha, her maid, the sale meant the collapse of her hopes of ever marrying Yasha, and a lifelong bondage to Yephodov, a poor, ineffectual clerk. To Varya, Madame Ranevskaya's adopted daughter, it meant a position as housekeeper on a nearby estate. To the landowner, Pischin, it was the confirmation of his philosophy. Investigators had found valuable minerals on his land, and he was now able to pay his debt to Madame Ranevskaya and to look forward to another temporary period of affluence. Fiers alone was unaffected. Departure of the family was the end of this old servant's life, for whatever it had been worth, but he was more concerned because Gaev, his master, had worn his light overcoat instead of a fur coat when he escorted the mistress, Madame Ranevskaya, to the station.

THE CHEVALIER OF THE MAISON ROUGE

Type of work: Novel
Author: Alexandre Dumas, father (1802-1870)
Type of plot: Historical romance
Time of plot: 1793
Locale: Paris
First published: 1846

Principal characters:
>GENEVIÈVE DIXMER, a young woman of aristocratic birth
>MAURICE LINDEY, an officer in the Civic Guard
>LOUIS LORIN, his faithful friend
>MONSIEUR DIXMER, a tanner and a royalist conspirator
>MORAND, his friend, the Chevalier of the Maison Rouge
>MARIE ANTOINETTE, Queen of France
>SIMON, a cobbler
>HÉLOÏSE TISON, an aide to the conspirators

Critique:

The Chevalier of the Maison Rouge is a particularly striking example of Dumas' genius in catching and holding the reader's interest. With a plot based on the hero's supposed love for Marie Antoinette, the novel tells of his several unsuccessful attempts to free her before she was sentenced to death and executed. The fact that the reader knows these attempts are bound to fail in no way diminishes the interest of a complex story in which the fabricated circumstances fit precisely into the actual ones. A champion of monarchy and of aristocratic virtues, Dumas has endowed his republican heroes with these same qualities. Maurice and Louis are republicans only for the sake of plot. The former is the ideal romantic lover; the latter is the faithful friend and perfect gentleman. The book can in no way serve as a manual of history, but it is captivating reading for amateurs of adventures in fiction.

The Story:

At the beginning of the year 1793, after the death of King Louis XVI on the guillotine, France was menaced at her borders by practically all of Europe at a time when the Convention was torn apart by dissensions between the Montagnards and the Girondins. One night in March, Maurice Lindey, a lieutenant in the Civic Guard, met a group of enlisted volunteers who were taking a woman to the guardhouse because she had no pass permitting her to be out at that time. The woman implored the officer for his protection against these men, who showed the effects of having drunk many toasts to their future victories. He decided to conduct her to the guardhouse himself, but she talked him into escorting her to her home.

Louis Lorin, Maurice's friend, had tried to persuade the lieutenant to avoid involving himself with an unknown woman who was so afraid of the guardhouse and who might well be a *ci-devant*, an aristocrat. But Maurice was already in love with her; he was afraid only that she was returning from a lovers' tryst. He escorted her home, but she refused to tell him her name, and once they had arrived in the old Rue Saint Jacques, in the center of the tanneries, with their horrible smell, she ordered him to close his eyes, gave him a kiss, and, leaving a ring between his lips, disappeared. The next morning he received a short note in which the woman gave him her thanks for his gallant conduct and said goodbye to him forever. This note he treasured with the ring.

Now that he had the lovely unknown woman on his mind he was not too upset

557

to learn that the same night the Chevalier of the Maison Rouge, back in Paris, had attempted a new conspiracy to free Marie Antoinette. The immediate consequence was that the Dauphin was taken away from the apartment where he was imprisoned with his mother, sister, and aunt. The boy was given to Simon, a shoemaker, to receive a so-called republican education.

On another evening Maurice went back to the same spot where the beautiful stranger had vanished. When he began reading all the names on the doors in the hope that love would prompt him to identify the right one, he was suddenly surrounded by seven men and thrown into a cave with his hands tied and his eyes blindfolded. Behind the door he could hear the men deliberating to determine whether he was a spy and whether they should kill him. The name of Mme. Dixmer was also mentioned. Maurice had gathered from their talk that she was the wife of one of the men, apparently the manager of a large tannery. The men continued talking, emphasizing that Mme. Dixmer must know nothing of this happening. Maurice wondered why a tanner would want to assassinate him.

Meanwhile, he had succeeded in freeing himself, and when the door was opened he jumped out, only to find himself in an enclosed garden where he found no visible means of escape. He leaped through a window and found himself in a room where a woman was reading. Dixmer followed him and ordered the woman to step aside so that he could shoot the intruder. Instead, she stretched out her arms to protect him. Geneviève Dixmer was the unknown woman of his previous encounter. Dixmer offered his apologies, explaining that he was using prohibited acids in his tannery business and that his smugglers had been afraid Maurice was an informer. Maurice was asked to stay for dinner, where he met Dixmer's business partner, Morand. At the end of the evening he was invited to return.

One day in May, Maurice was on duty at the Temple—the apartment where Marie Antoinette was held—when Héloïse Tison came to visit her mother, the prisoner's keeper. She was accompanied by a friend who was allowed to go upstairs. After they had left, a letter was discovered in Marie Antoinette's pocket, a note confirming the death of a friend. The handwriting was familiar to Maurice, and he wondered how Geneviève Dixmer could have anything to do with the queen. The next day Marie Antoinette asked to go to the top of the tower for a walk. After a while, turning to the east, she received signals from a window. Maurice thought he recognized Geneviève and immediately went to the Rue Saint Jacques, where he found everyone very busy with a new dye. He was amused at his own suspicions.

While he believed that Geneviève felt esteem rather than real love for her husband, Maurice was growing more and more jealous of Morand, whom for no reason at all he suspected of being in love with her. One day he did voice his jealousy; Geneviève pleaded with him to remain her friend. On the following day he received a note from her asking him to send a letter to her husband giving any reason he might think of for stopping his visits. Once more he complied with her wish.

His action greatly upset Dixmer and Morand, whose tannery business was only a cover to hide their conspiracies. Morand was the Chevalier of the Maison Rouge. After Geneviève refused to write to Maurice or to invite him back to their home, Dixmer himself went to see him. Maurice, true to his promise, refused to return. However, he became so lovesick that he could not do anything until he received a letter from Geneviève, in which, at her husband's insistence, she invited him to call once more. He had no suspicion that the conspirators had great need of him. They had bought a house close to the Temple and had worked all night to connect its caves with a trapdoor leading into the prison yard.

Geneviève having expressed a desire to see the queen, Maurice asked her to come to the Temple on the following Thursday. He also invited Morand. When a girl offered them some carnations, Maurice bought a bouquet for Geneviève. Later, as the queen walked by, on her way to the top of the tower, she admired the flowers and Geneviève offered her the bouquet.

Simon, who hated Lorin and Maurice because they protected the Dauphin against his cruelty, picked up a flower that had fallen from the bouquet and discovered a note hidden inside; but the note was blown away by the wind. After Simon had given the affair great publicity, the flower girl was found, tried, and condemned to death. The Chevalier of the Maison Rouge was unsuccessful in his efforts to rescue her, for she was executed immediately. She was Héloïse Tison. Her mother had contributed to her doom by joining her accusations to Simon's.

When the day set for the queen's escape arrived, Marie Antoinette asked to go into the yard for a walk. She was to sit by the trapdoor, then pretend to faint; during the confusion, she and her daughter and sister-in-law could be carried away through the tunnel. But as they were entering the yard, the queen's little black dog jumped forward and went barking toward the concealed trap. The conspirators were forced to retreat. Because the plot confirmed his earlier charge, Simon became the man of the day. Maurice fell under suspicion, together with his friend Lorin.

Lorin, determined to save his friend, insisted that he join the expedition which was to arrest the man who had bought the house to which the tunnel led. Maurice accepted, only to learn that Dixmer was the man. He realized that he had been a mere instrument in the hands of his alleged friends. When he arrived at the house, Geneviève said that she really loved him, and she promised to be his if

he would let the chevalier go free. He revealed the password to them, and the conspirators escaped. The house was burned down. As Maurice ran everywhere desperately calling for Geneviève, Lorin realized who the woman was. He followed his friend through the city on a fruitless search for his love, and finally took him home after he had become completely exhausted. There they found Geneviève waiting for Maurice.

Maurice decided to leave France in order to take Geneviève away. She was left alone to pack her few belongings while Maurice went to see Lorin. During his absence her husband came after her and forced her to go away with him.

In the meantime Marie Antoinette had been transferred to the Conciergerie. The chevalier managed to be hired as a turnkey there, replacing the former turnkey, whom he had bribed.

Dixmer also had a plan for the queen's escape. His design was to introduce himself in the Conciergerie as a registrar. He hoped to get into Marie Antoinette's room with Geneviève and kill the two keepers. Geneviève would then persuade the queen to change clothes with her and leave with Dixmer.

The Chevalier of the Maison Rouge had introduced into the queen's room a small file with which she was supposed to cut the bars of her window. Meanwhile, he would keep the jailers busy at the other window.

Unfortunately, the two attempts, taking place simultaneously, worked against each other, and Geneviève was arrested.

Maurice, having searched all Paris in order to find Geneviève again, had gone to live with Lorin after narrowly missing arrest in his own quarters. He and Lorin were definitely marked as suspects.

It was not until Marie Antoinette's trial, at which he met the chevalier, that Maurice learned what had happened to Geneviève. Every day he went to the Revolutionary Tribunal in the hope of finding her there. Finally she was brought in, and Maurice was surprised to see Lorin brought in also. The commissary who had come to arrest Maurice had arrested Lorin instead when Maurice was not to be found. Geneviève and Lorin were sentenced to death.

Maurice had seen Dixmer in the audience. After the trial he followed him and killed him during a quarrel. He took a pass which Dixmer, in order to harass his wife and accuse her of adultery, had secured for the purpose of entering the room where the prisoners were kept. Maurice ran to the waiting room and, handing the pass to Lorin, told him he, Lorin, was now free. But Lorin refused his friend's offer. Maurice was seized and all three died on the scaffold.

CHILDREN OF GOD

Type of work: Novel
Author: Vardis Fisher (1895-   )
Type of plot: Historical chronicle
Time of plot: 1820-1890
Locale: New York, Illinois, Utah
First published: 1939

Principal characters:
>JOSEPH SMITH, the founder of the Church of Latter-day Saints
>BRIGHAM YOUNG, the leader of the Church after Smith's death
>JOHN TAYLOR, a later leader of the Mormon Church

Critique:

Vardis Fisher calls his book an American epic. Certainly the material dealt with is of an epic character, for no one can doubt the bravery and the sincerity of the Mormons after reading this account of the great migration from New York to Illinois and Missouri and, finally, to Utah. Taking the bare bones of fact, Fisher rounded out the personalities and events of Mormonism in such manner that the facts seemed to take on flesh and come to life. The result is a novel in which history and fiction are one.

The Story:

In the early 1820's a young man in Palmyra, New York, had visions which led him to believe himself a prophet of the Lord. The young man was Joseph Smith and his visions were the basis upon which he built the Church of the Latter-day Saints, more commonly known as the Mormon Church. In those days his followers were few, being only his family and a handful of friends.

In March of 1830 the Book of Mormon was published. Shortly after it appeared, Joseph Smith ordained his brothers and the men of the Whitmer family as Latter-day Saints. After Joseph was reported to have cast out the personal devil of a man called Newel Knight, word of the miracle spread about the country near Palmyra and many were converted.

But with success came trouble. On one occasion a mob of men almost lynched the new prophet. On another, he was taken to court for trial. He realized that his life was no longer safe in the state of New York.

Joseph's three hundred followers left New York State for Ohio. Meanwhile Joseph sent two men, one of them Oliver Cowdery, his first convert, to travel beyond the Mississippi River for the purpose of converting the Indians and locating the place where the Saints were to build their Zion. In Ohio, Joseph Smith was again persecuted. One winter night a mob abducted him from his house and tarred and feathered him. Shortly afterward Joseph decided to take his flock to Missouri, and he went with a few of his followers to survey the country.

More trouble awaited him when he returned to Ohio. Several of his converts had set themselves up as prophets during his absence. Reports reached him that the people he had left in Missouri were being mobbed. Then one day two men came to offer their services to Joseph Smith. One was Brigham Young, the other Heber Kimball. Brigham Young was a great help to the Saints' community because he could make men do what he wished, something that Joseph Smith, the mystic, was never able to learn.

While the Saints in Ohio were facing internal strife, the people of the new faith in Missouri were being horsewhipped, murdered, and driven from their homes by mobs. Eventually Brigham Young was authorized to organize an army to march upon Missouri and rescue the Mormons there. At the last minute Joseph Smith went with it as leader. The expedition was doomed to failure. Cholera and Indians took their toll among the men. They never fought the Missouri mobs.

For the next few years the Saints prospered in Ohio. Joseph Smith and Brigham Young opened a Mormon-operated bank, which failed, along with many others, in the panic of 1837. The loss of their money turned the Saints against their leaders as nothing else had done, and Brigham Young and Joseph Smith fled to Missouri for their lives. They were soon joined by three hundred families from Ohio who remained true to Joseph's religion and prophetic power.

In Missouri mobs again harassed their settlements. The desperate Saints organized a retaliating secret society called the Danites or Destroying Angels. Finally the governor of Missouri ordered all the Mormons to leave the state or be killed. Again Joseph Smith and his leaders were tried for treason. Through a friendly guard they escaped execution.

The Saints settled next at Nauvoo, in Illinois, where Joseph Smith began the practice of plural marriages in an effort to keep the women in the church, who outnumbered the men, from becoming charity cases or harlots. Joseph himself soon had twenty wives. His first wife, Emma, made him send away all but two.

Joseph Smith never left Illinois. He was killed by a mob when he gave himself up to stand trial for treason a third time. Brigham Young then took over the leadership of the Mormons, not as a prophet, but as a leader. He decided that the only way for the Mormons to find peace was to leave the United States, to seek a place in the far West.

Trudging westward through the snow, three thousand Mormons started out under Brigham's leadership. Those left behind felt lost without their leader and soon there were fifteen thousand more people following Brigham westward.

In the spring of 1847 Brigham Young set out from his winter camp for the Rocky Mountains with a hundred and fifty picked men. The others were to follow later. Brigham had determined to settle south of the salt lake in Utah. By the winter of 1847 seventeen hundred Mormons were already in Utah. When Brigham learned that the Utah territory had been ceded to the United States by Mexico, he felt that the Mormons would never have a land of their own. The next winter five thousand of the Mormons lived through a year of intense cold and starvation rations. The third year in Utah brought a new problem to Brigham Young. California gold attracted thousands of rascals and adventurers, many of whom passed through the settlement of the Mormons on their way to the coast. Those scoundrels stole from the scanty stores of the settlers and made trouble among the women.

As the years passed, the Saints flourished. Brigham Young was elected governor of Utah Territory. In 1852 he took a bold step when he announced publicly what many people had long known or at least suspected, the practice of polygamy by the leaders of the Mormon Church. The hue and cry against the practice amazed and embittered Brigham, for he could say truthfully that it had maintained morality in the Mormon settlements.

In 1855 locusts demolished their crops. Many of the Saints turned against the practice of polygamy, for in times of famine a man could not secure enough food for his over-expanded family.

Two years later the Mormons heard that the Federal government had sent an army to deal with them. From their previous experiences, the Mormons knew they could expect little mercy. The territorial governor sent by the president was vigorously defied and the Mormons threatened to burn Salt Lake City and leave the country a desert as they had found it. Finally the president sent a pardon to the Mormons.

With General Grant in the White House, the Mormon problem again became a pressing one. Federal prosecutors invoked the anti-bigamy law and began to imprison Mormon leaders. Then the prosecutors attempted to indict the leaders, including Brigham Young, for murder. Young was never tried, however, for he died of natural causes.

After Young's death, the authorities secured more indictments in the hope that the Mormons would repudiate polygamy. They also moved against the cooperative stores and industries which had been founded, and attempted to deprive the Mormon Church of all assets in excess of fifty thousand dollars. The sum of those strains was too great. The president of the Mormon Council denounced plural marriages. No longer could the Mormon community hold itself apart in order to continue its existence. The Saints and the settlers from the East would live side by side in the new state of Utah.

THE CHILDREN OF HERAKLES

Type of work: Drama
Author: Euripides (c. 485 c. 406 B.C.)
Type of plot: C'assical tragedy
Time of plot: The age of legend
Loca'e: Before the temple of Zeus at Marathon
First presented: c. 430 B.C.

Principa! characters:
 IOLAUS, aged friend of Herakles
 COPREUS, hera!d of Eurystheus
 DEMOPHON, King of Athens
 MACARIA, Herakles' daughter
 ALCMENE, Herakles' mother
 EURYSTHEUS, King of Argos

Critique:

There are so many awkwardnesses in the structure of the *Children of Herakles* (the *Herakleidae*) that critics have suggested that important scenes must be missing or that, like *Alcestis*, it was not intended as a tragedy but as a substitute for a satyr play. Another suggestion is that since the *Herakleidae* was presented in the early years of the Peloponnesian War and glorifies the virtues of the Athenian city-state, Euripides depended upon the high patriotism of the play to carry it. The unity of the play lies in the fact that in the beginning Eurystheus threatens to slay the surviving relatives of Herakles, who are seeking refuge in Athens, and at the end of the play he is himself slain by command of Alcmene, the mother of Herakles.

The Story:

Iolaus, the aged warrior friend of the dead Herakles, together with Alcmene and the Herakleidae, the children of Herakles, had for years been wandering over Greece seeking a refuge from Eurystheus, King of Argos. No city had dared to take them in against the command of the powerful Argive ruler. At last the wanderers arrived in Athens. There, while resting at the temple of Zeus, they were immediately confronted by Copreus, the herald of Eurystheus, who demanded that they proceed at once to Argos and submit to death by stoning. Iolaus stanchly refused, and when Copreus seized the children a violent conflict ensued and Iolaus was thrown to the ground.

The chorus of aged Athenians immediately summoned their king, Demophon, who was warned by Copreus that his refusal to surrender the Herakleidae to the Argives would surely result in war. In response to Iolaus' plea, Demophon offered his protection on the grounds that the children of Herakles were gathered around the altar of Zeus, that they were bound to him by ties of kinship, and that the honor and freedom of Athens were at stake. Copreus sullenly departed, after warning that he would return with an army and punish Athens for its insolence. The grateful Iolaus praised the Athenians for their willingness to aid the helpless in an honest cause, but he refused to leave the temple until the issue with Argos was settled.

The Argive host appeared, led by Eurystheus himself. Demophon, who had consulted a variety of public and private oracles, came to Iolaus with the news that victory depended upon the sacrifice of some royal maiden and that he could not in good conscience slay his own daughter. When the distraught Iolaus offered to surrender himself to Eurystheus, Demophon pointed out that the Argive king desired only the children.

Macaria, daughter of Herakles, emerged

from the temple to offer herself, insisting that she be chosen even after Iolaus proposed that the victim be selected by lot. After she had been led away, a servant of Hyllus, son of Herakles, entered to announce that Hyllus had arrived with an army to aid the Herakleidae. The elated Iolaus summoned Alcmene from the temple to hear the good news. He was so overjoyed that in spite of his age he insisted on donning armor and setting off to take part in the battle.

Later a servant brought Alcmene tidings of victory and described how, after the cowardly Eurystheus had refused single combat with Hyllus, the rejuvenated Iolaus plunged into the fray and took Eurystheus prisoner. Alcmene was astounded that Iolaus had not killed him on the spot. When guards brought the bound Eurystheus before her, she demanded his immediate death.

The messenger of Demophon cautioned her that such an act would violate Athenian custom, but the vengeful Alcmene swore that she herself would kill Eurystheus if necessary. The Argive king explained that he had never had any personal quarrel with the Herakleidae and that he was merely forced to do as he did by the divine power of Hera, the deity of Argos. Nevertheless, he would not ask for mercy; in fact, since an old oracle had predicted it, he was quite willing to submit to death if his body would be buried at Pallene, where in the future his spirit could protect his former enemies. The bloodthirsty Alcmene then demanded that he be taken away from the city, slain, and cast to the dogs. The chorus, observing that so long as Eurystheus was not killed within Athens no stain of guilt would come upon the city, led him away to be executed.

CHILDREN OF THE GHETTO

Type of work: Novel
Author: Israel Zangwill (1864-1926)
Type of plot: Ethnocentric realism
Time of plot: Nineteenth century
Locale: London
First published: 1892

Principal characters:
    MOSES ANSELL, a pious Jew
    ESTHER, his daughter
    HANNAH JACOBS, a beautiful young Jewess
    REB SHEMUEL JACOBS, her father, a rabbi
    DAVID BRANDON, in love with Hannah
    MELCHITSEKEK PINCHAS, a poor poet and scholar
    MRS. HENRY GOLDSMITH, Esther Ansell's benefactress
    RAPHAEL LEON, a young journalist
    THE REVEREND JOSEPH STRELITSKI, minister of a fashionable synagogue
    DEBBY, a seamstress

Critique:

Children of the Ghetto, A Study of a Peculiar People is a story of the Jews of London, a novel which at the time of its publication uncovered a new vein of English fiction. The ghetto, as here presented, was a separate community continually struggling with the influx of destitute Poles, and the fierce, surging life within—a life both comic and tragic —was regulated by the canons of strict orthodoxy. In one sense this work is not a novel. There is no central plot, only a series of loosely grouped episodes, and the numerous characters are only vaguely connected in many instances. Although Zangwill wrote from a parochial point of view, the book is valuable for its descriptions of seething life, its study of racial strivings and discontents, and its warm, sympathetic character sketches.

The Story:

Moses Ansell accepted poverty as the natural condition of the chosen people. A pious man, he observed all the rituals of his religion, but even his meek wife, before she died, realized that he should have spent less time in prayer and more time working. His family consisted of Esther, a serious young girl, two smaller sons, a little daughter, and their complaining grandmother. The Ansells lived in one room in the ghetto. When the mother died, Benjamin, an older son, had been put in an orphanage.

One night Esther returned from the soup kitchen with a pitcher of soup and two loaves of bread. At the doorway of their room she fell and the soup spilled. The hungry family snatched at the bread. Becky Belcovitch, from the floor below, came to complain that the soup had leaked through the ceiling. When the Belcovitches heard what had happened, they sent up their own rations to the Ansells.

Malka Birnbaum was the cousin of Moses' dead wife. Occasionally, when the Ansells grew too hungry, she would give Moses a few shillings and berate him for his pious ineptitude. Malka had two daughters, Milly and Leah, by her first husband. Milly was married. Leah had become engaged to Sam Levine, a commercial traveler.

At the feast of redemption for Milly's infant son, Sam pretended that he had forgotten to give Leah a present. He took from his pocket an expensive ring and held it up for all to admire. Playfully he slipped it on the finger of Hannah Jacobs, the beautiful daughter of Reb Shemuel, while he repeated the words he had memorized for his marriage to

Leah. The horrified company realized at once what Sam was too secular to understand; he and Hannah were married according to the law. Hannah and Sam arranged for the ritualistic formality of a divorce after his next trip.

As compensation, Sam and Leah took Hannah to the Purim ball. There Hannah was greatly taken with David Brandon, a young South African immigrant who no longer observed orthodox practices. Hannah already had an earnest suitor, an impoverished poet and scholar named Pinchas. Although Reb Shemuel listened favorably to his bid for Hannah's hand, the indulgent rabbi refused to force his daughter to marry anyone she did not love.

Sugarman, the marriage broker, had a daughter, Bessie, who was in love with Daniel Hyams, but there was no talk of marriage because Daniel supported his aged parents. When the father saw that Daniel remained unmarried because he could not keep up two households, the old man pretended to receive word from a brother in America. With borrowed money the two old people took steerage passage for New York.

Sugarman, seeing that Becky Belcovitch was of an age to marry, thought he could arrange a match with Shosshi Shmendrik, a street hawker. Bear Belcovitch, her father, gave his consent. Becky, having other ideas, tried never to be at home when Shosshi came courting. One day Shosshi stationed his barrow in front of Widow Finkelstein's store. Because he started to leave without paying his sixpence rent, the determined widow harangued him in the street and continued the argument at his house. When she admitted to owning two hundred and seventeen golden sovereigns as well as her shop, Shosshi fell in love with her. Their marriage was a great success.

The disconsolate Pinchas met Wolf, a Jewish labor leader. When starving sweatshop workers struck for higher wages, Pinchas persuaded Wolf to let him address the strikers. In a speech filled with Messianic delusions, he asked them to support his candidacy for Parliament. In disgust the workers threw him out.

Occasionally Benjamin Ansell came to see his family, but he did not get on well with them. Only Esther, who had dared to look into a New Testament, sympathized with him. Word came from his school that the boy had pneumonia. In his dying delirium Benjamin spoke only Yiddish, and Moses, sitting by his bedside, rejoiced that his son died a real Jew.

When Hannah and David planned to marry, Reb Shemuel was apprehensive of her suitor's orthodoxy. David assured the rabbi that his family was orthodox and that he himself was a *cohen*, a priest. But Reb Shemuel declared they could never marry. Hannah had been divorced, and the law forbade a *cohen* to take a divorced woman. Hannah and David planned to run away to America. But after she had accompanied her father to the *Seder* services, Hannah realized the old ways were too strong for her to break. Heartbroken, she renounced David forever.

Ten years later wealthy Mrs. Henry Goldsmith entertained at a *Chanukah* dinner. Most of the guests were artists and intellectuals who had drifted away from the strict practices of Old Jewry. Among them was Raphael Leon, a young journalist. One topic of conversation was *Mordecai Josephs,* a new novel scandalous to West End Judaism, written by an unknown author named Edward Armitage. Sidney Graham, a young dilettante, praised the novel but criticized the crudity and immaturity of the writer. Raphael noticed that a shy, dark girl followed the conversation closely but said nothing.

The girl was Esther Ansell. Mrs. Goldsmith, after packing old Moses and the rest of his brood off to America, had adopted Esther and educated her. A graduate of London University, Esther was trying to decide upon a career. Unknown to all, she was Edward Armitage, the author of *Mordecai Josephs*.

567

Raphael's interest in her continued after he became editor of a Jewish paper, *The Flag of Judah,* financed by Mr. Goldsmith. Pinchas, the neglected poet, aspired to become a contributor. Raphael, unwilling to compromise between his principles and the wishes of his sponsor, was unhappy in his work.

At the theater Esther encountered Leonard James, the snobbish, vulgar brother of Hannah Jacobs. A short time later Leonard went to see Esther. They quarreled and he reminded her that her family had always been *Schnorrers,* beggars. Esther, feeling that he might be right, decided to abuse the generosity of the Goldsmiths no longer. When Raphael called, she told him her decision and announced that she was Edward Armitage.

Dissatisfied with himself, Raphael had an interview with the Reverend Joseph Strelitski, a fashionable minister who was, like Esther, of humble origins. Regarding himself as a hypocrite, a slave to wealth and outmoded ritual, Strelitski intended to resign his pastorate and go to America. Encouraged by his and Esther's examples, Raphael felt relieved when Mr. Goldsmith fired him and made Pinchas editor of the paper.

Esther, meanwhile, had returned to the ghetto to stay with Debby, a seamstress she had known years before. Surrounded by friends of her childhood, she felt herself drawn by family ties; she would go to America. She was glad when her publisher told her that her novel promised to be a success, for she would not go to her family empty-handed. On a ship loaded with Jewish emigrants she and Strelitski sailed for America. But there was no deep sadness in the parting when Esther said goodbye to Raphael. He would come to her later.

CHITA

Type of work: Novel
Author: Lafcadio Hearn (1850-1904)
Type of plot: Exotic romance
Time of plot: Nineteenth century
Locale: Louisiana coastal waters
First published: 1889

Principal characters:
 FELIU VIOSCA, a fisherman
 CARMEN VIOSCA, his wife
 CHITA, a foundling
 DR. JULIEN LA BRIERRE, her father

Critique:

Hearn's method of telling a story, his purpose, and his literary style are always distinctive. The style is always abrupt, an almost disdainful attitude on the part of the writer, as if he scorned any communication between himself and the reader. *Chita: A Memory of Last Island* is more, however, than a straight narrative. It is both poetry and story, for grained into the plot development is the exotic and dramatic description of the islands of the Louisiana coast and of a devastating hurricane that occurred there in the middle of the nineteenth century.

The Story:

Southward from New Orleans one passes settlements of many nationalities and races, Western and Oriental. Beyond lies an archipelago, the islands of which are Grande Pass, Grande Terre, and Barataria. Still to the south lies Grande Isle, a modern bathing resort, the loveliest island in the Gulf of Mexico. Last Island, forty miles west of Grande Isle, is now desolate, but at an earlier time it was the most popular of the group and a fashionable resort. The hotel there was a two-story timber structure with many apartments, a dining-room, and a ballroom. One night the sea destroyed it.

On the northwest side of each island are signs of the incessant influence of the wind and sea, for the trees all bend away from the water. All along the Gulf coast, and on the island beaches, are the ruins of hurricanes, skeletons of toppled build-

ings and broken tree trunks. The land itself is being eaten away.

The innocent beauty of summer on these islands is impossible to express. Years ago Last Island was immersed in the azure light of a typical July. It was an unusually lovely summer and the breathless charm of the season lingered on. One afternoon the ocean began to stir and great waves started to hurl themselves over the beaches, giving warning on Last Island that a hurricane was brewing. The wind, beginning to blow, continued for a few days to stir the water. A steamer, the *Star*, due that day, was not expected to arrive.

Captain Abraham Smith, an American, knew the sea and he knew his ship. Sensing that he might be needed, he had sailed for Last Island. As he approached he saw the storm rising. He ordered the excess weight of the *Star* tossed overboard to help her ride out the storm. On the island, however, the guests at the hotel continued to dance until they noticed water at their feet and the building began to be buffeted by the waves. Captain Smith spent the night rescuing as many as he could. Buildings were ripped apart, the shores were lashed by wind and wave, lakes and rivers overflowed, and by daybreak countless corpses floated on the stormy sea.

When the hurricane subsided, scavengers came to claim whatever plunder could be salvaged from the ruins and from the bodies of the dead.

On a tiny volcanic island lived Feliu Viosca, a fisherman, and his wife Carmen.

On the night of the terrible storm Carmen was awakened by the noise. Afraid, she aroused her husband, whose calmness comforted her, and he ordered her to return to sleep. In her dreams her dead child, dark-eyed Conchita, came to her.

The next day the fishermen, gathered at the shore, stood watching the wreckage and the bodies floating past. A flash of yellow caught Feliu's eye. In a moment he had stripped and was swimming out toward a child, still alive, clinging to her drowned mother. Feliu managed to rescue the baby and swim back to shore.

The half-drowned child was taken to Carmen, whose skillful hands and maternal instincts nursed the little girl into a warm, sound sleep; there was hope she would survive. Her yellow hair had saved her, for it was the flash of sun on her tresses that had caught Feliu's eye.

Captain Harris, of New Orleans, along with several other men, was sailing up and down the coast in search of missing persons, dead or still alive after the storm. Ten days after the rescue of the girl, Harris came to Viosca's wharf. Hardly able to communicate with the men, Feliu told them the story of his heroism, but cautioned them that if they wished to question the child they must proceed gently, since she was still not fully recovered from shock.

The child's Creole dialect was not comprehensible to anyone there until Laroussel, a Creole, began to question her. In her broken speech she told him that her Creole name was Zouzoune, her real one Lili. Her mother was called Adele and her father Julien. Nothing more could be determined. Realizing that the child's relatives might never be found, Harris decided to leave her with Feliu and Carmen, who promised to give her excellent care. Laroussel gave the little girl a trinket that had caught her eye. Although other searching parties stopped to see Feliu's waif, the child's identity remained a mystery. Meanwhile, near another island, a pair of bodies drifting in the sea had been identified as those of Dr. Julien La Brierre and his wife Adele. The doctor had survived, however; six months later he was in New Orleans looking at his own epitaph and that of his wife.

Dr. La Brierre had grown up in New Orleans. In maturity, to please his father, he had studied medicine in Paris. After his return to New Orleans he had fallen in love and had been wounded in a duel with a rival named Laroussel. Following the death of his father and mother, Julien had married Adele, and Zouzoune was born.

On the lonely island the small child, now called Chita, had become a member of the Viosca family. Gradually she adapted herself to the ways of her foster parents.

Years later Dr. La Brierre was practicing in New Orleans, a lonely and kindly physician. One year Edwards, an elderly patient of his, went to Viosca's Point, which Captain Harris had recommended for the sick man's recovery. While there, Edwards suffered a stroke. Hurriedly summoned, Dr. La Brierre arrived too late to help his patient.

Before the doctor could set out for home, he too became ill. Carmen nursed him. In the vague consciousness that accompanied his malady, the doctor saw Chita, whose resemblance to his dead wife greatly excited him. In his delirium he called out to Zouzoune, to Adele, while Carmen tried to calm him.

Reliving the horror of the hurricane that had taken Adele and Zouzoune from him, the sick man died.

THE CHOUANS

Type of work: Novel
Author: Honoré de Balzac (1799-1850)
Type of plot: Historical romance
Time of plot: 1799
Locale: Brittany
First published: 1829

Principal characters:

MARIE DE VERNEUIL, natural daughter of a duke
THE MARQUIS DE MONTAURAN, leader of the Chouans
MARCHE-À-TERRE, a Chouan
FRANCINE, Marie's maid
CORENTIN, agent of the Republic
MADAME DU GUA SAINT-CYR, a royalist in love with Montauran
HULOT, soldier of the Republic

Critique:

The Chouans was the first of Balzac's novels to gain recognition. It shows much unevenness in structure and the characters are but shallowly motivated; the action scenes, however, are well written. An obscure chapter in French history comes to life in this imitation of Scott's historical novels. Although few readers of Balzac are likely to place *The Chouans* high among his works, the author himself had the novel reprinted as part of *The Human Comedy* to represent "Scenes of Military Life." As such, it has a definite place in Balzac's work, aside from the picture presented of the struggles of the young Republic.

The Story:

The French Republic, in the years after the Revolution, had many enemies. Abroad, the remaining monarchies watched with cold disapproval the new government; at home, the survivors of the old aristocratic regime intrigued with all the dissident groups at odds with the central government in Paris. In Brittany peasants and smugglers, who came to be called Chouans, finally joined the aristocrats in guerrilla warfare against the Republic.

To put down the outbreak, Hulot, who commanded the Republican garrison at Mayenne, was on his way from Fougères with his conscripted Bretons. He was uneasy, for the Chouans were active and they would make every effort to rescue their comrades. When the Chouans did attack, he was partly prepared. Although the conscripts all got away, Hulot's vigorous defense got his Republican troops safely back to Mayenne. A short time later Hulot was ordered to escort the mail coach from Mayenne to Montagne. Passengers in the coach were Marie de Verneuil and her pretty maid Francine, who had become objects of great curiosity when they stopped at the inn in Mayenne. With them was a third traveler, Monsieur Corentin, a small, secretive man whom Hulot suspected of being a secret agent for the Republic. At Alençon the two women accepted an invitation to breakfast with Madame du Gua and her supposed son, the Citizen du Gua Saint-Cyr. Marche-à-Terre, a Chouan skulking nearby in his rebel uniform of goatskin, observed the party with distrust and sent to Madame du Gua a message warning her to beware of Marie, whom he suspected of being a Republican spy.

Hulot was also uneasy. He was sure that Madame du Gua's son was really the Marquis de Montauran, called Gars, the fiery leader of the Chouans. At last he forced his way into the dining-room to question the man. Marie, attracted to the handsome young man, came to his aid by producing a paper, countersigned by the Paris ministry, which notified all local authorities to obey the bearer. Ordered to retire, the old soldier was furious at having to obey a woman. A loyal Republican, however, he let the son go and announced his intention to resign his commission.

Since all were bound for Fougères, the next day Madame du Gua and her son set out in a carriage with Marie and Francine. Marie's letter had procured them an escort of soldiers to guard them through the dangerous Chouan territory. Once while they were ascending a long hill, Marie and the son walked up behind the coach. Their bearing was almost lover-like, and Madame du Gua seemed strangely jealous for a mother. Marie had little success in learning who the son really was. She in her turn was reticent about her own past.

The Chouans under an aristocratic leader ambushed the coach but were driven off by the Republican guard. The Chouan chief took the opportunity to whisper a warning against Marie to young du Gua.

After the excitement Madame du Gua announced that they were close to the family estate at Vivetière, and she and her son invited their companions to spend the night at the chateau. When the son promised safety for Marie and Francine and supper for the guards, the whole party went to the castle. Once inside, Marie saw that the hall was filled with insurgents who had come to lay plans for continuing the war against the Republic. Marie then realized that Madame du Gua's supposed son was in reality the Marquis de Montauran, the famous Gars. She knew also that she had fallen in love with the handsome rebel.

In spite of Montauran's promise of safe conduct, the jealous Madame du Gua ordered an attack on the Republican guard. Under the fierce Marche-à-Terre the Chouans massacred the guards and took Marie and Francine prisoner. Marche-à-Terre, however, saved Francine, whom he recognized as his former sweetheart. He was also able to rescue Marie, after

Madame du Gua had turned the girl over to the smugglers, and the two women were returned to Fougères in the coach.

In Fougères, Corentin rented a house for Marie and installed her as a great lady. She was tormented by her memories of Montauran and wondered if he really loved her. While walking near the city limits, she saw Madame du Gua and Montauran with a band of skulking Chouans. When Madame du Gua tried to kill Marie with a rifle shot, while Montauran looked on, Marie's love for him turned to hatred and a desire for revenge.

Marie tucked a jeweled dagger in her bodice and set out to kill Montauran. During her search she ran from some roving Chouans and took refuge in a cellar. In an abandoned scullery she found Marche-à-Terre and his band torturing a miser to get his gold. After helping the miser to escape, she was told of a nearby sanctuary, the cottage of Galpe-Chopine, who worked both for the Republicans and the Chouans. Galpe-Chopine's wife Barbette helped Marie to return to Fougères.

When Marie learned that the Chouans planned to give a ball, she resolved to attend. She induced Galpe-Chopine to guide her to St. James, where the aristocrats were gathering. By her great beauty Marie attracted the admiration of all the men, and when she told that she was the daughter of the Duke de Verneuil she removed the smirch on her reputation. Montauran, fascinated anew, escorted her from the ball.

Marie told Montauran her true story. Although she was only the natural daughter of the duke, she had been recognized by him. Unprovided for after his death, she had accepted the guardianship of a seventy-year-old friend of her father. Then, to her horror, she was accused of being the old man's mistress. After two years of adventures she became the wife of Danton. When he died she entered the service of the Republic. Her present mission was to win the love of Montauran and betray him to the government. Montauran, even after hearing her story could not restrain his love for her.

In Fougères, Corentin, now revealed as an agent of the Republic, determined to use Marie as a lure to draw Montauran to his death. The lovers finally decided to get married and flee the intrigues of France. A priest was procured and a small altar was set up in Marie's drawing-room. Then Marie sent word through Barbette to Montauran. Under cover of dense fog Montauran slipped into Fougères and the marriage ceremony was solemnized. But Corentin, who had been on the lookout, warned Hulot, commander of the Republican garrison, that the rebel leader could be captured easily. Hulot stationed a heavy guard around Marie's house, but because of the fog he could not be sure that Montauran was actually in the drawing-room.

In the morning Marie, seeing the guard, roused her husband. Montauran, in Chouan clothes, attempted to escape over the wall but was shot and captured. Marie, meanwhile, had put on Montauran's dress uniform and had gone out the street door. She too was shot down. The lovers, carried to the barracks, died there.

Disgusted with spies and intrigues, Hulot drove Corentin out of town.

A CHRISTMAS CAROL

Type of work: Novelette
Author: Charles Dickens (1812-1870)
Type of plot: Sentimental romance
Time of plot: Nineteenth century
Locale: London, England
First published: 1843

Principal characters:

EBENEZER SCROOGE, a miser
JACOB MARLEY'S GHOST
BOB CRATCHIT, Scrooge's clerk
TINY TIM, Cratchit's son
SCROOGE'S NEPHEW

Critique:

This story has become as much a part of the tradition of Christmas as holly wreaths, mistletoe, and Christmas carols. Dickens' skill with humor and character analysis are particularly evident. At the beginning of the story, we are made to dislike Scrooge for his miserly ways, but we are in sympathy with him as he is subjected to the tortures of his ghostly journeys. Dickens provides a psychological explanation for Scrooge's bitterness and desire to live apart from the rest of the world. At the same time he paves the way for Scrooge's reform, so that it comes as no surprise. It is entirely right that Scrooge should become an example of the meaning of Christmas among men.

The Story:

Ebenezer Scrooge was a miser. Owner of a successful counting-house, he would have in his bleak office only the smallest fire in the most bitter weather. For his clerk, Bob Cratchit, he allowed an even smaller fire. The weather seldom mattered to Scrooge, who was always cold within, never warm—even on Christmas Eve.

As the time approached for closing the office on Christmas Eve, Scrooge's nephew stopped in to wish him a Merry Christmas. Scrooge only sneered, for he abhorred sentiment and thought only of one thing—money. To him Christmas was a time when people spent more money than they should, and found themselves a year older and no richer.

Grudgingly Scrooge allowed his clerk, Bob Cratchit, to have Christmas Day off; that was the one concession to the holiday that he made. But he warned Cratchit to be at work earlier the day after Christmas. Scrooge left his office and went home to his rooms in a building in which he was the only tenant. They had been the rooms of Scrooge's partner, Jacob Marley, dead for seven years. As he approached his door, he saw in the knocker Marley's face. It was a horrible sight. Marley was looking at Scrooge with his eyes motionless, his ghostly spectacles on his ghostly forehead. As Scrooge watched, the knocker resumed its usual form. Shaken by this vision, Scrooge entered the hall and lighted a candle; then he looked behind the door, half expecting to see Marley's pigtail sticking out into the hall. Satisfied, he double-locked the door. He prepared for bed and sat for a time before the dying fire. Suddenly an unused bell hanging in the room began to ring, as did every bell in the house.

Then from below came the sound of heavy chains clanking. The cellar door flew open, and someone mounted the stairs. Marley's ghost walked through Scrooge's door—Marley, dressed as always, but with a heavy chain of cash boxes, keys, padlocks, ledgers, deeds, and heavy purses around his middle.

Marley's ghost sat down to talk to the frightened and bewildered Scrooge. Forcing Scrooge to admit that he believed in him, Marley explained that in life he had never done any good for mankind and so in death he was condemned to constant traveling with no rest and no relief from the torture of remorse. The ghost said that Scrooge still had a chance to save himself from Marley's fate. Scrooge would be visited by three spirits who would show him the way to change. The first spirit would appear the next day at the stroke of one. The next would arrive on the second night, and the last on the third. Dragging his chain, the ghost disappeared.

After Marley's ghost had vanished, Scrooge went to bed and in spite of his nervousness fell asleep instantly. When he awoke, it was still dark. The clock struck twelve. He waited for the stroke of one. As the sound of the bell died away, his bed curtains were pulled apart, and there stood a figure with a childlike face, but with long, white hair and a strong, well-formed body. The ghost introduced itself as the Ghost of Christmas Past, Scrooge's past. When the ghost invited Scrooge to go on a journey with him, Scrooge was unable to refuse.

They traveled like the wind and stopped first at Scrooge's birthplace. There Scrooge saw himself as a boy, neglected by his friends and left alone to find adventure in books. Next he saw himself at school, where his sister had come to take him home for Christmas. Scrooge recalled his love for his sister, who had died young. The ghost reminded him that she had had a son whom Scrooge neglected. Their next stop was the scene of Scrooge's apprenticeship, where everyone made merry on Christmas Eve. Traveling on, they saw a young girl weeping as she told young Scrooge that she realized he loved money more than he loved her. The ghost showed him the same girl, grown older but happy with her husband and children. Then the ghost returned Scrooge to his room, where he promptly fell asleep again.

When the Ghost of Christmas Present appeared, he led Scrooge through the city streets on Christmas morning. Their first stop was at the Cratchit home, where Bob Cratchit appeared with frail, crippled Tiny Tim on his shoulder. In the Cratchit home a skimpy meal became a banquet. After dinner Bob proposed a toast to Mr. Scrooge, even though it put a temporary damper on the holiday gaiety. Then the ghost and Scrooge crossed swiftly through the city where everyone paused to wish one another a Merry Christmas. As they looked in on the home of Scrooge's nephew, gaiety prevailed and Scrooge was tempted to join in the games. There, too, a toast was proposed to Scrooge's health. As the clock began to strike twelve, Scrooge found himself in his room, and the ghost of Christmas Present faded away.

With the last stroke of twelve, Scrooge saw a black-shrouded phantom approaching him, the Ghost of Christmas Future. The phantom extended his hand and forced Scrooge to follow him until they came to a group of scavengers selling the belongings of the dead. One woman had entered a dead man's room, had taken his bed curtains, bedding, and even the shirt in which he was to have been buried. Scrooge saw a dead man with his face covered, but he refused to lift the covering. Revisiting the Cratchits, he learned that Tiny Tim had died.

After seeing his empty counting-house and his own neglected grave, Scrooge realized that it was he who had lain on the bed in the cold, stripped room with no one to mourn his death. Scrooge begged the spirit that it should not be so, vowing that he would change, that he would forever honor Christmas in his heart. He made a desperate grasp for the phantom's hand and realized that the ghost had shriveled away and dwindled into a bedpost. Scrooge bounded out of bed and thanked Jacob Marley's ghost for his chance to make amends. Dashing into the street, he realized that it was Christmas Day. His first act was to order the largest turkey available to be sent anonymously to the Cratchits. He stopped a man whom the day before he had ordered from his counting-house for asking for a contribution, and to him Scrooge gave a large sum of money for the poor. Then he astounded his nephew by arriving at his house for Christmas dinner and making himself the life of the party.

Scrooge never reverted to his old ways. He raised Bob Cratchit's salary, improved conditions in his office, contributed generously to all charities, and became a second father to Tiny Tim. It was said of him thereafter that he truly knew how to keep Christmas well.

A CHRONICLE OF THE CONQUEST OF GRANADA

Type of work: History
Author: Washington Irving (1783-1859)
Time: 1465-1492
Locale: Spain
First published: 1829

Principal characters:
HENRY IV, King of Castile and León
FERDINAND V, King of Spain, his son
ISABELLA THE CATHOLIC, Queen of Spain
MULEY ABUL HASSAN, King of Granada
BOABDIL (EL CHICO), the last King of Granada
AYXA LA HORRA, his mother
ZORAYA, Abul Hassan's wife
EL ZAGAL, the rebel King of Andalusia
VIZIER ABEN COMIXA
THE COUNT OF TENDILLA

Washington Irving, youngest of the eleven children of a wealthy New York merchant, was sickly as a child. Unable to continue in school, he educated himself along lines that struck his fancy, and his studies included the Spanish language. One of the early books in his scattered reading was *Don Quixote,* which inspired in him a life-long interest in Spain and the Spanish people.

In 1825, while traveling in southern France, he decided to see the land of Cervantes, using as his excuse the need to go to Madrid to consult manuscripts dealing with Columbus. Out of this visit developed *A History of the Life and Voyages of Christopher Columbus* (1828). From material uncovered but unsuitable for this work, and from impressions of his travels, he wrote a chronicle of the conquest of Granada which he attributed to an imaginary historian, the Jesuit Fray Antonio Agapida. While in Granada he visited the Alhambra, then no national monument but a dirty, run-down building, and secured permission to live there while writing the tales contained in *The Alhambra* (1832).

In the introduction to the first edition of *A Chronicle of the Conquest of Granada,* Irving invented details of the life of Fray Antonio and affirmed that the original manuscript was in the Escorial Library. In a note to the 1850 revised edition, however, he confessed that the Jesuit priest was his own invention. He also admitted romanticizing some of the scenes and incidents of the history, but in this respect he was only doing what the Spaniards had done before, especially Ginés Pérez de Hita (c. 1544-c. 1619) in his *Civil Wars of Granada* (1595-1604), which he attributed to an imaginary Arabic contemporary.

The advantage of putting the account of the conquest of Granada into the mouth of a monkish zealot like Fray Antonio Agapida was to keep it in spirit with contemporary accounts by orthodox chroniclers of Spain. It also provided an explanation for its attitude toward religion and the throne, so much a part of the Spanish spirit in the fifteenth century.

After seven centuries of warfare between Moors and Christians, Aben Ismael, King of Granada, became weary of fighting in 1457 and bought a truce from King Henry IV of Castile and León. When his proud son, Muley Abul Hassan, inherited the throne in 1465, he stopped payment of the tribute. King Henry did nothing about the matter, but his successors, Ferdinand and Isabella, after amalgamating the kingdom in 1478 sent Juan de Vera as their ambassador to demand resumption of payment. The

Moorish monarch rebuffed the ambassador with the statement that the Moorish mint no longer coined money, only scimitar blades and the heads of lances.

Ferdinand listened to de Vera's report of the strength of the city, whose name means pomegranate, and the impossibility of direct siege, then made a punning threat that he would pick out the pomegranate's seeds one by one. Washington Irving's book tells with fascinating and romantic details how he kept that promise.

Granada in the late fifteenth century was a fortress city of parks, fountains, pools, and architectural gems still to be seen; but it was also a city of intrigue, as Irving bears witness. Among the women of Abul Hassan's harem was the captured daughter of a Christian warlord, Isabella Ximenes de Solís, better known to history by her Arabic name of Zoraya, the Morning Star. As mother of two of the king's sons, she schemed to place one of them on the throne of Granada instead of Abul Hassan's firstborn, Boabdil, the son of Princess Ayxa la Horra. Nobles in the court were taking sides in this intrigue, and one group was plotting to depose the king in favor of Boabdil.

Meanwhile, the ambitious Abul Hassan, unpunished for refusing to pay tribute, decided to break the unwritten truce and reconquer a poorly defended frontier town. Now that war with Portugal had ended, however, Ferdinand was free to retaliate by sending an army against the Moorish town of Alhama. Irving makes the campaign sound like a chess game. Troops from Granada marched to defend the town. Urged by Isabella, the powerful Duke of Medina Sidonia forgot his quarrel with the Marqués of Cádiz. The combined strength of the Spaniards drove Abul Hassan back to Granada, where his disappointed subjects revolted against him and crowned his son Boabdil, nicknamed El Chico, the young king.

By a wealth of details Irving keeps his account from being a dry catalogue of battles and proves that the war was fought during the age of chivalry. Moors and Christians vied to outdo each other in courtesy. Boabdil, captured by King Ferdinand, was released in exchange for Christian captives. Isabella, marching to visit her fighting husband, was allowed to pass by the Moors, who were unwilling to wage war against women. Fatima, niece of Boabdil's vizier, was captured by the Count of Tendilla while on her way to marry the governor of Tetuan. To ransom her, Boabdil offered a hundred Christians in exchange. Without waiting for their arrival, Tendilla loaded Fatima with jewels as a wedding present and escorted her home. The admiring king increased her ransom by twenty priests and a number of peasant women, and the delighted vizier started a correspondence with Tendilla that lasted through the siege and was useful in persuading the hesitant Boabdil of the uselessness of further fighting.

The author divides his study into two volumes, the first dealing with a succession of brief forays, and the second narrating the slow "picking" of the pomegranate seeds. While the world watched, Málaga, Granada's seaport for trade with Syria and Egypt, was besieged. The Grand Turk and the Soldan of Egypt stopped their feuding to send help to their Moorish brother monarch. Queen Isabella called on all Spaniards under the age of seventy to enlist in the Holy War, and she and her daughter, later to marry Henry VIII of England, came to cheer the fighters. Even the ancient Grand Cardinal of Spain donned armor and promised high pay to all who would follow him into battle.

Eventually the worried Boabdil offered to rule Granada as a vassal of Ferdinand if he were allowed time to prepare the minds of his subjects for the change; but with the capitulation of the last Moorish stronghold in sight, the Catholic monarch refused. When the Moors burned the camp of their besiegers, Ferdinand ordered a permanent city built, called Santa Fe, to prove his intentions of remaining in the field until Granada surrendered.

From legends and ballads, as well as histories, Irving reconstructed the last year of the siege. He told of the brave Moor who rode into the Christian camp and flung an insulting spear at the queen's tent and of Hernando Pérez del Pulgar, who answered the Moorish knight by stealing into Granada and fastening a scroll bearing the words "Ave María" to the door of the chief mosque. There were no pitched battles. At the king's command, Spanish soldiers refrained from fighting while they waited for the starving Arabs to capitulate. Finally, on November 25, 1491, a sixty-day truce was declared. Before it ended, Boabdil surrendered, and on January 2, 1492, he marched out of the fallen city. With the Count of Tendilla appointed governor of Granada, Spain concluded a crusade of reconquest that had lasted for seven and a half centuries.

CHRONICLES OF FROISSART

Type of work: History
Author: Jean Froissart (c. 1338-c. 1410)
Time: 1316-1399
Locale: England and Western Europe
First transcribed: 1373-1410

Jean Froissart, by being so much a man of his age, has become a man for all time. This unpriestly priest, this citizen celebrator of chivalry, took such an intense childlike joy in chronicling his times that he devoted an entire half-century to traveling, interviewing, writing and rewriting. He interviewed over two hundred princes in various courts from Rome and the Pyrenees to Edinburgh, and with such zest that he was a favorite of the nobles on both sides in the Hundred Years' War. In his own time his works were widely copied and —a sure sign of the value placed upon them—illuminated.

Although he recorded the Hundred Years' War on a colorful and unprecedented scale, he is not a reliable historian. Born in Valenciennes, now a city in France but at that time in the Low Country countship of Hainaut, Froissart was a Fleming who shifted his allegiance from one side of the conflict to the other, depending on the court that offered him patronage at the moment. Relying mostly on hearsay evidence from partisan observers, he never consulted official documents, many of which are still extant. As a result his history abounds in anachronisms, erroneous dates, garbled names, and impossible topography. More important, Froissart was afflicted with a psychological astigmatism; he was unaware that the fourteenth century marked the waning of the Middle Ages, and that he was the last of the medieval innocents. The Ottomans had penetrated deep into Europe in the East and Southwest; plagues were ravaging England and the Continent; the incessant wars were gradually increasing in ferocity; the peasants were challenging social order everywhere, the "universal" Church was split between Rome and Avignon—and Froissart was writing to praise famous men. The most significant historian to follow him was Philippe de Comines (c.1447-c.1511), whose *Memoirs* reflect a realism and disillusionment in startling contrast to Froissart's chivalric naïveté.

Froissart's purpose was clear: he wrote "in order that the honorable and noble adventures and feats of arms, done and achieved by the wars of France and England, should notably be registered and put in perpetual memory." His remarkable career was auspiciously launched in 1361 when he went to England as Queen Philippa's secretary and court historian. There he thoroughly ingratiated himself with the aristocracy and began a pro-English account of the wars from the time of Edward III in 1316 to the death of Richard II in 1399. Curiously enough, he makes no mention of Chaucer, a tacitly ignored rival, at court; and Chaucer reciprocated the slight. After the queen's death in 1369, Froissart returned to Valenciennes, went obscurely into business ("je me suis mis dans la marchandise"), and completed Book I of the *Chronicles* under the patronage of Robert of Namur, Philippa's nephew. A very large proportion of that version was directly plagiarized from his pro-English predecessor, Jehan le Bel, but Froissart's fame was such that Count Guy de Blois gave him first a prosperous living at Lestinnes and later a sinecure as a private chaplain. Under Count Guy's patronage Froissart traveled through France, making an especially fruitful trip in 1388 to Gaston de Foix in Orthez. During this period, he rewrote Book I and completed Books II and III, adopting a pro-French perspective on the wars. "Let it not be said," he prevaricates, "that I have corrupted this noble history through the favor accorded me by Count Guy de Blois, for whom I wrote it. No, indeed! For I will say nothing but the truth and keep a straight course without favoring one side or the other." The facts belie these lofty words.

In 1397 Count Guy de Blois died, a sot who had sold his patrimony, and Froissart gained a new patron in the Duke of Bavaria, who sent him again to England. Although Richard II, the new king, did not receive him cordially, when he retired to his home town eighteen months later, to revise and complete his work, it is interesting to note that the chronicles again took on a somewhat pro-English turn, whether subconsciously or by design.

Froissart more than returned the favors of his patrons by immortalizing them as heroes and heroines of chivalry, and he took immense delight in doing so: "I have taken more pleasure in it than in anything else. The more I work on these things, the more they please me, for just as the gentle knights and squires love the calling of arms and perfect themselves by constant exercize, so I, by laboring in this matter, acquire skill and take pleasure in it." What Froissart loved most was the resplendent panoply and pageantry of jousts and battle and the *Chronicles* are really a pastiche of anecdotes, great and small. His knights are invariably "noble, courteous, bold, and enterprising" and his ladies are eternally noble, beautiful, and gentle. It is no wonder that Sir Walter Scott said of Froissart, "This is my master!"

The *Chronicles* abound in dramatic vignettes: the Black Prince graciously submissive to his own prisoner, King John; the Duke of Brabant's envoy sick almost to death of the treachery he has unwittingly performed; King Henry IV meditatively feeding his falcons as he deliberates on the murder of deposed Richard; Gaston de Foix discovering a purse of poison on his treacherous son's person and unwillingly killing him; the blind King of Bohemia found dead in battle surrounded by the bodies of loyal guardsmen. In these narratives Froissart's style occasionally soars above the conventional rhetoric of the medieval romance. Johan Huizinga is surely too harsh when he says that "poverty and sterility" mark a "style wholly devoid of rhetorical qualities," for Froissart can range from the crude language of peasants and soldiers to the lofty rhetoric of the Bishop of St. Andrew's. A knight storming battlements in Spain leans over the wall to see the defenders, "ugly as monkeys or bears devouring pears." The Earl of Derby greets Pembroke after the battle of Auberoche: "Welcome, cousin Pembroke, you have come just in time to sprinkle holy water on the dead!" "Where is that son of a Jew's whore?" demands de Trastamara before the murder of Don Carlos.

Perhaps one of the finest little dramas concerns Edward III's love-game of chess with the Countess whom he has rescued from a Scottish siege:

When the chessmen arrived, the King, who wished to leave some possession of his with the Countess, challenged her, saying: "My lady, what stakes will you play?" And the Countess replied: "And you, Sire?" Then the King placed on the table a very fine ring, set with a large ruby, which he was wearing on his finger. The Countess said: "Sire, Sire, I have no ring as valuable as that." "Lady," said the King, "put down such as you have, it is indeed good enough."

The Countess, to please the King, took from her finger a gold ring, which was not of great worth. Then they played at chess together, the Countess playing as well as she could, in order that the King should not consider her too simple and ignorant; and the King made wrong moves, and did not play as well as he might. And there was scarce a pause between the moves but he looked so hard at the Countess that she lost countenance and fumbled her game. And when the King saw that she had lost a knight, a rook, or whatever it might be, he lost too to keep the Countess in play.

Froissart is by no means always so delicately perceptive. He can describe in gruesome detail the dismemberment of Hugh Despencer, the heart thrown into the fire, the head sent to London, and the pieces of his quartered body carried off to be displayed in other cities—and then calmly proceed with the narrative of the queen's joyous arrival for feasting in London. One feels a bizarre sense of the grotesque when Froissart asserts matter-of-factly that Galeas Visconti murdered his uncle "by bleeding him in the neck, as they are wont to do in Lombardy when they wish to hasten a person's end." He laments when captives are killed because they would have brought a good ransom. There are dozens of accounts of towns sacked and women and children murdered, all related without the least trace of compassion. Perhaps this detachment is explained by the fact that death was common (G. G. Coulton cites the fact that in proportion to the total population, more Christians killed each other then than they do now) or by Froissart's evident commitment to Boethian philosophy of the Wheel of Fortune, dramatically presented in one of the illuminated miniatures of an early manuscript.

Montaigne, who was a touchstone of the Renaissance just as Froissart was of the Middle Ages, said of the *Chronicles* that they were the "crude and unshapen substance of history." If he meant that they lacked any profound philosophical perspective, he was right. The simplicity of Froissart's mind can be seen in his obtuse declaration that "Mankind is divided into three classes: the valiant who face the perils of war . . . , the people who talk of their successes and fortunes, and the clerks who write and record their great deeds." Froissart was a man who could report, without realizing the realistic significance of his account, that French King John's Round Table of three hundred knights, who were to meet annually to tell their tales and have their heroism recorded, lasted only one year because all the knights perished in their foolhardiness.

Nevertheless, the *Chronicles* are rich in the sheer entertainment value of Gothic adventures. Froissart's account of the blazing day when Charles VI went mad is illustrative. As the troupe rode along, a page accidentally struck another's helmet with his spear:

> The King, who rode but afore them, with the noise suddenly started, and his heart trembled, and into his imagination ran the impression of the words of the man that stopped his horse in the forest of Mans, and it ran into his thought that his enemies ran after him to slay and destroy him, and with that abusion he fell out of his wit by feebleness of his head, and dashed his spurs to his horse and drew out the sword and turned to his pages, having no knowledge of any man, weening himself to be in a battle enclosed with his enemies, and lifted up his sword to strike, he cared not where, and cried and said: "On, on upon these traitors!"

Of greater horror are the descriptions of Sir Peter of Be'arn haunted by the ghost of a bear; or of the King of France at a marriage feast almost cremated alive when five of his squires dressed in pitch-covered linen for an entertainment brushed against a torchlight and were consumed in the flames. It is for these tales that Gray dubbed him "the Herodotus of a barbarous age," but it is for his celebration of chivalry that he was first translated into English by Sir John Bourchier, Lord Berners, in 1523-1525. In the preface to that work, Lord Berners cites a reason for reading the *Chronicles* that is still valid five centuries later: "What pleasure shal it be to the noble gentylmen of Englande to se, beholde, and rede the highe enterprises, famous actes, and glorious dedes done. . . ."

CICERO'S ORATIONS

Type of work: Speeches
Author: Marcus Tullius Cicero (106-43 B.C.)
First transcribed: 80-43 B.C.

When one thinks of the greatness of Rome and especially of its government, the name of Cicero is likely to come to mind. While a figure like Julius Caesar may symbolize the military greatness of imperial Rome, the figure of Cicero is a symbol of Roman justice and law, of the Roman Senate and its traditions, and of Roman greatness in philosophy and literature. Cicero is important in literature primarily for his orations and his numerous writings about oratory and rhetoric. As the author of these writings Cicero set a pattern in public speaking that is still alive in European culture. More than that, because of what he wrote and said, because of the viewpoints he held and defended, even to dying for them, Cicero became historically one of the great advocates of culture and conservatism.

Cicero took ten years to prepare himself as a lawyer before he appeared on behalf of a client in public. In those years of preparation he held, as he did all his life, that a thorough education is necessary for success in any activity. There have been exponents of oratory who have averred that manner is everything; Cicero disagreed, believing that matter is as inescapably a factor in oratorical success as is manner. In the *Orator,* one of his most mature pieces of writing on the art of oratory, Cicero wrote that his own success, like that of any orator, was more to be credited to his study of the philosophers than to his study of earlier rhetoricians, and that no one can express wide views, or speak fluently on many and various subjects, without philosophy. Although Cicero tried to make a science of rhetoric and saw profit in his own attempts at its systemization, he also realized that no simple set of formulas could ever make a great orator. As he put it, an eloquent man should be able to speak "of small things in a lowly manner, of moderate things in a temperate manner, and of great things with dignity."

In Cicero's time there were two prevalent styles in oratory, the Attic and the Asian. In the latter type, Cicero himself discerned two varieties, the one epigrammatic and euphuistic, dependent upon artful structure rather than importance of content, and the other characterized by a swift and passionate flow of speech in which choice of words for precise and elegant effect was a dominant factor. Cicero found both styles wanting in some degree and built his own style upon an eclectic combination of the two.

Fifty-eight speeches by Cicero are still extant, although not all have complete texts. The number of his speeches is unknown, but more than forty are known to have been lost. Not all the speeches Cicero wrote were delivered; sometimes he wrote them for an occasion which did not occur. His second *Philippic* is an example of such a speech. Marcus Antonius was so enraged by Cicero's first speech against him after the death of Julius Caesar that Cicero's friends persuaded the orator to leave the city of Rome temporarily. While absent from Rome, living at a villa near Naples, Cicero wrote the second *Philippic,* which was not spoken in the Senate or even published immediately. A copy was sent, however, to Brutus and Cassius, who enjoyed its invective against their enemy.

Not all of Cicero's speeches are of equal interest to a modern reader. His earliest extant oration, containing relatively little of interest, was delivered in a law court on behalf of Publius Quinctius. Cicero appeared for the defense, as he usually did, and spoke against Quintus Hortensius, the greatest lawyer in Rome at the time. Although Cicero won his case, it is difficult for a modern reader to retain interest in a case decided two thousand years ago when the stuff of the argument is largely points of law. But this speech, along with other early efforts, provided the opportunity for Cicero to prove himself. He made such a reputation that he was chosen to prosecute Caius Verres, who was accused of tyranny and maladministration in Sicily. Once again the famous Hortensius was Cicero's legal opponent. In the second oration he made against Verres, Cicero managed to produce such overwhelming evidence against the defendant that he went voluntarily into banishment. The evidence included chicanery designed to prevent the case from coming to trial, and even Hortensius could find little to say for the defendant. Although Cicero had no occasion to deliver five additional speeches he had written for the trial, scholars have judged that they are among Cicero's best and have found them excellent sources for material about Sicilian government, history, and art. Another of Cicero's noteworthy speeches is the one given in defense of Aulus Cluentius, who was tried and acquitted on a charge of having poisoned his father-in-law, who had tried a few years before to poison Cluentius.

Cicero's intent was to move his hearers, and his devices to insure victory in court were not always above reproach, as his speech in defense of Lucius Flaccus indicates. The defendant was accused of extortion while an administrator in Asia, and apparently Cicero could find little to say in his client's defense beyond impugning the Jews and Greeks who were witnesses against him, members of groups not much in favor in Rome. Of even greater interest is Cicero's defense of Aulus Licinius Archias, a poet of Greek descent whose status as a Roman citizen had been questioned. In this oration Cicero developed a long passage in praise of literature, saying that literature and its creators are of paramount interest to a nation because they afford excellent material for speeches, because they make

great deeds immortal by preserving them in writing, and because they give readers a useful and refreshing pastime.

Not all of Cicero's speeches were intended for courtroom presentation. Some were written for delivery in the Senate and some with a view to Cicero's own benefit. In 58 B.C. Cicero was exiled temporarily as a result of his activities in crushing the conspiracy of Catiline. When Pompey recalled him to Rome a year later, he thanked the Roman Senate in one speech for his recall; in another he thanked the Roman people generally; and in a third he made a request to the Senate for the return of his home, which had been taken over by Clodius for the state.

The most famous of Cicero's speeches are those he wrote against Marcus Antonius after the death of Julius Caesar. Cicero, a conservative, had not been favorable to the autocracy of Caesar and rejoiced when Caesar was assassinated. During an eight-month period in 44-43 B.C., when Marcus Antonius presumed to try to succeed Caesar, Cicero directed fourteen orations against him. These orations, passionate and sincere, are called the *Philippics*, after the famous speeches of Demosthenes against Philip, the father of Alexander the Great. In his first speech Cicero spoke with some moderation, speaking only of Antonius' public life and appealing to his sense of patriotism. In later speeches, especially the second *Philippic*, he made all sorts of attacks on Antonius' private life, accusing him of almost every conceivable type of immorality. Eventually Antonius had his revenge: when he, Lepidus, and Octavianus formed their triumvirate, Cicero was put to death.

Whether Cicero's *Orations* will ever again be popular with readers is doubtful. Orations of any kind are in little favor today. More than that, too few modern readers have the background in Roman history and culture needed to enjoy reading what Cicero wrote and said two thousand years ago.

THE CID

Type of work: Drama
Author: Pierre Corneille (1606-1684)
Type of plot: Romantic tragedy
Time of plot: Eleventh century
Locale: Seville
First presented: 1636

Principal characters:
DON FERNAND, King of Castile
DOÑA URRAQUE, Infanta, daughter of Fernand
DON DIÈGUE, father of Rodrigue
DON GOMÈS, father of Chimène
DON RODRIGUE, accepted suitor of Chimène
DON SANCHE, in love with Chimène
CHIMÈNE, daughter of Don Gomès

Critique:

In France, "Good as *The Cid*" became a proverb used to bestow high praise. *The Cid,* a tragedy in the neo-classical tradition, is generally ranked as the best of Corneille's works. The subject of the drama is man himself, and the hero determines his own fate in this tragedy of renunciation.

The Story:

Because she was the princess royal, the Infanta felt she could not openly love Rodrigue, a nobleman of lower rank. She encouraged, therefore, the growing attachment between Chimène and Rodrigue. Chimène asked her father, Don Gomès, to choose for his son-in-law either Rodrigue or Sanche. She awaited the choice anxiously; her father was on his way to court and she would soon hear his decision. Don Gomès chose Rodrigue without hesitation, chiefly because of the fame of Don Diègue, Rodrigue's father.

A complication soon arose at court. The king had chosen Don Diègue as preceptor for his son, the heir apparent. Don Gomès felt that the choice was unjust. Don Diègue had been the greatest warrior in Castile, but he was now old. Don Gomès considered himself the doughtiest knight in the kingdom. In a bitter quarrel Don Gomès unjustly accused Don Diègue of gaining the king's favor through flattery and deceit. He felt the prince needed a preceptor who would be a living example, not a teacher who would dwell in the past. In the quarrel, Don Gomès slapped his older rival. Don Diègue, too feeble to draw his sword against Don Gomès, upbraided himself bitterly for having to accept the insult. His only recourse was to call on his young son to uphold the family honor.

Torn between love and duty, Rodrigue challenged Don Gomès to a duel. After some hesitation because of Rodrigue's youth and unproved valor, Don Gomès accepted the challenge of his daughter's suitor. To the surprise of the court, Rodrigue, the untried novice, killed the mightiest man in Castile, piercing with his sword the man whom he respected as his future father-in-law.

Chimène now felt herself in a desperate plight because her love for Rodrigue was mixed with hatred for the murderer of her father. She finally decided to avenge her father by seeking justice from the king. Since she had the right to petition the king, Don Fernand was forced to hear her pleas. In the scene at court, Don Diègue made a strong counter-plea for his son, reminding the king that Rodrigue had done only what honor forced him to do—uphold the family name.

The king was saved from the vexing decision when fierce Moors assaulted the walls of Seville. Chimène awaited the outcome of the battle with mixed emotions. The army of Castile returned in triumph, bringing as captives two Moorish kings. And the man who had inspired and led the Castilians by his audacity was Rodrigue. The grateful king gave the hero a new title, The Cid, a Moorish name meaning "lord." The Infanta was wretched. Although her high position would not allow her to love Rodrigue, she could love The Cid, a high noble and the hero of Castile. She showed her nobility by yielding to Chimène's prior right.

Chimène was still bound to seek redress. The king resolved to test her true feelings. When she entered the throne room, he told her gravely that Rodrigue had died from battle wounds. Chimène fainted. The king advised her to follow the promptings of her heart and cease her quest for vengeance.

Still holding duty above love, however, Chimène insisted on her feudal right of a champion. Sanche, hoping to win the favor of Chimène, offered to meet Rodrigue in mortal combat and avenge the death of Don Gomès. Chimène accepted him as her champion. The king decreed that Chimène must marry the victor.

In private, Rodrigue came to Chimène. Indignant at first, Chimène soon softened when she learned that Rodrigue had resolved to let himself be killed because she wished it. Again wavering between love and duty, Chimène begged him to defend himself as best he could.

Sanche went bravely to meet Rodrigue who easily disarmed his opponent and showed his magnanimity by refusing to kill Chimène's champion. He sent his sword to Chimène in token of defeat. As soon as Chimène saw her champion approach with Rodrigue's sword in his hand, she immediately thought that Rodrigue was dead. She ran in haste to the king and begged him to change his edict because she could not bear to wed the slayer of her lover. When the king told her the truth, that Rodrigue had won, Don Diègue praised her for at last avowing openly her love. Still Chimène hesitated to take Rodrigue as her husband. The king understood her plight. He ordered The Cid to lead an expedition against the Moors. He knew that time would heal the breach between the lovers. The king was wise.

CINNA

Type of work: Drama
Author: Pierre Corneille (1606-1684)
Type of plot: Neo-classical tragedy
Time of plot: c. A.D. 10
Locale: Rome
First presented: c. 1640

Principal characters:
AUGUSTUS, Emperor of Rome
LIVIA, the empress
CINNA, the grandson of Pompey
MAXIMUS, his friend and fellow conspirator
AMELIA, engaged to Cinna
FULVIA, her confidante and companion
POLYCLITUS, once Augustus' slave, now freed
EVANDER, Cinna's freedman
EUPHORBUS, Maximus' freedman

Critique:

Although this play is widely known merely by its title, the subtitle, "The Mercy of Augustus" is more revealing. The theme of royal generosity and clemency made a timely commentary of special importance during the years of Louis XIV's minority, and because of this play its author received benefits from the great Richelieu, formerly his antagonist. The third of Corneille's great plays (the others are *The Cid* and *Horace*), *Cinna* displays the writer's unusual ability to utilize the so-called classical unities of time, place, and action heightened by noble sentiments concerning a superior person. The play is chiefly remembered today for Augustus Caesar's brilliant soliloquy on the confusion of good and evil, the nature of egotism and humility, and the strength and weakness that may exist in one person.

The Story:

Amelia, the daughter of Augustus' tutor, sought revenge for her father's death, and she had asked for vengeance as a provision of her marriage to Cinna, the grandson of Pompey and perhaps more deeply wronged than her loved one.

Her friend Fulvia felt that the plot against Augustus' life could be successful only if anger and hatred were not apparent, especially since Augustus held Amelia in such high esteem that courtiers often asked her to act as an intermediary in affairs at court. The two women debated the worth of Augustus as compared to the cruelties exercised to establish him in his high position. Amelia thought the winning of love through the destruction of a tyrant worth all the risk involved, but self-glorification seemed to Fulvia more obvious in the design than either love or desire for vengeance — a thought which almost caused Amelia to waver in deference to her endangered and beloved Cinna.

Cinna, however, felt the plot had an excellent chance of success. All the conspirators seemed to him as desirous of vengeance and as eager for the rewards of love as he himself, though their inspiration was the result of his oratorical eloquence in reciting his own as well as the historical grievances against the emperor — especially those of the proscripts who, like Amelia's father, deserved better than they received. Cinna himself would, while bearing the sacrificial cup at tomorrow's thanksgiving to the gods, strike home the dagger. His friend Maximus would hold back the mob while others would surround Cinna. Even though he proclaimed he cared not whether he lived or died as long as honor were upheld — an honor not unlike that of Brutus and Cassius, Amelia hastened to add — he believed that the people would then accept him as emperor.

Evander, a freed servant of Cinna, brought news that Augustus wanted to see both Cinna and Maximus, an event which upset their plans and struck fear into Amelia's heart. She retired to Livia's side while Cinna went to confront Augustus after each had sworn to die for the other.

Augustus prefaced his remarks by a long history of man's desire for the empty bauble of power and then asked the two young men to decide his fate, whether he should be the emperor or a private citizen. Both conspirators swore that Augustus, so much more noble than Julius Caesar, should remain supreme in power as the rightful ruler of a grateful empire. Although the sentiment redounded to Augustus' credit, neither felt it more than weakness to want a republic when a monarchy could be maintained. But Augustus was not convinced that five generations of struggle to eminence proved anything more than that the people wanted democracy. Cinna, disclaiming this idea, even citing his grandfather's claim on the throne as evidence, urged Augustus to name a successor who could carry on this Augustan age to posterity. Cinna was surprised to hear himself so named. Although Maximus wavered after such a noble act by their ruler, Cinna remained resolute in his bloody plan: he will kill Augustus, put his bloody hand in that of Amelia, and marry her on Augustus' tomb.

A short time later Maximus revealed to his companion and confidant Euphorbus that he too loved Amelia; the freedman in turn urged his former master to kill Cinna and gain not only the girl but

the emperor's gratitude. Maximus, after much argument, was repelled and yet intrigued by such a prospect. Just such a conflict existed in Cinna's breast as well; he loved the avenger but could not feel true hatred for the object, so dear was his own person to Augustus. Maximus suggested that these sentiments were enfeebling, though he felt the justice of their cause. Cinna, alone with his conscience, reasoned from cause to effect and decided to ask Amelia to release him from his promise of revenge.

Amelia greeted her lover with rejoicing, for she too had heard the news of Augustus' high regard for Cinna; she was, however, relentless in her desire for vengeance. When Cinna pleaded with her to return not only his love but that of Augustus as well, she replied that treason was the only answer to Augustus' tyranny. Finally he agreed to her demands, though not without a commentary on woman's ruthlessness.

In the meantime, perhaps thinking to better his own low position, Euphorbus went to Augustus with news of the plot against him. Augustus was more shocked at Cinna's treachery than at that of Maximus, who at least gave warning of his feelings, and he would have pardoned the latter had not Euphorbus lied and said that Maximus had committed suicide. In a soliloquy Augustus summarized the pity of it all. In the meantime Maximus proposed flight to Amelia as the best of a bad situation. When she spurned his love as traitorous to his friend, he in turn lamented the counsel of Euphorbus.

Augustus summoned Cinna and spoke of the leniency with which he had allowed his traditional enemy to live as recompense for ancient wrongs. For this, he declared, Cinna had planned to kill him at a religious ceremony in the Capitol. The emperor then offered all to Cinna, even though without the help of Augustus the young man could not succeed in his design. Cinna, unrepentant, refused to give Augustus satisfaction over his death.

Amelia and Livia then resolved the conflict, the former taking the blame on herself, even begging to die with Cinna; the lovers quarreled over the seeming break in love and honor, honor and love. Maximus then hastened to reveal his betrayal, through Euphorbus, of the plot. These circumstances moved Augustus to ask the friendship of those whom he most admired and loved. Amelia, the first to respond, was followed by the others, all moved by royal clemency. Livia commended her husband's generosity as a heavenly thing, a bright example to future rulers. Augustus humbly wished it would be so and appointed the morrow as the day of joyous sacrifice, doubly so because of the plotters' remorse and the forgiveness of the man against whom they had schemed.

CINQ-MARS

Type of work: Novel
Author: Alfred Victor de Vigny (1797-1863)
Type of plot: Historical romance
Time of plot: Seventeenth century
Locale: France
First published: 1826

Principal characters:

HENRI D'EFFIAT, Marquis of Cinq-Mars and a conspirator against
Richelieu
CARDINAL RICHELIEU, Minister of State
LOUIS XIII, King of France
ANNE OF AUSTRIA, Queen of France
MARIE DE GONZAGA, beloved of Henri Cinq-Mars
FRANÇOIS AUGUST DE THOU, fellow conspirator with Cinq-Mars

Critique:

Alfred de Vigny, poet and novelist, began this novel while he was still a lieutenant in the French army, before he settled down, after leaving military service, to make art, rather than war, his profession. However, the novel was not Vigny's only important contribution to French literature; he is also highly regarded for his poetry, much of which is written on themes of Christian religious tradition. His novel he based on true incidents in the history of the reign of King Louis XIII, and the novel parallels fact in the story of the conspiracy in which Cinq-Mars was involved. The characterization of Richelieu is an outstanding feature of the book. In this respect Vigny's writing differs from that of many twentieth-century historical novelists, most of whom hang a purely fictitious set of characters and a fictitious plot on the merest thread of historical background, bringing in, briefly, an actual person to give some semblance of reality to the story. *Cinq-Mars* has been called the first French historical novel.

The Story:

One June day in 1639, at the chateau of Chaumont in Touraine, young Henri d'Effiat, Marquis of Cinq-Mars, took leave of his family and set out, at the request of Cardinal Richelieu, Louis XIII's chief minister, to join the king's forces at the siege of Perpignan. Shortly after he left, a guest of his mother's, the Marshal Bassompierre, was placed under arrest at Richelieu's order, and sent in chains toward Paris and the Bastille. Young Cinq-Mars tried to release the marshal, but the haughty old soldier refused to be rescued. As if his flouting of the king's officers were not enough for a day, Cinq-Mars returned under cover of night to the chateau to bid goodbye again to Marie de Gonzaga, the beautiful Duchess of Mantua, who was staying with Cinq-Mars' mother at the chateau. He returned to bid her farewell again because the two, despite the differences of their stations, were very much in love.

Finally leaving Chaumont, Cinq-Mars, accompanied by a few servants, set out for Loudun. Upon his arrival, he found the town in a turmoil because a local clergyman, a monk named Urbain Grandier, was under trial as a magician. Charges against the monk had been made by order of Richelieu, who wished to do away with the independent cleric. The Abbé Quillet, Cinq-Mars' former tutor, had taken the clergyman's part and was just about to leave Loudun in secret, fearful for his own life. At the execution of Grandier, Cinq-Mars discovered that the man's assassins, for they were but that, had given him a red-hot cross to kiss. Seizing the cross, Cinq-Mars struck the judge's face with it, thus earning the enmity of one of Richelieu's most trusted agents.

After the execution Cinq-Mars hastened on his way to Perpignan. In the meantime, however, Cardinal Richelieu was making plans to use Cinq-Mars as a tool in undermining the authority of the king. The report of his agents about Cinq-Mars' actions with regard to the king's officers and Richelieu's agents made no difference to the cardinal, who felt he could shape the young man to his own ends.

Shortly after his arrival at Perpignan, Cinq-Mars was asked to join in a duel between a monarchist sympathizer and a cardinalist sympathizer, and on the monarchist's side. Immediately after the duel he found himself in the thick of an attack on the walls of the besieged city, along with the members of the king's own guard. He behaved so valiantly in the struggle that the captain of the guard introduced Cinq-Mars to the king, much to the disgust of Cardinal Richelieu, who himself had planned to introduce Cinq-Mars to the monarch.

The king took an immediate liking to Cinq-Mars, who had suffered a wound in the battle, and he made the young man an officer in the royal guards. During the battle Cinq-Mars had befriended the son of the judge whom he had struck with the cross at Loudun, and thereby he made a new friend, for the son was a bitter enemy of his father and hated all that his father and Richelieu stood for. At Perpignan, Cinq-Mars also renewed a friendship with a young aristocrat named de Thou, who was later to stand as close to him as a brother.

Two years passed. At the end of that time Cinq-Mars had become the confidant of Louis XIII, an important officer in the court, and the open and avowed enemy of Richelieu. He hated the minister of state for what Richelieu was doing to France, but more important was the fact that Cinq-Mars was ambitious to

win for himself honors and posts that might allow him to marry Marie de Gonzaga, who was being prepared against her will to become the Queen of Poland.

To accomplish his ends, Cinq-Mars had earned more and more of the king's confidence and had improved his influence with the nobility and the army. He also had gained the support of the Duke de Bouillon, who had been estranged from the king by Richelieu. De Bouillon was a strong support, for he had an army of his own in southern France. Cinq-Mars also gained the support of Gaston d'Orleans, the king's brother and another of Richelieu's enemies, and of Anne of Austria, the queen, who wished to protect her children, including the future Louis XIV, from the hatred and ambitions of Richelieu. The success of the plan to depose the minister lay in gaining the king's support for the plan and in securing aid from Spain. Cinq-Mars and his fellow conspirators were forced to deal with Spain on their own initiative, for neither King Louis nor his queen could assume responsibility for bringing Spanish troops into France. In addition, Louis XIII had for so long been under the influence of Cardinal Richelieu and his agents that he had little mind of his own and knew almost nothing of the problems, great and small, which daily beset those who guided the kingdom of France in those turbulent years of the 1640's.

Cinq-Mars, taking his chances, signed a treaty with Spain and sent a copy, concealed in a hollow staff, with a trusted messenger to Spain. Then he approached the king and secured the royal permission to revolt against Richelieu, after convincing the king that the revolt was not against the crown. Immediately afterward, as he was leaving the monarch's apartments, Cinq-Mars realized that an agent of the cardinal was on his way to seek an audience with King Louis. All Cinq-Mars could do was hope that the king would hold to the promise he had given the conspirators.

In order to insure his union with Marie de Gonzaga, Cinq-Mars had the duchess and himself affianced by a clergyman, an act which at that time was the equivalent of legal marriage. But in so doing Cinq-Mars revealed all his plans to the girl in the presence of the priest. Soon afterward he learned that the priest was not his own agent but a spy of Richelieu. Realizing that his plans were endangered, Cinq-Mars immediately went to Perpignan, which was to be the scene of the revolt.

Richelieu had all the time known what was afoot and had made his own plans. Having won over the armies, he knew he had nothing to fear in that quarter. He had also arranged that Marie de Gonzaga, in spite of her love for Cinq-Mars, was to become Queen of Poland. All that was left was to finish off Cinq-Mars and the other conspirators and prevent the treaty from reaching Spain. The messenger carrying the treaty was intercepted in the Pyrenees by the cardinal's agents and killed. In order to gain control of the conspirators, Richelieu pretended to resign his post as minister. King Louis realized within a few hours that he did not know enough about the affairs of the kingdom to rule France. He called back Richelieu and granted the minister's request to do as he pleased with the conspirators. Gaston d'Orleans was banished, while Cinq-Mars and de Thou were arrested at Narbonne, tried at Lyons by a secret court appointed by Richelieu, and beheaded. Marie de Gonzaga, pawn of the cardinal's political schemes, became Queen of Poland.

THE CIRCLE OF CHALK

Type of work: Drama
Author: Unknown; sometimes attributed to Li Hsing-Tao (n. d.)
Type of plot: Romantic comedy
Time of plot: Before the thirteenth century
Locale: Nanking and Peking
First presented: Thirteenth or fourteenth century

Principal characters:
CHANG-HI-TANG, a concubine
CHANG-LING, her brother
MR. MA, a rich mandarin and tax collector
MRS. MA, his wife
CHOW, an official of justice
CHU-CHU, a corrupt judge
PRINCE PO, in love with Chang-hi-tang

Critique:

A typical Chinese classical play in four acts (with a prologue) of the Yuan dynasty (1259-1368), *The Circle of Chalk* is remarkable for the beauty of its lyrical verse. The plot of the original play is concerned with a case of murder and a disputed son solved by a Solomon-like judge. The love affair between the prince and the commoner was introduced by the German adapter, who also widened the application of the symbolic circle of chalk.

The Story:

Chang-hi-tang, a beautiful girl of sixteen, was sold to a teahouse in Nanking by her mother. Her father, a market gardener and grower of silkworms, had been unable to pay his taxes, and in consequence he and his wife and children were driven from their home. Later, the father had hanged himself. Hi-tang's brother, Chang-ling, was opposed to her sale into the house of ill fame but, being a poor scholar, he could do nothing to help his family. He took a part of the money paid for his sister and left Nanking to seek his own fortune.

On her first night in the teahouse, Hi-tang met Prince Po, one of the emperor's many sons, and the young man was struck with her beauty and many accomplishments. The girl drew a circle of chalk to symbolize her fate. But be-

fore their love could be fulfilled, another man visited the teahouse. Mr. Ma, the mandarin and tax collector, outbid the prince and bought Hi-tang as his concubine.

One year later, Hi-tang had given birth to a boy. Mr. Ma, though a man given to sensual pleasure and money-seeking, felt real love for the concubine. Naturally, his childless lawful wife was jealous.

One day Chang-ling, in beggar's rags, appeared at the door of Mr. Ma's house. Hi-tang did not at first recognize him. Then he told her that he had joined a secret society, the Brotherhood of the White Lotus, whose purpose was to take revenge on the oppressors of the poor. Mr. Ma's name was marked in the blacklist, and the gangsters intended to murder him and plunder and burn his house. Hi-tang tried to dissuade her brother by consulting the oracle. She drew a circle and threw a knife. Instead of striking inside the circle, the knife cut the chalkline; it seemed the gods did not approve of the crime. Chang-ling then agreed to reconsider the case. Hi-tang gave him her fur jacket to protect him from cold.

Mrs. Ma, who had seen the stranger, reported to Mr. Ma that Hi-tang had been talking to a man, obviously a lover, and had given away her fur jacket. Mr. Ma was satisfied when Hi-tang said that the man was only her brother.

On the same day Chow, an official of justice in the local courts, was invited to Mr. Ma's house to discuss a legal point. Mr. Ma was thinking of getting a divorce and raising Hi-tang to the rank of wife. Divorce to Mrs. Ma would mean the loss not only of her position but also of the inheritance of Mr. Ma's property. Even if she remained the head wife, as Chow explained to her, the concubine and her boy would be the heirs to the property and she could expect to receive only a certain amount of allowance, as she was childless. She was desperate. But Chow was actually her paramour, so she could depend on his help.

Her solution came when Mr. Ma wanted a drink: she put in the tea the poison brought by Chow. It was Hi-tang who served the tea, so she became the suspect when Mr. Ma dropped dead after taking the drink. She was put under arrest and sent to the prison.

Chu-chu, the local judge, accepted a bribe from Mrs. Ma. Her position was further strengthened by the testimony of a midwife who declared that it was really Mrs. Ma who had given birth to the child and that of two coolies who remembered how they were entertained at a feast in celebration of the birth of Mrs. Ma's child. Mrs. Ma swore that Hi-tang had murdered her master in order to obtain the child and the inheritance. Chow suggested the motive of revenge since Mr. Ma had caused the death of her father. Hi-tang, who had been kneeling inside a circle of chalk, was therefore convicted and sentenced to death.

At that moment a courier arrived from Peking with the news that the old emperor had died. The new emperor had ordered that all death sentences be suspended and that the judges and judged alike be summoned to Peking for imperial investigation. So Hi-tang's life was saved for the time being. Chang-ling, who had been in the crowd of people watching the trial, was angry at the kind of justice his sister received; he expressed his indignant doubt that the new emperor would be any more just than the old. His blasphemy was overheard and he, too, was put in the block.

Hi-tang suffered greatly on the way to Peking under the escort of two soldiers. In a big snowstorm she saw her brother, also guarded by two soldiers, struggling onward. When he collapsed, she took off her mantle to buy a glass of wine to revive him. The soldiers had their drinks, too, but did not pay, much to the chagrin of the innkeeper. Chu-chu, Chow, Mrs. Ma, and the child were traveling in sedan chairs.

In the Imperial Palace the young emperor, who was Prince Po, kept thinking of the teahouse girl whom he had been unable to marry in Nanking a year before. When the prisoners from Nanking were brought before him, he and Hi-tang immediately recognized each other, but their recognition was not noticed by anyone else. He questioned her about her life in the teahouse and suggested that surely she remembered the young prince she had met on the night she entered the place. But it was his official duty to reëstablish justice in China before he could declare his love again. He ordered a circle of chalk to be drawn on the floor wherein the child was placed. The two women were to pull the boy out of the circle, one grasping each arm. She who succeeded in pulling him out would prove herself his mother. Mrs. Ma won with one pull, since Hi-tang pulled only gently, not making the least effort. The emperor asked her why she did not pull with enough strength to win. Hi-tang answered that a child's arms were tender and that to pull him hard would hurt him. Since a mother would never harm her own child, it was decided that Hi-tang was the child's real mother. Also, Mrs. Ma having sworn on oath that the false mother was also the murderess, the murder case was easily solved.

The emperor left his rod of justice in Hi-tang's hand and let her pass sentence on the criminals. She pronounced the judgment that Chow and Chu-chu be deprived of their offices and Mrs. Ma should make herself a cup of tea; the kind of tea she should make was left to her conscience to decide. The emperor approved this judgment and appointed as Chu-chu's successor Hi-tang's brother Chang-ling, whose crime had been pardoned when his criticism of the corruption in government found a sympathetic listener in the emperor, who shared the young scholar's zeal for reform.

After the court had been dismissed, the emperor held Hi-tang for a private talk. She told him that she had had a dream on the first night she was brought to Mr. Ma's house. She was alone, dozing, and she dreamed that a young lord climbed to her bed and loved her as a husband would his wife. The young man was Prince Po. And it was not a dream, for the prince had not given up his desire even after he was outbid, but had followed her to Mr. Ma's house and ravished her while she was still a virgin. Thus, the prince had begotten the child. Hi-tang was made empress.

CLARISSA HARLOWE

Type of work: Novel
Author: Samuel Richardson (1689-1761)
Type of plot: Sentimental romance
Time of plot: Early eighteenth century
Locale: England
First published: 1747-1748

Principal characters:

CLARISSA HARLOWE, a young woman of family and fortune
ROBERT LOVELACE, her seducer
JOHN BELFORD, Lovelace's friend
WILLIAM MORDEN, Clarissa's cousin
ARABELLA, Clarissa's older sister
JAMES, Clarissa's older brother

Critique:

This novel is unusual for the modern reader because of its style. It is an epistolary novel, made up entirely of letters written by the various characters to each other, in which characterization and plot are revealed to the reader. The drawbacks to this form of novel are its tediousness and its superfluities. One wonders how the characters found the time during their adventures to pen such long, involved, and painstaking letters. It is also difficult for a twentieth-century reader to follow Clarissa's logic. Her decision to die, rather than marry the man who had seduced her, is not of a pattern to be quickly assimilated by a mind conditioned to the pragmatism of the modern world. The book is, in spite of sentimental theme and physical bulk, Richardson's best novel.

The Story:

Robert Lovelace, a young Englishman of a noble family, was introduced into the Harlowe household by Clarissa's uncle, who wished Lovelace to marry Clarissa's older sister, Arabella. The young man, finding nothing admirable in the older girl, fell deeply in love with Clarissa, but he quickly learned that his suit was balked by Clarissa's brother and sister. James Harlowe had disliked Lovelace since they had been together at Oxford, and Arabella was offended because he had spurned her in favor of Clarissa. Both were jealous of Clarissa because she had been left a fortune by their grandfather and they had not.

James Harlowe, having convinced his mother and father that Lovelace was a profligate, proposed that Clarissa be married to Mr. Solmes, a rich, elderly man of little taste and no sensibility. When Solmes found no favor in the eyes of Clarissa, her family assumed she was in love with Lovelace, despite her protestations to the contrary.

Clarissa refused to allow Solmes to visit with her in her parlor or to sit next to her when the family was together. Her father, outraged by her conduct, ordered her to be more civil to the man he had chosen as her husband. When she refused, saying she would never marry a man against her will, not even Lovelace, her father confined her to her room.

Lovelace, smitten with the girl's beauty and character, resolved to seduce her away from her family, partly out of love for her and partly in vengeance for the insults heaped upon him by the Harlowe family.

He was greatly aided in his scheme by the domineering personalities of Mr. Harlowe and his son. They took away Clarissa's trusted maid and replaced her with a girl who was impertinent and insolent to the young woman. They refused to let her see any member of the family, even her mother. Clarissa's only adviser whom she could trust was Miss Howe, a friend and correspondent who advised her to escape the house if she could, even if it meant accepting Lovelace's aid and his proposal of marriage.

One evening Lovelace slipped into the garden where Clarissa was walking and entreated her to elope with him. Thinking only to escape her domineering father, she went with him after some protest. Lovelace told her she would be taken to the home of Lord M——, a kinsman of Lovelace, who would protect her until her cousin, Colonel Morden, could return to England and arrange for a reconciliation between Clarissa and her family. Lovelace was not as good as his word, however, for he took her to a house of ill repute, where he introduced her to a woman he called Mrs. Sinclair. Inventing reasons why he could not take her to Lord M——'s house, he persuaded the bewildered girl to pass as his wife, for the time being, and he told Mrs. Sinclair that Clarissa was his wife with whom he could not live until certain marriage settlements had been arranged. Clarissa permitted him to tell the lie, in the belief that it would prevent her father and her brother from discovering her whereabouts.

In Mrs. Sinclair's house she was almost as much a prisoner as she had been in her father's home. Meanwhile her family had disowned her and refused to send her either money or clothes. Indeed, her father declared she was no longer his daughter and he hoped she would have a miserable existence in both this world and the next.

This state of affairs was distressing to Clarissa, who was now dependent upon Lovelace for her very existence. He took advantage of the circumstances to press his love upon her without mentioning his earlier promises of marriage. Clarissa tried to escape and got as far as Hampstead before Lovelace overtook her. There he had two women impersonate his cousins to convince Clarissa that she should return to her lodgings with them. Upon her return to Mrs. Sinclair's house, they filled her with drugs and later Lovelace raped her. A few days later Clarissa received from Miss Howe a letter in which she learned that she was in a house in which no woman of her station would be seen. Again Clarissa tried to escape, this time by calling for aid from a window. Lovelace finally promised to leave her unmolested until she could get aid from her cousin or from Miss Howe.

Lovelace left London for a few days to visit Lord M——, who was ill. While he was gone, Clarissa contrived to steal the clothes of a serving-girl and escape from the house, but within a day or two Mrs. Sinclair discovered Clarissa's whereabouts and had her arrested and imprisoned for debt. When John Belford, a friend of Lovelace, heard of the girl's plight, he rescued her by proving the debt a fraud. He found shelter for Clarissa with a kindly glove-maker and his wife. Tired of her miserable existence, Clarissa began to go into physical decline, in spite of all that the apothecary and doctor secured by John Belford could do for her.

She spent her time writing letters in an effort to secure a reconciliation with her family and to acquaint her friends with the true story of her plight. She refused to have anything to do with Lovelace, who was by that time convinced that he loved her dearly. He wished to marry her, to make amends for the treatment she had suffered at his hands, but she refused his offer with gentle firmness.

As she declined in health, Clarissa's friends did what they could to have her family forgive her. When her father and brother refused to receive her, she went to an undertaking establishment and bought a coffin which she had fitted as she wished, including a plaque which gave the date of her death as the day on which she left her father's house.

On his return to England Colonel Morden tried to raise her spirits, but his efforts failed because he, too, was unable to effect any change in the attitude of the Harlowe family. He also had an interview with Lovelace and Lord M—. The nobleman and Lovelace assured him that their family thought very highly of Clarissa and wished her to marry Lovelace and that Lovelace wanted to marry her. But even her cousin was unable to persuade Clarissa to accept Lovelace as a husband.

Everyone, including the Harlowe family, saw that Clarissa was determined to die. Her father and brother lifted their ban upon her ever entering the Harlowe house; her sister was sorry she had been cruel to Clarissa; and the mother was convinced that she had failed in her duty toward her daughter. They all wrote to Clarissa, begging the girl's forgiveness and expressing their hope she would recover quickly and be reunited with her family. Their letters, however, arrived too late, for Clarissa had breathed her last.

Clarissa was returned to her father's house for her funeral. She was interred in the family vault at the feet of the grandfather whose fortune had been one of the sources of her troubles. Lovelace, who was quite broken up at her death, was persuaded by Lord M— to go to the continent.

There Clarissa was avenged. Lovelace met Colonel Morden in France, and early one winter morning Clarissa's cousin fought a duel with her betrayer. Lovelace was mortally wounded by a thrust through his body. As he lay dying, he expressed the hope that his death would expiate his crimes.

CLAUDIUS THE GOD

Type of work: Novel
Author: Robert Graves (1895-   )
Type of plot: Historical chronicle
Time of plot: A.D. 41-54
Locale: Rome, Britain, the Near East
First published: 1934

Principal characters:
> TIBERIUS CLAUDIUS DRUSUS NERO GERMANICUS, Emperor of Rome
> MESSALINA, his third wife
> CALPURNIA, his mistress
> AGRIPPINILLA, his fourth wife
> LUCIUS DOMITIUS, later called Nero, Agrippinilla's son and Claudius' grandnephew
> HEROD AGRIPPA, Tetrarch of Bashan

Critique:

Claudius the God and His Wife Messalina is characterized by meticulous care of detail and scrupulous handling of incident and character. Graves' technique is such that he is able to re-create a strikingly vivid picture of the life and the times about which he writes. A sequel to *I, Claudius,* this novel is, nevertheless, an entity in itself.

The Story:

When the Emperor Claudius was the neglected scholar of the Claudian family, before his accession to the throne, one of his friends and well-wishers was Herod Agrippa. The Emperor Tiberius had imprisoned Herod for treasonous sentiments, but when Caligula came to the throne he made Herod Tetrarch of Bashan. When Caligula was murdered and Claudius proclaimed emperor by the palace guards, Herod was back in Rome on official business.

Claudius' position was a difficult one at first, especially so as the result of popular opinion that he was a cripple, a stammerer, and an idiot. The Roman Senate did not expect much of such a man and certainly not a capable handling of public affairs after Caligula's four years of misrule. But Claudius immediately began a program of reforms, among them a reorganization of the Senate, a stabilization of the state's finances, and the abolition of many of Caligula's cruel decrees. To carry out his widespread program Claudius appointed many new ministers of state. To his wife, Messalina, he entrusted the office of the Director of Public Morals, as she had been most helpful in reorganizing the Senate list. To his loyal friend, Herod, Claudius gave the lands of Judea, Samaria, and Edom. Then in the open market place before an immense crowd Claudius and Herod made a solemn pact of friendship and loyalty.

Soon after Claudius' ascent to the throne his son Brittanicus was born, followed approximately eleven months later by a daughter named Octavia. After the birth of his second child, Messalina came to Claudius and requested his permission to move into an apartment in the new palace and thus live apart from him. Claudius ruefully agreed to her plan. Messalina's real desire to move to the new palace was greater freedom than she could enjoy under the eyes of Claudius, and her removal to her new quarters began a life of debauchery, licentiousness, political intrigue, bribery, cheating, and murder. Claudius was so busy with matters of state that seven years passed before he heard rumors of Messalina's depravities.

After beginning a public works program, sending an expedition into Ger-

CLAUDIUS THE GOD by Robert Graves. By permission of the author and the publishers, Random House, Inc. Copyright, 1934, by Harrison Smith & Robert Haas, Inc.

many to recover the eagle standard lost by Varus' army, and putting down a minor revolt at home, Claudius turned his attention to the conquest of Britain. The war was hastened by the detention of Roman trading ships by Togodumnus, who was joint ruler with his brother Caractacus, and also by the rapid spread of the Druid cult through Britain and France. Claudius sent Aulus Plautius to Britain with a large invasion force and the promise of additional legions if Roman losses exceeded a certain figure. Aulus managed to cross the Thames and capture London. Then he camped just outside London to await the arrival of Claudius and reinforcements. A decisive battle took place at Brentwood Hill, a ridge between London and Colchester. The Romans won it by means of Claudius' armchair strategy. At the age of fifty-three Claudius fought his first battle, won it, and never fought again. In Britain he was deified as a god and upon his return to Rome he received a full triumph.

He now had to turn his attentions to the East, where for some time he had been receiving disquieting reports regarding Herod Agrippa and his plot to establish a united Jewish empire. Herod had been making secret alliances with neighboring princes and potentates, and he hoped to obtain the support of the Jews by declaring himself the long-awaited Messiah. Claudius realized that affairs had progressed to the stage where there was little he could do to forestall Herod's plans. Herod, at the great festival at which he proposed to proclaim himself the Messiah, permitted neighboring rulers to address him as God without bothering to correct their error. At that moment an owl flew into the arena. Herod remembered a prophecy that when next he saw an owl his death would be near and the number of days left to him would be the same as the number of hoots. The owl hooted five times; five days later Herod was dead. His plot to set up a Jewish kingdom collapsed.

About eight years after they were married, Messalina came to Claudius with a strange tale. Barbillus the astrologer had predicted that her husband would die within thirty days, not later than the Ides of September. She proposed that Claudius' death might be averted if he permitted her to divorce him in order to remarry Silius, her former husband. Claudius finally gave in to her pleading. But the whole story was a ruse to rid herself of Claudius so that she might marry Silius; the two were plotting Claudius' murder and their own accession to the throne. Her marriage to Silius was announced for September tenth, but on the fifth of September, while Claudius was out of the city, she married Silius. Calpurnia, a former mistress of Claudius, finally told him the whole truth regarding Messalina and her behavior throughout their marriage. Claudius tried and executed over one hundred people, most of them the men with whom Messalina had committed adultery. Messalina herself was killed by an officer of the palace guards.

Claudius married again, this time his niece, Agrippinilla, the mother of Lucius Domitius, later the emperor Nero. He no longer took any interest in life but allowed the affairs of state to be handled by Agrippinilla and his ministers. Claudius adopted Lucius and made him joint heir with Brittanicus. Lucius became of age first, and Agrippinilla, who wished to see her son sole ruler of Rome, poisoned Claudius. His death was concealed from the people until the empire had been secured for Nero. Thus Claudius, Emperor of Rome and a Roman god, ended his troubled reign.

THE CLAYHANGER TRILOGY

Type of work: Novel
Author: Arnold Bennett (1867-1931)
Type of plot: Domestic realism
Time of plot: 1870-1895
Locale: England
First published: 1910, 1911, 1915

Principal characters:
EDWIN CLAYHANGER, a businessman
HILDA LESSWAYS, his wife
MAGGIE CLAYHANGER, Edwin's sister
MR. INGPEN, Edwin Clayhanger's friend
GEORGE CANNON, Hilda's first husband
DARIUS CLAYHANGER, Edwin's father

Critique:

In *The Clayhanger Trilogy (Clayhanger, Hilda Lessways, These Twain)* Bennett depicted the middle class of late nineteenth-century England with sympathy and understanding. He, unlike the naturalistic novelists, was not after ugliness for its own sake. Though the region he drew was one of the least picturesque in England's industrial Midlands, he did not see its ugliness alone; in it he perceived a homely beauty. Certainly, if the events of the work do not linger brilliantly in the mind, the characters will be remembered clearly and long.

The Story:

In 1872 sixteen-year-old Edwin Clayhanger left school to aid his father in the Clayhanger printing shop. His father had disregarded Edwin's request that he be allowed to go to school and study to be an architect. Old Darius Clayhanger was a self-made man who had risen from a boyhood experience in the workhouse to the position of affluence he held in the Midland community, and it was his desire that his work be carried on by his only son. Since he was a complete tyrant in the home, no one dared to cross him.

Several years later Darius Clayhanger built a new house in a more pretentious part of town. Edwin became friendly with the Orgreave family, who lived next door. The elder Orgreave was an architect, with whom Edwin spent many hours discussing his own interest in that profession. Unknown to Edwin, the oldest Orgreave daughter, Janet, fell in love with him.

Edwin met Hilda Lessways at the Orgreave home. She was an orphan living in Brighton with the sister of a former employer, George Cannon, who wished to marry her. Although she was attracted to Edwin, she returned to Brighton and soon married Cannon. At the time of her marriage she gave Cannon her small patrimony to invest for her.

A year later Hilda returned to visit the Orgreaves. During that year she had learned that her husband had been married earlier and that her marriage to him was void. On this second visit she fell in love with Edwin and promised to marry him, for no one knew of her marriage at Brighton. Then, learning that she was to have a baby, she returned to Brighton. She wrote to Janet Orgreave, saying that she was married and asking Janet to inform Edwin. He, deeply hurt, turned himself entirely to his father's business, for his father had become mentally ill.

Hilda, meanwhile, had had her child

and had named him George Edwin, after its father and Edwin Clayhanger. She managed a rooming-house owned by her husband's sister. Cannon, discovered by his first wife, was sentenced to serve a two-year prison term for bigamy. After his release he was again imprisoned for ten years for passing a forged check. The money he had imprudently invested for Hilda was lost when the hotel corporation, whose shares he had bought, collapsed. Hilda was no longer financially independent.

After his father's death, Edwin and his sister Maggie continued to live alone in the Clayhanger house. Both of them became old-maidish in their habits, although many young women, including Janet Orgreave, would have gladly married Edwin, whose printing business continued to prosper and grow.

Edwin became quite fond of Hilda's son, who was living temporarily with the Orgreaves. When George Edwin became ill with influenza, it was Edwin who sent for the doctor and notified Hilda.

Although neither spoke openly of their feelings, Hilda and Edwin renewed their affection for one another when they met at the sick child's bed. When he was well again, George Edwin and his mother went back to Brighton. Nine years had passed since Edwin and Hilda first had met. Hilda was still struggling along with the failing boarding-house at Brighton.

Months later Edwin went to see Hilda and found her penniless and about to be evicted. Edwin paid her bills, and Hilda told him all that had happened to her, explaining that her marriage was void and her child illegitimate. Edwin returned home but at last he resolved to marry Hilda quietly. He met her in London, where they were married. They then moved into the Clayhanger house and Maggie went to live with a maiden aunt. Edwin also adopted Hilda's son and gave him his name.

Edwin, long having had his own way, was accustomed to a certain routine in his home and to making his own de-

cisions. But Hilda was a person of equally strong personality, and Edwin felt that she was trying to make him conform too much to her own domestic views and habits. Worst of all, she attempted to influence Edwin in business affairs, a realm which he thought was solely his own.

A few months after the marriage, the aunt with whom Maggie Clayhanger was living became seriously ill. During her last days, Mr. Ingpen, Edwin's business friend was injured in a factory accident. At Ingpen's request, Edwin went to his rooms to destroy some letters and pictures, so they would not be found if Ingpen died in the hospital. There Edwin found a woman asleep. She was Ingpen's mistress, a woman whose husband was incurably insane. Edwin was disturbed for his friend, but Ingpen laughed and said that the situation was best as it was because he did not want to be trapped in a marriage.

When Edwin's aunt died, her estate was left to the children of Edwin's younger sister, Clara. Edwin and Maggie were pleased, but Hilda thought that she and Edwin should have received part of the estate. Her selfishness irked Edwin. He felt that he was rich enough and that his nieces and nephews deserved the money. Seriously thinking that a divorce was the answer to his present situation, he recalled with nostalgia his bachelor days. The only bright ray in his life seemed to be George Edwin, his stepson, who was studying the elements of architecture with the aid of John Orgreaves. Edwin hoped that his son might now have the chance to become an architect.

On a visit to a nearby city, Hilda and Edwin were taken to inspect a prison. There they saw George Cannon. He was released soon afterward when he was found to be innocent of the forgery charge. Cannon then went to Edwin, unknown to Hilda, and Edwin gave him money to go to America. Edwin never expected to see the money again, but he wanted to get the man out of the country. He was also bothered by the fact that Hilda had been in correspondence with Cannon's other wife.

The climax of Edwin's unhappiness with Hilda came on Christmas day, when she took him to see a house in the country. She tried to force him into buying it by diplomatic moves and conversations with their friends and family, so that Edwin would appear foolish if he did not buy the house.

After a violent argument with his wife, whom he accused of being grasping, underhanded, and dishonest, Edwin left the house in a rage. But after a long walk in the cold winter night he realized that his marriage and his wife meant a great deal to him. He saw in his mind that he had to make concessions for his wife and for the fact that they had been married so late in life that they had already fixed their habits. Finally he saw, in his mind, his friend Ingpen, who was unable to marry the woman he loved.

He went back to the house to reconcile himself with Hilda. His faith in human nature was completely reëstablished when he found in the mail a check from America for the money he had lent to George Cannon.

CLIGÉS

Type of work: Poem
Author: Chrétien de Troyes (c. 1150-c. 1190)
Type of plot: Chivalric romance
Time of plot: Sixth century
Locale: England, Brittany, Germany, and Constantinople
First transcribed: Before 1164

Principal characters:

ALEXANDER, heir to the Greek Empire
SOREDAMORS, Sir Gawain's sister, King Arthur's niece
CLIGÉS, son of Alexander and Soredamors
ALIS, Alexander's brother, later regent for Cligés
FENICE, a German princess, later Empress of Greece
KING ARTHUR
QUEEN GUINEVERE
SIR GAWAIN, Cligés' uncle, a knight of King Arthur's court
THESSALA, a necromancer, Fenice's nurse
JOHN, an artisan in stone

Critique:

This metrical romance, the second in chronological order of the surviving tales of Chrétien de Troyes, marks also the second period in that writer's work, one devoted to combining materials from the Arthurian cycle with classical elements drawn from Ovid, Vergil, Statius, and others. It is generally held that the central situation, the duping of Alis through the drinking of a potion, reflects the influence of an early Byzantine story, now lost, and there is some resemblance to the account of the wife of King Solomon who deceived her husband in the same way. The fusion of the materials, based as it may have been on a lost medieval manuscript, is clearly original, however, and delightful in its subtleties. Also interesting is the fact that this tale contains the writer's most detailed analysis of the anatomy of love, a matter of absorbing interest to the medieval audience.

The Story:

Alexander, the older son of the Emperor of Greece and Constantinople, scorned to receive knighthood in his own country. Having heard of the famed King Arthur of Britain, the young prince was determined to emulate the brave and courteous knights of that monarch's court and to win knighthood by his own merits. Accordingly, he swore never to wear armor on his face or helmet upon his head until King Arthur himself should gird on his knightly sword. At last he was allowed to have his own way in spite of the disapproval of his father and his mother's grief at being separated from her son, and he set sail at once for Britain. With him went twelve noble companions and a store of rich treasure.

When Alexander and his friends arrived at the royal court in Winchester, King Arthur and Queen Guinevere welcomed them with gracious speech. All who saw him were impressed by the young Greek, not alone for his generosity but for his strong character and handsome appearance as well. Sir Gawain, a knight of great prowess and the nephew of the king, took him for his friend and companion, and King Arthur, about to make a journey into Brittany, included the young man in his retinue. On the trip Alexander and the damsel Soredamors, sister of Sir Gawain, fell deeply in love. Since each felt that such a love was hope-

CLIGÉS by Chrétien de Troyes, from ARTHURIAN ROMANCES by Chrétien de Troyes. Translated in prose with introduction, notes and bibliography, by W. W. Comfort. From EVERYMAN'S LIBRARY. By permission of the publishers, E. P. Dutton & Co., Inc. All rights reserved.

less, they did nothing but grow pale and sigh and tremble, so that Queen Guinevere, observing them, mistook their lovesickness for the effects of the heaving sea.

King Arthur remained in Brittany through the summer, and during that time the young lovers were much perplexed and distressed by emotions they were unable to reveal to each other. At the beginning of October messengers arrived with news that Count Angrès, who had been entrusted with the rule of the kingdom during the king's absence, was raising an army and preparing to withstand King Arthur on his return. Angered by this traitorous deed, the king transported a great host across the Channel and prepared to lay siege to London, where Count Angrès had assembled his forces. Prince Alexander and his twelve companions were knighted while the king's army was encamped outside the city walls. Queen Guinevere's gift to the young knight was a white silk shirt on which Soredamors had embroidered strands of her own hair, indistinguishable from the golden thread of the design.

When Count Angrès and his army slipped away from the city under cover of night and retreated to the strong castle at Windsor, King Arthur and his troops pursued the traitors and besieged the fortress. During the siege Alexander displayed great bravery and prowess. One night, while he was in attendance on the queen, Guinevere noticed that the gold thread on his shirt was tarnishing but that the golden hair of Soredamors was as lustrous as ever. So the damsel's deed was disclosed and Alexander rejoiced to wear on his person a token of the lady to whom he had vowed undying devotion.

A short time later Windsor Castle was taken through his wit and valor. He and several of his companions dressed in the armor of vanquished traitor knights and then went by a secret path into the fortress, where they killed many of the enemy and captured Count Angrès. For this deed Alexander was awarded a gold cup which the king had promised to the most valiant of his knights. In the meantime, believing Alexander killed during the fighting inside the castle, Soredamors had revealed her love for the young prince. After the battle the knight received three joys and honors as the reward for his valor: the town he had captured, a kingdom in Wales, and, greatest of all, the hand of Soredamors.

From this union was born a handsome son, Cligés. Meanwhile, in Constantinople, the emperor died without hearing again from his older son, and Alis, the younger heir, assumed the rule of the empire after receiving a report that Alexander was also dead. Hearing that his brother had taken the crown, Alexander set out to reclaim his kingdom, accompanied by his wife, his small son, and forty valiant knights from King Arthur's court. When Alis learned that his older brother was alive, an amicable arrangement was made whereby Alis would rule in name only and the affairs of the kingdom would be entrusted to Alexander. Also, Alis promised never to marry or have heirs, so that Cligés would in time reign over Greece and Constantinople. Before Cligés had grown to manhood, however, Alexander died of a pestilence and Soredamors of grief.

Not long afterward advisers began to urge Alis to take a wife, with the result that the emperor was moved to break the oath made to his brother. The bride proposed was the daughter of the Emperor of Germany, the Princess Fenice, prophetically named for the phoenix bird. The princess had previously been affianced to the Duke of Saxony, however, and that incensed nobleman felt that he had a prior claim to her hand. While arrangements for the wedding were being made, Cligés and Fenice fell deeply in love. About the same time the duke sent his nephew to proclaim that his uncle's claim to the princess would be defended against the Greeks. His defiant speech so angered Cligés that he challenged the young Saxon to trial by arms and in the melee unhorsed him and

605

routed his followers. By this time, although Fenice loved Cligés dearly, she prudently decided that she would not yield herself to either the uncle or the nephew; and with the help of her nurse Thessala, a sorceress, she planned to remain a virgin. A potion served unwittingly, to the bridegroom by his nephew made it seem to the emperor that in his dreams he possessed his bride, though he never did so in reality.

On the return trip to Constantinople, the nephew of the Duke of Saxony set an ambush for the travelers. When Cligés killed the treacherous knight and the duke offered a reward for Cligés' head, that resourceful young knight cut off the head of an enemy and affected a disguise as his father had done before him. Fenice was abducted, however, during the battle that followed. Overtaking her captors, Cligés killed all but one, who survived to carry to the duke news of what happened. The conflict ended when Cligés, inspired by his love for Fenice, defeated the duke in single combat. The lovers then parted, Fenice going to Constantinople with her husband and Cligés traveling to England, there to fulfill his father's wish that he receive knighthood at the hands of King Arthur.

At a great tournament on the plain before Oxford, Cligés, changing his armor each day, defeated King Arthur's most valiant knights and bore himself so bravely that he became the subject of much speculation concerning his origin and whereabouts, for the young warrior retired to his lodgings every night and kept away from the feasting that followed each day's tourney. As the Black Knight he defeated mighty Sagremore; as the Green Knight, Sir Lancelot of the Lake; as the Vermilion Knight, Sir Perceval of Wales. On the fourth day, disguised as the White Knight, he would have defeated Sir Gawain, his uncle, if King Arthur had not intervened. Then Cligés appeared in his own person and at the royal banquet revealed his name and told his story, to the pleasure and as-tonishment of all. King Arthur and Sir Gawain, in particular, were delighted to find their young kinsman so brave in conduct, so pleasing in modesty and knightly courtesy.

On his return to Greece, Cligés learned that Fenice had missed him as much as he had desired her. Since their great love could no longer be denied, they were able, with the help of Thessala and an artful stonecutter, to devise a plan that would ensure their happiness. From the artisan, John, Cligés got possession of a tower in which the builder had constructed hidden chambers with secret entrances and exits. Thessala then concocted a potion which put Fenice into a trance so deep that all except three skeptical physicians from Salerno believed her dead. But the three doctors were slain by a mob of indignant women before they could restore Fenice to consciousness by acts of torture, and the body of the empress was placed, amid great mourning throughout the kingdom, in a sepulcher which John had built. From there she was taken in secret by Cligés, restored to life, and hidden in one of the secret chambers of the tower.

There, for a year and two months, they were free to take their pleasure with each other as they pleased. At the end of that time Fenice began to pine for the out of doors, and John revealed a secret door which opened upon a walled garden filled with beautiful blooming trees and flowers. Cligés and Fenice had much joy in their hidden paradise until, one day, a hunter searching for his lost hawk climbed the wall and saw the lovers asleep in each other's arms. Although Cligés awoke and wounded the hunter, the man escaped to tell the emperor of what he had seen. Alis dispatched troops to the tower, but Cligés and Fenice had already fled. Arrested, John accused the emperor of having tried to wrong Cligés by marrying and expecting to produce an heir; then the artisan revealed how Alis had been tricked by the potion he had drunk on his wedding night, so that he had never possessed his wife except in his dreams. The emperor swore that he could never again be happy until he had taken his revenge for the shame and disgrace that had been put upon him.

In the meantime Cligés and Fenice, with Thessala's aid, had eluded their pursuers and enlisted the aid of King Arthur, who promised to fill a thousand ships with knights and three thousand more with men-at-arms in order to help Cligés regain his rights. Before the mighty expedition could set sail, however, messengers arrived in Britain with word that Alis had died of rage and grief because the lovers had escaped him. With Fenice, Cligés returned to rule over Greece and Constantinople, and there the two lived happily in love, as husband and wife, lover and mistress.

Since that time, however, every emperor, remembering the story of Fenice and her potions, has had little confidence in his empress and has kept her closely guarded, attended by no man except one who has been a enunch since his boyhood.

THE CLOISTER AND THE HEARTH

Type of work: Novel
Author: Charles Reade (1814-1884)
Type of plot: Historical romance
Time of plot: Fifteenth century
Locale: Holland, Germany, France and Italy
First published: 1861

Principal characters:
GERARD ELIASON, a young artist
MARGARET BRANDT, his betrothed
DENYS, a Burgundian bowman
MARGARET VAN EYCK, sister of Jan Van Eyck
GHYSBRECHT VAN SWIETEN, a burgomaster

Critique:

The two outstanding features of this novel are its photographic details of fifteenth century European life, and the vivid character portrayal of Denys, the Burgundian crossbowman. Reade did tremendous research in order to achieve his accurate descriptions of fifteenth century European life. His Denys is one of the most delightful characters in English literature. Among the variety of literary types found in *The Cloister and The Hearth* are the long letter, poetry, dramatic dialogue, the tale within the tale, and picaresque romance. The description of the Catholic Church and clergy in the late Middle Ages is illuminating.

The Story:

Gerard, the son of Elias, a Dutch cloth and leather merchant, and Katherine, his wife, developed at an early age his talent for penmanship and illuminating. At first he was aided by the monks of the local convent for which he was destined. When the monks could teach the young artist no more, he became the pupil of Margaret Van Eyck, sister of the famous painter, Jan Van Eyck. She and her servant, Reicht Heynes, encouraged the lad to enter a prize art competition sponsored by Philip the Good, Duke of Burgundy and Earl of Holland.

On his way to Rotterdam to an exhibit of the entries, Gerard met an old man, Peter Brandt, and his daughter, Margaret, who sat exhausted by the way-side. He went with them into the town. There he took to the Princess Marie, daughter of Prince Philip, a letter of introduction from Dame Van Eyck. Impressed by the lad's talent, the princess promised him a benefice near his village of Tergou as soon as he had taken holy orders. He won a prize in the contest and returned to Tergou wondering whether he would ever again see Margaret Brandt, with whom he had fallen in love.

Gerard, learning accidentally from Ghysbrecht Van Swieten, Tergou's burgomaster, that the old man and his daughter lived in Sevenbergen, a nearby village, began to frequent their cottage. Ghysbrecht disclosed to Katherine, Gerard's mother, that the young man was interested in Margaret Brandt. A quarrel ensued in the family, Elias threatening to have Gerard imprisoned to prevent his marrying. Margaret Van Eyck gave Gerard money and valuable advice on art and recommended that he and the girl go to Italy, where Gerard's talents were sure to be appreciated. Gerard and Margaret Brandt became betrothed, but before they could be married the burgomaster had Gerard seized and put in jail. He was rescued at night from the prison by Margaret, his sweetheart, Giles, his dwarf brother, and Kate, his crippled sister. In the rescue, Giles removed from a chest in the cell some parchments which the villainous Ghysbrecht had

608

hidden there. At Sevenbergen, Gerard buried all of the parchments except a deed which concerned Margaret's father.

After an exciting pursuit, Gerard and Margaret escaped the vicinity of Tergou. They separated, Margaret to return to Sevenbergen, Gerard to proceed to Rome. On the way, he was befriended by a Burgundian soldier named Denys, and the pair traveled toward the Rhine. They went through a variety of adventures together.

In Sevenbergen, meanwhile, Margaret Brandt fell sick and was befriended by Margaret Van Eyck. Martin, an old soldier friend of the young lovers, went to Rotterdam where he procured a pardon for Gerard from Prince Philip. Dame Van Eyck gave a letter to Hans Memling to deliver to Gerard in Italy, but Memling was waylaid by agents of the burgomaster and the letter was taken from him.

Gerard and Denys came upon a company of Burgundian soldiers on their way to the wars and Denys was ordered to ride with them to Flanders. Gerard was left to make his solitary way to Rome. Later Denys, released because of wounds received in the duke's service, set out for Holland, where he hoped to find Gerard. Elias and Katherine welcomed him in Tergou when he told them that he had been Gerard's comrade. Meanwhile old Brandt and Margaret disappeared from Sevenbergen, and Denys searched all Holland for the girl. They had gone to Rotterdam, but only the burgomaster knew their whereabouts. When Margaret practiced medicine illegally, she was arrested and sentenced to pay a large fine. In order to stay alive, she took in laundry. Denys discovered Margaret in Rotterdam and the pair returned to Tergou, where Gerard's family had become reconciled to Gerard's attachment to the girl.

Gerard made his dangerous way through France and Germany to Venice. From there he took a coastal vessel and continued to Rome. When the ship was wrecked in a storm, Gerard displayed bravery in saving the lives of a Roman matron and her child. He went on to Rome and took lodgings, but he found work all but impossible to obtain. He and another young artist, Pietro, decorated playing cards for a living. Finally through the good graces of the woman whose life he had saved in the shipwreck, Gerard was hired to decorate manuscripts for Fra Colonna, a leading classical scholar.

Hans Memling brought to Rome a letter, sent by Ghysbrecht, which gave Gerard the false news that Margaret had died. Gerard forsook the Church and in despair threw himself into the Tiber. But he was saved and carried to a monastery, where he recovered and eventually took monastic vows. He became Brother Clement of the Dominican Order. After a period of training he was sent to teach at the University of Basle, in Switzerland. Meanwhile, in Holland, Margaret gave birth to Gerard's son.

Brother Clement received orders to proceed to England. Preaching as he went, he began the journey down the Rhine.

In Rotterdam, Luke Peterson became Margaret's suitor. She told him he could prove his love for her by seeking out Gerard, but Luke's and Brother Clement's paths were fated not to cross. The priest went to Sevenbergen, where he was unable to find the grave of Margaret. He proceeded to Rotterdam, and there Margaret heard him preach without recognizing him as Gerard. He next went to Tergou to see Ghysbrecht. The burgomaster was dying; he confessed to Brother Clement that he had defrauded Margaret of wealth rightfully hers. On his deathbed Ghysbrecht made full restitution.

When Brother Clement left the burgomaster, he returned to Rotterdam and took refuge in a hermit's cave outside the city. There he mortified himself out of hatred for mankind.

Margaret, having learned his whereabouts through court gossip, went to him, but he repulsed her in the belief that she was a spirit sent by Satan. Margaret took her son to the cave in an attempt to win back his reason. Brother Clement's acquaintance with his son, also named Gerard, brought him to his senses. Margaret by shrewd argument persuaded him to come with her to Gouda, where he would be parson by arrangement with church authorities. They lived in Gouda, but apart, Gerard tending his flock and Margaret assisting him in his many charitable works.

After ten years at Gouda, Margaret died of the plague. Gerard, no longer anxious to live after her death, died two weeks later. Their son, Gerard, grew up to be Erasmus, the world-famous sixteenth-century Biblical scholar and man of letters.

THE CLOSED GARDEN

Type of work: Novel
Author: Julian Green (1900-   )
Type of plot: Psychological realism
Time of plot: 1908
Locale: France
First published: 1927

Principal characters:
ANTOINE MESURAT, a retired teacher
ADRIENNE, his daughter
GERMAINE, her invalid older sister
DR. DENIS MAURECOURT, a physician
MADAME LEGRAS, a neighbor

Critique:

It has been said that the inspiration for *The Closed Garden—Adrienne Mesurat* in the original edition—was a painting by Utrillo. Certainly the novel has the sunlit yet melancholy dullness we find in many of Utrillo's street scenes. Julian Green has also been compared with Emily Brontë for the intensity of his atmosphere and with Balzac for his realistic rendering of French provincial life. But these comparisons are true only in part. Green is himself first of all, with his own powers and compelling insights. In this novel there is a constant clashing of motives and wills among members of a single household; and the limitation of characters and scene gives added force to the story of Adrienne Mesurat, who falls in love with a man to whom she had never spoken, commits a crime of violence, and goes mad. Julian Green's mastery of his somber theme makes this novel a classic of its kind, just as the writer himself, born in Paris of American parents, is one of the most distinguished writers of his literary generation abroad.

The Story:

Adrienne Mesurat lived with her father, a retired writing-master, and Germaine, her invalid older sister, in a small, ugly villa in the country town of La Tour l'Evêque. The routine of the household was simple, for Antoine Mesurat lived only to indulge his own quiet tastes. Three meals a day, his morning and evening walks, his favorite newspaper, an occasional game of *trente-et-un*—these were his pleasures. In his tranquilly stubborn manner he was a complete domestic tyrant, and the idea that his daughters might be unhappy with their lot never crossed his mind.

There had been a time when callers came to the villa, for the Mesurats owned enough property to attract young men of the district. But old Mesurat considered his daughters superior to the sons of provincial tradesmen and lawyers and laughed complacently at their proposals of marriage. Finally the visits ceased. In the uneventful round of Adrienne's days a strange passerby in the street, local gossip her father brought back from his walks, and the succession of tenants who each summer rented the Villa Louise on the corner became items for speculation and comment. So matters might have gone on indefinitely if Adrienne had not, in the summer of her seventeenth year, fallen suddenly in love.

She had been gathering flowers beside a country road when a carriage passed her and she saw in it a slight man of middle age, who half lifted his hat as the vehicle went by. Adrienne recognized him as Dr.

Maurecourt, a recent arrival in the town. A feeling of gratitude and adoration filled her because he had noticed her. For the rest of the summer she walked the same road every day, but the doctor never rode that way again.

At last Adrienne hit upon another plan. Each night, after Germaine had gone to her room and Mesurat had settled himself in the parlor for his evening nap, she would steal out of the house. From the corner on which the Villa Louise stood she could see the front of the Maurecourt dwelling, and the sight of its lighted windows gave her a deep feeling of happiness. Once she saw Maurecourt on the street. Later she felt that she had to see him again at any cost. One day, while cleaning, she discovered that she could also watch his house from the window of Germaine's room. As often as possible she went there and sat, hoping to see him enter or leave by his front door.

Germaine, surprising Adrienne in her bedroom, became suspicious. That night the older sister was awake when Adrienne returned quietly from her evening vigil. Mesurat, informed of what had happened, ordered Adrienne to play cards with him after dinner the next day. Under her father's suspicious gaze, she played badly. Enraged, he accused her of stealing out nightly to meet a lover. From that time on she was allowed to leave the house only when she went walking with her father. Again she saw Maurecourt on the street. Thinking that if she were hurt he would be called to attend her, she thrust her arms through the windowpane. Her father and sister bandaged her cuts, much to her despair.

Germaine's sickness grew worse. Mesurat, refusing to acknowledge her serious condition, insisted that she get up for her meals. One morning, after he had berated her at breakfast, Germaine confided her intention of leaving home, and she borrowed five hundred francs from Adrienne's dower chest to pay her fare to a convent hospital. Adrienne was glad to see her sister go; she hoped to occupy the room

from which she used to watch Maurecourt's house. Mesurat, surprised and furious, was puzzled to know how Germaine had arranged for her flight and where she had secured money for her train fare.

In June, Madame Legras had become the new tenant of the Villa Louise. Adrienne and her father had met the summer visitor at a concert and Madame Legras had invited the young girl to call. After Germaine's flight Adrienne went to see her new neighbor. Madame Legras was affable but prying. Confused by questions about a possible lover, Adrienne had a strange attack of dizziness.

That night Mesurat angrily ordered her to produce her dower box. Seeing that five hundred francs were missing, he accused her of plotting with Germaine to outwit him. While he stood reviling her from the head of the stairs, Adrienne ran against him in the dark. He fell into the hall below. Dazed and frightened by her deed, Adrienne went to bed.

The cook stumbled upon Mesurat's body the next morning, and Madame Legras, aroused by the disturbance, summoned Maurecourt. Although there were some whispers that the old man's end might not be all it seemed, the verdict was one of accidental death. Germaine did not return for the funeral. Before long Adrienne, to her dismay, found herself lonelier than ever. A feeling of lethargy possessed her much of the time. When the prioress wrote asking for money in Germaine's name or lawyers sent legal papers for her signature, she disregarded them. Nothing seemed to matter except the time she spent with Madame Legras, who had assumed a protective attitude toward the girl. But at last Adrienne began to realize that Madame Legras suspected the truth about Mesurat's death, and her sly looks and pointed remarks seemed intended to lead the girl into a trap.

One day Adrienne decided to go to Montfort. There, walking the streets, she imagined that people were staring at her. She spent the night in Dreux, where a young workman accosted her. Later, frightened because she did not remember why she had gone away, she returned to La Tour l'Evêque after sending Maurecourt a card telling him of her unhappiness.

Shortly after her return she collapsed and had to be put to bed in the Villa Louise. Madame Legras, undressing her, found a love letter which she gave to the doctor when he came in response to her summons. That night Adrienne awoke and went back to her own home. Maurecourt went to see her there the next day. When she confessed her love, he told her that he was sick and soon to die. Overcome by his visit, she was barely able to rouse herself when Madame Legras appeared and demanded an immediate loan in order to pay some pressing debts. While she looked on helplessly, the woman emptied the dower chest of its gold coins. Then she removed the watch and chain Adrienne was wearing and dropped them into her purse.

A short time later, when the cook brought word that Madame Legras had left town very suddenly, Adrienne realized that the servant also knew her guilt. Dazed, she sat vacant-eyed when Maurecourt's sister called to reproach her for her shameless behavior. At nightfall she left the house and wandered toward the lighted square, where a fête was in progress. Suddenly she turned and ran toward the dark countryside. There some peasants found her a few hours later. She could not tell them her name. She was mad.

THE CLOUDS

Type of work: Drama
Author: Aristophanes (c. 448-385 B.C.)
Type of plot: Social satire
Time of plot: Fifth century B.C.
Locale: Athens
First presented: 423 B.C.

Principal characters:
STREPIADES, an Athenian gentleman
PHIDIPPIDES, his son
SOCRATES, a Sophist philosopher

Critique:

The Clouds is one of the best known of Aristophanes' many comedies. This Greek master, recognized as a leading playwright in his day and still acknowledged as the foremost of comedy writers, colors this play with an air of buffoonery and raillery, sometimes savage and biting. The attacks on the Sophists, the logic lessons that Socrates administers to Strepiades, and the lesson that Phidippides gives his father, gave the Athenian audience moments of high entertainment. Aristophanes rejected the school of Sophists, whom he considered irreverent and artificial, and he satirized their teachings in *The Clouds*.

The Story:

Strepiades, a rich gentleman of Athens, was plunged into poverty and debt by his profligate son, Phidippides. Hounded by his son's creditors, Strepiades pondered ways and means to prevent complete ruin. Hearing reports that the Sophists taught a new logic which could be used to confuse one's creditors and so get one out of debt, Strepiades saw in the Sophist teachings a possible solution to his problem. He pleaded with Phidippides to enter the school of the Sophists and learn the new doctrines. When Phidippides, more interested in horse-racing than in learning, refused to become a pupil, Strepiades denounced his son as a wastrel and decided to enroll himself.

He went to the Thoughtery or Thinking-School, which was the term used for the classroom of the Sophists, and asked to see Socrates, the philosopher. After Strepiadies had explained his purpose, Socrates proceeded to demonstrate several logical conclusions of the new school. More certain than ever that the new logic would save him from ruin and disgrace, Strepiades pleaded until Socrates admitted him to the Thoughtery.

Unfortunately, Strepiades proved too old to master the Sophist technique in the classroom. Socrates then decided that Strepiades could learn to do his thinking outdoors. But when Socrates put questions concerning poetry to Strepiades, his answers showed such complete ignorance that Socrates finally admitted defeat and returned to the Thoughtery. Strepiades, disgusted with his own efforts, decided that he would either make Phidippides go to the Sophist school or turn him out of the house.

Approached a second time by his father, Phidippides again protested against enrolling in the school but finally yielded to his father's demands. Strepiades felt that all now would be well.

Some time afterward Strepiades went to learn what progress his son had made. Socrates assured him that Phidippides had done well. At this news, Strepiades felt sure that his plan had been a good one and that the new logic, as learned by his son, would soon deliver him from his creditors. He asked Socrates to call Phidippides from the classroom. When Phidippides emerged, Strepiades greeted him between tears and laughter, and said it was fitting that he should be saved by the son who had plunged him into debt.

He asked Phidippides to demonstrate his new learning, and Strepiades was amazed by the cunning of the new logic. At that moment one of Strepiades' creditors appeared to demand money that was owed him for a horse. Strepiades, confident that the Sophist-taught Phidippides could turn the tables on any creditor in the law court, refused to pay, ignoring threats of court action. He treated a second creditor in the same way and went home convinced that the new logic, as argued by Phidippides, would save him in the pending law suits.

It became a different matter, however, when Phidippides proceeded to demonstrate the Sophist teaching at home. Arguing that Strepiades had beaten him often for his own good, Phidippides buffeted his father during a family argument and declared that he was beating Strepiades for his own good. The old man protested, but with the new logic Phidippides silenced his protests and threatened to beat his mother on the same principle.

Strepiades realized that the Sophists could justify all manner of evil with their tricky logic. Thinking the teachings dangerous to the youth of Athens, he took a torch and set fire to the Thoughtery. As Socrates and the Sophist disciples screamed their objection, the Thoughtery went up in flames. Strepiades watched it burn, certain that he had eliminated an evil.

THE COCKTAIL PARTY

Type of work: Drama
Author: T. S. Eliot (1888-   )
Type of plot: Social criticism
Time of plot: Mid-twentieth century
Locale: London
First presented: 1949

Principal characters:
    EDWARD CHAMBERLAYNE, a lawyer
    LAVINIA, his wife
    JULIA, a meddling woman
    CELIA, a sensitive young woman
    PETER, in love with Celia
    ALEX, a meddling man
    SIR HENRY HARCOURT-REILLY, at first unidentified

Critique:

The Cocktail Party, a verse play, was an immediate success on Broadway. The style, the clever comedy, the sharp social criticism—all were factors in its ready acceptance. That Eliot's intelligent comedy should win a wide audience is another token of his place among men of letters. The penetrating social analyses concern the present fetish of psychiatry, the dullness of cocktail parties and those who give them, and the meaning of success. Although the play is a comedy, Eliot has used it to give new light on contemporary civilization.

The Story:

The Chamberlaynes were giving a cocktail party in their London flat. The atmosphere was somewhat strained because Lavinia, the hostess, was not there, and Edward, her bumbling husband, hastily invented a sick aunt to account for her absence. Alex, as usual, had an exotic story to tell, for he traveled widely and knew everyone. Julia, a sharp-eyed and sharp-tongued family friend, missed the point of his tale and wondered why Alex and the Maharaja were up a tree. Julia usually missed the point of stories she heard.

The assembly demanded that Julia give her inimitable imitation of Lady Klootz and the wedding cake. They had all heard the story before, except possibly Edward, who forgot stories, and an unidentified and unintroduced guest. Somehow Julia got off on a family who had a harmless son, and the story never did get told. The harmless son was a fascinating person: he could hear the cries of bats. Then Peter had to tell of a scenario which he had written and which, unfortunately, never was produced.

To Edward's relief, the guests prepared to leave. Only the stranger remained. He drank gin with Edward for a while, and Edward was compelled to confide in him. Lavinia was not really at her aunt's house; she had simply left with no explanation. The stranger pointed out that her leaving might be a blessing, since Lavinia was demanding and practical. But Edward was uneasy, without knowing exactly why he wanted Lavinia back. The stranger promised that the erring wife would return within twenty-four hours if Edward would ask for no explanations. He warned also that both Lavinia and Edward might be greatly changed. The stranger, full of gin, broke into song as he left the apartment.

Julia, returning for her glasses, had Peter in tow. The glasses were in Julia's bag all the time, and she departed again, leaving behind an agitated Peter. The young man wanted to confide in Edward.

He had fallen in love with Celia after attending many concerts with her, and she had been very friendly. Lately, however, she had been unresponsive. He asked if Edward would intercede for him.

At this juncture Alex came gaily back. Edward was irritated. He asked Peter and Alex to lock the door when they left so no one else would wander in. Alex archly went to the kitchen, intent on whipping up a meal for the lone Edward. He succeeded in using up all the fresh eggs in some outlandish concoction.

At last, after answering the phone several times, Edward settled down in solitary comfort to play patience. Then the doorbell rang and in came Celia. She had divined that Lavinia had left Edward, and now she thought it would be a good time for Edward to seek a divorce so that he and Celia could marry. Edward agreed, but in spite of his repeated assurances of continued love, Celia was uneasy, for she sensed a change in him. Edward then confessed that Lavinia was coming back and that he almost wanted her back. He scarcely knew why, for until his wife left he had wanted only Celia. Celia was discomfited at her faint-hearted lover. When Julia returned once more, this time to invite Edward to dinner, Celia escaped into the kitchen. There, under pretext of getting a lunch for the lone Edward, she ruined Alex's concoction completely.

The next day the stranger returned. Again he warned Edward that by wanting Lavinia to return he had set in motion forces beyond his control. When she returned, she would be a stranger and Edward would be a stranger to her. But since Edward had made his choice he had to abide by it. After admonishing Edward to receive any visitors who might come, the mysterious stranger left by the back stairs.

Celia was the first to arrive. She had come at Julia's request, apparently in response to a telegram from Lavinia. While they were together, Celia had a chance to look at Edward carefully; he seemed to her only a rather comic middle-aged man. She could laugh now at her infatuation.

Peter arrived in response to Alex's invitation. Alex had also received a wire, ostensibly from Lavinia. He had time for some reproachful remarks to Celia and then announced he was leaving for Hollywood.

Lavinia herself arrived next, surprised to find Peter and Celia and disclaiming any knowledge of telegrams to Alex and Julia. When the latter two got there, the mystery deepened. At length the guests departed and Lavinia turned expectantly to Edward. But he had little to say. He reproached her for her overbearing ways, and she twitted him for being unable to make decisions. When she suggested Edward was on the verge of a nervous breakdown, he was angered but interested in the possibility. He resolved stoutly not to visit any doctor Lavinia might recommend, and stalked off to his club.

In Sir Henry's offices, preparations were being made to receive patients. The first was Edward, who was surprised to see that Sir Henry was his mysterious stranger. In the consultation Edward told why he had wanted Lavinia back: she had dominated him so long that he was incapable of existence without her. Sir Henry then brought in Lavinia, the better to have the whole problem threshed out.

During the conversation it was revealed that Lavinia had left because of Edward's disgraceful affair with Celia. Edward, somewhat shaken to learn that she had known of the affair, grew confident again when Lavinia confessed she had been infatuated with Peter. Sir Henry diagnosed their trouble as mutual fear: Edward was afraid he could not make successful love to any one and Lavinia was afraid she was completely unlovable. The doctor assured them that they had every requirement for a successful life together. They had a mutual fear and hatred of each other, and both were quite mediocre people. They left, moderately reconciled.

Julia arrived at the doctor's office to ask how successful her scheming had been. It had been she who had induced Sir Henry to step in, and Alex had abetted her.

Celia also came in for a consultation. She had vague feelings of guilt and sin and wanted to take a rest cure. After talking with her, Sir Henry recognized that she was an outstanding person, that her destiny called her. He advised her to be at ease and do whatever she had to do.

Two years later the Chamberlaynes were giving another cocktail party to many of the old crowd. They were smugly settled in their mediocrity and even made a pretense of being in love. To them the inanities of cocktail parties were their measure of social standing. Peter came in hurriedly. He had been a great success in America. He now had money and renown of a sort. His destiny had been a material one. Alex arrived next. He was just back from bearing the white man's burden on a tropical island. He reported Celia's death. Celia had been a nurse on the island. She had been killed in a native rebellion. Her destiny had called her to martyrdom for the love of humanity.

COLLECTED POEMS

Type of work: Poetry
Author: Walter de la Mare (1873-1956)
First published: 1941

Walter de la Mare published his first book of poems, *Songs of Childhood,* in 1902, his last, *O Lovely England,* in 1953, three years before his death; and his career, spanning more than half a century, was productive to the end. Since five books of new lyrics and a supplementary volume of earlier verse followed the 1941 edition of his *Collected Poems,* this collection cannot in any sense be regarded as complete. Rather, it marks an interval stage of revision and regrouping of work which de la Mare wished to preserve and present in its final form. A number of the poems have been slightly altered from their original versions; others have been regrouped by subject matter, and some have been omitted from earlier single volumes. Most of these have been reprinted in a second series, *Collected Rhymes and Verses* (1944). In the light of these changes it seems certain that at the time the poet considered this volume the definitive edition of his most serious work.

"Delamarian" has come to stand for that blending of supernal beauty and the supernatural, nature and mankind tinged delicately with "theotherworlde," as Henry C. Duffin, friend and critic of the poet, has styled it. *Poems: 1906* opens on this note in "Shadow":

> Even the beauty of the rose doth cast,
> When its bright, fervid noon is past,
> A still and lengthening shadow in the
>   dust,
>   Till darkness come
> And take its strange dream home.

The poem concludes with recognition of the "dark and livelong hint of death" which is the shadow of life haunting us into eternity. In this first group is an-

other poem, "England," which presents the other side of his brightest coin:

> No lovelier hills than thine have laid
>   My tired thoughts to rest:
> No peace of lovelier valleys made
>   Like peace within my breast.

The poem continues with a celebration of the woods, "a refuge green and cool," and seas that "like trumpets peal," and concludes:

> Thine be the grave whereto I come,
>   And thine my darkness be.

Neither the sonnets nor the attempts to re-create characters from Shakespeare are equal to de la Mare's lyric or descriptive poems, though the selections which are recalled from childhood display his unique ability to "become as a little child," often with startling results, as in "Fear" or "Echo," in which phantasms arise and will not be put down. Then, too, the lovely idyl which is childhood takes shape in "The Mermaids" and "Myself," but always with a touch of strangeness, a shadow.

The Listeners (1912) contains the title poem, too well-known to be repeated but beloved by all, and many others which exhibit the same masterly blending of clear, singing music and the twilight atmosphere of a world of fantasy and dreams, qualities that made his poetry popular. "All That's Past" suggests in modern runes the wonder and antiquity of winds, brooks, minerals, the rose, and immemorial man:

> Very old are we men;
>   Our dreams are tales
> Told in dim Eden
>   By Eve's nightingales;

We wake and whisper awhile,
  But the day gone by,
Silence and sleep like fields
Of amaranth lie.

From this past, against the background of "Arabia" or other romantic, distant lands, Walter de la Mare takes his reader on a pilgrimage from light to shadow, from the real to the unreal. "Martha," one of the unreal, tells stories "in the hazel glen" of fairies and gnomes that the poet makes real. For those who believe that de la Mare is limited in subject and mood, "The Keys of Morning" presents the poignant wisdom of a child, Louisa, who faces death with an understanding beyond that of adults.

Motley (1918) and *The Veil* (1922) mark the maturation of the delamarian style: the most exact and exacting words in the most carefully chosen places, the rhythmic cadences more syllabic than metered, the rhymes more individually and unmistakably set in a perfection of sentiment. Here, too, the poet's themes match the times, for de la Mare was against the Philistines, "Mrs. Grundy," and all those who gloat in righteousness. Here is one of the most perfect poems, "Music," which takes one away from this earth to the place where "all her lovely things even lovelier grow." The antique though rememberable past comes forth and the poet reaches a synthesis with time.

As critics have remarked, a newer realism is discernible in the later poems. "The Old Angler," obviously a stylized person, fishes in eternity though he himself, his boat, and his surroundings are often naturalistically displayed. "Titmouse" is an exercise of the physical senses with symbolic overtones:

This tiny son of life; this spright,
By momentary Human sought,
Plume will his wing in the dappling
    light,
Clash timbrel shrill and gay—
And into time's enormous nought,
    Sweet-fed, will flit away.

In this section great love lyrics appear, and also humor—that most difficult element to place in lyric poetry—as in "Maerchen":

Soundless the moth-flit, crisp the death-
    watch tick;
Crazed in her shaken arbour bird did
    sing;
Slow wreathed the grease adown from
    soot-clogged wick:
    The Cat looked long and softly at
    the King.

The section closes with "An Epitaph" (de la Mare wrote many such, all wonderful):

Last, Stone, a little yet;
And then this dust forget.
But thou, fair Rose, bloom on.
For she who is gone
Was lovely too; nor would she grieve to
    be
Sharing in solitude her dreams with
    thee.

The Fleeting (1933) is full of surprises, new cadences, startling themes, odd forms. "The Feckless Dinner-Party," for example, contains all these and satiric thrusts against an inane society madly orbiting to death, and led by a butler, Toomes. Here, too, is "Slum Child," de la Mare's bitterest criticism of a society which allows a child to go frightened and unloved into "evil, filth, and poverty" as "epitome of man's disgrace"; yet there is hope of finding "living bread in stones" and "a self beyond surmise." Echoes of an early note, however, sound with the same chill magic in such a fine though macabre poem as "The House":

"Mother, it's such a lonely house,"
The child cried; and the wind sighed.
"A narrow but a lovely house,"
    The mother replied.

"Child, it is such a narrow house,"
The ghost cried; and the wind sighed.
"A narrow and a lonely house,"
The withering grass replied.

If the poet could not pass a graveyard without stopping, neither can the reader overlook the resulting poems, especially the epitaph of "Isaac Meek" who "inherited the earth" or that of "J——H——: Aged 34" who sleeps "Beneath a Motionless Yew," remembered faintly by his ancient widow.

Memory (1938), containing as it does echoes from earlier poems, even a reworking of earlier themes under similar titles, returns to the essential de la Mare of childhood, of ancient ways, of shadows extended backward in time, all expressed in the short lyric, the close-cropped line, the sentient rhyme, the evocative symbol. The title poem suggests that memory is a "strange deceiver" who brings back the relevant and irrelevant, "poor and trivial, rich and rare," but refuses to yield "grave fact and loveliest fantasy." The poet then cites, autobiographically though symbolically, instances of memory's caprices.

The loss of a child, "Sallie's Musical Box," is as poignant a short lyric as exists in the language:

Once it made music, tiny, frail, yet sweet—

Bead-note of bird where earth and elf-land meet.
Now its thin tinkling stirs no more, since she
Whose toy it was, has gone; and taken the key.

Here, again, is the earlier theme of lost rapture, but now without the Blakian quality noted in the earlier *Songs of Childhood*.

Walter de la Mare may have considered this his last volume of poems, published as it was when he was sixty-eight. Fortunately, some of his loveliest writing, like the beautiful and moving "Winged Chariot," came later. In this book, however, the last lines of the last poem, "Snow," appropriately epitomize his unique poetry:

A marvel of light,
Whose verge of radiance seems
Frontier of paradise,
The bourne of dreams.

O tranquil, silent, cold—
Such loveliness to see:
The heart sighs answer,
Benedicite!

COLLECTED POEMS, 1934-1952

Type of work: Poetry
Author: Dylan Thomas (1914-1953)
First published: 1952

When Dylan Thomas died at the age of thirty-nine he was, for a poet in this century, extraordinarily popular. His poetry had been read and admired for years; a paean of praise greeted his collected works, and still more appreciation was accorded him after his death. However, many reputable critics, fellow poets, and general readers have disliked, derided, and dismissed his work on the grounds that it is merely sibylline raving. These contradictory reactions are explained by the fact that Thomas was primarily a violently emotional poet. The strength of his feelings thus either forcibly attracts or repels his readers.

The poems make an emotional impact, on first reading, that subsequent analyses will not displace. With the exception of Ezra Pound, Thomas is probably the most obscure of the great poets of this century. Whether he is a major or a minor poet will be established only by the evaluation of critics in the future, as no contemporary can have the necessary perspective to place a poet accurately in such a hierarchy. Undeniably, Dylan Thomas' poetry is great in kind; to what degree, posterity will decide.

A poet who is both very obscure and very popular is an anomaly, but Thomas is not in this position by virtue of belonging to a particular school of verse, nor by writing in a recognized poetic convention. Nor is he socially or politically committed. His poetry is an affirmation of life: "These poems are written for the love of man and in praise of God, and I'd be a damn' fool if they weren't." The truth of this assertion in the introductory note to his volume of collected verse is shown in every successful poem that he wrote. His early poetry is egocentric;

he was writing of his own private feelings in these poems of birth, death, and sex, and the glory he found in these themes was entirely personal. His later poems show a far wider human interest and an increasing concern for mankind.

Throughout his work a unity of vision is apparent. He sees death in birth and resurrection in death. He is aware of the hate in all love and of the power of love to transcend suffering. He comprehends the simultaneous glory and corruption in life, and the fact that all forms of life are interdependent and inseparable. "I see the boys of summer" is a dialogue between the young poet who sees the destruction of the future in the present, and the adolescent boys living their first passionate and confusing loves. The successive images of light and dark, heat and cold, throughout the poem emphasize this contrast. The poem is filled with pleasure and pain conjoined, and with gain and loss. The polarity of these emotions is explicitly stated in the final, joyful image:

O see the poles are kissing as they cross.

"If I were tickled by the rub of love" is a difficult poem, to be understood by remembering the comprehensiveness of Thomas' idea of life. In the context of the poem, "tickled" appears to mean completely involved with, or wholly absorbed by, but the term necessarily retains the connotations of amusement and enjoyment. "Rub," as well as having sensual implications, also means doubt, difficulty, or strain. The poet says that if he were "tickled by the rub of love," he would not fear the fall from Eden or the flood; if he were "tickled" by the birth of a child, he would not fear death or war. Desire is spoken of as devilish and is provoked by

> . . . the drug that's smoking in a girl
> And curling round the bud that forks her eye.

This harsh image is followed by a statement of the poet's consciousness that he carries his own old age and death already within him.

> An old man's shank one-marrowed with my bone,
> And all the herrings smelling in the sea,
> I sit and watch the worm beneath my nail
> Wearing the quick away.

The feeling of fear is strong, and neither love, sex, beauty, nor birth is the "rub"; the solution is in wholeness or unity:

> I would be tickled by the love that is:
> Man be my metaphor.

Thomas' poetical development is unusual in that the thought in his later poems is usually not at all obscure. These poems are also less clotted with material; there are fewer esoteric symbols; ideas are developed at greater length, and tension is relaxed. The close attention to rhythm and structure persists, and the evocative power of his language is enhanced. Thomas' genius lay in the brilliant and highly personal use of the words with which his penetrating perception is communicated. The ambiguity of his language parallels the reciprocal nature of his images. He delights in punning and the various meanings of a word or image will often reverberate throughout an entire stanza.

"Poem on his birthday" is a good example of his method. The last poems are often, as this one is, set in the Welsh countryside. The heron is always in his poems a religious or priestly symbol. In the first stanza "herons spire and spear"; in the third, "herons walk in their shroud," and in the ninth he writes of the "druid herons' vows" and of his "tumbledown tongue"—this last a beautifully fused image of the action of the tongue of a pealing bell and the impetuous voice of the poet. In the tenth stanza he speaks of the "nimbus bell' which is a magical goal. By this use of compound images Thomas explores and thoroughly penetrates his subject. All aspects of the experience are involved, and pain, happiness, grief, and joy are equally present in this expression of unified sensibility.

This inclusive view of the universe is sometimes incoherent in his early poems, sometimes illuminating. One of the finest of his early poems is titled "The force that through the green fuse drives the flower." The symbolism here is not obscure and the emotions are controlled by the form of the poem. The third line of each of the four five-line stanzas has only three or four words and is the main clause of the three-line sentence in which the theme of each stanza is stated. The last two lines of each stanza begin with the words "And I am dumb. . . ." After the dramatic first two lines the short solemn third lines ready the reader for the equally forceful antithesis. The poem ends with a rhyming couplet:

> And I am dumb to tell the lover's tomb,
> How at my sheet goes the same crooked worm.

The theme of the poem is that the forces of nature are the same as those that drive man and that these forces both create and destroy. The careful structure of this poem is typical of Thomas' craftsmanship. He has been called undisciplined. He is not, but his unfettered imagination can confuse his meaning and his symbolism remains, in spite of painstaking analysis, almost inexplicable.

The sonnet sequence, "Altarwise by owl-light," is Thomas' most difficult poetry. The sonnets contain lines and passages of great beauty, and the overall movement, from horror and suffering toward the idea of the redemption of man by the Resurrection of Christ after the

Crucifixion, is clear. But the sequence as a whole remains too compressed and fragmentary to be successful. Thomas has failed mainly to communicate the bases of the intense suffering and hope that he so obviously felt.

In "After the funeral," an elegy for a cousin, Ann Jones, Thomas expresses both his own grief and the character of the dead woman. It is, as the poet points out, written with a magniloquence that exceeds the subject's,

> Though this for her is a monstrous image blindly
> Magnified out of praise. . . .

This manner contrasts so sharply with the humble and suffering woman that the poignancy of the portrait is increased. His grief

> Shakes a desolate boy who slit his throat
> In the dark of the coffin and sheds dry leaves.

The clear-sighted description of the woman after the expression of such grief is very moving:

> I know her scrubbed and sour humble hands
> Lie with religion in their cramp, her thread-bare
> Whisper in a damp word, her wits drilled hollow,
> Her fist of a face died clenched on a round pain.

The sonnet sequence and the elegy give some indication of Thomas' later themes, where religious faith and a concern for mankind are evident.

During the second world war Thomas spent several years in London, where he was deeply moved by German air raids on the city. This reaction is very clear in his fourth volume, *Deaths and Entrances*. The well-known "A refusal to Mourn the Death, by Fire, of a Child in London" is both an affirmation of Christian faith and an expression of cold fury at such a death. The poet feels that the event was too great for grief and that no elegy should be written for the child until the end of the world. Writing of grief at the time would be as if to murder her again:

> I shall not murder
> The mankind of her going with a grave truth.

The child is representative of all mankind and of all London's dead, a view which gives her a certain greatness:

> Deep with the first dead lies London's daughter.

The last line of the poem is ambivalent; it communicates both the irrevocability, finality, and cruelty of death and the Christian belief of the deathlessness of the soul:

> After the first death there is no other.

After the war Thomas was concerned to recapture in his poetry the world of his childhood. The rhythm of these poems is more relaxed and flowing than that of his early work, and the landscapes are glowing and full of color and wonder. These lyrics are poems in praise of the created world. Thomas' skill with words and rhythm evokes the whole Welsh countryside, and his unique imaginative vision makes the places his own. He has here communicated his great reverence and love of life. The unified vision of life remains, and Thomas is still aware of the presence of death in life, although this is no longer a cause of anguish as it was in the early poems.

In "Fern Hill," Thomas describes his youth on a farm. He has re-created youthful feeling that the whole world was his; there is an atmosphere of timelessness, a lulling of the consciousness of time's destruction, which the poet in recapturing his youthful feeling has conveyed without negating his manhood's knowledge.

Dylan Thomas was a highly emotional poet whose lyrics express a unified vision of life. His poetry contains many of the aspects of birth and death, fear, grief, joy, and beauty. From the violent, anguished poems of his youth, his power over his "craft or sullen art" increased until he was able to channel his special mode of feeling in ways which enabled him to speak for all men:

And you shall wake, from country
    sleep, this dawn and each first dawn,
Your faith as deathless as the outcry of
    the ruled sun.

Type of work: Novel
Author: Gerald Griffin (1803-1840)
Type of plot: Domestic tragedy
Time of plot: Late eighteenth century
Locale: Ireland
First published: 1828

Principal characters:

EILY O'CONNOR, a beautiful girl of the lower classes
HARDRESS CREGAN, a spirited young man of wealth
ANN CHUTE, a young woman of the upper classes, in love with Cregan
KYRLE DALY, a college friend of Cregan, in love with Ann Chute
DANNY MANN, Cregan's villainous servant
MRS. CREGAN, Hardress Cregan's mother

Critique:

Gerald Griffin was a dramatist and poet as well as a novelist, but his chief claim to fame is The Collegians, which was extremely popular in the years immediately after its publication. The story is more familiar to Americans in drama form, having been dramatized by Dion Boucicault under the title of The Colleen Bawn, a play which capitalized upon the melodramatic qualities of the novel. Griffin attempted to do for the Irish and Ireland what Sir Walter Scott had done in portraying Scotland and the Scottish people, and like Scott, Griffin was intensely interested in the folk traditions, customs, and personalities of the people about whom he wrote. The pages of The Collegians are filled with items of Irish folklore and more than a little attention has been paid to capturing the language of the peasants.

The Story:

Hardress Cregan and Kyrle Daly had been companions in their college days, in spite of the fact that Kyrle was of the middle classes and Hardress was the son of an Irish gentleman. Their respective ranks were close enough, however, so that they could respect one another and not be ashamed of their friendship. After leaving college they maintained the same close relationship, for they lived not far from each other. In fact, Kyrle, who had begun the study of law, became a suitor for the hand of Hardress' cousin, Ann Chute, a suit in which Kyrle had the good will of his friend.

Hardress Cregan, a spirited young man, lived more for sports and good times; he was actually shy in the presence of women, although he was bold enough in the face of danger. He was also disdainful of people from the lower classes. As an example of his attitude for them, one morning Kyrle's family watched from a window of their house as Hardress ran down some fishermen with his yacht, when such action could have been averted by a slight shift of the yacht's tiller.

That same day Kyrle set out for Chute Castle to attend the races and to press his suit with Ann Chute. He did not know that on board Hardress' yacht was a young woman of the lower classes, Eily O'Connor, daughter of a rope-maker, whom Hardress had secretly married a month before. The young woman was beautiful, but Hardress was afraid to make his marriage public, for he knew that his mother expected him to make a marriage with a young woman of wealth and position. He had taken Eily on board his yacht and was sailing with her up the coast, where he intended lodging her in the cottage of his servant's sister, close to his family's home. She had consented to go with him and to stay away from her father's home only because Hardress had promised to acknowledge her publicly as his bride within a matter of days. Hardress knew that he was safe in settling her with the sister of his servant, Danny Mann, because Danny, a hunchback, was devotedly loyal to his headstrong master.

At Chute Castle that same afternoon Kyrle's suit for the hand of Ann was ended. The girl told Kyrle in definite terms that she could not marry him, although she loved no one else. That night Kyrle met Hardress at the cottage where the latter had taken Eily. Kyrle was too distraught to notice anything unusual in the fact that the girl was with his friend. Hardress promised to do everything he could to assist Kyrle in marrying Ann.

Ann, asked to stay at the home of Hardress' parents, accepted the invitation. A few days after her arrival she confided to a sick old huntsman that she was in love with Hardress. Just before the old man died, he told his master that someone was in love with the young man. He did not, however, tell who loved him, but Hardress' mother soon realized the love Ann had for her son. Approving of the match, even though the young people were cousins, she threw them together at every opportunity. When Hardress tried to avoid Ann, his mother upbraided him bitterly. Her attitude completely prevented the young man from revealing his marriage to Eily.

Eily, meanwhile, grew restive when her husband refused to acknowledge her as his bride, for even the people with whom she stayed did not know that Hardress was her husband. As the weeks went by she realized that she had outworn her welcome among the peasants with whom she was quartered. Above all, she found her husband acting very strangely when he visited her. The girl asked him the reasons for his strangeness and for his reluctance to admit to the world that she was his wife. When she did, he burst out in anger, pointing out that he had married below his station and was very sorry he had done so. It was then

that he realized that he was in love with Ann. Leaving the cottage in a rage, he met his confidential servant, the hunchbacked Danny Mann. The servant was so devoted to his master that he promised to do away with the girl if Hardress wished her out of the way. His offer, a shocking one, brought Hardress to his senses, although he was still torn between his duty to his unacknowledged wife and his love for Ann.

At home the love for him that Ann openly showed, as well as his mother's wishes that he· marry the girl, increased the young man's perplexities. Gradually his desire to marry Ann overcame his sense of duty to his secret bride.

In the meantime Eily decided to let someone know of her marriage. Leaving the cottage, she went to see an uncle, the parish priest in a village not far from where she was staying. She told her uncle that she was married, but obedience to her husband kept her from telling who the husband was. Upon her return to the cottage she met Danny Mann, who gave her a letter from Hardress. Finally yielding to temptation and resolving to be rid of Eily, he had commissioned Danny to spirit her out of Ireland and put her on a boat bound for Canada. In the letter he told his wife of his decision; Eily, still obedient to her husband, submitted to his wishes.

But Danny misinterpreted his master's commands and murdered the girl. Too late, Hardress realized what had happened, but in spite of the blood on his hands he determined to marry Ann. His hope was that Danny would disappear for good and that the crime would never be discovered. As plans were being made for the wedding, Hardress began to act rather strangely. No one knew of the crime that was preying on his mind; people put his strange actions down to cowardice and illness.

Quite by chance, a short time before the date set for the marriage, Eily's body was discovered. At the inquest nothing was learned of the girl's death. Although the coroner suspected foul play, it seemed as if Hardress' plans were to work out successfully. Then, on the day before the marriage, Danny returned and was captured by the authorities. For a time it seemed as if fate were with the criminals. Hardress was able to effect his servant's escape, but Danny continued to linger in the neighborhood, much to Hardress' dismay. Discovering the servant, he beat the hunchback unmercifully. In revenge, Danny went to the authorities and confessed his crimes, implicating his master. Hardress, a few hours before his wedding, was taken from his home and sent into exile as a criminal. Danny Mann was hanged.

A happy ending of the tragedy came when, some months later, Ann married Kyrle Daly, who she found was really a better man and more worthy of her love than wealthier and more spirited Hardress Cregan.

COLOMBA

Type of work: Novel
Author: Prosper Mérimée (1803-1870)
Type of plot: Romantic adventure
Time of plot: Early nineteenth century
Locale: Corsica
First published: 1840

Principal characters:
COLONEL SIR THOMAS NEVIL, an Irish officer serving in the English
army
LYDIA NEVIL, his daughter
ORSO DELLA REBBIA, a lieutenant in the French army
COLOMBA DELLA REBBIA, his sister
LAWYER BARRICINI, blood enemy to the della Rebbias

Critique:

A tale of vengeance, *Colomba* tells the story of the blood enmity between two Corsican families, one honorable, the other cowardly. Although primitive customs of the Corsicans are contrasted with the civilized manners of two British subjects, the savage Corsicans do not fall short in honor and courage. Adventure and romance form the background for this story of a girl who would not rest until she saw her father's death avenged.

The Story:

When Lydia Nevil and her father, Colonel Nevil, first met Lieutenant Orso della Rebbia, they were impressed with that young man's good looks and his obvious pride in his native Corsica. Although Colonel Nevil and Orso had been on opposite sides in the Napoleonic Wars, each admired the other's bravery and courage. The Nevils were on their way to Corsica when they met Orso, a trip they hoped would provide release from boredom for Lydia and good hunting for her father. Orso, a lieutenant under Napoleon, was going home on half pay now that the wars were over and his leader had been defeated.

A short time after the party arrived in Corsica, Orso's sister Colomba joined them. From her and Orso, the Nevils learned the story of the della Rebbia family. The father had been murdered from ambush and no one had paid for the

crime. But Colomba firmly believed that Lawyer Barricini had been responsible for her father's death, the two families having been blood enemies for generations, and she demanded that Orso avenge the death. Orso, having been absent from Corsica for many years, did not feel the old passionate hatred of his kin, and he was satisfied that the law had rightly cleared Barricini, there being no proof that he was guilty of murder. Colomba, sharing the fiery passions of her ancestors, was determined that her brother should uphold the honor of their family. Lydia, on the other hand, pleaded with Orso to let the law settle such matters; she felt that to avenge the death would be to commit murder.

There had been evidence in the case, the bloodstained notebook of the murdered man, in which he had printed part of a name before he died. Barricini, as mayor of the village, had impounded the book, and when it was offered in evidence the name appeared to be that of a bandit in the district. Colomba believed that Barricini had torn out the original page and himself printed the bandit's name. No one believed her story but some peasant friends who were also bandits, and their testimony was of no value.

Orso and Colomba left the Nevils for a time and returned to their native village, the colonel and Lydia promising to visit them later. Not long after their return the prefect called on them and said that he had proof that Barricini was not guilty of the crime of which Colomba accused him. A thief, now imprisoned, had confessed that he had written a letter that had started the trouble between Barricini and the slain della Rebbia. Colomba, not impressed, said that Barricini, fearing that she would prevail upon her brother to seek out their enemy and kill him, had no doubt bribed the prisoner to make a false confession.

The prefect invited Orso to accompany him to the Barricini house, there to settle the matter peacefully. The prefect, who also had a letter for Orso from Lydia, promised that he would hand over the letter when the young man made the call. But the next morning Colomba told the prefect's servant that her brother had sprained his ankle; she asked the prefect to call at their home. When the prefect arrived, accompanied by Barricini and his two sons, Colomba confronted them with one of her friends, a bandit who said that he had been in prison with the thief supposed to have confessed to writing the letter. The bandit said that the prisoner had received many visits from Barricini's son and that the prisoner displayed a great deal of money for one so notoriously poor. Orso, convinced by this evidence, accused Barricini of forgery, perhaps murder. He struck one of the sons and promised to seek true vengeance later. The prefect, promising to investigate the whole matter, asked Orso to refrain from violence until the investigation was complete.

Orso wrote to Barricini's son, however, and challenged him to a duel with guns. Barricini promptly sent the note to the public prosecutor as evidence that Orso had threatened his family. Orso then wrote to Lydia, whose letter to him had stated that she and her father were on the way for their visit, and asked the Nevils not to come until she heard from him again. He wished to spare them the danger of a feud. Learning that his letter had not reached Lydia in time, he proposed to intercept the Nevils on their way to the village.

In order to stir her brother to violence, Colomba slit the ear of his favorite horse. Convinced by his sister that his enemies had done the deed, enraged Orso swore he would avenge his honor, for to slit the ear of an enemy's horse was a mortal challenge.

On his way to meet the Nevils, a friendly child warned Orso that his enemies were waiting to ambush him, but he refused to turn back. When he reached a thicket, he was attacked from two sides and injured in the arm. With one arm he discharged his heavy gun twice and killed both his attackers. Realizing that they were the two sons of Barricini, he knew that he would be arrested for murder. He took refuge with some bandits friendly to his family.

Lydia and Colonel Nevil, arriving in the village, learned of Orso's disappearance, and they joined Colomba in fears for his safety. At last the bandits sent word that Orso had escaped and was hiding with them. Believing in his innocence, Lydia convinced her father that Orso had only defended himself against his would-be assassins. In fact, Colonel Nevil told the prefect that he and Lydia had heard Orso's gun fire twice after two lighter guns had been fired. The colonel's reputation convinced the prefect that Orso had acted in self-defense.

Colomba and Lydia visited Orso in his hideout. As the two young people declared their love for each other they were interrupted by the arrival of the police. Orso fled again. Colomba and Lydia were seized and returned to the prefect. By that time the prefect had proof that Orso had acted in self-defense, which carried no charge of murder. He demanded, however, that Orso surrender to the authorities so that the affair could be settled legally.

After his surrender Orso was found innocent of any crime. He and Lydia married and went to Italy. Colomba and

Colonel Nevil accompanied them. Although Colomba soon learned the dress and manners of polite society, she often longed for her wild life in Corsica. One day she saw an old man who had almost lost his senses. She learned that he was old Barricini, who had been forced to flee Corsica after Orso's vindication. Now he was a broken man, mourning the loss of his sons and his honor. He confessed to Colomba that he had indeed torn the page out of the notebook and substituted another name for his own. Colomba had no sympathy for the old man. She felt that his plight was due to his own evil and was glad that her father's blood was now completely avenged.

THE COMEDY OF ERRORS

Type of work: Drama
Author: William Shakespeare (1564-1616)
Type of plot: Farce
Time of plot: First century B.C.
Locale: Ancient Greece
First presented: c. 1592

Principal characters:
SOLINUS, Duke of Ephesus
AEGEON, a merchant of Syracuse
ANTIPHOLUS OF EPHESUS, and
ANTIPHOLUS OF SYRACUSE, twin brothers, sons of Aegeon and Aemilia
DROMIO OF EPHESUS, and
DROMIO OF SYRACUSE, twin brothers, attendants of above twins
AEMILIA, Aegeon's wife
ADRIANA, wife to Antipholus of Ephesus
LUCIANA, Adriana's sister
A COURTESAN

Critique:

The Comedy of Errors is a farce-comedy at times bordering on slapstick. The situations make the farce, the characters being only incidental to the plot. It required a nimble wit to place each character at the right place at the exact time to increase the confusion already existing in the story. Here Shakespeare had no subtle moral, no lyrical expression of love, no purpose of any kind but to entertain with scenes of hilarious confusion. The reader must enter wholeheartedly into the spirit of fun and gaiety or his time is wasted. Absent is the perfection of structure and characterization of Shakespeare's later works, but nowhere does he surpass The Comedy of Errors in simple, side-splitting fun.

The Story:

Aegeon, a merchant of Syracuse recently arrived in Ephesus, was to be put to death because he could not raise a thousand marks for payment of his fine. The law of the time was that a native of either land must not journey to the other on penalty of his life or the ransom of a thousand marks. But when Solinus, Duke of Ephesus, heard Aegeon's story, he gave the merchant one more day to try to raise the money.

It was a sad and strange tale Aegeon told. He had, many years ago, journeyed to Epidamnum. Shortly after his wife joined him there she was delivered of identical twins. Strangely enough, at the same time and in the same house, another woman also bore twin boys, both identical. The second wife and her husband were so poor that they could not care for their children, and so they gave them to Aegeon and his wife Aemilia, to be attendants to their two sons. On their way home to Syracuse, the six were shipwrecked. Aemilia and the two with her were rescued by one ship, Aegeon and the other two by a different ship. Aegeon did not see his wife and the two children in her company again. When he reached eighteen years of age, Antipholus, the son reared by his father, grew anxious to find his brother, and he and his attendant set out to find their missing twin. Now they too were lost to Aegeon, and he had come to Syracuse to seek them.

Unknown to Aegeon, his son and his attendant had just arrived in Ephesus. Antipholus and Dromio, his attendant, met first a merchant of the city, who warned them to say that they came from somewhere other than Syracuse, lest they suffer the penalty already meted out to Aegeon. Antipholus, having sent Dromio to find lodging for them, was utterly bewildered when the servant returned and said that Antipholus' wife waited dinner for him. What had happened was that the Dromio who came now to Antipholus was Dromio of Ephesus, servant and attendant to Antipholus of Ephesus. Antipholus of Syracuse had given his Dromio money to pay for lodging, and when he heard a tale of a wife about whom he knew nothing he thought his servant tricked him. He asked the servant to return his money. But Dromio of Ephesus had been given no money and professed no knowledge of the sum. He was beaten soundly for dishonesty. Antipholus of Syracuse later heard that his money had been delivered to the inn; he could not understand his servant's joke.

A short time later the wife and sister-in-law of Antipholus of Ephesus met Antipholus of Syracuse and, after berating him for refusing to come home to dinner, accused him of unfaithfulness with another woman. Not understanding a thing of which Adriana spoke, Antipholus of Syracuse went to her home to dinner, Dromio being assigned by her to guard the gate and allow no one to enter. Thus it was that Antipholus of Ephesus arrived at his home with his Dromio and was refused admittance. So incensed was he that he left his house and went to an inn. There he dined with a courtesan and gave her gifts intended for his wife.

In the meantime Antipholus of Syracuse, even though almost believing that he must be the husband of Adriana, fell in love with her sister Luciana. But when he told her of his love, she called him an unfaithful husband and begged him to remain true to his wife. Dromio of Syracuse was pursued by a kitchen maid whom he abhorred; the poor girl mistook him for Dromio of Ephesus, who loved her.

Even the townspeople and merchants were bewildered. A goldsmith delivered to Antipholus of Syracuse a chain meant for Antipholus of Ephesus and then tried to collect from the latter, who in turn stated that he had received no chain and accused the merchant of trying to rob him.

Antipholus and Dromio of Syracuse decided to get out of the seemingly mad town as soon as possible, and the servant was sent to book passage on the first ship leaving the city. But Dromio of Syracuse brought back the news of the sailing to Antipholus of Ephesus, who by that time had been arrested for refusing to pay the merchant for the chain he had not received. Antipholus of Ephesus, believing the servant to be his own, sent Dromio of Syracuse to his house to get money for his bail. But before that Dromio returned with the money, Dromio of Ephesus came to Antipholus of Ephesus, naturally without the desired money. Meanwhile Dromio of Syracuse took the money to Antipholus of Syracuse, who had not sent for money and could not understand what his servant was talking about. To make matters worse, the courtesan with whom Antipholus of Ephesus had dined had given him a ring. Now she approached the other Antipholus and demanded the ring. Knowing nothing about the ring, he angrily dismissed the wench, who decided to go to his house and tell his wife of his betrayal.

On his way to jail for the debt he did not owe, Antipholus of Ephesus met his wife. Wild with rage, he accused her of locking him out of his own house and of refusing him his own money for bail. She was so frightened that she asked the police first to make sure that he was securely bound and then to imprison him in their home so that she could care for him.

At the same time Antipholus and Dromio of Syracuse were making their way toward the ship that would carry them away from this mad city. Antipholus was wearing the gold chain. The merchant, meeting them, demanded that

Antipholus be arrested. To escape, Antipholus of Syracuse and his Dromio fled into an abbey. To the same abbey came Aegeon, the duke, and the executioners, for Aegeon had not raised the money for his ransom. Adriana and Luciana also appeared, demanding the release to them of Adriana's husband and his servant. Adriana, seeing the two men take refuge in the convent, thought they were Antipholus and Dromio of Ephesus. At that instant a servant ran in to tell Adriana that her husband and Dromio had escaped from the house and were even now on the way to the abbey. Adriana did not believe the servant, for she herself had seen her husband and Dromio enter the abbey. Then Antipholus and Dromio of Ephesus appeared before the abbey. Aegeon thought he recognized the son and servant he had been seeking, but they denied any knowledge of him. The confusion grew worse until the abbess brought from the convent Antipholus and Dromio of Syracuse, who instantly recognized Aegeon. Then all the mysteries were solved. Adriana was reunited with her husband, Antipholus of Ephesus, and his Dromio had the kitchen maid once more. Antipholus of Syracuse was free to make love to Luciana. His Dromio was merely freed. Still more surprising, the abbess turned out to be Aegeon's wife, the mother of the Antipholi. So the happy family was together again. Lastly, Antipholus of Ephesus paid his father's ransom and brought to an end all the errors of that unhappy day.

COMMENTARIES

Type of work: History
Author: Gaius Julius Caesar (102 or 100-44 B.C.)
Time: First century B.C.
Locale: Western Europe
First transcribed: c. 51 B.C.

Principal personages:
JULIUS CAESAR, Roman governor and general in Gaul
VERCINGETORIX, rebel leader of the Gauls
ORGETORIX, a chieftain of the Helvetii
DIVITIACUS, a Gaul loyal to the Romans
ARIOVISTUS, a chieftain of the Germanic tribes

Two thousand years ago the Roman Empire expanded north and westward into the area now known as France and Germany, and in 59 B.C. Julius Caesar, already famous as a general and administrator, was appointed to govern the Roman territories inhabited by the Gauls. When he went to Gaul he faced a situation requiring strong, active government, and as he proceeded he kept records of the events of his governorship, a record eventually to be known as Caesar's *Commentaries.* The *Commentaries* are an important record for posterity, despite the fact that many generations of English-speaking schoolchildren learning Latin have found them repugnant as a classroom exercise. Scholars and general readers have wished that Caesar had left a more complete record than he did. To expect a detailed history in the *Commentaries* is, however, to misunderstand the writer's purpose. His intention was not to write a definitive history of the period of the Gallic Wars, but rather to put down in writing what he considered, as the Roman general and administrator, most important.

No one can understand the *Commentaries* without having some concept of the flux of migration and its consequent pressures in Europe during the first century before Christ. The Gallic peoples were under pressure from the Germanic peoples across the Rhine River, tribes that coveted the rich lands of the Gauls and were, in their turn, under pressure from migrations still farther to the east. Rome faced a double threat from the Germanic tribes. First, they were pressing constantly southward; eventually they would invade and dismember the Roman Empire. The Germanic tribes also threatened Rome indirectly by the unrest they created in Gaul. Being a man of action and a clear analyst of the situation confronting Rome, Caesar took war home to the Germans.

In the *Commentaries* he gives a chronological account of his activities in Gaul from the time of his succession to the governorship of Gallia Narbonensis in 59 B.C. to the end of the Gallic revolt led by Vercingetorix late in the same decade. During those years Caesar and his Roman legions were set first against one group of tribes and then another. Most of the sections of the book carry such headings as "Campaign against Ariovistus," "Expedition against the Unelli," "First expedition into Germany," and "Siege and Sack of Avaricum." Only two sections, the first section of Book I and the second section of Book VI, are not about actual battle operations or preparations. The former is a description of Gaul and its inhabitants; the latter, an account of customs of the Gauls and Germans.

In his comments about the Gauls, Caesar stirs the imagination and stimulates curiosity by giving only enough information to make the reader wish more had been written; for example, an account of the druids' place in Gallic culture and the religious rites at which the druids officiated would be welcome. In some other cases, however, Caesar taxes the imagination, as in reporting certain kinds of animals as existing in the Hyrcanian Forest. One such animal is an elk that is captured, says Caesar, by partly cutting trees the elk leans against to rest; the animal has no joints in the legs and once down cannot rise. Caesar also reports a fabulous ox with but one horn growing from the middle of the forehead. Such reports, when compared with other natural histories of the period, do not detract from the value of the *Commentaries,* for in Caesar's time such reports were generally taken seriously, however absurd they may seem today.

Caesar's account of the Gallic Wars reminds us that war has been a continual factor in human affairs. As one example of the fury and effectiveness of war in ancient times, Caesar comments at the end of his account of the battle with the Nervii: "This battle being ended, and the name and nation of the Nervii almost reduced to annihilation, their old men, together with the boys and women whom we have stated had been collected together in the inlets and the marshes, when this battle had been reported to them, convinced that nothing was an obstacle to the conquerors, and nothing safe to the conquered, sent ambassadors to Caesar with the consent of all who survived, and surrendered themselves to him; and in recounting the calamity of their state, they said that their senators were reduced from six hundred to three; that of sixty thousand men who could bear arms, scarcely five hundred remained." Another example of the character of these ancient wars is the siege of Avaricum, at which, according to Caesar, scarcely eight hundred people of all ages and both sexes escaped the city when it was taken, out of a population of forty thousand; the rest were killed.

Caesar the Roman administrator is apparent throughout the *Commentaries.* He writes in an impersonal fashion, however, much as though he were preparing a favorable report to the Roman Senate. Only rarely does an individual come through to the reader as a real personality. Even Caesar himself, whose name figures more largely than any other, remains an official and a general, rather than a clearly visualized person. The Gallic and Germanic chieftains who opposed him are little more than names, and the same is true of the lieutenants who served under him. The only outstanding exception to this general statement is the passage concerning Sextius Baculus who, sick though he was, arose from his bed and saved the day for the Romans, rallying their forces when they were attacked in a camp at Aduatuca and fighting bravely until he had to be carried back to rest.

Of particular interest to English-speaking readers are those portions of the *Commentaries* which deal with Britain and Caesar's invasions of Britain. Most of us know all too little about the early history of that part of our heritage, and Caesar's account is the earliest in any Roman documents. Caesar tells of his first expedition, an abortive one, made in 55 B.C., and his second and more successful attempt the following year, an invasion which paved the way for the Roman occupation that was to last until the fifth century after Christ. For his second invasion he built and assembled a fleet of more than eight hundred vessels, a logistical success noteworthy in any era of history. This fleet carried two thousand cavalrymen with their mounts, and five Roman legions, each consisting at that time of about five thousand men.

Caesar was a remarkable man, one of the greatest in human history, in the sense that greatness may be defined as leaving an indelible mark on the pages of history. Few such men have lived; fewer still have left written records for posterity; and none has ever left a document to compare with Caesar's *Commentaries.* The book occupies a unique place in the written records of the Western world. In addition to its value as history, it also deserves to be read as an example of the concise report presented with a style and flavor all its own.

THE COMPLEAT ANGLER

Type of work: A treatise on sport, nature, and human conduct
Author: Izaak Walton (1593-1683); added to by Charles Cotton (1630-1687)
Time: Seventeenth century
Locale: England
First published: 1653; fifth edition with the Cotton additions, 1676

Principal characters:
PISCATOR, a fisherman
VENATOR, a hunter
AUCEPS, a falconer
PISCATOR JUNIOR
VIATOR, a traveler

One of the most modest and unassuming books ever written, *The Compleat Angler* has preserved its quality of evergreen freshness through more than three hundred editions since its first appearance in 1653. Its importance as a practical handbook on the angler's art has long since passed, although its appeal remains perennial to anyone who has ever sat for hours on the bank of a creek, with a cane pole and a can of worms, while waiting patiently for a horny-headed chub to take the hook, or has crept up behind some bushes at dawn to lay a fly in water swirling around a shaded rock where the riffle is guarded by hungry trout. What survives is the pastoral beauty of woodland, meadow, and stream, charmingly yet vividly drawn; the mood of pure pleasure that a sport like fishing holds for the contemplative man; and above all the author's ability to convey a message of fellowship and peace to all "honest, civil, quiet men" in an age of turmoil and revolution.

Izaak Walton, who wrote *The Compleat Angler* in a decade of religious and political ferment, himself remained serene and detached from the disturbances of his age. Aptly subtitled "The Contemplative Man's Recreation," his book is addressed to the "honest angler." "We anglers," he declares, "all love one another." In his Epistle to the Reader prefacing the third edition, he wrote:

And though this discourse may be liable to some exceptions, yet I cannot doubt but that most readers may receive so much pleasure or profit by it as may make it worthy the time of their perusal, if they be not very busy men. . . . And I am the willinger to justify the pleasant part of it because though it is known I can be serious at seasonable times, yet the whole Discourse is, or rather was, a picture of my own disposition, especially in such days and times as I have laid aside business and gone a-fishing with honest Nat. and R. Roe; but they are gone, and with them most of my pleasant hours, even as a shadow that passeth away and returns not.

Even a believer in the unstrenuous life—the indoors man or woman—will be charmed by Izaak Walton, whose book is a highly personal treatise on the art of angling, a work of fascinating though not always reliable natural history, an anthology of reflective passages on the condition of man, and an example of the almost lost art of graceful writing.

The author opens his discourse on a fine, fresh morning in May when Piscator, by stretching his legs up Tottenham Hill, overtakes Venator and Auceps. The latter is headed toward "a friend's house who mews a hawk for me, which I now long to see," and Venator hopes "to bestow another day or two in hunting the Otter." As the three walk along, each extols his favorite sport. First Auceps describes the beauty of his falcons as they soar high into his element, the Air. Venator commends his element, the Earth, and praises the pleasure of men who hunt "the stately Stag, the generous Buck, the wild Boar, the cunning Otter, the crafty Fox, and the fearful Hare." Both Auceps and Venator look somewhat down their noses at angling, believing it to be an easy art, but Piscator is so persuasive in defense of his element, Water, and so convincing on the importance of fish and the antiquity of his sport that, after Auceps drops off to see his hawk, Venator decides he would like to learn more from his new friend, the fisherman. Piscator agrees that they shall first spend one day in hunting the otter, a notorious killer of fish, and then Venator shall begin his education in the art of angling

At the stream Piscator demonstrates his skill by catching a chub (for it is the middle of the day and trout will not bite before evening) and when Venator objects to wasting time on such a rough, tasteless fish, Piscator proves the chub can be made delicious by proper dressing. The next day's instruction is on the catching of trout. Says Piscator, "The Trout is usually caught with a worm, or a minnow, which some call a Penk, or with a fly, *viz.* either a natural or an artificial fly: concerning which three I will give you some observations and directions." The names of the best worms for trout are strange to twentieth-century ears: there is the Lob-worm, the Brandling, the Gilt-tail, the Twachel. But with charming detail Piscator tells where to find them and how to put them on the hook. He commends minnows highly, for "a large Trout will come as fiercely at a Minnow, as the highest mettled hawk doth seize on a partridge, or a greyhound on a hare."

Venator is unsuccessful in his first try at trout, but Piscator catches three brace. When he loses a big one his comment is a model of restraint for fishermen: "Nay, the Trout is not lost; for pray take notice, no man can lose what he never had." When Venator insists that he should learn to tie artificial flies, Piscator names twelve kinds "to angle with upon the top of the water," among them the Moorish-

fly and the Dark-Drake-fly. Then he gives instructions for the tying of flies and how to fish with them. All of this chapter on the trout is charmingly interspersed with references to and quotations from Bacon, the classics, and the Bible.

So it is with the other types of angling and other fish. For Piscator is thorough and his lessons take Venator (by now, of course, an ardent angler) from the grayling to the salmon to the tench to the eel to the gudgeon to the miller's thumb. Walton rounds off Part I of *The Compleat Angler* with discussions of rivers and fish ponds ("and how to order them") and with directions for making a line.

Written by Walton's young friend Charles Cotton, whose additions are now an integral part of the text, Part II returns (this time with Piscator Junior and Viator) to what is obviously the great love of both authors, fishing for trout. Here we have more directions on technique (including one called "Daping, Dabbing, or Dibbling") and more on what flies are best for what months; August, for instance, demands a Harry-Long-Legs, "the body made of bear's dun and blue wool mixed, and a brown hackle-feather over all." But Cotton, like Izaak Walton, is also a lover of fish well cooked, and so he includes a recipe for trout that is, to say the least, elaborate; among the ingredients (aside from the trout) are beer, white wine, salt, lemon rind, horse-radish root, "a handsome little fagot of rosemary, thyme, and winter-savory," butter, and ginger. Having exhausted the possibilities of angling at the top, the middle, and the bottom for trout and grayling, Piscator Junior concludes his instructions to Viator by apologizing for having "tired you sufficiently."

But no one can grow tired (either sufficiently or insufficiently) of *The Compleat Angler*. True, a great deal of the information it contains is of little value to the present-day fisherman who may never see the Trent or the Severn, never feel on the end of his line a barbel or a bleak. He will, however, revel in Izaak Walton's

638

(and Cotton's) tender consideration for the smallest detail of angling, and through the whole book he will feel the presence of the author, a man of charm, scholarship, and propriety. He will even find a special kind of morality, for Sir Izaak at one point apparently fears he may be making the sport *too* attractive: he suggests that a time be set when each man should "leave fishing, and fall to his business." Most of all, Walton is a writer. His style is polished and gentle, as befits a description of angling, and his sentences move at a leisurely pace, the pace of a man carefully working up a trout stream. As long as there are fish in rivers and readers who enjoy good writing, *The Compleat Angler* will be read and loved.

COMRADES

Type of work: Drama
Author: August Strindberg (1849-1912)
Type of plot: Comic realism
Time of plot: Late nineteenth century
Locale: Paris
First presented: 1888

> *Principal characters:*
> AXEL, an artist
> BERTHA, his wife, also an artist
> ABEL, her woman friend, an ardent feminist
> WILLMER, a dandified author
> DR. ÖSTERMARK, a doctor, Axel's friend
> MRS. HALL, his divorced wife
> CARL STARCK, a happily married army officer

Critique:

The problem of marriage—the responsibilities of each of the parties, the proper relationship between them, the respective rights, duties, and privileges of each—concerned the thrice-divorced Strindberg, both as a person and as an artist, throughout his adult life. Along with this problem, the complications introduced into it by the feminist movement strongly concerned him also. While his Scandinavian contemporaries, Henrik Ibsen and Bjørnstjerne Bjørnson, were defending the rights of women in their plays, Strindberg was pleading the cause of masculine supremacy. His relatively early play *Comrades* is an example of his attempt to deal with this problem through comic means. Here he is illustrating the impossibility of a marriage based on equal rights and, along with it, the shallowness, meanness, and actual viciousness of those females who aspire to masculine prerogatives. However, though they obviously have Strindberg's sympathy, the triumphant males here seem little better than the conniving females whom they defeat. The play, inferior to the best of Strindberg, is an excellent example of his early work and interests.

The Story:

When Dr. Östermark visited his painter friend Axel, he found that Axel was married to a young feminist named Bertha, herself an aspiring artist. Axel explained the conditions of his marriage: the two were to live, not as husband and wife, but as comrades, each with equal rights, each free to achieve artistic expression in his own way. Dr. Östermark, a widower who, earlier in life, had been divorced, was dubious about the whole thing.

While they were talking, a male model arrived. Axel explained that the model was hired for Bertha and that he, forced to paint commercially to pay for Bertha's art lessons, could not afford one. Carl Starck, a Swedish army officer, and his wife joined the company. They were shocked that the model posed in the nude and that Bertha was left alone with him.

After the company had gone, Bertha returned. There was a slight altercation over finances, but Bertha kept the argument subdued because she had a favor to ask of Axel. Both had submitted paintings to an important show. It seemed certain that Axel's would be accepted by the jury, but there was much doubt about Bertha's. She begged Axel to use his influence—especially on the wife of the jury's chairman—to have her painting accepted. At first Axel claimed that to do so would be unsporting, but Bertha and her two friends, the masculine female, Abel, and the effeminate male, Willmer, finally convinced him to make the attempt. They even talked him into wearing the ribbon to a Russian decoration which he had vowed never to wear.

Axel carried out his wife's mission, returned, and then left again as the result of an argument. During his absence Abel arrived with the news that Axel's own painting had been rejected by the jury. A subsequent letter confirmed her statement. Bertha was triumphant. She and Abel gloated over the downfall of the male.

After Abel had gone, Bertha was visited by a Mrs. Hall, who explained that she was the divorced wife of Dr. Östermark. The doctor, she claimed, had left her penniless with two young daughters twenty years before. Hearing that Dr. Östermark was in Paris and that Bertha was a leading feminist, she had come to Bertha for help in devising a plan of vengeance. Bertha promised that she would present Mrs. Hall and her two daughters to the unsuspecting doctor at a masquerade party which she and Axel were to give the following evening.

Bertha planned that the party was also to further Axel's humiliation: she had ordered a dancing girl's costume for him to wear. When Axel returned, the quarrel over finances was resumed. Bertha taunted Axel with the charge that he was quibbling because her painting had been accepted and his had not. This charge angered him. When he saw his costume for the masquerade, he left again, completely enraged.

Abel and Bertha devised still another humiliation for Axel: they planned to arrange for the rejected painting to be brought home during the party. While they were contemplating their success, Willmer arrived with liquor and tobacco which they had ordered as supplies for a pseudo-masculine orgy. Willmer agreed to see that the painting was brought in at the right time. When he tried to make love to Bertha, she slapped and insulted him. As he left, Abel warned Bertha that it was dangerous to turn a friend into an enemy.

Bertha waited hours that night for Axel to come home. When he finally did come in, she attempted to placate him with genuinely feminine wiles, but he informed her that it was too late for her to become feminine; he had regarded her as a comrade for too long. Besides, he had just been with a woman who was truly a woman. His intentions were to divorce her. Also, having learned from Willmer that she had mismanaged his finances, he intended to demand financial reparations as well. Bertha was reduced to purely female pleading, but Axel was adamant. His only concession was to hold off the proceeding until after the party.

At the party, everything went wrong for Bertha. Axel refused to wear the effeminate costume. Starck recognized Mrs. Hall's daughters as a pair of prostitutes who had once accosted him and a fellow officer. Then Dr. Östermark, confronted by Mrs. Hall, who by that time was too drunk to stand, revealed that he had divorced the woman twenty years before because she was a confirmed dipsomaniac and that the two daughters were not his at all but the results of a subsequent marriage or liaison.

Bertha's final blow was the return of the rejected painting, not Axel's, but Bertha's. Axel confessed that, like a good comrade, he had switched numbers on the paintings so that Bertha's might have the advantage of his name. The advantage had not been enough, it proved, to overcome the poor workmanship. When Willmer admitted arranging for its return during the party, Axel threw him out bodily.

Bertha now resorted to taunts inspired by jealousy. Axel was getting rid of her, she claimed, because he was in love with Abel. Axel assured her that the notion was preposterous—no more feminists for him. He had, he admitted, a womanly woman to take her place.

Defeated, Bertha begged to be allowed to see him again. He would see her, he agreed, but in the place where one ought to see comrades, in the café. At home he would see his wife.

COMUS

Type of work: Masque
Author: John Milton (1608-1674)
Type of plot: Moral allegory
Time of plot: The age of myth
Locale: Kingdom of Neptune
First presented: 1634

Principal characters:
ATTENDANT SPIRIT, later disguised as Thyrsis
COMUS
THE LADY
THE ELDER BROTHER
THE SECOND BROTHER
SABRINA, the River Nymph

Critique:

The masque, popular in sixteenth- and seventeenth-century England, was originally composed of dancing, pageantry, and processions. Masques were performed in the homes of noblemen and were usually presented by the nobility themselves. The music and scenery were composed and designed by well-known musicians and architects. Ben Jonson introduced the anti-masque to these performances: the presence of non-noble and usually uncouth characters, who were in sharp contrast to the chief characters. Thus plot and character increased in importance, whereas in earlier times music and scenery had taken precedence over these. *Comus* was first presented to the Earl of Bridgewater at Ludlow Castle in honor of his appointment as Lord President of Wales and was performed by his three children. The Earl and Countess appeared in the final scene. In this work the poetry is more sensuous in its imagery than in Milton's earlier *Arcades*, and the structure is more complex and architectonic; the masque thus marks an important advance in his poetic development. Although *Comus* is not an example of the conventional masque (it would more properly be called a pastoral drama), it is important because, by its verse structure and its wealth of classical imagery used to further Puritan philosophy, it foreshadows Milton's later epic poetry.

The Story:

The Attendant Spirit came into a wild wood, far from his usual abode outside Jove's court, far above the dirt and hubbub of the world. He was on earth only to show the rare mortals before him some of the ways to godly virtue. He spoke of the plight of the children of Neptune, ruler of many island kingdoms, who were traveling to visit their father. Their path lay through a dark and treacherous wood where their lives would have been in danger if Jove had not sent the Spirit to protect them. The chief danger was Comus, son of Bacchus and Circe. He lived in the wood and possessed a magic wine which, when drunk by thirsty travelers, gave them the heads and inclinations of wild animals. The Spirit disguised himself as a shepherd to guide the children of Neptune. He left when he heard Comus and his band of bewitched travelers approaching.

Comus, invoking joy and feasting, drinking and dancing, declared that the night was made for love and should be so used before the sun revealed the revels of his band and turned them to sinfulness. His followers danced until he stopped them, sensing the approach of a girl whom he immediately wished to enchant.

The Lady entered, drawn to the scene by the noise of the revelers. Unwilling as she was to meet such people, she nevertheless felt that they were the only hope she had of finding her way out of the

643

wood. Because she had been tired by her walking, her brothers had left her to find wild fruit for refreshment, but night had fallen before they could return and they were unable to find her again. Meanwhile, a dark cloud had covered the stars. The Lady called and sang to the nymph, Echo, to guide her to her brothers.

Comus, delighted with the song she sang, decided that the Lady should be his queen, and in the disguise of a village boy he greeted her as a goddess. The Lady reproved him and said that she wanted help to find her companions. After questioning her about them, he said that he had seen two such young men gathering fruit and that it would be a delight to help her find them. Comus added that he knew the woods perfectly and that he would therefore lead the Lady to her brothers. She replied that she would trust him. They left the clearing together.

The two brothers arrived and the elder called to heaven for the moon and stars, so that they might see their way. Failing this, he wished to see the lights of someone's cottage. The Second Brother, adding that even the sound of penned-up flocks would help them, expressed great fear for his sister's fate. The Elder Brother insisted that the Lady's perfect virtue would protect her. The Second Brother said that beauty such as hers needed to be guarded and that she could easily be in danger in such a place. The Elder Brother repeated that he had great hope for her safety as she was armed by chastity. Nothing could violate this; the very angels in heaven would protect her.

Hearing someone approaching, the brothers called out to him. When the Attendant Spirit greeted them, they thought they recognized him as their father's shepherd, Thyrsis. He anxiously asked where their sister was and, hearing that she was lost, told them that Comus dwelt in the wood. He added that he had overheard Comus offer to escort a lady to her companions. Fearing that she was their sister, he had himself left to find the brothers. That news plunged the Second Brother into complete despair. The Elder Brother, maintaining that virtue could be attacked but not injured, declared that they must find Comus and fight him for their sister; but the Attendant Spirit warned them that swords would not help them against Comus. He said, however, that he had been given a magic herb that was effective against all enchantments. He instructed the brothers to break the glass in Comus' hand when they found him and to seize his wand.

In Comus' palace, meanwhile, the Lady refused his wine and attempted to leave, but she was restrained by a threat to transfix her in her chair. When she declared that Comus could not control her mind, he propounded his hedonistic philosophy, saying that she should enjoy her youth and beauty, not cruelly deny them. She replied that she would never accept anything from him, since only the good man can give good things. Comus argued that in rejecting him she was denying life, and the plentiful gifts of nature by her abstinence; beauty should be enjoyed, not left to wither like a dying rose. The Lady decided that she must refute these arguments with her own: nature's gifts are for the temperate to use well, and excess of luxury only breeds ingratitude in men. She feared that Comus could never understand this doctrine; and she felt that if she attempted to explain, her conviction would be so strong that his palace would tumble around him. Comus was impressed by her argument, which seemed to him inspired by Jove himself, yet he determined to try again to persuade her. As he began to speak, the brothers rushed in, broke his glass on the ground, and overwhelmed his followers.

Comus himself escaped because they had not captured his wand. The Attendant Spirit despaired of freeing the Lady until he remembered that he could summon Sabrina. This river nymph would help them, since she loved the virtue that the Lady personified. By song he summoned her in the name of Neptune and Triton to save the girl. As Sabrina rose from the river, she sang of the willows and flowers that she had left. She freed the Lady by sprinkling on her the pure and precious water from her fountain. The Attendant Spirit gave Sabrina his blessing and prayed that the river should always flow in good measure and that its banks would be fertile.

The Attendant Spirit then told the Lady that he would lead them to Neptune's house, where many friends were gathered to congratulate him. In Ludlow Town, at the President's castle, country dancers led the Lady and her two brothers before the Earl and the Countess, who impersonated Neptune and his Queen. There the Attendant Spirit praised the young people's beauty, patience, and honesty, and their triumph over folly; then he announced his return to his natural home in the Gardens of Hesperus, for his task was done. If any mortal would go with him, however, his way was the path of virtue.

CONFESSIONS

Type of work: Spiritual autobiography
Author: Saint Augustine (Aurelius Augustinus, 354-430)
Time: 354-399
Locale: Tagaste, Carthage, Rome, Milan
First transcribed: 397-401

> Principal characters:
> SAINT AUGUSTINE
> MONICA, his mother
> ADEODATUS, his natural son
> FAUSTUS, Bishop of the Manichaean sect
> AMBROSE, Bishop of Milan
> ALYPIUS, a friend from Tagaste

"My *Confessions,* in thirteen books," wrote Saint Augustine, looking back from the age of sixty-three at his various writings, "praise the righteous and good God as they speak either of my evil or good, and they are meant to excite men's minds and affections toward him. . . . The first through the tenth books were written about myself, the other three about the Holy Scripture."

In the year before his death, writing to Darius, he declared: "Take the books of my *Confessions* and use them as a good man should. Here see me as I am and do not praise me for more than I am."

The *Confessions* was a new form in literature. Others, like Marcus Aurelius, had set down meditations, but this was more. Others had written biographies and autobiographies, but again Saint Augustine did not follow their model. True, he does tell about his life, but his method is a departure from a narrative of dates and events. He was more interested in his thievery of pears than in more important actions, and he makes the fruit as meaningful in his life as the Old Testament symbolism of the apples in the Garden of Eden. Other episodes are selected because of their revelation of the grace and provision of God. As he wrote: "I pass over many things, hastening on to those which more strongly compel me to confess to thee." In fact, his life story might be looked on as a parallel to the parable of the Prodigal Son, with his heart "restless till it finds its rest in God"; and he brings

his account to an end, after his struggles to free himself from pride and sensuality, with his return to his home at Tagaste. Half his life still lay ahead of him.

Although his friends, his teachers, and his mother appear in the *Confessions,* they lack any physical details by which one may visualize them. Two lines cover the death of his father. Neither name nor description is given to his mistress and the mother of his child, nor of the friend whose death drove him from his native city. Detail was of less importance to Saint Augustine than theological meditation and interpretation.

Taking his text from the psalmist who would "confess my transgressions unto the Lord," this work is one long prayer beginning, "Great art thou, O Lord, and greatly to be praised," and ending with the hope that "thus shall thy door be opened."

From the very first, the consolation of God's mercy sustained Saint Augustine. His memories of infancy made him wonder what preceded that period, as later he theorized about what had been before the creation. His pictures of himself crying and flinging his arms about because he could not make his wants known were symbols to him of the Christian life, even as the acquisition of facts about this early period from his mother impressed on him the need for help from others to gain self-knowledge.

Though his mother Monica was a devout Christian and her son had been brought up in that faith, young Aurelius Augustinus was more interested in Aeneas than in God. Once, at the point of death from a stomach ailment, he begged to be baptized, but his mother refused to have him frightened into becoming a Christian. So he went on, reading Latin and disliking Greek, and taking special delight in the theater. A frank but modest description of his many abilities, the gift of his God to one not yet dedicated to God, ends the first book of this revealing work.

Book II concentrates on the sixteenth year of lazy, lustful, and mischievous Aurelius. He and his companions robbed a pear tree, not because they wanted the fruit, since they threw it to the swine, but because it was forbidden. His confession that he loved doing wrong made him ponder his reasons for wandering from the path of good and becoming a "wasteland."

When he traveled to Carthage to study, at the age of nineteen, his chief delights were his mistress and the theater. In the course of his prescribed studies he read an essay by Cicero, *Hortensius,* now lost, urging the study of philosophy. Remembering his mother's hopes that he would become a Christian, he tried to read the Scriptures; but he found them inferior in style to Cicero. However he did become involved with a pseudo-Christian sect, founded by the Persian religious teacher Mani (c.216-277), because he approved of their logical approach to the problems of evil and good, represented by the dualistic concept of the universe. During the nine years that he was a Manichaean, his mother, encouraged by a dream that he would eventually see his error, kept loyally by him.

Back in Tagaste, he wrote plays, taught rhetoric, and lived with a mistress. He had no patience with a bishop, sent by his mother, to instruct him in Christianity. He was equally scornful of a magician who offered to cast spells to insure his success in a drama competition. He thought he was sufficient to himself,

and by his own efforts he won a rhetoric contest.

His temporary interest in astrology ended when he was unable to prove that successful divinations were more than chance. The death of a dear friend, who during his last illness became a Christian and denounced the life Aurelius was leading, so profoundly affected him that he returned to Carthage. There, still following the Manichaean beliefs, he wrote several essays, now lost. He was soon to be disillusioned. Faustus, reputed the most learned of Manichaean bishops, came to Carthage, and Aurelius Augustinus went to him to clear his religious doubts. But he found Faustus more eloquent than logical. Hoping to improve himself, this teacher of rhetoric then went to Rome, where students were reported to be less rowdy than those in his classes in Carthage. In Rome, malaria, the teaching of the skeptics who upset his confidence in the certainty of knowledge, and above all, the lack of classroom discipline induced him to accept the invitation of officials to go to Milan and resume his teaching career in that city.

In Milan he enjoyed the companionship of two friends from Tagaste, Alypius and Nebridius. His mother, coming to live with him, persuaded Bishop Ambrose to try to convert her son. About the same time efforts to get him married and to regularize his life caused a break with his mistress, who on her departure left him with his young son Adeodatus.

The group around the young rhetorician often discussed philosophy, and in Neo-platonism he found an answer to his greatest perplexity: If there is a God, what is the nature of His material existence? Now he was ready to study Christianity, especially the writings of Saint Paul. In Book VII, which describes this period of his life, appears one of Saint Augustine's two ecstatic visions, a momentary glimpse of the One.

Book VIII recounts his conversion. Anxious to imitate those who had gained what he himself sought, he listened to an account of the conversion of the orator Marius Victorinus. While returning home, still upset and uncertain, he heard a child chanting: "Pick it up and read it." Taking these words as God's command, he opened the Bible at random and found himself reading Romans XIII, 13: "Put on the Lord Jesus Christ." Convinced, he called Alypius, and they found Monica and reported to her their newly acquired convictions.

Giving up his teaching, Saint Augustine prepared for baptism, along with his friend and Adeodatus. He was baptized by Bishop Ambrose during Easter Week, A.D. 387. Then the party set out to return to Tagaste. During their journey, and following another moment of Christian ecstasy, Monica died at Ostia on the Tiber. Her son's *Confessions* contains touching chapters of affection and admiration for her; sure of his faith at the time of her death, however, he fell into no period of abject mourning such as that which had followed the death of his friend at an earlier time.

With Book X, Saint Augustine turned from episodes of his life to self-analysis, detailing the three steps of the soul's approach to God, passing from an appreciation of the beauties of the outside world to an introspective study of itself, and ending with an inexplicable anticipation of the blessedness of the knowledge of God, the "truth-given Joy," that crowns the soul's pilgrimage.

Book XI represents one of Saint Augustine's great contributions to Christian thought, the analysis of time. Pondering the mysteries of creation in an "eternal world," he saw it not as measured by "the motion of sun, moon, and stars," but as determined by the soul, the past being its remembrance; the present, its attention; and the future, its anticipation. He wrote: "The past increases by the diminution of the future, until by the consumption of all the future, all is past."

The last two books present speculation on the methods of creation and on the truth of the Scriptures, with most of the chapters devoted to interpretation of the opening verses of Genesis. The Old Testament account is open to many interpretations, and the final book of the *Confessions* deals with both the material and allegorical possibilities of the story of the Creation. At the end, Saint Augustine acknowledges the "goodness" of creation, and meditates on verses describing the rest on the Seventh Day. He begs that God will bestow the rest and blessedness of that Sabbath in the life eternal that is to come.

The *Confessions*, a work filled with the spirit of a sincere, devout faith, lays the groundwork for Saint Augustine's more formal treatises, *On the Trinity* and *The City of God*.

CONFESSIONS

Type of work: Autobiography
Author: Jean Jacques Rousseau (1712-1778)
Time: 1712-1765
Locale: Switzerland, France, England
First published: 1784

> *Principal personages:*
> JEAN JACQUES ROUSSEAU, French writer and philosopher
> ISAAC ROUSSEAU, his father
> LOUISE DE WARENS, a Catholic convert and divorcee
> CLAUDE ANET, a domestic, Madame de Warens' lover
> DENIS DIDEROT, celebrated French encyclopedist
> FRIEDRICH MELCHIOR GRIMM, a writer
> LOUISE D'ÉPINAY, a French woman of letters
> THÉRÈSE LEVASSEUR, a servant girl, Rousseau's mistress
> COMTESSE D'HOUDETOT, sister-in-law of Madame d'Épinay

Rousseau's *Confessions* is the result of the attempt of a famous but psychotic romantic to speak fully and honestly of his own life. It is famous as a literary expression of a writer's remembrance of things past, more revealing through its signs of passion and prejudice than through its recording of the facts of his experience. The book serves as autobiography only to the extent that it can be checked against other, more objective, reports; but whatever its bias, the *Confessions* is Rousseau's work, and it reflects the man as he was at the time of its writing.

To some extent Rousseau undoubtedly succeeded in his effort to write an autobiography of such character that he could present himself before "the sovereign Judge with this book in my hand, and loudly proclaim, Thus have I acted; these were my thoughts; such was I. With equal freedom and veracity have I related what was laudable or wicked, I have concealed no crimes, added no virtues. . . ." Only a person attempting to tell all would have revealed so frankly the sensual satisfaction he received from the spankings administered by Mlle. Lambercier, the sister of the pastor at Bossey, who was his tutor. Only a writer finding satisfaction either in truth or self-abasement would have gone on to tell that his passion for being overpowered by women continued through-

out his adult life: "To fall at the feet of an imperious mistress, obey her mandates, or implore pardon, were for me the most exquisite enjoyments; and the more my blood was inflamed by the efforts of a lively imagination, the more I acquired the appearance of a whining lover." Having made this confession, Rousseau probably found it easier to tell of his extended affair with Madame de Warens at Annecy and of his experiences with his mistress and common-law wife, Thérèse Levasseur.

Rousseau records that he was born at Geneva in 1712, the son of Isaac Rousseau, a watchmaker, and Suzanne Bernard. His mother died at his birth, "the first of my misfortunes." According to the son's account of his father's grief, Isaac Rousseau had mixed feelings toward his son, seeing in him an image of Suzanne and, at the same time, the cause of her death. Rousseau writes: ". . . nor did he ever embrace me, but his sighs, the convulsive pressure of his arms, witnessed that a bitter regret mingled itself with his caresses. . . . When he said to me, 'Jean Jacques, let us talk of your mother,' my usual reply was, 'Yes, father, but then you know we shall cry,' and immediately the tears started from his eyes."

Rousseau describes his first experiences with reading. He turned to the romances that his mother had loved, and he and his father sometimes spent the entire night reading aloud alternately. His response to these books was almost entirely emotional, but he finally discovered other books in his grandfather's library, works which demanded something from the intellect: Plutarch, Ovid, Molière, and others.

He describes with great affection how his Aunt Suzanne, his father's sister, moved him with her singing; and he attributes his interest in music to her influence.

After his stay at Bossey with Pastor Lambercier, Rousseau was apprenticed to an engraver, Abel Ducommun, in the hope that he would succeed better in the engraver's workshop than he had with City Registrar Masseron, who had fired him after a brief trial. Ducommun is described as "a young man of a very violent and boorish character," who was something of a tyrant, punishing Rousseau if he failed to return to the city before the gates were closed. Rousseau was by this time, according to his account, a liar and a petty thief, and without reluctance he stole his master's tools in order to misplace them.

Returning from a Sunday walk with some companions, Rousseau found the city gates closing an hour before time. He ran to reach the bridge, but he was too late. Reluctant to be punished by the engraver, he suddenly decided to give up his apprenticeship.

Having left Geneva, Rousseau wandered aimlessly in the environs of the city, finally arriving at Confignon. There he was welcomed by the village curate, M. de Pontverre, who gave him a good meal and sent him on to Madame Louise de Warens at Annecy. Rousseau expected to find "a devout, forbidding old woman"; instead, he discovered "a face beaming with charms, fine blue eyes full of sweetness, a complexion whose whiteness dazzled the sight, the form of an enchanting neck. . . ." He was sixteen, she was twenty-eight. She became something of a mother to him (he called her "Maman")

and something of a goddess, but within five years he was her lover, at her instigation. Her motive was to protect him and to initiate him into the mysteries of love. She explained what she intended and gave him eight days to think it over; her proposal was intellectually cool and morally motivated. Since Rousseau had long imagined the delights of making love to her, he spent the eight days enjoying thoughts more lively than ever; but when he finally found himself in her arms, he was miserable: "Was I happy? No: I felt I know not what invincible sadness which empoisoned my happiness: it seemed that I had committed an incest, and two or three times, pressing her eagerly in my arms, I deluged her bosom with my tears."

Madame de Warens was at the same time involved with Claude Anet, a young peasant with a knowledge of herbs who had become one of her domestics. Before becoming intimate with Rousseau she had confessed to him that Anet was her lover, having been upset by Anet's attempt to poison himself after a quarrel with her. Despite her generosity to the two young men, she was no wanton; her behavior was more a sign of friendship than of passion, and she was busy being an intelligent and gracious woman of the world.

Through her efforts Rousseau had secured a position registering land for the king in the office at Chambéry. His interest in music, however, led him to give more and more time to arranging concerts and giving music lessons; he gave up his job in the survey office.

This was the turning point of his life, the decision which threw him into the society of his times and made possible his growing familiarity with the world of music and letters. His alliance with Madame de Warens continued, but the alliance was no longer of an intimate sort, for he had been supplanted by Winzenreid de Courtilles during their stay at Les Charmettes. Winzenreid came on the scene after the first idyllic summer, a period in his life which Rousseau describes as "the short happiness of my life." He tells of rising with the sun, walking through the woods, over the hills, and along the valley; his delight in nature is evident, and his theories concerning natural man become comprehensible. On his arrival Winzenreid took over physical chores and was forever walking about with a hatchet or a pickax; for all practical purposes Rousseau's close relationship with Madame de Warens was finished, even if a kind of filial affection on his part survived. He describes other adventures in love, and although some of them gave him extreme pleasure, he never found another "Maman."

Rousseau, having invented a new musical notation, went to Paris hoping to convince others of its value. The system was dismissed as unoriginal and too difficult, but Rousseau had by that time been introduced to Parisian society and was known as a young philosopher as well as a writer of poetry and operas. He received an appointment as secretary to the French ambassador at Venice, but he and M. de Montaigu irritated each other and he left his post about a year later.

Returning to Paris, Rousseau became involved with the illustrious circle containing the encyclopedist Diderot, Friedrich Melchior Grimm, and Mme. Louise d'Épinay. He later became involved in a bitter quarrel with all three, stemming from a remark in Diderot's Le Fils naturel, but he was reconciled with Diderot and continued the novel he was writing at the time, La Nouvelle Héloïse. His account of the quarrel together with the letters that marked its progress is one of the liveliest parts of the Confessions.

As important an event as any in Rousseau's life was his meeting with Thérèse Levasseur, a needlewoman between twenty-two and twenty-three years of age, with a "lively yet charming look." Rousseau reports that "At first, amusement was my only object," but in making love to her he found that he was happy and that she was a suitable successor to "Maman." Despite the difficulties put in his way by her mother, and despite the fact that his attempts to improve her mind were useless, he was satisfied with her as his companion. She bore him five children who were sent to the foundling hospital, against Thérèse's will and to Rousseau's subsequent regret.

Rousseau describes the moment on the road to Vincennes when the question proposed by the Academy of Dijon—"Has the progress of sciences and arts contributed to corrupt or purify morals?"—so struck him that he "seemed to behold another world." The discourse that resulted from his inspired moment won him the prize and brought him fame. However, it may be that here, as elsewhere in the Confessions, the actual circumstances have been considerably altered by a romantic and forgetful author.

The Confessions carries the account of Rousseau's life to the point when, having been asked to leave Bern by the ecclesiastical authorities as a result of the uproar over Émile, he set off for England, where David Hume had offered him asylum.

Rousseau's Confessions offers a personal account of the experiences of a great writer. Here the events which history notes are mentioned—his literary triumphs, his early conversion, his reconversion, his romance with Madame d'Houdetot, his quarrels with Voltaire, Diderot, and churchmen, his musical successes—but they are all transformed by the passionate perspective from which Rousseau, writing years after most of the events he describes, imagines his own past. The result is that the Confessions leaves the reader with the intimate knowledge of a human being, full of faults and passions, but driven by ambition and ability to a significant position in the history of literature.

CONFESSIONS OF AN ENGLISH OPIUM EATER

Type of work: Essays
Author: Thomas De Quincey (1785-1859)
Type of treatise: Confession and fantasy
Time of treatise: Early nineteenth century
Locale: England and Wales
First published: 1821

Principal characters:
THOMAS DE QUINCEY, the narrator
ANN, a prostitute

Critique:

This book is one of those works about which all educated people have heard but which few have read, in spite of the sensational subject, addiction to drugs. The modern reader has little patience with deliberate displays of erudition, with protracted sentimentality, with latinate periodic sentences, and with apostrophes to this abstraction or to that inanimate object. De Quincey was a conscious stylist in his attempt to give prose writing the imaginative and emotional qualities of poetry. But he was also prolix; and it is for this prolixity, perhaps, that he goes largely unread today. Still, *Confessions of an English Opium Eater* is worth reading: De Quincey forbore admirably here, hewing to or staying close to his theme throughout. As an inspiration to human beings who have succumbed to any pernicious habit and who despair of ever breaking free, the work is invaluable.

The Story:

When Thomas De Quincey was about twenty-eight years of age, intense stomach pains drove him to take opium for relief. These stomach pains were a legacy from hardships that he endured as an adolescent.

De Quincey's father had died when the boy was seven. Thomas, the joint responsibility of four guardians, was sent to school, where he became an excellent Greek scholar. Later, at the Manchester Grammar School, he was so superior to his teachers in Greek that he soon felt a desire to leave the school. His guardi-

ans being against this plan, however, he asked an old friend for money, received it, and planned to make his escape from a school which he felt had nothing to offer him intellectually.

The day of his escape came. When the groom of his hall was carrying his book-laden trunk down a narrow stairway, the man slipped and fell, the trunk clattering noisily to the floor below. Young De Quincey was sure he would be caught. But the incident, miraculously, did not arouse the curiosity of the resident master, and the youth was able to get away.

Seventeen-year-old De Quincey headed westward, walking through Wales, where, in Bangor, he took a room. His landlady was the ex-servant of a bishop's family. On one of her regular visits to the bishop's house, she disclosed that she was taking in lodgers. When she reported her disclosure to De Quincey, he took exception to the tenor of her remarks concerning him, moved out of her house at once, and found lodging in inns. That type of lodging being relatively expensive, the young man soon found himself reduced to eating only once a day, and this a meal of only coffee or tea. The mountain air of Wales and the walking made him abnormally hungry, so that his having to subsist off berries and charitable handouts hurt him physically. As time went by, he managed to earn a meager living by writing letters for the illiterate and by doing odd jobs. But the damage to his health had been done.

His travels then took him from Wales

to London, where, utterly destitute and afraid to reveal himself to any friends of his family, he lived for several months on little more than a small ration of bread; also, at that time, he slept out of doors. At last, in cold weather, an acquaintance gave him shelter in a large, almost empty house, where De Quincey's companion was a ten-year-old girl. Pains in his stomach prevented his ever getting a proper night's sleep; consequently, he slept by fits and snatches both day and night. The master of the house was a legal representative of money-lenders, but despite the man's apparent lack of principles De Quincey found him generous in his way. The little girl appeared to be a servant in the large house, which was situated near Soho Square.

De Quincey walked the streets and often sat all day in parks, until Ann, a sixteen-year-old street-walker, befriended him. One night, when he had a violent attack of his stomach complaint, Ann spent part of her scant savings on wine and spices for him.

Soon afterward he met an old family acquaintance who gave him money, thus ending De Quincey's period of extreme poverty. Previously, he had been afraid to appeal to family friends for help for fear that his guardians would send him back to the grammar school. That he might have taken on literary work of some kind never occurred to him. Now, solvent for the moment, he made arrangements to get an advance on his patrimony, which would not be legally his until his twenty-first birthday.

After saying goodbye to Ann, he took a coach to Eton to get a signature that was required for an advance on his patrimony. At Eton he called upon an acquaintance, young Lord Desart, who invited him to breakfast. Finding that he could not keep down the food, he took wine to his great comfort. Lord Desart, who was only eighteen, was reluctant to sign for security, but he finally consented. De Quincey returned to London, where he found that Lord Desart's signature did not impress the money-lenders with whom he was negotiating for the advance. Again he was threatened with hardship; again, however, he was saved, for his reconciled relatives sent him to Oxford University. Meanwhile, before he left London, he searched unsuccessfully for Ann. She was nowhere to be found, and he never saw her again.

De Quincey, now nineteen, made frequent weekend trips to London from Oxford. One Sunday, while in the metropolis, he suffered agonies from neuralgic pains in the head, and a fellow student whom he encountered recommended opium for relief. He thereupon bought a small amount of laudanum, the tincture of opium, from an apothecary. He returned to his room and took the prescribed amount. The result seemed phenomenal to him; all his pain ceased, and he knew boundless pleasure. There was no intoxication, as from wine or spirits; there was only a protracted sense of being utterly at peace with the world and with himself. The opium uplifted the intellect rather than the animal spirits, and when its effect wore off there was no period of depression such as spirits induced.

As a college student, De Quincey's two great pleasures were to hear Grassini, an Italian soprano who often sang in London, or to take opium and afterward join the Saturday night crowds in the London markets. Even greater than these pleasures, however, was that of withdrawing himself at the time when the opium had reached its maximum effect on his mind, so that he could get the most complete enjoyment from his opium-induced dreams and visions.

De Quincey left Oxford. In 1812 he took a cottage, where he studied German metaphysics and continued to take opium once a week. His health was apparently never better. Even after eight years of taking opium, he was able to say that he had not become a slave to the drug; he was still able to control the amount taken and the intervals between doses.

But a recurrence, in 1813, of his old stomach disorder led him to take the drug every day. That he was already partially addicted was a secondary reason for his increased use of opium. For two years he took three hundred and twenty grains of opium daily, but at last he was able to reduce the amount to forty grains. Staying on that allowance, he experienced the happiest year of his life.

About that time a Malay, traveling afoot, stopped for a night at the cottage. De Quincey was impressed by the aspect and garb of the Oriental. Before the man left the next morning, De Quincey gave him enough opium, divided into three parts, to kill a man if taken all at once. The Malay clapped all three pieces into his mouth and departed. De Quincey felt concern for several days, but to his relief he never heard or read of the untimely death of a Malay in his part of Great Britain.

In his little cottage in the mountains of northern England, De Quincey, in the winter of 1816-1817, knew complete happiness in his experience with opium. Deep snows, heavy rains, a snug cottage, a roaring fire, a large collection of good books, plenty of tea, and daily consumption of laudanum brought him idyllic happiness.

But matters changed. Having become addicted to the daily taking of opium, it became impossible for him to reduce his daily allowance without bringing on abnormal perspiration and excruciating abdominal pains. He soon lost interest in reading and the study of mathematics and philosophy. A friend sent him David Ricardo's *Principles of Political Economy and Taxation*. The book aroused him from his lethargy long enough to write for publication on that popular subject. Then, unable to write a preface for his work, he shelved the project. He neglected household responsibilities. At night he lay awake in his bed, processions of visions passing through his mind.

These visions consisted largely of scenes from the English Civil War and from ancient Rome. Soon he found it difficult to distinguish between the real and the unreal. Furthermore, other dreams and visions took him into frightful abysses. Constantly depressed, he lost all normal sense of space and time, and he often had the sensation of having lived through a millennium. Also, he found himself able to recall insignificant events of his childhood, details which he had never been conscious of remembering.

The opium dreams were periodic in subject matter: there were nights during which he dreamed historical scenes; then there was a period of architectural dreams —vast piles of buildings and enormous cities; these were followed by dreams of water—lakes, lagoons, vast oceans; and next a period of dreams in which countless human faces presented themselves in peculiar situations to his mind's eye.

In May, 1818, his dream visions took on an Oriental theme. At times he was in Egypt, then in China, or in India. Where in previous dream sequences he had known only spiritual horrors, in these Oriental ones he sensed physical horror from reptiles and frightful birds.

In the summer of 1819, De Quincey, still addicted to opium, dreamed of a graveyard in his own little valley. In the dream he arose and walked out of his cottage yard to enjoy the air. He thought he saw an Oriental city and, beneath a palm tree, Ann, the street-walker friend of his youth. She did not speak; the dream faded and he found himself walking with her in the streets of London. In 1820 one vision was so terrifying in its profundity and breadth that he awoke and declared that he would never sleep again.

Finally, he reasoned that he would surely die if he continued to take opium and that he might die in the attempt to break the habit. With so little choice, he

654

decided to try, at least, to free himself from opium. He reduced his ration gradually and finally broke free, thus proving to himself that an addict may end a habit of seventeen years' duration.

CONFESSIONS OF FELIX KRULL, CONFIDENCE MAN

Type of work: Novel
Author: Thomas Mann (1875-1955)
Type of plot: Social realism
Time of plot: Early twentieth century
Locale: Germany, Paris, Lisbon
First published: 1954

Principal characters:

FELIX KRULL, alias Armand, a hotel employee, alias the Marquis de Venosta
ENGELBERT KRULL, his father
FRAU KRULL, his mother
OLYMPIA, his sister
HERR SCHIMMELPREESTER, his godfather
MÜLLER ROSE, an actor and a friend of Engelbert Krull
MME. HOUPFLÉ, a sentimental novelist
DOM ANTONIO JOSÉ KUCKUCK, a Portuguese museum director
DONA MARIA PIA KUCKUCK, his wife
SUSANNA ("ZOUZOU") KUCKUCK, their daughter
THE MARQUIS DE VENOSTA, a wealthy young nobleman
ZAZA, the marquis' mistress

Critique:

Thomas Mann, who had left Nazi Germany in 1933 and who became an American citizen in 1944, returned in 1952 to Switzerland. There he wrote *Felix Krull.* Preliminary work to this novel had been published as early as 1922, but only after the nightmare of Hitler and World War II was over did Mann find time and the mood to continue writing about Felix Krull, a character who surprised some of his readers, accustomed as they were to a steady flow of more metaphysically inclined characters and unprepared for the diary of a confidence man. Shortly after publication of the book, the world knew that Felix Krull would be the last character created by the pen of the great Thomas Mann. Many Germans consider Mann the only writer worthy to continue the tradition of classical German literature as established by Goethe and Schiller. It is most unfortunate for Mann's readers in general, and for readers of this novel in particular, that the greater part of Felix Krull's adventures will remain a secret forever. The present book, subtitled *The*

Early Years, indicates that more volumes of Krull's confessions were planned, but so far nothing has been found among Mann's papers that leads readers to hope for more information about the fate of Felix Krull, the confidence man.

The Story:

Felix Krull was born in the Rhine Valley, the son of a champagne maker named Engelbert Krull. Townspeople considered the Krull family upper class, but frowned on the easygoing way of life in the Krull household; Engelbert Krull, for one thing, showed too much interest in one of his female employees. A number of fun-loving friends, led by Felix' godfather, Herr Schimmelpreester, were frequent guests at Krull's gay parties. Early in life Felix and his sister Olympia were allowed to take part in the festivities.

The greatest experience of Felix' youth was a dramatic performance starring a famous actor, Müller Rose. Since the actor was a friend of Engelbert Krull, Felix was allowed to visit backstage. When he saw the actor removing his make-up, he was completely disillusioned. For a long time he marveled at the impressions an actor could create. Before long Felix himself became an actor. He decided to prolong the vacation period in school by falsifying his father's signature on absentee notes, but he gained much more satisfaction when he was able to feign sickness to such a degree that the family doctor was at a loss for explanations.

Unfortunately, the champagne business did not prosper. Krull's champagne was bottled in a most exquisite manner, yet the wine was of such a low quality that even Herr Schimmelpreester spoke of it only with disdain. The loss of his business and consequently his fun-loving friends was too much for Engelbert Krull, and he shot himself. Herr Schimmelpreester recommended that Frau Krull open a rooming house in Frankfurt. For sister Olympia he provided employment in a light opera company. For Felix he arranged an apprenticeship in a Paris hotel, but the problem of military conscription prevented Felix' departure. Thus he was free to explore city life in Frankfurt, although lack of financial means left for him only the role of an outside observer. He studied the behavior of society at theaters and learned from window displays what was recommended for gentlemen. With equal interest he studied the lives of prostitutes. So far his only affair had been with one of his father's female employees. This experience was enriched when he met Rosza. While her procurer was in jail he became her lover.

In order to follow Herr Schimmelpreester's advice about employment in Paris, Felix had two alternatives left: to serve his military term before departure or to be excused entirely from service. Felix decided on the latter. After careful preparation he gave an impressive performance at the army medical examination center. While declaring dramatically his desire to serve the fatherland, he managed to convey the most unfavorable information about his background, and

he crowned his performance with a pretended epileptic fit. Seemingly heartbroken because of his rejection, he left for Paris. During the confusion at customs inspection he inadvertently, as he assured himself, slipped the jewel case of a woman traveler in his suitcase.

In Paris he found himself the lowest member of the hotel hierarchy. With the help of a roommate he sold some of the stolen jewels. As an elevator operator in a luxury hotel, he made every effort to please his customers, especially the women. The hotel director gave him the name Armand. One of the guests in his elevator turned out to be the original owner of the jewel case, Mme. Houpflé, the wife of a rich Strassburg merchant. When Armand realized that the woman did not suspect him of the theft, he was very considerate toward her and was rewarded with an invitation to visit her during off-duty hours.

He became her lover. Mme. Houpflé enjoyed especially the humiliating aspect of the affair, and talked about her need to be humiliated. Armand considered the moment appropriate for confessing the theft of the jewel case. Surprisingly, Mme. Houpflé enjoyed the confession because it increased her abasement, and she suggested that he should rob her of all her valuables. He gladly obliged.

After he had sold the valuables, he rented a room in town. A dual life began: during the day he was Armand the hotel employee, and during the night Felix Krull, man about town. Thanks to his excellent manners he was soon promoted to the post of waiter. Difficulties arose when the sixteen-year-old daughter of a wealthy family fell hopelessly in love with him, and when the Scottish Lord Strathbogie was determined to have Armand as his valet. To all offers Armand said no; freedom to do as he pleased seemed to him the most valuable goal in life.

His favorite customer was the young Marquis de Venosta, who enjoyed the witty remarks of waiter Armand. The nobleman's mistress, a Parisian dancing girl named Zaza, also approved of him because he did not fail to call her Madame la Marquise. It was de Venosta who finally discovered Armand's double life when he came across Felix dining in a famous restaurant.

A great dilemma had developed for de Venosta. His parents, not approving of his relationship with Zaza, planned to send him on a trip around the world. Because he found the thought of parting from Zaza unbearable, the marquis was happy to find in Felix a sympathetic listener. Felix explained that the only way for him to stay with Zaza would be to let someone else assume his identity and travel under his name. Delighted with the idea, de Venosta decided that Felix was the best candidate.

After elaborate preparations and much coaching Felix received a letter of credit and took the train to Lisbon. On the way he met Dom Antonio José Kuckuck, director of the Museum of Natural History in Lisbon. Impressed by the high social standing of his fellow traveler, the professor explained the outline of his philosophy. Felix found in the professor's theories an explanation of his own being; all developments of natural history seemed to him only steps toward himself. The professor's opinion that all phases of de-velopment were still with us and around us gave Felix a clue to the stage-like appearance of the world. He accepted gladly an invitation to visit Kuckuck in Lisbon.

When he met Dona Maria Pia Kuckuck and her daughter Susanna, called Zouzou, Felix was impressed by the beauty of the two women, who were in turn equally impressed by the handsome "Marquis." Determined to kiss Zouzou before his departure, but finding his time in Lisbon running short, Felix wrote a letter to "his parents," presenting his stay in Lisbon in such a favorable light that they agreed to the postponement of the scheduled trip to South America. Under the pretext of wanting to show some of his drawings to Zouzou, Felix met her secretly in Kuckuck's garden. The incident resulted in a kiss, which was suddenly interrupted by Dona Maria. Sternly she asked "the Marquis" to come into the house, where she reprimanded him for abusing her hospitality. Outspoken Dona Maria wanted to know why Felix could not appreciate maturity instead of asking satisfaction from childishness. When Dona Maria threw herself into his arms, he realized that his attempted seduction of the daughter had ended with his unforeseen conquest of the mother.

THE CONFIDENCE MAN

Type of work: Novel
Author: Herman Melville (1819-1891)
Type of plot: Social satire
Time of plot: Nineteenth century
Locale: The Mississippi River
First published: 1857

Principal characters:
THE CONFIDENCE MAN
CHARLES NOBLE, a talkative passenger
MR. ROBERTS, a merchant
PITCH, a frontiersman
MARK WINSOME, a mystic
EGBERT, his disciple

Critique:

The Confidence Man: His Masquerade is a quiet but bitter castigation of mankind. Episodic in structure, it relentlessly reveals man's utter lack of faith in man and, at the same time, discloses the facility with which most men can be duped. This, Melville's last major fiction, rivals Mark Twain's late works for gloom, pessimism, and misanthropy. However, Melville's career-ending novelette, *Billy Budd, Foretopman,* written more than thirty years later, exhibits none of these harsh and cynical characteristics.

The Story:

Aboard the steamboat *Fidele,* in dock at St. Louis, a group of passengers stood reading a placard which offered a reward for the capture of an impostor from the East—a confidence man. A deaf-mute beggar joined the group and began displaying a slate on which he wrote several mottoes praising the virtue of charity. Jeered at by the crowd, the deaf-mute lay down and slept on the forecastle as the steamboat pulled out for New Orleans.

A short time later Black Guinea, a crippled Negro, appeared on deck to beg for pennies, which he skillfully caught in his mouth. A man with a wooden leg broke up this cruel game by loudly accusing the Negro of fraud, but Black Guinea protested his innocence and, in reply to an Episcopal clergyman's request for references, described several persons

on the boat, all of whom, along with Black Guinea himself and the deaf-mute as well, were one and the same man—the confidence man. After the clergyman left to find one of these references, only a kindly country merchant gave Black Guinea alms, an act which had unfortunate consequences, since he dropped one of his business cards while he was fishing in his pocket for a coin.

To this merchant, Mr. Roberts by name, the impostor introduced himself as John Ringman. Pretending that he had met Mr. Roberts six years earlier, on a business matter, Ringman won his confidence and talked him out of a sum of money. To repay Mr. Roberts, Ringman gave him a tip on some valuable stock which could be bought aboard ship from the president of the Black Rapids Coal Company.

Next, Ringman accosted a college student who was reading Tacitus. Before Ringman could make a pitch for money, the student left in embarrassment at a lecture Ringman was delivering on the decadence of Tacitus.

The confidence man appeared next as a solicitor of funds for the Seminole Widow and Orphan Society. In this disguise he was recognized as one of Black Guinea's references by the Episcopal clergyman. The clergyman gave his alms for Black Guinea and was prevailed upon to contribute to the Seminole Fund also.

In the same disguise the impostor gulled a widow and a gentleman into donating to the fund. Somewhat reluctantly, the gentleman also contributed to a plan for the world-wide consolidation of all charities.

Disguised as Mr. Truman, the president of the Black Rapids Coal Company, the impostor met the student again. Ironically, since he prided himself on his cynicism and circumspection, the student insisted on buying some stock, despite the impostor's feigned reluctance to sell. The good merchant, Mr. Roberts, was also pleased to purchase some of the shares which his friend Ringman had recommended. During the conversation which followed this transaction, Mr. Roberts happened to mention the presence of a sickly old miser aboard ship and thus informed the confidence man of another victim.

The confidence man succeeded in gulling the miser twice: once by selling him some of the bogus stock and once, posing as an herb doctor, by selling him a supply of Omni-Balsamic Reinvigorator, guaranteed, if taken with confidence, to cure a consumptive cough.

A Missouri frontiersman's scorn for herbs and natural healing transformed the herb doctor into a representative of an employment agency, the Philosophical Intelligence Office. This Missourian, named Pitch, had resolved to purchase machinery to work his farm rather than rely on another boy, having had thirty-five unpleasant experiences with as many boys. Through brilliantly specious rhetoric the impostor persuaded him to hire still another boy.

The impostor appeared to Pitch once more, this time disguised as Francis Goodman, a friendly world traveler and cosmopolitan. But Pitch, brooding over his own gullibility, was in no mood for fellowship. After trying unsuccessfully to dispel Pitch's misanthropic melancholia, the cosmopolitan moved on in search of more susceptible prey.

He was accosted by one Charles Noble, a garrulous passenger who, having overheard the colloquy with Pitch, was reminded of another bitter frontiersman: Colonel John Moredock, a notorious Indian hater. Goodman being agreeable, Noble proceeded to narrate a long tale of Moredock's vendetta against Indians and to expound the philosophy of Indian-hating.

Needless to say, the confidence man was appalled by such a misanthropic tale. Finding that Noble shared his feeling, Goodman agreed to split a bottle of port with him. Over their port, the two found that they shared a high regard for wine, but their incipient friendship was strained by Goodman's suspicion that Noble was trying to get him drunk. Cordiality and noble sentiments prevailed, however, until Goodman asked Noble to prove his professed confidence in mankind by lending him fifty dollars. This startling request produced such a violent reaction that the friendship would have ended then and there had not Goodman pretended that he had been joking. Confidence restored, Goodman told the story of Charlemont, an aristocrat of singularly peculiar behavior, as a prelude to another request for a loan. Before Goodman could make his appeal, Noble abruptly retired.

A passenger who had been watching the two men warned Goodman to beware of Noble's companionship. Goodman had difficulty in extracting a comprehensible reason for this warning because the passenger turned out to be Mark Winsome, a mystic philosopher of no plain, ordinary tongue. Finally, Winsome stated clearly that Noble was a confidence man. Of course the real confidence man expressed incredulity, whereupon Winsome withdrew, leaving behind a disciple, a young man named Egbert, to explain the Winsome mystic philosophy, which was, in effect, quite practical.

To explore the philosophy on a practical level, Goodman suggested that Egbert use it to answer a hypothetical request for a loan. Steadfastly and consistently Egbert rejected the plea and finally told a long story to illustrate the folly, the tragedy, of loans between friends. Disgusted by such complete cynicism, the confidence man retreated.

Still in the guise of the cosmopolitan, he visited the ship's barber shop. There he succeeded in cheating the barber out of the price of a shave but failed, ultimately, in persuading the barber to extend credit to his customers.

Later that night, in the gentleman's sleeping cabin, the confidence man found only one person still awake, an old man reading the Bible. Though he mouthed pious sentiments attesting his faith in mankind and God, the old man eagerly bought a traveler's lock and a money belt from a child peddler and accepted a counterfeit detector as a premium. Commenting that the two of them put equal trust in man and God, the confidence man led the old gentleman, who was now carrying a life preserver, off to bed.

CONINGSBY

Type of work: Novel
Author: Benjamin Disraeli (1804-1881)
Type of plot: Political romance
Time of plot: 1832-1840
Locale: England and Paris
First published: 1844

Principal characters:
HARRY CONINGSBY, a young nobleman
MARQUIS OF MONMOUTH, his grandfather
SIDONIA, a wealthy young Jew, Coningsby's friend
EDITH MILLBANK, Coningsby's sweetheart
OSWALD MILLBANK, Edith's father
MR. RIGBY, a member of Parliament
LUCRETIA, a young Italian noblewoman, later Lord Monmouth's wife
FLORA, a member of a troupe of actors

Critique:

Coningsby occupies a special position in literature because of its varied aims. Not only is it the literary history of young Harry Coningsby's fortunes, but it is an important political treatise as well. In it Disraeli traced the decline of the Whig and Tory factions and the developments which led to the birth of the Conservative Party. The characters may be readily identified with real personages of the time.

The Story:

Harry Coningsby was fourteen when he met his grandfather, the Marquis of Monmouth, for the first time. He had been placed in his grandfather's charge when he was still very young with the understanding that his widowed mother, a commoner, was never to see him again. He had been turned over, sight unseen, to the care of Mr. Rigby, a member of Parliament who sat for one of Lord Monmouth's ten boroughs.

Lord Monmouth, who preferred to live abroad, had returned to his native land in 1832 in order to help fight the Reform Bill. Hearing favorable reports of his grandson, he had ordered Mr. Rigby to bring the boy from Eton to Monmouth House. Unfortunately, young Coningsby was unable to put out of his mind thoughts of his mother, who had died when he was nine, and he burst into tears at the sight of his grandfather. Lord Monmouth, dis-

gusted by that sign of weakness, ordered him to be led away. He thought to himself that the sentimental boy's future probably lay with the church.

Fortunately, the boy became friendly with the marquis' guests, Princess Colonna and her stepdaughter, Lucretia. The princess passed on such glowing descriptions of Coningsby to his grandfather that they were on excellent terms by the time he returned to school.

At Eton one of Coningsby's close friends was Oswald Millbank, a manufacturer's son. When Coningsby left Eton in 1835 he went to explore Manchester's factories before going to Coningsby Castle to join his grandfather. During his journey he visited the Millbank mills. Oswald was abroad, but he was hospitably greeted by his friend's father. At the Millbank mansion Coningsby met beautiful but shy young Edith Millbank and learned from her Whig father that he favored the rise of a new force in government—a natural aristocracy of able men, not one composed of hereditary peers.

Before departing for Coningsby Castle, young Coningsby was tempted to inquire about the striking portrait of a woman which graced the dining-room wall. His host, much upset by his question, made a brusque, evasive answer.

Lord Monmouth, backing Mr. Rigby for reëlection to Parliament, had returned to his borough and scheduled an elaborate program of dances, receptions, and plays, to gain a following for his Conservative candidate. Princess Colonna and Lucretia were again his grandfather's guests. Coningsby had no need, however, to confine his attentions to them, for as Lord Monmouth's kinsman and possible heir he found himself much sought after. He found time also to encourage Flora, a member of the troupe of actors entertaining the marquis' guests. The girl was shy and suffering from stage fright.

Here Coningsby met Sidonia, a fabulously wealthy young Jew. Coningsby found his new friend impartial in his political judgments, not only because his fortune allowed him to be just but also because his religion disqualified him as a voter. Sidonia taught him, during their lengthy discussions, to look to the national character for England's salvation. He believed that the country's weakness lay in developing class conflicts.

Lucretia made a brief effort to attract Coningsby when she observed the favor in which his grandfather held him, but before long she found Sidonia, a polished man of the world, more intriguing. But Sidonia was not to be captured. He was attracted by others' intellects, and Lucretia could not meet him on his own level.

After his holiday Coningsby went to Cambridge for his last years of study. During his first year there King William IV died and the Conservative cause fell in defeat. Mr. Rigby was, as he had been for many years, the candidate from his borough, and with the marquis to back him his victory seemed certain until Mr. Milbank entered the field. The manufacturer and the marquis had been enemies for many years, and their feud reached a climax when Millbank not only bought Hellingsley, an adjoining estate which Lord Monmouth had long coveted, but also defeated his lordship's candidate.

Prepared for the worst, the defeated Mr. Rigby went to Monmouth House, where the marquis was in residence. He was pleasantly disappointed, however, for his employer's thoughts were not on him. Lord Monmouth was preparing to marry Lucretia, who, if she could not have the man she desired, was determined at least to obtain power and riches through marriage.

A year after the wedding Coningsby was invited to join his grandfather and his bride in Paris at Christmas time. Stopping at his banker's on his way through London, he was given a package of his mother's correspondence. In the packet was a locket, with an exact copy of the portrait he had seen at Millbank. It was a picture of his mother.

While visiting an art gallery in Paris with Sidonia, Coningsby again met Edith Millbank, who was traveling with her relatives, Lord and Lady Wallinger. Coningsby, who fell in love with her immediately, was distressed to hear reports that Sidonia intended to marry her. Finding the couple conversing on familiar terms one evening, he regretfully decided to withdraw from the scene. He returned to England.

Disappointed in love, Coningsby devoted himself to his studies for the remainder of his stay at Cambridge. Then, learning that Edith had not married and that Sidonia was no more than an old family friend, he went to Coningsby Castle in order to be near the Millbanks.

Coningsby spent every possible moment with Edith and her family during the next few weeks. When her father discovered the lovers' feelings, he asked Coningsby to leave. He would not, he explained, submit his daughter to the same fate the young man's mother had suffered at Lord Monmouth's hands. In this manner Coningsby learned that his mother had once been Mr. Millbank's fiancée.

Leaving Hellingsley, Coningsby went on a sea voyage from which he was called home by the marquis. Parliament faced another crisis, and Lord Monmouth had decided that Coningsby should stand as his candidate. Coningsby refused, for he was of the opinion that men should cut across party lines to establish recognition of the bond between property and labor.

The same day Lord Monmouth faced his rebellious grandson he separated from Lucretia, who had proved unfaithful.

The marquis died at Christmas of that year. Most of his fortune he left to Flora, who was his natural daughter. Coningsby was cut off with the interest on ten thousand pounds.

Deeply disappointed in his expectations, Coningsby gave up his clubs and most of his friends and began to study law. He had resigned himself to the prospect of years of drudgery when Mr. Millbank repented his decision. The manufacturer withdrew his candidacy in the 1840 election to back Coningsby as the Tory candidate. Mr. Rigby was his rival candidate, but he was easily defeated.

Not many months later Edith became Coningsby's bride and went with him to live at Hellingsley, their wedding present from Mr. Millbank. As a final blessing, though not an unmixed one, Flora, who had always been weak, died, leaving the fortune she had inherited to the man who had befriended her many years before at Coningsby Castle.

THE CONJURE WOMAN

Type of work: Novel
Author: Charles Waddell Chesnutt (1858-1932)
Type of plot: Regional romance
Time of plot: Post-Civil War
Locale: North Carolina
First published: 1899

Principal characters:
THE NARRATOR
ANNIE, his wife
UNCLE JULIUS, his colored coachman
AUNT PEGGY, the conjure woman

Critique:

The first important American novelist of Negro descent, Charles Chesnutt has given us pure folktale and regional romance in *The Conjure Woman.* Uncle Julius is a very real person, one who does not waste his stories on any occasion. Each tale has a motive, some for the benefit of Julius himself, others for the benefit of his white employers. His stories are fantasy in the purest form, but so delicately, so fancifully told that the reader grieves or rejoices, just as Uncle Julius wants him to. Charles Chesnutt has portrayed the old Negro retainer with fidelity and understanding.

The Story:

When the Narrator's wife began to suffer ill effects from the severe Great Lakes climate, he began to look around for a suitable place to take her. He had been engaged in grape culture in Ohio, and when he learned of a small North Carolina town that seemed to offer what he needed in climate and suitable land, he decided to buy an old, dilapidated plantation and settle there. An untended vineyard was already on the place; with a little care and expense the vines would flourish once more.

On the day that he took his wife Annie to look at the plantation they happened upon an ancient Negro who called himself Uncle Julius. He advised them not to buy the plantation because it was goophered. Seeing they did not know that anything goophered was bewitched (conjured), the old colored man asked permission to tell them the story of the vineyard.

Many years before the war, when Uncle Julius was still a slave, the plantation owner had made many thousands of dollars from the grapes. Because the master could never keep the slaves from eating the rich grapes and stealing the wine made from them, he conceived the idea of having Aunt Peggy, a conjure woman living nearby, put a goopher on the vines. She made one that said that any Negro eating the grapes would die within a year. Most of the slaves stayed away from the grapes, but a few tried them in spite of the conjure—and they all died. When a new slave came to the plantation, no one remembered to tell him about the conjure, and he ate some of the grapes. So that he would not die, Aunt Peggy made him a counter-goopher. Then a strange thing happened. Every year, as the grapes ripened, this slave became so young and sprightly that he could do the work of several men, but in the fall, when the vines died, he withered and faded. This strange action went on for a year or two, until the master hit upon the idea of selling the slave every spring when he was so strong, and buying him back cheaply in the fall. By this transaction he made money each year.

One year the master hired an expert to prune his vines, but the expert cut them out too deeply and the vines were ruined. Soon afterward the slave who had bloomed and withered with the vines died also. Some said he died of old age, but Uncle Julius knew that it was the goopher that finally overcame him. Uncle Julius advised strongly against buying the land because the conjure was still on.

The Narrator bought the plantation, however, and it prospered. Later he learned that Uncle Julius had been living in a cabin on the place and sold the grapes. He always suspected that the story was told to prevent ruination of the old man's business. He gave Uncle Julius employment as a coachman, and so the former slave was well cared for.

At another time Annie wanted a new kitchen, and her husband decided to tear down an old schoolhouse on the place and use the lumber from it for the new building. Uncle Julius advised him against the plan. Strangely enough, that schoolhouse was goophered, too. The story was that a slave called Sandy was borrowed by others so often that his woman was afraid they would be separated forever. She was a conjure woman, and so she turned him into a tree. Each night she would turn him back into a man, and they would slip into her cabin until morning, when she would again change him into a tree. One day the woman was sent away from the plantation before she could change Sandy into a man. While she was away the master had the tree that was Sandy cut down to build a new kitchen. The slaves had a hard time felling the tree, which twisted and turned and tried to break loose from the chains. At last they got it to the sawmill. Later the house was built, but it was never much use. The slaves refused to work there because at night they could hear moaning and groaning, as if someone were in great pain. Only Sandy's woman, when she returned, would stay in the building, and she, poor girl, went out of her mind.

Uncle Julius advised against using goophered lumber for the new kitchen. It also seemed that Uncle Julius needed the old schoolhouse for his church meetings. The goopher would not bother the worshipers; in fact, the preaching would help Sandy's roaming spirit. There was nothing for the wife and her husband to do but buy new lumber for her kitchen. No one would want to use goophered wood.

When the Narrator was about to buy a mule to use in cultivating some land, Uncle Julius warned him against mules because most of them were conjured. Uncle Julius did, however, know of a horse for sale. After his employer bought the horse, which died within three months, Uncle Julius appeared in a new suit he had been admiring for some time.

One day, when Annie felt depressed and listless, Uncle Julius told her and her husband about Becky, a slave traded for a horse. Taken away from her child, she grieved terribly. Aunt Peggy, the conjure woman, turned the baby into a hummingbird so that he could fly down to his mother and be near her and soothe her. Later the conjure woman arranged to have Becky and her baby reunited. But Uncle Julius knew that she would never have had all that trouble if she had owned the hindfoot of a rabbit to protect her from harm. The story seemed to cheer Annie, and her husband was not surprised later to find Uncle Julius' rabbit's foot among her things.

When the Narrator prepared to clear a piece of land, Uncle Julius warned him that the land was goophered and told him a harrowing tale about a slave turned into a gray wolf and tricked into killing his own wife, who had been changed into a cat. Although the gray wolf was said to haunt the patch of land, it did not seem to bother a bee tree from which Uncle Julius gathered wild honey.

One day Annie's sister Mabel and her

fiancé quarreled bitterly. Uncle Julius had another story for them about Chloe, a slave who ruined her life because she was jealous. Chloe listened to a no-account rival and believed his story that her lover was meeting another woman. When she learned that she had lost her lover because she allowed her jealousy to trick her, she sorrowed and died. Even the conjure woman could not help her. Mabel listened to the story and then ran to her fiancé, who just happened to be close to the spot where Julius had stopped their carriage. Later on the young man seemed to develop a special fondness for Uncle Julius. After the wedding he tried to hire the old Negro into his service, but Uncle Julius remained faithful to his employers. He thought they needed his advice and help.

A CONNECTICUT YANKEE AT KING ARTHUR'S COURT

Type of work: Novel
Author: Mark Twain (Samuel L. Clemens, 1835-1910)
Type of plot: Social satire
Time of plot: Sixth century
Locale: England
First published: 1889

> *Principal characters:*
> THE CONNECTICUT YANKEE, the Boss
> CLARENCE, a page
> KING ARTHUR
> SANDY, wife of the Boss
> MERLIN, a magician

Critique:

Buried beneath a layer of wit is the serious social satire of Mark Twain's imaginative chronicle. The glorified days of knight errantry are exposed as a form of childish barbarism. The Connecticut Yankee finds instead of the legendary gallantry a cruel system of feudalism where the common people are abused and impoverished. Examining the Yankee's ideas about democracy, one can discern Mark Twain's own principles. He demonstrates that a government is good only insofar as the bulk of the people benefit by it.

The Story:

Struck on the head during a quarrel in a New England arms factory, a skilled mechanic awoke to find himself being prodded by the spear of an armored knight on horseback. The knight was Sir Kay of King Arthur's Round Table and the time was June, A.D. 528 in Merrie England, as a foppish young page named Clarence informed the incredulous Yankee, when his captor took him back to white-towered Camelot. The Yankee remembered that there had been a total eclipse of the sun on June 21, 528. If the eclipse took place, he was indeed a lost traveler in time turned backward to the days of chivalry.

At Camelot the Yankee listened to King Arthur's knights as they bragged of their mighty exploits. The magician, Merlin, told again of Arthur's coming. Finally Sir Kay told of his encounter with the Yankee, and Merlin advised that the prisoner be thrown into a dungeon to await burning at the stake on the twenty-first of June.

In prison the Yankee thought about the coming eclipse. Merlin, he told Clarence, was a humbug, and he sent the boy to the court with a message that on the day of his death the sun would darken and the kingdom would be destroyed. The eclipse came, and at the right time, for the Yankee was about to be burned when the sky began to dim. Awed, the king ordered the prisoner released. The people shouted that he was a greater magician than Merlin.

The court demanded another display of his powers. With the help of Clarence, the Yankee mined Merlin's tower with some crude explosives he had made and then told everyone he would cause the tower to crumble and fall. When the explosion took place, the Yankee was assured of his place as the new court magician. Merlin was thrown into prison.

The lack of mechanical devices in King Arthur's castle bothered the ingenious New Englander, and the illiteracy of the people hurt his American pride in education. He decided to make the commoners more than slaves to the nobility. He had a title of his own by this time, for the people called him the Boss.

A CONNECTICUT YANKEE AT KING ARTHUR'S COURT by Mark Twain. Published by Harper & Brothers.

As the Boss, he intended to modernize the kingdom.

His first act was to set up schools in small communities throughout the country. He had to work in secret, for he feared the interference of the Church. He trained workmen in mechanical arts. Believing that a nation needed a free press, he instructed Clarence in the art of journalism. He had telephone wires stretched between hamlets, haphazardly, however, because there were no maps by which to be guided.

When Sir Sagramor challenged the Boss to a duel, the court decided that he should go upon some knightly quest to prepare himself for the encounter. His mission was to help a young girl named Alisande, whose story he could not get straight. With many misgivings he put on a burdensome coat of mail and on his heavy charger started off with Sandy, as he called her. Sandy was a talkative companion who told endless tall tales as they traveled through the land. Along the way the Boss marveled at the pitiable state of the people under the feudal system. Whenever he found a man of unusual spirit he sent him back to Clarence in Camelot, to be taught reading, writing, and a useful trade. He visited the dungeons of the castles at which he stayed and released prisoners unjustly held by their grim masters.

In the Valley of Holiness he found another opportunity to prove his magic skill. There a sacred well had gone dry because someone, according to legend, had bathed in it. When he arrived, Merlin, now released from prison, was attempting magic to make the spring flow. With a great deal of pomp and flourish, the Boss repaired a leak in the masonry at the bottom of the well. As the well filled, Merlin went home in shame.

By chance the Boss came upon one of his telephone installations in a cave nearby. He talked to Clarence, who told him that King Arthur was on his way to the Valley of Holiness to see the flowing spring. He returned to the spring to find a fake magician assuring the gaping pilgrims that he could tell what anyone was doing at that moment. The Boss asked him about King Arthur. The magician said that he was asleep in his bed at Camelot. The Boss grandly predicted that the king was on his way to the Valley of Holiness. When the king did arrive, the people were again awed by the Boss's magic.

Anxious that King Arthur be convinced of the sufferings of his people, the Boss suggested that he and the king disguise themselves as commoners and travel as pilgrims through the country. The Boss knew that Arthur was not to blame for his own social doctrines; he was a victim of his place in society. On their journey the king proved to be courageous and kind.

Misfortune soon overtook them. They were seized by an earl and sold as slaves, because they were unable to prove themselves free men. The slaves were taken to London, where the Boss picked the lock that held him and escaped. The rest of the slaves were ordered to be hanged after his escape. But the Boss located one of his telephones and called Clarence in Camelot, ordering him to send Sir Lancelot and an army of knights to London to save their king from hanging.

The Boss came back to Camelot in glory, but not for long. He still had to fight a duel with Sir Sagramor—in reality a battle between Merlin and the Boss. Merlin professed to cover Sir Sagramor with an invisible shield, but the credulous knight was invisible to no one but himself. The Boss wore no armor, and so on the field of the tournament he was able to dodge the charging knight until Sir Sagramor grew tired. Then the Boss lassoed him and pulled him from his horse. When Sir Sagramor returned once again to the field, Merlin stole the Boss's lasso. There was no alternative; the Boss shot Sir Sagramor with his gun. Then he challenged all the knights of the Round Table. He had only twelve shots in his two revolvers, but fortunately, when he had killed eleven of the charging knights, the line wavered and gave up.

Three years passed. By this time the Boss had married Sandy and they had a little girl. He and Clarence were planning to declare a republic after the death of Arthur, for the sixth-century kingdom was now a nineteenth-century land with schools, trains, factories, newspapers, the telephone and the telegraph. Although the code of chivalry had been abolished, the knights still insisted on wearing their armor. Then little Hello-Central, the Boss' daughter, became ill, and he and Sandy took the child to the seashore for recuperation. On their return, the Boss found Camelot in a shambles. Only Clarence remained to tell him the story. There had been a battle between King Arthur and Sir Lancelot over Queen Guinevere. The king was dead, and by interdict the Church had destroyed the work of the Boss. Clarence and the Boss built a fortress surrounded by an electrically charged barrier. In a battle with the surviving chivalry of England the Boss was stabbed. When an old woman came to the fortress from the enemy lines and offered to nurse him, no one recognized her as Merlin. The magician cast a spell on the Boss and declared that he would sleep for thirteen hundred years. And, indeed, the Yankee did awake once more in the nineteenth century.

CONQUISTADOR

Type of work: Poem
Author: Archibald MacLeish (1892-   )
Time: Early sixteenth century
Locale: Mexico
First published: 1932

> *Principal personages:*
> BERNÁL DÍAZ, called del Castíllo, the narrator
> DIEGO VELÁSQUEZ, Spanish administrator in Cuba
> HERNÁN CORTÉS, conqueror of Mexico
> MONTEZÚMA, Emperor of the Aztecs

Conquistador: In his truly fine poem Archibald MacLeish makes this word whistle and flash like a blade of Spanish steel. But there are no overblown heroics here. Avoiding the stale approach of the historian, of "this priest this Gómara with the school-taught skip to his writing," MacLeish turns over the telling of his story to Bernál Díaz, an old man who in his youth was a soldier with Cortés and who confines his tale to " 'That which I have myself seen and the fighting.' . . ." The result, as Díaz rambles on with simple eloquence, becomes an impressionistic, sensual record of the bravery and the brutality, the sickness of defeat and the tingle of triumph that are all a part of conquest.

Díaz' narrative follows the exploits of the first Spanish conquerors of Mexico under the leadership of Cortés, but the story is neither complete nor fully connected. Episodic and broken, it is what a veteran would remember when he is old and going blind. Wisely, MacLeish does not force Díaz into passing moral judgment on the Spaniards or the Indians, into pondering tricky questions on the rights of the conquerors and the conquered. Of the massacre of the natives at Cholúla, Díaz says simply:

> They died slowly with much pain like serpents:
> Our hands were lame with the sword when the thing was done. . . .
>
> *And who are ye to be judge of us . . . ?*

When Díaz does exercise judgment it is mainly to deride the men who were "not there": Vespucci, who gave his name to two continents, but who was unknown in Cuba and Mexico; Velásquez, who tried to restrain Cortés and his men, to block them, to take credit for their victories. Such touches make this truly Bernál Díaz' story, not MacLeish's, and by this sublimation of the author's personality to that of his narrator, MacLeish has given the story an absorbing reality. But it is, of course, MacLeish's poetic talent that turns *Conquistador* into one of the finest long poems of this century.

For his stanza form MacLeish has chosen a variation on terza rima and by skillful shifting of the rhythm he avoids monotony; by delicate use of assonance and consonance he creates a sensuous music that is felt as well as heard. Listen to (and feel) these stanzas describing the life of Cortés' men in a rare time of peace among the Indians:

> And the girls they gave us for love with the scented hair:
> The green light through the leaves: the slow awakening:
> How there were many and small birds in the air then. . . .
>
> We were like those that in their lands they say
> The steers of the sun went up through the wave-lit orchards
> Shaking the water drops and those gold naked

Girls before them at their dripping
horns!
And they ate the sea-doused figs with
the salt taste:
And all their time was of kine and of
sea and of morning:

This passage reveals the subtle, musical
effects of his technique. In the first
stanza there is the unobtrusive "scen-ken-
then" of terminal assonance and the outright rhymes of "hair" and "air"; in the
second, "say-wave-nake" and "orchards-
naked"; and in the third, "horns-morn,"
with an echo of the second stanza in
"taste" and, as a kind of fillip, the internal "time-kine" combination. Such in-
genuity, while sustaining a clear thought,
calls for the highest technical skill. All is
so cleverly done that one must almost
ponder the lines to realize the effects of
imagery and tonal pattern.

Oddly enough, the major flaw in *Conquistador* is a result of MacLeish's decision to let the whole story be Díaz'. In
achieving unity and reality and the balance between hardship and glory that is
the soldier's lot, the poet has played down
the overall drama and climaxes to the
point of flatness. The death of Montezúma, for instance, becomes little more
important than the death of a favorite
war stallion. Here is the way Díaz describes it:

And the smoke coiled on the cold
stones: and we went by

Dawn on the wall-head there: and
Montezúma
Clad in the gold cloth: gilded: and he
smiled:
He climbed by the stair and smiling
and they slew him:

Even Cortés himself is presented as a
shadowy figure, more a symbol of leadership than a man. ("This is Cortés that
took the famous land.") Perhaps this is
the way the soldier sees the great men;
perhaps it is only history and legend that
lifts the leaders above the led.

But Díaz, the narrator, is certainly no
shadow. He emerges from the poem as a
full character, fiercely alive and tenderly
human. In his preface Díaz calls himself
"an ignorant sick old man," but he takes
pride that he fought in the battles, that
he was there. Disclaiming any desire for
fame, he mourns, as death comes closer,
that his youth is past, that his companions are nearly all gone. Yet he remem-
bers that once

We were the lords of it all. . . .
Now time has taught us:
Death has mastered us most: sorrow
and pain
Sickness and evil days are our lives'
lot:

Now even the time of our youth has
been taken:
Now are our deeds words: our lives
chronicles:
Afterwards none will think of the night
rain. . . .

By remembering the night rains, the
mountains, the windy ditches, the taste
of melons, Díaz elevates a story that
might have been a dry chronicle of battles to the level of high poetry. He is a
professional soldier with a keen eye for
military strategy, but he is also a sen-
sualist, a man whose memory holds vivid
impressions of a strange land that was
alternately a paradise and a hell. He can
catch the details of the fighting, of the
drums rolling "like the thud in the ear of
a man's heart"; he can take satisfaction
in the Spanish cannons that mow down
scores of Indians as the link chain slashes
their bellies. But equally well he can
describe a market in an Indian town: the
corn, the fish, the hides "smelling of
oak," the sellers of "lettuces washed cool"
and of henequen, the makers of rope and
"of stone masks of the dead and of stone
mirrors." The reader of *Conquistador* can
see, hear, and feel with Díaz.

When the wars are over, the conquest
complete, Díaz disparages the colonists
who come like lice to build their Spanish
cities. For him "the west is gone now"

and *Conquistador* ends with his final dream:

> O day that brings the earth back bring again
> That well-swept town those towers and that island. . . .

The literature of the United States has been criticized for its failure to produce an epic in poetry or prose which records and matches the epic event in our history: the opening of the American West. All we have been able to come up with, some say, is the stylized "Western" of the paperbacks, the movies, and the television programs that is like a stale joke repeated over and over. MacLeish has chosen to go south to Mexico for his story and in doing so he has avoided stumbling onto any well-worn paths. An American has written a great poem about the history of our continent. *Conquistador* is an epic.

THE CONSCIOUS LOVERS

Type of work: Drama
Author: Sir Richard Steele (1672-1729)
Type of plot: Sentimental comedy
Time of plot: Early eighteenth century
Locale: London
First presented: 1722

> *Principal characters:*
> YOUNG BEVIL, a young gentleman of fortune
> SIR JOHN BEVIL, young Bevil's father
> INDIANA DANVERS, a girl befriended by young Bevil
> LUCINDA SEALAND, engaged to young Bevil
> MR. SEALAND, Lucinda's father
> MR. MYRTLE, young Bevil's friend, in love with Lucinda Sealand
> MR. CIMBERTON, a suitor for Lucinda Sealand's hand

Critique:

The Conscious Lovers, often called Steele's finest play, began the vogue of sentimental comedy and marked a departure from the comedy of manners popular during the late eighteenth century. In this drama the virtues of the true gentleman, as opposed to those of the wit and fop, are clearly demonstrated. The characters are frankly middle-class people instead of the nobility. The lovers are frank in their affections and the father is portrayed as the object of filial affection, whereas in earlier drama he had been the object of ridicule, often a bar to the enjoyment of a fortune. As a social reformer Steele advanced two doctrines: the abolishment of marriage as simply a contractual affair, and the absurdity of the barbaric practice of dueling. The latter doctrine he had presented earlier in a famous number of *The Spectator*. Steele, unlike earlier dramatists of the period, sought to give good examples to his audiences.

The Story:

Young Bevil, a gentleman of some fortune, was engaged to marry the daughter of Mr. Sealand. Although he was not in love with the girl, he had agreed to marry her at his father's request. On the day of the marriage, however, there was some doubt that the marriage would take place, for the bride's father had discovered that Bevil was paying the bills of a young woman he had brought back from France. Fearing that the young woman, called Indiana, was Bevil's mistress, Mr. Sealand did not want to see his daughter married to a man who kept another woman.

The fathers did not know that Bevil had sent a letter to Lucinda Sealand which gave her his permission to break off the marriage at that late date. Bevil had done so because he knew that Lucinda was really in love with his friend, Mr. Myrtle, and because he himself wanted to marry Indiana. Shortly after the letter was sent, Sir John's valet told young Bevil that the marriage would probably be broken by Mr. Sealand. Bevil then confided in the servant that Indiana was the daughter of the British merchant named Danvers, who had disappeared in the Indies soon after the ship in which Indiana, her mother, and her aunt had been traveling to join him had been captured by French privateers.

Shortly afterward Myrtle arrived at Bevil's apartment and told his friend that a third marriage arrangement was in the wind that day. Mrs. Sealand was trying to wed her daughter to Mr. Cimberton, a queer fellow with peculiar ideas about wives and a great deal of money; Mrs. Sealand was willing to overlook strange notions in favor of the fortune her daughter might marry. The only thing that prevented the marriage contract from being settled that day was the non-appearance of Cimberton's wealthy uncle. Bevil suggested to Myrtle that he and Bevil's servant Tom, an artful rascal, disguise themselves as lawyers and go to the Sealand house in an attempt to prevent the marriage or, at least, to find out what could be done to keep the contract from being signed.

Meanwhile Indiana's aunt was cautioning her against the attentions of Bevil. The aunt could not believe, despite Indiana's reports of Bevil's behavior, that the young man was helping Indiana and paying her bills without intending to make her his mistress. As they continued to argue, Bevil himself appeared. Indiana tried to learn in private conversation what his intentions were, for she loved him very much. He would only reply that he did everything for her because he found pleasure in doing good. Wanting him to love her, she felt rather hurt. Secretly, Bevil had promised himself that he would never tell her of his affection as long as his father had not given permission for a marriage to her.

At the Sealand house, in the meantime, Lucinda was subjected to the humiliation of an inspection by Mr. Cimberton, who in company with Mrs. Sealand looked at Lucinda as he might look at a prize mare he was buying for his stable. While they were talking over her good and bad points, Myrtle and Bevil's servant, disguised as lawyers, put in their appearance. They learned very little, except that Mrs. Sealand was determined to wed her daughter to Cimberton as soon as possible. Upon leaving the house, Bevil's servant received a letter from Lucinda for his master. Myrtle, who was of a very jealous disposition, suspected duplicity on Bevil's part and instantly sent him a challenge to a duel.

Myrtle appeared at Bevil's apartment a few minutes after his challenge. Bevil refused at first to be a party to a duel, out when Myrtle heaped many insults upon Bevil and Indiana, calling the latter Bevil's whore, his language so enraged Bevil that he said he would fight. A moment later Bevil regained control of himself. Realizing how foolish a duel would be, he showed Myrtle the letter from Lucinda, which only thanked Bevil for giving her permission to break off the wedding.

Sir John and Mr. Sealand met. Mr. Sealand refused to go on with the marriage that day until he had satisfied himself as to the relationship between Indiana and Bevil. Sir John agreed to wait until the investigation had been made.

Bevil and Myrtle decided to make one more attempt to terminate the possible marital arrangements of Mrs. Sealand for her daughter. Myrtle disguised himself as Cimberton's uncle and went to the Sealand house. There Lucinda discovered his identity, but she kept it from her mother and the unwelcome suitor.

At the same time Mr. Sealand had gone to Indiana's home. As soon as he entered the house Indiana's aunt recognized him as someone she had known before, but she decided not to reveal herself to him. Questioned, Indiana said that she had been befriended by Bevil but that he had made no effort to seduce her. Her deportment and her narrative assured Mr. Sealand that there was no illicit relationship between the two. When she had finished her story, telling of her lost father and the capture of herself, her mother, and her aunt by French privateers, he asked her father's name. She told him it was Danvers. Mr. Sealand then announced that Indiana was his long-lost daughter, and he identified some trinkets she had as those belonging to his first wife and their child. When Indiana's aunt appeared, identifying herself as Mr. Sealand's sister, he recognized her at once. He told them that he had changed his name after undergoing certain difficulties in the Indies.

Mr. Sealand readily agreed to a marriage between his new-found daughter and Bevil. At that moment Sir John, young Bevil, and a group from the Sealand house arrived. Sir John, hearing the news, was pleased at the prospect of a marriage between Indiana and his son. Bevil, anxious to aid his friend Myrtle, then requested that a marriage be arranged between his friend and Lucinda Sealand. Cimberton tried to intercede on his own behalf until Mr. Sealand informed him that only half his fortune would now go to Lucinda. Cimberton, who was more anxious for the money than the girl, departed in a huff, whereupon Myrtle, who was still disguised as Cimberton's uncle, threw off the disguise and claimed Lucinda for his bride.

THE CONSOLATIONS OF PHILOSOPHY

Type of work: Philosophical prose and verse
Author: Anicius Manlius Severinus Boethius (c. 480-524)
First transcribed: 523

When Theodoric, Ostrogoth king of Italy, imprisoned his minister Boethius because he suspected him of plotting with the Emperor Justin The Elder, he inadvertently encouraged the writing of a masterpiece. For Boethius was a philosopher with the intellectual and spiritual resources of a Socrates, and until his death he used the time in prison not only in consoling himself by philosophical reflections but also by writing a book of prose and verse in which Philosophy, pictured as a fair lady, reconciles him to his condition. She consoles Boethius by giving him substantial amounts of Platonic philosophy, but she manages to give her message a distinctive character which we may take as a reflection of the author's own philosophic temperament.

Philosophy's consolations, metaphysically defended and poetically adorned, amount to this message: God is blessedness; trust in Him.

The Consolations of Philosophy is important historically because it made Platonism an important element in the thought of the Middle Ages, and it is important philosophically and as literature because it presents a calm and inspiring use of Plato's ideas. Also it secures for Boethius a place in the history of philosophy. It cannot be defended, however, as a Christian work unless one is willing to call Plato a Christian. Controversy continues over the question of whether Boethius was a Christian, and it is significant that although everyone knows and admits that *The Consolations of Philosophy* is his work, that knowledge by no means settles the question one way or the other, although it tends to support the negative case. Only the fact that Boethius is *reputed* to have written a number of tracts explaining and supporting certain theological points of Christian dogma leads anyone to suppose that Boethius was a Christian.

Like Dante's *Vita Nuova* (c. 1292), which may have been influenced by *The Consolations of Philosophy*, Boethius' work alternates prose and verse, but unlike the *Vita Nuova* the prose passages do not merely explain the circumstances under which the verses were written but contain the body of the work: a dialogue between Boethius and Philosophy.

The First Book begins with a verse in which Boethius complains about the coming of old age and sorrows. A woman with a grave appearance, a clear eye, and of indeterminate age and height appears to him and objects to the presence of the "tragical harlots" of poetry. It turns out that she is Philosophy and that she has come to Boethius to help him in his time of trouble. She reminds him that philosophers have often suffered because of criticizing wicked men; Socrates is but one of many who have been punished for speaking the truth.

Boethius then tells Philosophy of his political difficulties, and concludes by suggesting that wicked men often prosper while the innocent suffer. In a poem addressed to God, "Creator of the Sky," Boethius asks, ". . . why should punishments/ Due to the guilty, light on innocents?" and goes on to complain that ". . . now the highest place/ Giveth to naughty manners greatest grace,/ And wicked people vex/ Good men, and tread unjustly on their necks. . . ."

In this manner Boethius presents the problem of evil as the subject matter of his work. The answer, when it comes after several books of discussion, is that evil is nothing, all manner of fortune is good, adversity makes virtue possible, God knows what He is doing, and all is for the best.

Baldly stated, such an answer would

satisfy no one, particularly a suffering man. But Boethius reached this answer only after leisurely, charming discourse on value, man's condition, the nature of God, and the uses of philosophy.

After Boethius has complained to Philosophy, Philosophy reminds him that he believes that God created all things; it would be odd if he had doubt about God's concern for the end of all things, including men. She continues, in a striking passage:

"But I would have thee answer me to this also; dost thou remember that thou art a man?" "Why should I not remember it?" quoth I. "Well, then, canst thou explicate what man is?" "Dost thou ask me if I know that I am a reasonable and mortal living creature? I know and confess myself to be so." To which she replied: "Dost thou not know thyself to be anything else?" "Not anything."

"Now I know," quoth she, "another, and that perhaps the greatest, cause of thy sickness: thou hast forgotten what thou art . . ."

In Book Two, Philosophy tells Boethius that Fortune is always changeable; that is her nature. Philosophy then determines that nothing is more precious to a man than himself, and nothing of himself is more important than his happiness. But in what does happiness consist? Not in wealth, for no matter how much a man has, he wants more; material goods fail to satisfy him, and covetous men endanger him. Not in power and honors, for they are given to the undeserving as well as to the deserving, and that spoils them for all men; furthermore, power and honor will not keep a man from giving way to lusts that can destroy him. Nor does happiness reside in fame, for a man who loves fame expects only glory in this life, yet after death he has nothing.

Philosophy agrees with Aristotle that all men love happiness, but the usual goods which men pursue neither consist in happiness nor bring happiness. Even pleasure is not happiness, for it enslaves a man and turns his attention away from what could make him happy. Philosophy decides that only the Sovereign God is true goodness, happiness, and blessedness. Anything else which is ever good, such as power, fame, and pleasure, is good because it is not in addition to, but part of, the blessedness which is God. The substance of God consists in goodness. This argument comprises the content of Book Three.

In the following book Philosophy argues that if nothing is more powerful than God and God is goodness, then evil cannot be absolute and evil men cannot truly triumph. Philosophy agrees with Plato that "only wise men can do that which they desire"; wicked men do what pleases them but not what they would do if they were to choose action capable of leading to happiness. The evil are punished by the fact of doing evil; they deprive themselves of the good which would otherwise be theirs. Wickedness makes men into beasts: the violent are like wolves; the angry, like dogs; the treacherous, like the fox; the outrageous, like the lion; the fearful, like the deer; the slow and stupid, like the ass; the inconstant, like the birds; the lustful, like sows. "So that he who, leaving virtue, ceaseth to be a man, since he cannot be partaker of the divine condition, is turned into a beast."

In considering God's Providence, Philosophy tells Boethius, one is forced to the conclusion that evil "hath no place left for it at all." Therefore, "all manner of fortune is good." If it sometimes seems that the wicked prosper and the virtuous suffer, it is because men do not always realize the value of adversity, how adversity challenges man's spirit and makes him virtuous.

In Book Five Philosophy assures Boethius that man has free will even though everything is a manifestation of God's Providence. God's contemplation does not prevent the free exercise of man's reason and will. The necessity of doing well is one which man's spirit imposes on itself "since you live in the sight of your Judge, who beholdeth all things."

CONSUELO

Type of work: Novel
Author: George Sand (Mme. Aurore Dudevant, 1804-1876)
Type of plot: Historical romance
Time of plot: Eighteenth century
Locale: Venice, Bohemia, Vienna
First published: 1842

Principal characters:
CONSUELO, a singer
ANZOLETO, her betrothed
PORPORA, her music master and godfather
COUNT RUDOLSTADT, a Bohemian nobleman
ALBERT, his son
CORILLA, Consuelo's rival
JOSEPH HAYDN, a composer

Critique:

Although George Sand was one of the most popular novelists of the nineteenth century, her style seems somewhat tedious to present-day readers. The plot of *Consuelo,* interesting as it is, suffers at times from the excessive detail with which the thoughts and movements of the main characters are depicted. The author's many literary skills are exhibited, however, in this novel. Her descriptive passages are beautiful and moving, and her intimate knowledge of music and musicians enabled her to write convincing characterizations of many of the people whom Consuelo met in her travels. All told, *Consuelo* is well worth the effort spent reading it, for its virtues at least balance, if not outweigh, its defects.

The Story:

At the church of the Mendicanti in Venice, Consuelo was the most gifted of all the pupils of the famous teacher, Porpora. Consuelo was a poor orphan child, and Porpora had made her his goddaughter. Before the death of her mother, Consuelo had promised that she would one day become betrothed to Anzoleto, another poor musician of Venice.

Through the efforts of Anzoleto, Consuelo was engaged as the prima donna at the theater of Count Zustiniani, replacing Corilla, who had also been Porpora's student. Consuelo was a great success, but Anzoleto, who had also been engaged in the theater at the insistence of Consuelo, was not much of a musician and was not well received. Anzoleto, afraid that he would be discharged, pretended to be in love with Corilla, thinking that he would be safe if both singers were in love with him.

Porpora had never liked Anzoleto, and at last he contrived to have Consuelo visit Corilla's home. When they found Anzoleto there, Consuelo was so hurt that she left Venice at once, vowing that she would never set foot on the stage again, and renouncing the false Anzoleto forever.

From Venice Consuelo went to Bohemia, where she was engaged by Count Rudolstadt as a companion for his niece, Amelia. This young noblewoman had been betrothed to young Count Albert Rudolstadt, but she feared him because he seemed to be insane. Albert often had visions in which he saw scenes of the past and often imagined himself to be the reincarnated body of some person long dead.

When Albert first heard Consuelo sing, he called her by her name, even though she had taken another name to hide her unhappy life in Venice. Albert told Consuelo and the whole family that she was his salvation—that she had been sent to remove the curse from him. Consuelo was bewildered.

Albert often disappeared for many

days at a time, no one knew where. Consuelo followed him, but could never find his hiding place until the night she descended into a deep well and found steps leading to a grotto where Albert and an idiot called Zdenko spent many days together. Zdenko loved Albert more than his own life; when he saw Consuelo coming into the well, he thought she wanted to harm Albert and almost killed her. Consuelo escaped from Zdenko and found Albert, and after she spoke soothingly to him he ceased his mad talk and seemed to regain normal behavior. She persuaded him to return to his family and not to go back to the grotto without her. Albert told Consuelo that he loved her and needed her; but although she no longer loved Anzoleto, she could not forget how she had once loved him, and she asked Albert to wait a while for her answer.

Albert's father and the rest of the family were grateful to Consuelo for helping restore Albert to his senses. The father, Count Rudolstadt, even told Consuelo that he would give his consent to a marriage between his son and her, for the old gentleman believed that only Consuelo could keep his son sane. While Consuelo was debating whether she loved Albert and could accept the honor, Anzoleto, having deserted Corilla, came to the castle in search of her. Consuelo slipped away from the castle, leaving a note for Albert. She went to Vienna to rejoin Porpora.

Without funds, Consuelo had great difficulty in reaching Vienna, and had to walk most of the way. In her travels, she met Joseph Haydn, a young composer who had been on his way to the castle to find her; he had hoped he could persuade her to take him to Porpora, under whom he wished to study. Dressed as a peasant boy, Consuelo accompanied Haydn to Vienna. One night they took refuge in the home of a canon of the Church. While they were there, Corilla came to the door, seeking a safe place to give birth to her child. Consuelo had

pity on her former enemy and took Corilla to an inn, where she helped to deliver the child. From a maid, Consuelo learned that Anzoleto was the father. Corilla did not recognize Consuelo, who continued to wear the disguise of a boy.

When Joseph and Consuelo finally reached Vienna, the girl found Porpora overjoyed to see her again. Haydn became Porpora's pupil, and Consuelo sang for the Empress. Then Corilla, who had also come to Vienna and learned that it was Consuelo who befriended her during the birth of her child, arranged for Consuelo to sing in the theater there. Corilla hoped to seal the lips of Consuelo, who knew of the illegitimate child and knew also that Corilla had abandoned the baby in the home of the canon who had given Consuelo and Joseph shelter. Anzoleto was never heard from again.

Consuelo wrote to Albert, telling him that she was almost ready to return to him, but Porpora intercepted the letter and tore it up. Consuelo waited in vain for a reply from Albert. At last, Porpora told her that he had received a letter from the count, saying that he did not wish his son to marry an actress, and that Albert had concurred in the decision. Consuelo so trusted her godfather that she believed him, not realizing how ambitious Porpora was for her musical career.

Porpora went with Consuelo to accept a theater engagement in Berlin. On the way they met the brother of Count Rudolstadt. Albert had asked his father to have someone at a certain place on the road on a specific day and at a specific hour, saying that the messenger was to bring the travelers he would meet there to the castle at once. Albert was very ill, and Consuelo persuaded Porpora to allow her to go to Albert. When she arrived at the castle, she learned that his father had received a letter from Porpora saying that he would never consent to a marriage between Consuelo and Albert and that Consuelo herself had renounced Albert. It had been the deathblow. Albert grew very weak and begged Consuelo to marry him before he died so that his soul could find peace; he still believed that only through Consuelo could he find salvation. So the marriage vows were repeated, and Albert, crying that he was now saved, died in Consuelo's arms.

Consuelo stayed with her husband all night, leaving him only when he was carried to his bier. She then bade Albert's family goodbye, refusing to accept any of the fortune which was now hers. Then she left the castle and went to join Porpora in Berlin, where Frederick the Great himself worshipped both her beauty and her art.

THE COPPERHEAD

Type of work: Novel
Author: Harold Frederic (1856-1898)
Type of plot: Regional romance
Time of plot: 1860's
Locale: Four Corners, New York
First published: 1893

Principal characters:
ABNER BEECH, a farmer
HURLEY, his hired man
JEFF, his son
ESTHER HAGADORN, Jeff's sweetheart
JEE HAGADORN, a cooper, Esther's father
NI HAGADORN, his son
JIMMY, an orphan

Critique:

The Copperhead is the story of the fortitude of one man in opposition to his neighbors. Although Harold Frederic deplores the irrationality of society in time of stress, the true significance of the theme lies in the thought that it is impossible properly to judge, much less to condemn, a man for his political views unless one comes to understand the personal motivations of the man himself. The story is seen through the eyes of a young boy who himself plays little part in the action. The local descriptions are vivid and a sense of realism is carried by the heavily flavored dialects and regional locutions of the farmers who live in the community of Four Corners.

The Story:

Abner Beech was a stalwart, shaggy man, who had often been supervisor of his district. Jimmy, who was an orphan, went to live with him when he was six or seven years old. Abner was a town leader, a great reader, and he owned more books than most people did in Dearborn County, located in northern New York State.

For some reason, Abner Beech violently hated the Abolitionists. The first Abolitionist in Dearborn County, as far as Jimmy knew, was old Jee Hagadorn, but now nearly everyone except Abner Beech shared the old man's sentiments.

Because the Anti-abolitionists were attacked from the pulpit every Sunday at church meeting, Abner and Jimmy finally stopped going to church. Then someone spread the rumor that Abner's milk had not been accepted at the communal cheese factory because he had put water into it. At that time Abner's household became real outcasts in Four Corners.

One day in August, Abner came home early from the field. He was furious because he learned that Jeff, his only son, had been seen walking with Esther Hagadorn, the daughter of his enemy. Abner sent Jimmy to call Jeff home. When Jimmy found Jeff and Esther, the young man gave the boy his fishing pole and told him to tell Abner that he was going to Tecumseh to enlist in the Union Army. When Jimmy told Jeff's parents what Jeff had said, they took the news calmly. They had already guessed his intention, for on that same day an entire group of boys from the area had gone off to enlist.

Abner's hired man also enlisted, and Abner hired an Irish widower, Hurley, who had been doing odd jobs in the neighborhood. Hurley was also an Anti-abolitionist, the only one in the area besides Abner. It was understood in Abner's household that Jeff's name should never be mentioned, and Abner refused to show regret over the departure of his only son.

In late September, Hurley and Jimmy went to Octavius to buy some butter firkins; Abner refused to buy firkins from Jee Hagadorn, who lived close by. In Octavius Hurley and Jimmy learned of the terrible battle at Antietam, in which a number of the boys from Dearborn County had taken part. Hurley got into a fight when some of the citizens taunted him for being a Copperhead, a Northerner who sympathized with the Southern cause in the Civil War.

On the way home from Octavius, Jimmy went to see Jee Hagadorn. Jimmy found Esther there, worrying about Jeff. Jee came home elated because Lincoln had signed the Emancipation Proclamation.

A fortnight later the Beech household learned that Jeff Beech and Byron Truax had been reported missing after a battle in the South.

The work on the farm continued. Warner Pitts, Abner's former hired man, came home on furlough as an officer. A hero to the townspeople, one day he called Abner a Copperhead. Ni Hagadorn, Jee's son, did not like Warner Pitts, and so he went to Abner's house to tell him that he was going south to try to find Jeff. Abner refused, however, to give Ni any money to help him on his journey.

The local citizens were beginning to feel that the North was not carrying on the war as vigorously as they expected. On election day, November 4, Jimmy accompanied Abner and Hurley to the polls. Abner voted proudly, but the inspector said that Hurley's naturalization papers were not in order and that he could not vote. When a fight started, another inspector then said that Hurley could vote. A few days later it was learned that the Abolitionists had lost in that congressional district. Abner was overjoyed, believing that this defeat would lead to peace and an end of what he called murder. To celebrate, Janey, one of the hired girls, made a big bonfire.

The next day Jimmy was in bed with a cold. To the amazement of everyone, Esther Hagadorn came in and asked to speak to Abner. When Abner came home he was civil to Esther and asked her to stay to supper. Esther said that there was a rumor to the effect that Copperheads were spreading clothes that had smallpox in them and that the local citizens were fearful and angry. She said that Abner's bonfire to celebrate the voting results had made them even angrier and that they were planning to come for Abner that night. Esther then accepted Abner's invitation to remain and have supper with them.

The townspeople arrived to tar and feather Abner and Hurley and to ride them on a rail. Abner, however, stood firm, a loaded shotgun on his arm. Suddenly Jimmy realized that the house was afire. He fainted.

Jimmy regained consciousness later that night. It was snowing, and the house had been completely burned. With some of the furniture that they were able to rescue, Abner and his wife, M'rye, had improvised a home in the cold barn. Esther, still with them, had regained the friendship of M'rye, since they were both able to talk about Jeff again.

Jimmy, unable to sleep that night, overheard Esther talking to Abner. Abner said that he believed that the townspeople had started a fire for the tarring and feathering and that, because of the strong wind, his house had caught fire accidentally. Esther said that Abner was really liked and respected by the townspeople but that they could not be expected to behave reasonably because so many husbands and sons were now involved in the war.

At that point Jee Hagadorn arrived in search of his daughter. Abner pulled off Jee's wet boots and gave him some warm socks. They had breakfast in near silence. Suddenly Ni Hagadorn appeared. He told M'rye that Jeff had been only slightly hurt and was due home any day. M'rye suddenly ran out of the barn, where she found Jeff returned from the war after having lost his left arm.

While everyone was welcoming Jeff and offering condolences, an unexpected visitor arrived. He was Squire Avery, who wanted, on behalf of the townspeople, to apologize for the events of the previous night. Hoping to let bygones be bygones, he asked Abner to send milk to the cheese factory again. He also wanted to have a house-raising bee for Abner's new house and to lend him money if he needed it. Abner, filled with the spirit of forgiveness, said that all of these kindnesses were nearly worth the house burning. He and M'rye expressed the hope that Jeff and Esther would marry.

CORIOLANUS

Type of work: Drama
Author: William Shakespeare (1564-1616)
Type of plot: Historical tragedy
Time of plot: Third century
Locale: Rome, Corioli, and Antium
First presented: c. 1609

Principal characters:

CAIUS MARCIUS CORIOLANUS, a noble Roman
TITUS LARTIUS, and
COMINIUS, generals against the Volscians
MENENIUS AGRIPPA, friend of Coriolanus
TULLUS AUFIDIUS, general of the Volscians
SICINIUS VELUTUS, and
JUNIUS BRUTUS, tribunes of the people
VOLUMNIA, mother of Coriolanus
VIRGILIA, wife of Coriolanus

Critique:

The Tragedy of Coriolanus, a powerful study of a man's willful spirit and his inability to follow the advice of those who would help him, moves with a fluency not found in all of Shakespeare's plays. This faster tempo is the result, chiefly, of a terseness of line and a highly compact unity of plot. The play is devoid of prolonged soliloquy and subplot to divert the attention, with the whole action so closely geared to the. title character that the play leaves but a single impression upon audience and reader alike.

The Story:

Caius Marcius, a brilliant soldier, was attempting to subdue a mob in Rome when he was summoned to lead his troops against the Volscians from Corioli. The Volscians were headed by Tullus Aufidius, also a great soldier and perennial foe of Marcius. The hatred the two leaders had for each other fired their military ambitions. Marcius' daring as a warrior, known by all since he was sixteen, led him to pursue the enemy inside the very gates of Corioli. Locked inside the city, he and his troops fought so valiantly that they overcame the Volscians. Twice wounded, the victorious general was garlanded and hailed as Caius Marcius Coriolanus.

On his return to Rome, Coriolanus was further proclaimed by patrician, consul, and senator; and he was recommended for the office of consul, an appointment whole-heartedly approved by the nobles. Because the citizens also had to vote on his appointment, Coriolanus, accompanied by Menenius Agrippa, went to Sicinius and Brutus, the plebian tribunes, to seek their approval.

The people had long held only contempt for Coriolanus because of his arrogance and inhumane attitude toward all commoners. Although coached and prompted by Menenius to make his appeal as a wound-scarred soldier of many wars, Coriolanus was not able to bring himself to solicit the citizens' approval. He could only request and demand their support, which he got from individuals approached at random on the streets.

But Brutus and Sicinius, as representatives of the common people, were not willing to endorse the elevation of Coriolanus to office. Voicing the opinions of many citizens in their accusations against Coriolanus for his abuses in denying the people food from the public storehouses and for his insolence, Brutus and Sicinius urged the citizens to rescind their votes for Coriolanus. They pointed out that his military prowess was not to be denied, but that this very attribute would result in further suppression and misery for the people. Coriolanus' ambitions, they pre-

686

dicted, would lead to his complete domination of the government, thereby destroying their democracy.

The repeated pleading by Menenius, Cominius, and the senators that Coriolanus relent and approach the tribunes civilly in order to realize his political desires gave rise to Volumnia's admonition that he take the measures advised and gain the election. Volumnia, appealing to his responsibility as a Roman, pointed out that service to one's country was not shown on the battlefield alone and that Coriolanus must use certain strategies and tactics for victory in peace as well as in war.

Coriolanus misconstrued his mother's suggestions. She had taught him arrogance, nurtured his desires in military matters, and boasted of his strength and of her part in developing his dominating personality. Because of her attitude, Coriolanus inferred that his mother in her older years was asking for submissiveness and compliance. Although he promised Volumnia that he would deal kindly with the people, it was impossible for him to relent.

Virgilia, his wife, who had never condoned his soldiership, lent her pleas to those of the group, but he spurned her appeal to his vanity as a capable political leader and to his responsibility as a father and husband.

Coriolanus' persistence in his derision and mockery of the citizens led to an uprising against him. Drawing his sword, he would have stood alone against the mob, but Menenius and Cominius, fearing that the demonstration might result in an overthrow of the government, prevailed upon him to withdraw to his house before the crowd assembled.

Coriolanus, mistaking the requests of his friends and family that he yield to the attitudes of the common people for denials of loyalty and devotion to him, displayed such arrogance that he was banished from Rome. Tullus Aufidius, learning what was happening, prepared his armies to take advantage of the civil unrest in Rome.

Coriolanus, in disguise for protection against the many who would avenge the deaths of those whom he had killed earlier, went to Antium to offer his services to Aufidius against Rome. When Coriolanus removed his disguise, Aufidius, who well knew the Roman's ability as a military leader, willingly accepted his presence and his offer to aid in the Volscian campaign. Aufidius divided his army in order that he and Coriolanus each could lead a unit, thereby broadening the scope of his efforts against the Romans. Aufidius foresaw in his plan the possibility of avenging his earlier defeats by Coriolanus. When they had taken Rome, Aufidius thought, the hatred the Romans held for Coriolanus would make easy his dominance over the arrogant patrician.

The Romans heard with dismay of Coriolanus' affiliation with Aufidius; their only hope, it was claimed, was to appeal to Coriolanus to spare the city. Although Menenius and Cominius blamed the tribunes for the banishment of Coriolanus, they went as messengers to the great general in his camp outside the gates of Rome. Unsuccessful in their efforts, Cominius returned to inform the citizens that Coriolanus, in spite of old friendships, would not be swayed in his intentions to annihilate the city. Coriolanus could not, Cominius reported, take time to find the few grains who were his friends among all the chaff that he intended to burn.

Menenius, sent to appeal again to Coriolanus, met with the same failure, Coriolanus maintaining that his ears were stronger against the pleas than the city gates were against his might. Calling the attention of Aufidius to his firm stand against the Romans, he asked Aufidius to report his conduct to the Volscian lords. Aufidius promised and praised the general for his stalwartness. While Coriolanus was vowing that he would not hear the pleas of another Roman, he was interrupted by women's voices calling his name.

The petitioners were Volumnia, Virgilia, and young Marcius, his son. Reaffirming to Aufidius his determination to demolish Rome, he told the callers he would not be moved, and he urged Aufidius to observe his unyielding spirit. Volumnia answered that their requests for leniency and mercy were in vain since he had already proclaimed against kindliness; therefore, they would not appeal to him. She also declared that he made it impossible for them to pray to the gods; they could not pray for victory for Rome, because such supplication would be against him, and to pray for his success in the campaign was to betray their country. Volumnia suggested that she was not seeking advantage for either the Romans or the Volscians. Asking only for reconciliation between the two governments, she declared that Coriolanus would be a hero to both sides if he could arrange an honorable peace between them.

Moved by his mother's reasoning, Coriolanus announced to Aufidius that he would frame a convenient peace between the two forces. Even Aufidius declared that he had been moved by Volumnia's solemn pleas and wise words. Volumnia, Virgilia, and young Marcius returned to Rome, there to be welcomed for the success of their intercession with Coriolanus.

Aufidius withdrew to Antium to await the return of Coriolanus and their meeting with the Roman ambassadors. But as Aufidius reviewed the incidents of the day, he realized that peace would nullify his plan for revenge against Coriolanus. Also, he was aware of the favorable regard the Volscians had for the Roman. He had to remove the man who had been his conqueror in war and who might become his subduer in peace. At a meeting of the Volscian lords Aufidius announced that Coriolanus had betrayed the Volscians by depriving them of victory. In the confusion he stabbed Coriolanus to death. Regretting his deed, he then eulogized Coriolanus and said that he would live forever in men's memory. One of the Volscian lords pronounced Coriolanus the most noble corpse that was ever followed to the grave.

THE CORSICAN BROTHERS

Type of work: Novel
Author: Alexandre Dumas, father (1802-1870)
Type of plot: Adventure romance
Time of plot: 1841
Locale: Corsica and Paris
First published: 1845

Principal characters:

ALEXANDRE DUMAS, narrator of the story and traveler in Corsica
LUCIEN DE FRANCHI, a Corsican at whose home Dumas spent a night
LOUIS DE FRANCHI, Lucien's brother, and a law student in Paris
EMELIE, a married woman with whom Louis is in love
M. DE CHATEAU-RENAUD, Louis' rival for Emelie's affections

Critique:

The story of Lucien and Louis, two brothers unlike in temperament and interests, yet held together by a bond which stretches even beyond the grave, is in the true romantic vein. The pace of the novel never lags; its colorfulness is in the florid, robust tradition of French romanticism.

The Story:

In March, 1841, Alexandre Dumas was traveling, with his horse and guide, on the island of Corsica. One day he arrived at the top of a hill overlooking the towns of Olmeto and Sullacaro; and in accordance with the custom followed by travelers on that island, he surveyed the scene before him in order to decide at whose house he would spend the night. Hospitality was an ancient art on Corsica, where it was considered an honor to entertain a guest without recompense. From his vantage point Dumas decided upon a house which his guide informed him was the Sullacaro property of Madame Savilia de Franchi.

The weary traveler was cordially welcomed by Madame de Franchi and shown to the room of her absent son, Louis. She promised that her other son would soon be home and would pay his respects on his arrival. A few minutes later young Lucien de Franchi knocked at the guest's door.

Dumas gathered from the youth's conversation that there was little likeness between the twin de Franchi brothers in appearance or tastes. Lucien, browned and robust, was dressed in riding clothes. He could not, he said, be forced to leave his native mountains. Louis, he declared, was a student who had spent most of his time indoors with his books. In spite of variance in interests, Lucien continued, they were devoted to each other.

So that they might continue their conversation while he dressed, Lucien invited the guest to his room, a chamber in contrast with that of the absent Louis. The student's room was furnished in the modern French manner and filled with books. Lucien's furniture was all of the fifteenth and sixteenth centuries, and the walls were hung with weapons of every type. Lucien exhibited two pistols, each bearing a similar date and inscription on its butt, which had belonged to his father and mother.

When the two men rejoined Madame de Franchi, she anxiously asked Lucien if he had anything to tell her about Louis. He replied that he had not. To the guest Lucien explained that the brothers, born attached and cut apart, experienced like impressions at the same time. Because he had felt melancholy for the past few days, he knew his brother must be in trouble. He knew Louis was not dead, however, for if he had been he would have seen his twin in a vision.

At dinner Lucien explained that he had to go out later, as he had been chosen mediator to bring to an end an ancient vendetta between the Orlandi and Colonna families. That evening Lucien was to meet with the leader of the Orlandi clan at a ruin about a league from town so that a reconciliation might take place the following day. He invited Dumas to accompany him.

In the moonlight they climbed a hill on which stood the ruins of an old house which had belonged to an ancestress of the de Franchis, a woman who some four hundred years before had become involved in a feud with the de Guidice family. The pistols in Lucien's room celebrated the end of the vendetta, concluded when his parents had simultaneously killed two brothers, the last of their hereditary enemies.

The head of the Orlandi clan agreed, after some urging, to bring his family to Sullacaro the following morning so that a peace treaty with the Colonna clan might be signed. After Lucien had shot a pheasant, he and his guest began their descent to the town.

The following morning Dumas was on hand to witness the conciliation of the Orlandi and Colonna families as they marched from either end of the town to stand before the church. After a pact had been signed before the village notary, the clan leaders attended mass together.

That afternoon Dumas was forced to leave for Paris. After exchanging his hunting belt for one of Lucien's daggers, he started for the coast. Lucien had given Dumas a letter for his brother, and Madame de Franchi had begged that he himself should deliver it. The author sought out the young man immediately on his arrival in Paris. Louis was not at home. In answer to a note left by Dumas, he came to call the next day. Dumas was surprised at the resemblance between Louis and his brother. In response to inquiries, the young man admitted that he had been suffering from a bitter private grief. Unfortunately, he was in a hurry and could not stay long that day. It was

agreed that he and Dumas would meet the following night at an opera ball.

When he kept his appointment with his new friend, Louis appeared distraught and at first did not want to accompany Dumas to a supper party to be given after the ball by D—, a friend of the writer. When he understood, however, that a M. de Chateau-Renaud would be present and that this gentleman had a bet with his host that he would bring a certain unidentified personage with him, the Corsican declared he would go.

At the party Dumas and Louis discovered that de Chateau-Renaud had gambled on bringing a young married woman with him and on being able to present her before four o'clock. The couple arrived only a few minutes before the hour, the man forcing rather than escorting his companion. When she realized, from the few words which de Chateau-Renaud let slip to their host, that she had been the object of a bet, she insisted on leaving immediately and asked Louis to take her home. When the young man consented, he was challenged by de Chateau-Renaud. Although he had never handled a weapon, Louis accepted the challenge.

Later that day Dumas called on his young friend and agreed to serve as a second in the duel. Louis explained that Emelie, the young woman whose cause he had championed, had been entrusted to his care by her husband, a sea captain. Deeply in love with her, he had made every effort to conceal his passion. When, to his dismay, he realized she was carrying on an affair with de Chateau-Renaud, he had attempted to reprove her but had been accused of jealousy for his pains. Then, by chance, he had been invited to D—'s party, where Emelie had appeared as the result of de Chateau-Renaud's wager.

The duel, with pistols, was to take place next morning at nine. Dumas arrived at Louis' rooms at seven-thirty and found the young man writing a letter in which he informed his mother and brother that he was writing in a lucid interval, but that he would soon be dead of brain fever. He explained to Dumas that he had been visited by his father the previous night and been told that he would die. Not wishing his family to know the true circumstances of his death, he asked his friend to send the letter so that Lucien would not come to Paris seeking vengeance and so, perhaps, be killed.

The young Corsican died, as he had predicted. A bullet entered below his sixth rib, and came out just above his hip on the other side of his body. Dumas mailed the letter as he had promised.

Five days later he was surprised by a visit from Lucien, who could not yet have learned of his brother's fate. The Corsican declared he had been out riding the day his brother was killed, and at the moment of Louis' death he had felt as though a bullet had pierced him also. To Dumas' astonishment, he showed an inflamed mark below the sixth rib on his own body. The following morning he had set out for Paris, with his mother's blessing.

Two days later Lucien stood facing de Chateau-Renaud on the spot where his brother had fallen. An instant later de Chateau-Renaud lay dead, a bullet through his head, and Lucien shed his first tears since Louis' death.

THE COSSACKS

Type of work: Novel
Author: Count Leo Tolstoy (1828-1910)
Type of plot: Psychological realism
Time of plot: Nineteenth century
Locale: The Caucasus
First published: 1863

Principal characters:

OLYENIN, a Russian aristocrat
MARYANKA, a Cossack girl
LUKASHKA, a young Cossack, betrothed to Maryanka
UNCLE YEROSHKA, an old Cossack retired from service

Critique:

The Cossacks is one of Tolstoy's lesser known and shorter novels, but in it is one of the finest pictures of Cossack life and the Cossack people in all Russian literature. Against that primitive background Tolstoy placed two psychological problems. The first is that of a young man who wants to love and who wants to fit into society. The second problem is that of the difficulty of a primitive society in accepting the domination of a higher culture. In the reactions of a Russian aristocrat and a Cossack girl one sees quite clearly the same problems that occurred when a body of Russians appeared in a Cossack village to aid in defending the borders. The two groups could not at all times admire, respect, or conceive affection for one another, despite the fact that they were allied against a strong and determined foe.

The Story:

Olyenin, a young Russian aristocrat, decided to leave the society of Moscow and enter the army as a junior officer for service in the Caucasus. There were a number of reasons for his decision: he had squandered a large part of his estate, he was bored with what he considered an empty life, and he was in some embarrassment because of a love affair in which he could not reciprocate the woman's love.

Olyenin left the city after a farewell party one cold, wintry night. He and his servant, Vanyusha, traveled steadily southward toward the Caucasus, land of the Cossacks. The farther Olyenin went on his journey the better he felt about the new life he was about to begin. In a year's service he saw the opportunity to save money, to rearrange his philosophy, and to escape from a mental state which did not permit him to love. He was sure that in a new environment he could become less egocentric, that he could learn to love others as he loved himself.

Shortly after he joined his unit, he was one of a force sent out along the Terek river line to guard against depredations by the tribes who lived in the mountains and on the steppes south of the river. The troops were to reinforce the Cossacks who lived in the narrow strip of verdant land which bordered the river. Olyenin's unit was stationed in the village of Novomlin, a small settlement of houses and farms with a population of less than two thousand people, mainly Cossacks.

The Cossack men spent their time in hunting and standing guard at posts along the Terek river, while the women tended the homes and farms. When Olyenin's unit moved into the village, he, as an aristocrat, was not assigned duties with the troops, and so his time was largely his own.

The Cossacks did not like the Russian troops, for there were years of enmity and different cultures to be reconciled. Olyenin, quartered in the house of a Cossack ensign, soon learned that he was not welcome. They were accepting him and his servant only because the household had to take them in.

In the house lived an ensign, his wife, and their daughter Maryanka. The girl had been spoken for in marriage by a young Cossack, Lukashka, a hero in his village because he had saved a boy from death by drowning and had killed a mountain tribesman who had attempted to swim across the river during a raid. Olyenin quickly became infatuated with Maryanka. He did not know how to act in her presence, however, because he was bewildered by the possibility of a love affair between himself and the young, uncultured Cossack girl.

Olyenin made friends with Lukashka, whom he met at an outpost while hunting, and Uncle Yeroshka, an old Cossack whose days of service were over. In Yeroshka's company Olyenin went hunting almost every day. He disliked drinking bouts, gambling at cards with the other officers, and the pleasure they found in pursuing the women of the village whose husbands and sweethearts were away on duty. Olyenin was happier alone or with Yeroshka hunting in the woods along the Terek, where he could try to work out his emotional problems.

At last Olyenin began to feel that he could be happy through generosity to others. He discovered that he enjoyed giving a horse to Lukashka and presenting old Yeroshka with small gifts that meant little to Olyenin but a great deal to the old man. In addition, Olyenin won the respect of the Cossacks by his ability to shoot pheasants on the wing, a new feat to the Cossacks, who had never even seen it done before.

As time passed Olyenin became more and more aware of Maryanka's presence. When the girl's parents announced that she was formally engaged to young Lukashka, the announcement made Olyenin decide that he, too, was really in love with her. He turned over in his mind the possibilities that such a love would entail. He could not imagine taking the girl back to Moscow, into the so-

ciety to which he had expected to return after his tour of duty, nor could he imagine settling down for life in the Cossack village. Although his stay there meant a great deal to him, he knew that he could never be happy following the primitive life he saw there, for he had too many ties, both social and material, in the world he had temporarily left.

While Olyenin helped Maryanka pick grapes in the vineyards, he had an opportunity to declare his love. Maryanka neither became angry nor repulsed him, although she gave him little encouragement. Later Olyenin, able to press his suit at various times, promised to marry the Cossack girl. She, on her part, refused to say that she would marry him, for she too realized the difficulties such a marriage would bring about. Unlike most of the Cossack girls, she was not free with her favors and refused to let either Olyenin or Lukashka share her bed. Lukashka, well aware of what was happening, was not worried; he felt that the situation would right itself because he was actually the better man of the two.

One day a small band of marauders from across the Terek appeared a short distance from the village. When the Cossacks, accompanied by Olyenin, made a sortie against them, the outlaws tied themselves together, so that they could not run away while they made a stand against the Cossacks. After the battle Lukashka, wounded by a gunshot, was carried back to the village, where it was discovered that he could not recover from his wound. Maryanka, faced with the death of the man her parents had chosen as her husband, realized that her life and people were widely separated from Olyenin and the culture for which he stood. Deciding that she could never have any lasting affection for the Russian, she told Olyenin bluntly of her decision. Olyenin requested a change of duty to another unit. Permission for the transfer having been granted, he and his servant left the village and the kind of life he never could learn to accept.

THE COUNT OF MONTE-CRISTO

Type of work: Novel
Author: Alexandre Dumas, father (1802-1870)
Type of plot: Historical romance
Time of plot: Nineteenth century
Locale: France
First published: 1844

Principal characters:
EDMOND DANTÈS, a young sailor
MERCÉDÈS, his sweetheart
FERDINAND MONDEGO, a rival
M. DANGLARS, an ambitious shipmate
M. VILLEFORT, a deputy
VALENTINE, his daughter
ABBÉ FARIA, a prisoner at Chateau D'If
CADEROUSSE, an innkeeper
M. MORREL, a shipping master
MAXIMILIAN, his son
ALBERT, Mondego's son
HAIDEE, An Albanian

Critique:

The Count of Monte-Cristo is a good story, and that seems to be its chief merit. The characters are flat; they remain courageous, avaricious, kind, loyal, selfish or treacherous, in the conventional mold the author has set for them. But in spite of many defects the novel remains a great work in literature, for the story of the Count of Monte-Cristo is still a breath-taking experience for all who read his adventure, a dramatic tale filled with mystery and intrigue.

The Story:

When Edmond Dantès sailed into Marseilles harbor that day in 1815, he was surrounded by enemies. His shipmate, Danglars, coveted his appointment as captain of the *Pharaon*. Ferdinand Mondego wished to wed Mercédès, who was betrothed to Edmond.

Danglars and Ferdinand wrote a note accusing Edmond of carrying a letter from Elba to the Bonapartist committee in Paris. Caderousse, a neighbor, learned of the plot but kept silent. On his wedding day Edmond was arrested and taken before a deputy named Villefort, a political turncoat, who, to protect himself, had Edmond secretly imprisoned in the dungeons of the Château D'If. There

Dantès' incarceration was secured by the plotting of his enemies outside the prison, notably Villefort, who wished to cover up his own father's connections with the Bonapartists.

Napoleon came from Elba, but Edmond lay forgotten in his cell. The cannonading at Waterloo died away. Years passed. Then one night Edmond heard the sound of digging from an adjoining cell. Four days later a section of the flooring fell in and Edmond saw an old man in the narrow tunnel below. He was the Abbé Faria, whose attempt to dig his way to freedom had led him only to Edmond's cell. Thereafter the two met daily, and the old man taught Edmond history, mathematics, and languages. In Edmond's fourteenth year of imprisonment Faria, mortally ill, told Edmond where to find a tremendous fortune should he escape after the old man's death. When death did come, the abbé's body was placed in a sack, and Edmond conceived the idea of changing places with the dead man, whom he dragged through the tunnel into his own bed. Jailers threw the sack into the sea. Edmond ripped the cloth and swam through the darkness to an islet in the bay.

At daybreak he was picked up by a

gang of smugglers with whom he worked until a stroke of luck brought him to the island of Monte-Cristo, where Faria's fortune awaited him. He landed on the island with the crew of the ship, and, feigning injury in a fall, persuaded the crew to leave him behind until they could return for him. Thus he was able to explore the island and to find his treasure hidden in an underground cavern. He returned to the mainland and there sold some small jewels to provide himself with money enough to carry out his plans to bring his treasure from Monte-Cristo. There he learned that his father had died and Mercédès, despairing of Edmond's return, had married Ferdinand.

Disguised as an abbé, he visited M. Caderousse to seek information of those who had caused his imprisonment. M. Villefort had gained fortune and station in life. Danglars was a rich banker. Ferdinand had won wealth and a title in the Greek war. For this information Edmond gave Caderousse a diamond worth fifty thousand francs.

He learned also that his old shipping master, M. Morrel, was on the verge of bankruptcy. In gratitude, because Morrel had given the older Dantès money to keep him from starvation, Edmond saved Morrel's shipping business.

Edmond took the name of his treasure island. As the Count of Monte-Cristo he dazzled all Paris with his fabulous wealth and his social graces. He and his mysterious protégée, a beautiful girl named Haidée whom he had bought during his travels in Greece, became the talk of the boulevards.

Meanwhile he was slowly plotting the ruin of the four men who had caused him to be sent to the Château D'If. Caderousse was the first to be destroyed. Monte-Cristo had awakened his greed with the gift of a diamond. Later, urged by his wife, Caderousse had committed robbery and murder. Now, released from prison, he attempted to rob Monte-Cristo but was mortally wounded by an escaping accomplice. As the man lay dying,

Monte-Cristo revealed his true name— Edmond Dantès.

In Paris, Monte-Cristo had succeeded in ingratiating himself with the banker, Danglars, and was secretly ruining him. Ferdinand was the next victim on his list. Ferdinand had gained his wealth by betraying Pasha Ali in the Greek revolution of 1823. Monte-Cristo persuaded Danglars to send to Greece for confirmation of Ferdinand's operations there. Ferdinand was exposed and Haidée, daughter of the Pasha Ali, appeared to confront him with the story of her father's betrayal. Albert, the son of Mercédès and Ferdinand, challenged Monte-Cristo to a duel to avenge his father's disgrace. Monte-Cristo intended to make his revenge complete by killing the young man, but Mercédès came to him and begged for her son's life. Aware of Monte-Cristo's true identity, she interceded with her son as well, and at the scene of the duel the young man publicly declared his father's ruin had been justified. Mother and son left Paris. Ferdinand shot himself.

Monte-Cristo had also become intimate with Madame Villefort and encouraged her desire to possess the wealth of her stepdaughter, Valentine, whom Maximilian Morrel, son of the shipping master, loved. The count had slyly directed Madame Villefort in the use of poisons, and the depraved woman murdered three people. When Valentine herself succumbed to poison, Maximilian went to Monte-Cristo for help. Upon learning that his friend Maximilian loved Valentine, Monte-Cristo vowed to save the young girl. But Valentine had apparently died. Still Monte-Cristo promised future happiness to Maximilian.

Meanwhile Danglars' daughter, Eugénie, ran off to seek her fortune independently, and Danglars found himself bankrupt. He deserted his wife and fled the country. Villefort having discovered his wife's treachery and crimes, confronted her with a threat of exposure. She then poisoned herself and her son

Edward, for whose sake she had poisoned the others. Monte-Cristo revealed his true name to Villefort, who subsequently went mad.

But Monte-Cristo had not deceived Maximilian. He had rescued Valentine while she lay in a drugged coma in the tomb. Now he reunited the two lovers on his island of Monte-Cristo. They were given the count's wealth, and Monte-Cristo sailed away with Haidée never to be seen again.

THE COUNTERFEITERS

Type of work: Novel
Author: André Gide (1869-1951)
Type of plot: Psychological realism
Time of plot: Early 1920's
Locale: Paris
First published: 1925

Principal characters:
EDOUARD, a writer
OLIVIER MOLINIER, his nephew
GEORGE MOLINIER, Olivier's younger brother
VINCENT MOLINIER, Olivier's older brother
BERNARD PROFITENDIEU, Olivier's friend and Edouard's secretary
LAURA DOUVIERS, Edouard's friend
COMTE DE PASSAVANT, a libertine
ARMAND VEDEL, Laura's brother and Olivier's friend

Critique:

The Counterfeiters traces the behavior pattern of a group of youths, each stimulated by intimate contact with an older individual. It is generally considered Gide's finest novel and one of the noteworthy novels in contemporary fiction. The author's ability to create real characters, to understand them and present them for our understanding, is remarkable. His intention is to show that man must follow the dictates of his own heart and ignore convention, if he wishes to find full expression and happiness.

The Story:

When seventeen-year-old Bernard Profitendieu discovered an old love letter of his mother's and realized that he was an illegitimate son, he left a scathing letter for the man whom he had considered his real father and ran away from home. He spent that night with his friend, Olivier Molinier. Olivier told him of his Uncle Edouard, a writer, who would be arriving from England the following day, and also of a woman with whom his older brother Vincent was involved.

The next morning Bernard left before Olivier had awakened. For a time he wondered what to do. He idly decided to go to the station and watch Olivier meet his uncle.

That same morning Vincent visited his friend, the notorious homosexual, Comte de Passavant. He was disturbed over his affair with Laura Douviers, a married woman whom he had met while both were patients in a sanatorium. Upon her release she had followed Vincent to Paris.

Edouard was returning to Paris because of a promise to Laura. He had known her before her marriage, and had told her to call upon him whenever necessary. He was also looking forward to seeing his nephew Olivier, of whom he was very fond. So excited was he, in fact, that, after checking his bag, he threw away his checkroom ticket. But the meeting with his nephew was unsatisfactory.

Bernard, unobserved, had watched the meeting between the two. He picked up the checkroom ticket Edouard had dropped and claimed the bag. In it he discovered a large sum of money, which he quickly pocketed; Edouard's journal, which he read without scruple; and Laura's supplicating letter.

With no definite plan in mind, he called on Laura. Laura was disturbed by the young man who knew so much about her affairs, but his actions became understandable when Edouard arrived and Bernard admitted the theft of the bag. Bernard said that he had stolen it as a means of getting in touch with Edouard. Edouard was very much taken with the young man's impudent charm. When Bernard suggested that he might fill the role of a secretary, Edouard agreed.

A few days later, with Bernard as his secretary, Edouard took Laura to Switzerland. Bernard wrote to Olivier in glowing terms about his new position. Olivier was jealous of Bernard, who, he felt, had taken his place in Edouard's affections. He decided to take an editorial assignment offered him by Comte de Passavant.

In the meantime Bernard fell in love with Laura. When he confessed his love, Laura showed him a letter from her husband, begging her to come back to him with her child and Vincent's. She had decided to return to him. Bernard and Edouard returned to Paris.

A letter arrived from Olivier to Bernard. He was in Italy with de Passavant, and he wrote complacently about the wonderful journal they intended to publish. Bernard showed the letter to Edouard, who failed to realize that the letter disguised the boy's real feelings of jealousy and hurt.

Bernard, although still acting as Edouard's secretary, had enrolled in the Vedel School and was living in the Vedel household. The Vedels were Laura's parents and Edouard's close friends. Edouard was particularly fond of Rachel, Laura's older sister, and it distressed him to see that she was devoting all her time and energy to managing the school.

Bernard told Edouard about some children, including George Molinier, Olivier's younger brother, who were engaged in some underhanded activities. The boys, as Bernard was soon to learn, were passing counterfeit coins.

Olivier returned to Paris to get in touch with Bernard. The meeting between the two was strained. As they parted, Olivier invited Edouard and Bernard to a party which de Passavant was giving that evening. Olivier then went to call on another old friend, Armand Vedel, Laura's younger brother. Armand refused the invitation to the party, but suggested that Olivier ask his sister Sarah to go in his place. Bernard, who was living at the school, was to serve as her escort.

The party was an orgy. Olivier became drunk and quarrelsome. Edouard led him from the room, and Olivier, ashamed, begged his uncle to take him away.

Bernard escorted Sarah home. Her room was beyond Armand's, and her brother handed Bernard the candle to light the way. As soon as Bernard had gone into her bedroom, Armand bolted the door. Bernard spent the night with Sarah.

The next morning he found Edouard attempting to revive Olivier. The boy, after spending the night with his uncle, had risen early in the morning on the pretext that he wanted to rest on the sofa. Getting up later, Edouard had discovered his nephew lying on the bathroom floor unconscious, the gas jets turned on. Edouard nursed Olivier until the boy recovered. When Olivier's mother went to see her son, she expressed to Edouard her concern for George and his wayward habits. Edouard promised to speak to George. He also learned that Vincent had gone away with Lady Griffith, a friend of de Passavant.

A few days later Edouard received a call from M. Profitendieu, Bernard's foster father. Ostensibly he had called in his office as magistrate to ask Edouard to speak to his nephew George, who was suspected of passing counterfeit coins. But it soon became evident that the real object of his visit was to inquire about Bernard. Since the boy had left home, Profitendieu had worried about him. He wanted very much to have him home once more.

Meanwhile Bernard's affair with Sarah

698

had attracted Rachel's attention, and she asked him to leave the school. Bernard went to Edouard, who told him of the interview with Profitendieu. For some time Bernard had regretted the harsh letter he had written, and the hatred he had felt for his foster father had changed to sympathy and fondness. It was evident that Bernard was no longer needed as Edouard's secretary. He decided to return home.

Armand had succeeded Olivier as editor of de Passavant's journal. He went to see Olivier and showed him a letter from an older brother in Egypt. The writer told of a man with whom he was living who was almost out of his mind. From what he could gather from the fellow's ravings, the man had been responsible for his woman companion's death. Neither Armand nor Olivier guessed that the man was Olivier's brother Vincent.

George and his friends caused a tragedy at their school. Boris, the young grandson of an old friend of Edouard, had been invited to join a secret society if he would perform the act of initiation —stand up before the class and shoot himself through the temple. It was understood that the cartridge would be a blank. One of the boys, however, substituted a real bullet for the dummy, and when Boris, pale but resolute, walked to the front of the class and shot himself, the joke became a tragedy. The experience was terrible enough to bring George to his senses.

Olivier having completely recovered, Edouard settled down again to writing his book, with a great sense of peace and happiness.

THE COUNTESS DE CHARNY

Type of work: Novel
Author: Alexandre Dumas, father (1802-1870)
Type of plot: Historical romance
Time of plot: 1791
Locale: France
First published: 1853-1855

Principal characters:
COUNT OLIVIER DE CHARNY, aide to King Louis XVI
COUNTESS ANDRÉE DE CHARNY, his wife
SEBASTIAN, her illegitimate son
DR. GILBERT, the boy's father
COUNT ALESSANDRO DI CAGLIOSTRO, assumed name of Joseph Balsamo
KING LOUIS XVI
QUEEN MARIE ANTOINETTE
HONORÉ MIRABEAU

Critique:

The Countess de Charny is the concluding novel of a series dealing with historical personages and events before and during the period of the French Revolution. Other novels of the group are *Memoirs of a Physician, The Queen's Necklace,* and *The Taking of the Bastille.* Dumas drew much of his material for this novel from Michelet's *History of the Revolution.* The story, told in the Dumas manner, carries the conviction of the reader by means of dramatic scenes and rapid movement.

The Story:

In the days following the fall of the Bastille, King Louis XVI and Queen Marie Antoinette were forcibly escorted to Paris by troops under the command of General Lafayette. With the king were his most trusted aides, Count Olivier de Charny, the Marquis de Favras, and a commoner but also a close and trusted friend of the king, Dr. Gilbert. During the commotion of the king's return, an agent of the powerful and mysterious Cagliostro learned from the king's locksmith, Gamain, of the construction of a secret door in the quarters in Paris where the king was to be confined. He immediately reported this information to Cagliostro. It was suspected by Cagliostro that the secret door would be used in the future to allow the king's escape with his

family.

Meanwhile, young Sebastian Gilbert, disturbed by reports of riots in Paris, left his foster home in the country in order to seek his father, for whose safety he feared. In Paris, Sebastian met the Countess Andrée de Charny, whom he immediately felt was his mother. She, in turn, recognized him as her own long-lost son. What Sebastian did not know, however, was that he had been born out of wedlock when the countess, then known as Mademoiselle de Taverney, had been attacked by Dr. Gilbert, at that time only a humble peasant, fifteen years before. Later, when she became the wife of Count de Charny and gained the favor of Queen Marie Antoinette, she procured from the queen a *lettre de cachet* and had Dr. Gilbert locked in the Bastille where he stayed until it was captured by the rioting populace.

Years had brought a philosophic calm to Dr. Gilbert and he now sought to expiate his early crime by doing deeds of charity to all who would accept his services.

Sebastian, sensing his mother's hatred for his own father, ran away and was run over by a carriage in the streets of Paris soon after leaving the countess' apartment. Dr. Gilbert, arriving soon after in search of his son, quickly traced the boy to a small house where Sebastian

700

had been taken after the accident. Dr. Gilbert administered to him and he recovered.

Count de Charny, knowing nothing of his wife's early misfortune, could not understand why their relationship had remained so distant throughout their married life; the countess had been fearful that her husband would discover the story of her earlier life. Now, however, the count had little time to think of his own affairs because of the rapid movements of events and the dangers facing the king and his family.

Soon after the royal family's arrival in Paris, King Louis summoned de Charny and asked him to go on a mission to the Marquis de Bouille and procure his aid in securing troops to cover the king's escape. Dr. Gilbert, meanwhile, tried to convince King Louis to put his trust in Honoré Mirabeau, who was then the man of the hour and held the respect of the French people. The king's only chance was to agree with Mirabeau and sign the revolutionary principles. Although the king listened to Dr. Gilbert's advice, he still decided to bide his time until more favorable circumstances arose.

In the meantime the National Assembly grew more restless. Many people were brought to trial, among them the Marquis de Favras, whose execution was practically certain. His sole chance of reprieve was offered to him by Cagliostro, who guaranteed him a sure escape. Favras declined, however, and in the end went nobly to his death.

In desperation the king finally agreed to follow Dr. Gilbert's advice and joined forces with Mirabeau. Mirabeau's own popularity began to wane, however, when one of Cagliostro's agents distributed pamphlets accusing Mirabeau of betraying the revolutionary cause. A short time later Mirabeau, who had been suffering from a lung condition, died. On his deathbed he managed to scrawl a message to the king, urging him to flee while time still remained. The king and his family immediately began preparations for their flight.

On the night before the royal party was to leave, Cagliostro paid Dr. Gilbert a visit. He told Dr. Gilbert that he knew of the king's plans for escape and that he was willing to offer assistance in order to assure that King Louis and his family would have a safe journey. Dr. Gilbert, who was quite fatalistic, declined Cagliostro's offer; he felt that what must be would be.

The night of departure arrived. The king and his family escaped through the secret door and thus were able to elude the guards stationed around their quarters. Accompanying the royal family were Count de Charny and M. de Malden, another trusted nobleman dedicated to the king's cause. The flight had been carefully planned. Long before, arrangements had been made to have fresh horses waiting for the king's carriage at regular stations along the route, and at a bridge near Someville the Marquis de Choiseul was waiting with a company of dragoons to accompany the king on his journey.

Sudden difficulties developed when the king's carriage broke down and caused a delay of four hours. Meanwhile, at Someville, the marquis' troops were being threatened by the local populace and there was imminent danger of the arrival of nationalist troops. After waiting as long as he could, the marquis was finally forced to retire with his dragoons. When the royal family finally did reach Someville, the king was recognized by a revolutionary patriot, Jean Drouet, who immediately fled to inform nationalist troops quartered not too far away. De Charny, exchanging his tired horse for a fresh one, immediately set out in pursuit of Drouet. He finally caught up with him, only to discover that neither of his pistols was loaded when he fired at Drouet. The informant escaped in the woods and finally made contact with the nationalist troops. A short time later the troops arrived in Someville, where the king was being detained by the villagers.

In order to avoid bloodshed, King Louis agreed to an armed escort back to Paris. On their arriving in the city the king and his family were threatened by large groups of people. De Charny, trying to defend the king, attempted single-handedly to fight a hostile mob and barely escaped with his life.

Although de Charny had, throughout his career, devoted his chief energies to the defense of the monarchy, his wife had always been in his thoughts. After his escape, and in the presence of the royal family, Dr. Gilbert disclosed to the count his wife's secret of her illegitimate child. The doctor explained that only her great love for de Charny had kept her from revealing her shame and expressing her true feelings for her husband. De Charny immediately returned to Andrée and the two were happily reunited.

A COUNTRY DOCTOR

Type of work: Novel
Author: Sarah Orne Jewett (1849-1909)
Type of plot: Regional romance
Time of plot: Mid-nineteenth century
Locale: Oldfields, Maine
First published: 1884

> *Principal characters:*
> NAN PRINCE, a student of medicine
> MRS. THACHER, her grandmother
> DR. LESLIE, her guardian
> MISS NANCY PRINCE, her aunt

Critique:

Sarah Orne Jewett's *A Country Doctor* is a good example of the local color novel. The plot is simple and subordinated to the description of the environment and the customs and habits of the people therein, but the novel is a highly successful and satisfying book.

The Story:

One cold winter night while Mrs. Thacher and two of her neighbors were sitting around the stove and gossiping about neighborhood activities, they were interrupted by a noise at the door. Adeline Thacher Prince had fallen on the doorstep. In her arms she held her infant daughter, Nan. Dr. Leslie was sent for at once but by the next day Adeline was dead. According to her wishes, Dr. Leslie became the little child's guardian, though she lived with her maternal grandmother.

Nan's mother had left home to go to work in a textile mill in Lowell. There she had fallen in love with a young man from Dunport, Maine, and after a short courtship she had married him. The marriage had been far from happy. Adeline had inherited a wild, rebellious tendency, and it was whispered in Dunport that she had eventually taken to drink. She resented, furthermore, the opposition of her husband's family to the marriage, especially the views of her husband's sister, Miss Nancy Prince. After Adeline's husband died, she tried for a time to support herself and the child. When she could do so no longer, she trudged back to Oldfields to die in her mother's home.

Little Nan seemed to exhibit some of her mother's characteristics, for she was mischievous and inclined to pleasure. Her grandmother often thought her a trial, but to Dr. Leslie she was something quite different. One day Nan retrieved a fallen bird with a fractured leg and applied a splint, as she had seen Dr. Leslie do to his patients. The doctor began to wonder if Nan had not inherited some tendency toward medicine which her father had had. He did not insist that she go to school. He thought that the training she received in the woods and the fields was far more beneficial than any she would obtain in the schoolroom.

When Mrs. Thacher died, Nan went to live with Dr. Leslie. Between the two there was a great feeling of affection. Nan, who continued to go out on calls with the doctor, exhibited much interest in his work. The time came at last for her to be sent to boarding-school. At first she was shy and rather backward in her studies, but after a while she made admirable progress. She would have been completely satisfied with her life if she had not wondered, from time to time, about the mysterious aunt of whom she had heard only rumors. Mrs. Thacher had never explained anything of the girl's family background to her, and Nan had conjured up the figure of a wealthy aristocratic relative who would one day send for her. Miss Prince, who had inherited a large estate, regularly sent money to Dr. Leslie to provide for Nan's upkeep. The doctor never touched a penny of it. When Adeline had died, Miss Prince had asked for the custody of the child, but Mrs. Thacher and Dr. Leslie had refused her request.

When Nan grew older, she told Dr. Leslie of her desire to study medicine. Although the doctor was aware of the difficulties she would face, he approved heartily of her interest. But the town of Oldfields did not, and many were shocked at the idea of a woman doctor. Nan continued her studies in the doctor's books, however, and acted as his nurse. That training she was to continue at a medical school in a nearby city.

When the time came for her to leave Oldfields, Nan wrote a brief note to her aunt, Miss Prince, and asked if she might visit her father's sister. Miss Prince, although she feared that Nan might be like her mother, consented to receive her niece. On Nan's arrival in Dunport, Miss Prince, genuinely pleased with her, helped Nan to make friends and openly acknowledged her young relative. But when Nan expressed her wish to study medicine, everyone was shocked, even Miss Prince, who in a large measure blamed Dr. Leslie for Nan's unladylike desire for a professional career. Nan, although made unhappy by her aunt's ob-jections, remained adamant.

Her aunt and her friends, however, sought to lead her astray from her work. Miss Prince had a favorite friend, young George Gerry, to whom she intended leaving her money. When Nan grew fond of George, everyone hoped that they would marry. One day, during an outing, Nan and George stopped at a farmhouse, and Nan treated a farmer who had thrown his arm out of joint. Sometime later, George asked Nan to marry him. She refused, both because she wanted to become a doctor and because she was afraid that her inherited characteristics might cause her to be a bad wife.

At last she told her aunt that she would have to return to Oldfields. On her arrival, the doctor, who had been apprehensive that Nan might have been influenced by Miss Prince and her money, was pleasantly surprised. She was the same Nan she had been before, and all the more ambitious for a successful medical career.

Nan went away to study. When she returned, Dr. Leslie was older and needed more help in his practice. Nan settled down in Oldfields and slowly the community accepted her. Before many years passed she had succeeded Dr. Leslie in the affections of the men and women of the village.

THE COUNTRY DOCTOR

Type of work: Novel
Author: Honoré de Balzac (1799-1850)
Type of plot: Naturalism
Time of plot: Early nineteenth century
Locale: Southern France
First published: 1833

Principal characters:
PIERRE JOSEPH GENESTAS, a soldier
DR. BENASSIS, physician and mayor
LA FOSSEUSE, a social waif

Critique:

The plot of *The Country Doctor* is spare and concise. The various country folk appear only as incidental to the busy doctor's life, for the main narrative thread concerns only Genestas' visit and its consequences. For most readers the true interest of the novel lies in Benassis' present existence and the mystery of his past. Interesting as the people are, they appear only as sketches. Genestas himself is but half drawn. The reader would like to know more about La Fosseuse and Judith, but they are shadowy types. The good doctor, however, emerges as one of Balzac's real creations; his is a sympathetic portrayal. The book belongs to the unfinished series of novels, "Scenes of Country Life."

The Story:

Pierre Joseph Genestas had long been a simple soldier. He always did his duty well and silently; this lack of ostentation and his reserved nature made his promotion slow. He had followed Napoleon from Egypt to Moscow, but the monarchy showed him little gratitude or recognition for his services. Now he rode slowly along a mountain road in the direction of the Grande Chartreuse to seek out Dr. Benassis.

A rather sullen peasant woman gave him a drink of milk and pointed out Benassis' house, but when he got there the doctor was out. When he finally found the man he sought, Genestas came upon a strange scene. A cretin was on his death-bed in a miserable hovel. It seemed to Genestas that the whole village must have crowded around the humble cottage in a remote section of the town, for they regarded the dying cretin with superstitious awe. As the religious procession entered the hut, Genestas and the doctor took their leave, the soldier curious about what he had seen. Benassis told him that not long before he had been stoned in the same poor quarter of the town.

Eight years ago, when Benassis first came to practice in the village, the place had only seven hundred inhabitants; now there were two thousand. Once the district where the cretin died had been a settlement of mental defectives. Benassis, as the only health official in the town, had condemned the district and removed all but one of the cretins to an asylum. This change had been accomplished against the will of the village, but gradually the inhabitants had come to understand the doctor's unselfish wisdom.

Although the village was not far from Grenoble, the peasants could not trade with the big city because there was no road between the town and the village. Benassis' first project had been to build a road across the valley. Now it was a broad straight highway lined with Lombardy poplars, and the peasants' carts went constantly to Grenoble with produce.

Benassis, having been elected mayor, was shrewd enough to get the former

705

mayor on his side. Many projects, all encouraged and financed by the mayor, brought jobs and money to the town. There were tile works, an osier-basket works, a mill, and many more farms. With selfless devotion the mayor had built up both the population and the prosperity of the village.

On the excuse that his old wounds needed attention, Genestas arranged to stay for a time with the mayor. When he was ready to go to bed the first night, he found his own room comfortable, even luxurious. By contrast, Benassis' room was monastic in simplicity. Genestas resolved to pierce the secret of this strange doctor-mayor.

In the morning Genestas made the rounds with his doctor host. They visited two houses of mourning where the fathers had just died. Among the poorer folk death was a natural occurrence; among the richer people the father's death was a sign for much lamentation, many visitors, and elaborate mourning garments. The contrast emphasized the fact that Benassis was equally at home with all classes, and equally welcome.

From one house to another the pair continued that whole day. Everywhere the fields were carefully cultivated and the stock was cleanly housed. Laborers were busy clearing new land in the level spots and draining marshes. Everywhere the peasants gave credit to Benassis for inspiration.

Near evening the two men called on La Fosseuse, a strange but beautiful girl who lived alone. She was supported by Benassis, for she had no talent with which to earn a living. Left an orphan, she had been brought up in a rich household, but the family had cast her out when she was sixteen. For years she had been forced to beg. Her body was frail and her spirit was changeable. All she could do was sew, but her attention wandered often and she seldom did much work. Genestas was impressed by the great devotion La Fosseuse showed toward Benassis.

That evening at dinner Genestas met the priest, the notary, the former mayor, and the justice of the peace. These dignitaries also showed great faith in Benassis' leadership. Truly the doctor was a great man.

On impulse Benassis confided to Genestas the secret of his life. Benassis had been born into a rich family. His father had sent him to good schools and eventually to Paris to study medicine. At first Benassis was a willing student, but before long he lost interest in his studies. Because his strict father gave him only a small allowance, the gay life of Paris was far beyond his reach. He met a devoted young girl and lived with her in contentment. Under her influence he regained his zest for work.

When his father died, Benassis inherited a fortune. On his return to Paris he was determined to cut a social figure, and he quickly ran through the inheritance after casting off his devoted mistress. Two years later, learning that the girl was dying, he went to see her. He made her a deathbed promise that he would care faithfully for their son.

Soon afterward he fell in love with the young daughter of a very religious family. On the advice of an older man, Benassis kept secret the story of his dead mistress and his child, and the family came to look on him as a man of upright character and their own son. Finally his conscience forced him to tell the girl of his past; in sorrow she renounced him. It was a crushing blow to Benassis. The final misfortune came when his son died. In expiation Benassis had buried himself in the little village in the Grande Chartreuse and there devoted himself to the poor and miserable peasants of the region.

Genestas was much affected by the story. A bond of sympathy with the doctor led him to tell his own story.

Genestas, with one of his friends, had been quartered in the house of a Jewish family in Poland after the retreat from Moscow. Judith, the daughter, had attracted him greatly, but she married his friend. Shortly afterward, when the friend was killed in battle, he left Judith pregnant. Before his death, however, he asked Genestas to marry Judith and look after the baby. After much scheming Genestas got Judith to Paris, where her son was born. Genestas married her on her deathbed and took her son as his own.

The boy, Adrien, was living with a tutor. He was well educated but in poor health. Although he was sixteen, he looked twelve. Genestas wanted Benassis to take the boy into his own home and rebuild his health. After seeing Adrien, Benassis declared he was only run-down, not consumptive, as had been feared. Benassis let the boy run with the village hunter and soon he was strong and healthy. His care of young Adrien was only one of his many good works throughout the countryside.

Genestas was given a regiment at Grenoble, his first real command. One day he received a letter from Adrien; Benassis was dead. Tired out, he had succumbed to a chill. Genestas hurried to the village, to be told on his arrival that Benassis had already been buried. Sorrowing workmen were erecting over his grave a huge mound topped with a monument. Weeping, La Fosseuse lay beside the grave.

THE COUNTRY HOUSE

Type of work: Novel
Author: John Galsworthy (1867-1933)
Type of plot: Social criticism
Time of plot: Early twentieth century
Locale: England
First published: 1907

Principal characters:
GEORGE PENDYCE, heir to Worsted Skeynes
MRS. HELEN BELLEW, separated from her husband
HORACE PENDYCE, George's father
MARGERY PENDYCE, his mother
THE REVEREND HUSSELL BARTER, rector at Worsted Skeynes
GREGORY VIGIL, Mrs. Bellew's guardian
CAPTAIN BELLEW, her husband
MR. PARAMOR, the family lawyer

Critique:

Before the two world wars had shaken the institutions of the world to the breaking point, the English country house was symbolic of many of the strongest traditions of the aristocracy. In this novel we see what happens when one such house is threatened with disrepute and, perhaps, eventual destruction because of the careless attitude of one of its sons. Galsworthy also gives a vivid account of the prejudices and feelings of English society, including the pettiness of some of its members. Everything, however, remains indestructible and, through the deft handling of one of its more insignificant members, society comes away without even a blemish.

The Story:

In the fall of 1891, Horace Pendyce invited several people to Worsted Skeynes, his country estate, for a hunt. Little had been changed at Worsted Skeynes since the time of Mr. Pendyce's great-great-great-grandfather. Mr. Pendyce, as head of the house, naturally took a conservative political stand and expected each member of his family to follow suit.

Included in the party for the hunt was George Pendyce, the oldest son of Horace and Margery Pendyce, who now spent most of his time in London and who had recently become interested enough in racing to buy his own horse and have him trained for that sport. There was also Mrs. Helen Bellew, a very attractive young woman who had separated from her husband simply because they had grown tired of one another and who, it was being rumored, now encouraged the attentions of George. Needless to say, in the English country society of that time separation of married couples was still frowned upon and for a lady in such a position to favor at all the attentions of a gentleman was for her to invite criticism. Unfortunately, at a dance given by Mrs. Pendyce during the week of the hunt, the young couple were seen to kiss each other passionately. The observer was the Reverend Hussell Barter, rector of the parish of Worsted Skeynes and another member of the party.

Soon after the week of the hunt Gregory Vigil, cousin of Mrs. Pendyce and guardian of Mrs. Bellew, who was himself in love with his beautiful ward, decided that Helen's situation was intolerable and had gone on quite long enough. After consulting Mrs. Pendyce on the matter, he approached his lawyer, Mr. Paramor, on the subject of divorce. Paramor advised against it, however, on the grounds that there must be some very tangible reason for the lady's wanting a divorce and also because of the fact that such an act was always extremely public and painful, even for the one bringing the action. Helen Bellew was subject to certain charges, unknown to her guardian, because of her growing relationship with George Pendyce.

When Mr. Vigil decided to go on with the action, Mrs. Pendyce took up the matter with the rector, without, however, suspecting in the least his strong feelings against both divorce and Mrs. Bellew. Mr. Barter objected, of course, because of what he considered an immoral act which he himself had witnessed. In his mind it was the husband, Captain Bellew, who had been wronged, and he felt it his Christian duty to make that gentleman aware of the action that was about to be taken against him. Consequently, Captain Bellew began proceedings before Gregory Vigil had had time to do so on behalf of Mrs. Bellew.

In the meantime George had fallen in love with Mrs. Bellew to the extent that he felt he could not live without her, and he was willing to allow his name and reputation to be dirtied in the divorce courts in order that he might then marry the woman. Besides, he had also fallen very heavily into debt through gambling on the horses. This combination of circumstances proved too much for the conservative Mr. Pendyce; no Pendyce had ever been a gambler and certainly none had ever been involved in a divorce suit. When George had finally lost all his money and was forced to sell his horse to pay his debts, and when the papers had been served naming him corespondent in the case of Bellew vs. Bellew, Mr. Pendyce resolved to take action. Rather than see the estate and heritage of the family fall into the hands of one so irresponsible, he decided to disinherit George, unless his son would promise never to see the woman again. If George would agree to do this, Mr. Pendyce had Captain Bellew's word that he would drop the divorce proceedings. But George refused.

Mrs. Pendyce, however, would not consent to her husband's action. Because of a very tender and somewhat sympathetic feeling for her firstborn child, she threatened to leave Mr. Pendyce if he carried out his decision. She was as good as her word. Having a small income of her own, she felt that she could keep herself and George with some measure of comfort if not with the luxury they had known at Worsted Skeynes. Her first steps were to go to London, find George, and attempt to get him to fulfill his father's demands. When this effort failed, she went to see Helen Bellew to see if she would give up George. By this time Mrs. Bellew was as tired of George as she previously had been of her husband, and she was quite willing—in fact, she desired—never to see George again.

Meanwhile, Mr. Pendyce was highly upset by his wife's leaving him; such an act was so very much out of keeping with the tradition in which he lived. He was, therefore, quite relieved to see her when she returned to their home. However, Horace Pendyce was far too proud a man to write to Captain Bellew and acknowledge that his son had been discarded in the same way that the captain himself had been. Thus the danger of divorce proceedings, with the subsequent harm to the family reputation, was as great as ever. Again it was Mrs. Pendyce, only an insignificant part of the social system as Mr. Pendyce thought of it, who was able to solve the problem. She took it upon herself to visit Captain Bellew and ask him to drop proceedings. Because he had instituted the whole action as a kind of self-defense and because he was so much impressed by a real lady, he agreed to do so. So the Pendyce name, the country house, and the whole system of society were again preserved.

THE COUNTRY OF THE POINTED FIRS

Type of work: Novel
Author: Sarah Orne Jewett (1849-1909)
Type of plot: Regional romance
Time of plot: Late nineteenth century
Locale: Maine seacoast
First published: 1896

Principal characters:
MRS. TODD, a New England herbalist
MRS. BLACKETT, her mother
WILLIAM, her brother
THE BOARDER, a writer
ESTHER, William's sweetheart
MRS. HIGHT, Esther's mother

Critique:

In this book there are few episodes that could be called exciting. Instead, the interest lies in character portrayal and nature description. Each chapter can stand alone as a local-color sketch, a self-contained unit. For one who wishes to explore the deep springs of New England character, however, this book is pleasant and leisurely reading.

The Story:

A woman writer came one summer to Dunnet Landing, a Maine seacoast town, to find seclusion for her work. She boarded with Mrs. Almira Todd, a friendly widow and the local herb doctor. Besides having a garden full of herbs, Mrs. Todd often roamed far afield for rarer specimens. The boarder sometimes took care of Mrs. Todd's sales of herbs and birch beer when Mrs. Todd was away.

At last the boarder realized that she must get to work on her book and give up the society of Mrs. Todd in the day-time. The boarder found the village schoolhouse a quiet place for her writing, and she spent most of her days there. One morning she was surprised to have a visit from old Captain Littlepage, a retired seaman who seldom left his house. For a time he spoke seriously of the great English poets. When he saw that the boarder did not laugh at him, he launched upon a long narrative. It seemed that he had been shipwrecked upon a small island and had met there another sailor who had been to the North Pole. He told Captain Littlepage of a town of ghosts he had discovered. It was Captain Littlepage's theory that in this town souls awaited their passage into the next world. The old man's narrative stopped suddenly as his mind returned to the present. The boarder helped him home and told no one about his strange story.

On another day Mrs. Todd took her boarder out to Green Island, where Mrs. Todd's mother lived. Mrs. Blackett was over eighty, her daughter past sixty. Mrs. Blackett still did her own work and kept house for her son William, who was past fifty. William was a bashful man, but he found a friend to his liking in the boarder. Mrs. Todd and the boarder gathered some herbs before they left the island, and Mrs. Todd showed her the spot offshore where her husband had gone down in his boat.

Mrs. Fosdick came to visit Mrs. Todd. The two old ladies and the boarder often spent their evenings together. One night Mrs. Todd told of her husband's Cousin Joanna, who had lived on Shell-heap Island. Disappointed in love, Joanna went to live alone on the tiny island. Passing fishermen often left presents on the shore for her, but no one ever visited her. Finally Mrs. Todd and the minister went to see her, for the minister was worried about the state of Joanna's soul. They found Joanna living comfortably but simply. Satisfied with her lonely life, she could not be induced to return to the mainland. Joanna lived out her life on the island and was buried there.

Late in August Mrs. Todd took her boarder and Mrs. Blackett to the Bowden family reunion. They hired a carriage and drove far inland to the family seat. All the Bowdens for miles around came to the reunion, and Mrs. Blackett was one of the privileged guests because of her age. For once Mrs. Todd forgot her herbs and spent the entire day in the enjoyment of the society of her friends. William had not come to the gathering because of his bashfulness. Mrs. Blackett treasured every moment of the day, for she knew it was one of the last reunions she would attend.

One day the boarder stood on the shore below Dunnet Landing. There she met Mr. Tilley, one of the oldest fishermen in the village. Mr. Tilley was reserved toward strangers, but he had at last accepted the boarder as a friend and he invited her to visit him that afternoon. When the boarder arrived, he was knitting some socks. The two friends sat in the kitchen while Mr. Tilley told the boarder about his wife. She had died eight years before, but her husband had never got over his sorrow. He kept the house just as she had left it. Proudly he showed the boarder the seldom-used parlor and Mrs. Tilley's set of china. She left the cottage feeling the loneliness that surrounded the old fisherman.

When the clear, cool autumn came, it was time for the boarder to leave. Mrs.

Todd helped her pack and get her belongings down on the wharf for the steamer. Mrs. Todd took her leave of the boarder before she left the house. From the deck of the steamer the boarder watched Dunnet Landing fade into the distance. She recalled a day of the past summer when William had come to the mainland. He was going trout fishing in an inland stream. Self-consciously he asked the boarder to go with him. They caught no fish, but William took her afterward to see Mrs. Hight and her daughter Esther. The boarder stayed to talk to Mrs. Hight, while William went out to speak to Esther, who supported her aged and crippled mother by tending sheep. As William and the boarder left, she realized that William and Esther were lovers.

When the boarder returned to Dunnet Landing in the spring, Mrs. Todd told her that Mrs. Hight had recently died and that Esther and William were to be married immediately. He was to come to the mainland the next day if the weather proved good.

Early in the morning Mrs. Todd was up to watch for a sail from Green Island. Finally she saw it approaching. Then neighbors began to drop in to inquire why William was coming to the mainland. After the ceremony William and Esther stopped for a moment at Mrs. Todd's house before returning to the island. Mrs. Todd and the boarder accompanied the pair to the landing to see them off. The older woman expressed no emotion at the leavetaking; but as she and the boarder returned to the house, they walked holding hands all the way.

THE COUNTRY WIFE

Type of work: Drama
Author: William Wycherley (1640?-1716)
Type of plot: Comedy of manners
Time of plot: Seventeenth century
Locale: London
First presented: 1673

Principal characters:
MR. HORNER, a gallant alleged to be impotent
MR. PINCHWIFE, a jealous husband
MRS. PINCHWIFE, his dissatisfied wife
ALITHEA, Mr. Pinchwife's sister, a society woman
HARCOURT, a gallant in love with Alithea

Critique:

This play is the epitome of the spirit of the reign of Charles II. The plot is presented with Restoration boldness, depending as it does on the supposition of Horner's impotence and his amorous adventures with various wives who have been gulled into believing that he is incapable of feelings for the opposite sex. While the main device of the play is frankly indecent, the handling of the theme, particularly in the dialogue, is brilliant. Clever dialogue and the whimsicality of Mrs. Pinchwife's naïveté save the drama from approaching pornography, however, and raise the play to the realm of art. Because of the deftness of the handling, the reader usually finds himself laughing, along with the characters, at the duplicity of the women and their lover.

The Story:

Mr. Horner, a gallant with a bad reputation for seduction pretended that he had been made impotent through disease and caused word of his misfortune to be spread throughout the town by his quack doctor. Immediately, men who had been afraid to let him meet their wives for fear of seduction hastened to assure him that he could come to their homes and escort their women anywhere.

Horner's old companions among the town gallants teased him unmercifully and at first the women would have nothing to do with him. Among his friends was Jack Pinchwife, who was vastly afraid of being made a cuckold. He had not even let it be known that he was married. His wife was a woman from the country; she, he thought, did not know enough about fashionable city life to think of taking a lover.

Pinchwife made the mistake, however, of escorting his wife to a play, where she was seen by Horner and some of his friends. When Pinchwife returned to his lodgings, his wife, tired of being kept locked in the house, asked her husband to let her go walking. A relative, a woman from the town, spoke for her as well. Pinchwife became angry with both: at his wife for wanting to go out and at his relative who had, he claimed, been corrupting her morals. Pinchwife foolishly told his wife what she was missing in town life—plays, dinners, parties, and dances—and so aroused her interest in all that he was attempting to keep from her for the sake of his own honor.

When a party of women came to take his wife to the latest play, Pinchwife refused to let her go or even to see the visitors. He gave out the excuse that she had smallpox. The excuse failed. At the same time Horner and some other gallants came to call.

The women were urged by their husbands to let Horner take them to the theater, but they, in disgust, refused, until Horner himself whispered to one of them that the rumor spread about his impotency was untrue. Mrs. Pinchwife was forgotten and left behind.

After some time Mrs. Pinchwife became melancholy because she wished to enjoy the gayety her husband told her about but refused to let her see. At last Pinchwife agreed to take her to a play if she would dress as a man. On the way to the play, accompanied by Pinchwife's sister Alithea, they met the sister's fiancé, a simpleton who let his friend, Harcourt, pay court to Alithea. She, realizing that her fiancé was a fool, tried to treat Harcourt coolly, even though her fiancé was angry with her for doing so.

Before they arrived at the theater they met Horner. Pinchwife, in spite of all he had heard about Horner's impotence, was worried lest Horner penetrate Mrs. Pinchwife's disguise. Horner, recognizing Mrs. Pinchwife, teased the jealous husband by kissing the young "gentleman" and telling "him" the kiss was for his sister, Mrs. Pinchwife. Horner, in addition, told the "young man" that he was in love with Mrs. Pinchwife.

The following morning Alithea was dressed to marry her fiancé. The bridegroom came with a parson, actually Harcourt in disguise. Harcourt was still determined to take Alithea for his own, if he could. After some discussion the marriage was put off for a day.

Meanwhile Pinchwife tried to force his wife to send a letter calculated to discourage Horner's attentions, but she substituted a love letter for the one her husband had dictated. After taking the letter, Pinchwife locked her in her room and told her to stay away from the window.

In his own rooms, Horner held a discussion with his quack doctor and told him how well his scheme to fool husbands was working. In proof, a well-bred woman came to his rooms, but the opportunity was lost when her husband followed her. A few moments later two other women arrived, much chagrined when they found Horner entertaining other visitors.

Pinchwife, knowing nothing of the substitution, delivered the letter. Upon his return home he found his wife writing another love letter to Horner. Angered, he drew his sword, but he was interrupted by the entrance of Alithea's fiancé.

Mrs. Pinchwife lied her way out of the situation by saying she was writing the letter for Alithea, who, she said, was in love with Horner. Pinchwife, knowing that Horner was of as good family and as wealthy as his sister's fiancé, thought that by marrying Alithea to Horner he could keep his wife away from the rake. When he agreed to take Alithea to Horner, his wife disguised herself in Alithea's clothing and presented herself as Alithea to be taken to Horner's lodgings.

Pinchwife unsuspectingly took his wife to Horner and left to get a clergyman to marry the couple. On the way he met his sister's fiancé, who was puzzled by Pinchwife's tale. When they met the real Alithea, all were confused.

Shortly after Pinchwife had gone, three women appeared at Horner's lodgings. During the visit all three discovered that Horner had enjoyed their favors, while they each thought he was hers alone. After they left, Horner got rid of Mrs. Pinchwife after some little trouble; she wanted to leave her husband and live with Horner.

Pinchwife, Alithea, Harcourt, and the fiancé all arrived to clear up the mystery of the disguised Alithea. The men accused Horner of double-dealing, and Pinchwife threatened the gallant with his sword. Mrs. Pinchwife, who had been loitering nearby, entered the room. To save the honor of all concerned, Alithea's maidservant took the blame for lying. The doctor came in unexpectedly and testified again to the impotency of Horner. His report put all husbands at their ease again. Only Mrs. Pinchwife, who had been unable to leave her husband or to have Horner's favors, was out of sorts.

THE COURTESAN

Type of work: Drama
Author: Pietro Aretino (1492-1556)
Type of plot: Satiric comedy
Time of plot: Early sixteenth century
Locale: Rome
First presented: 1534

Principal characters:
MESSER MACO, a would-be courtier
MAESTRO ANDREA, a clever charlatan
SIGNOR PARABOLANO, a nobleman
VALERIO, a gentleman, Parabolano's chamberlain
ROSSO, a rogue, Parabolano's groom
ALVIGIA, a procuress
ARCOLANO, a baker
TOGNA, his young wife

Critique:

Pietro Aretino's biting satire earned him the title "The Scourge of Princes." No one, no institution, in sixteenth-century Europe was immune to his barbs— not even the Papacy. In *The Courtesan* (*La Cortegiana*) he is settling an old score. Driven from the Papal court in fear of his life (upon which an attempt was actually made by the Papal favorite Giberti in 1525), Aretino long nursed a grudge against the headquarters of the Holy See. The knaves, fools, and lechers who constitute the *personae* of this drama are supposed to be typical of the courtiers who fawned upon the Medici Popes and of their own minions who in turn fawned upon them, duping them whenever they could. But in spite of his personal grievance, Aretino's satire here is not personal. He is ridiculing the kind of pretentiousness that exists in any age. This universality, plus the unabashed ribaldry of the action, makes *The Courtesan* a perennially entertaining piece.

The Story:

Messer Maco, a wealthy Sienese fop and a fool, came to Rome with the intention of becoming a cardinal. Upon his arrival he met Maestro Andrea who informed him that he would first have to be a courtier. Maco then announced his desire to become a courtier, and Andrea obligingly promised to transform him into one.

Signor Parabolano, learning that Maco was in town, ordered his groom, Rosso, to have all the lampreys he could find sent to Maco as a gift of welcome. When Parabolano left, Rosso made fun of his master's love affairs to the other servants. Valerio, Parabolano's faithful chamberlain, overheard him and ran him off. Rosso swindled a fisherman out of his lampreys by posing as a servant of the Pope. When discovered, he convinced the authorities that the fisherman was mad.

Maco received his first lesson in being a courtier. He was instructed in being, among other things, a blasphemer, a gambler, an adulator, a slanderer, an ingrate, a whore-chaser, an ass, and a nymph.

Next, Rosso visited Alvigia, a procuress. Rosso, having overheard Parabolano talking in his sleep, had thereby learned that his master was in love with the matron Livia. If, he told Alvigia, he could successfully pander to his master's lust, he would be secure in his favor and could also be revenged on Valerio, Parabolano's chamberlain. Alvigia agreed to help the groom.

Meanwhile, Maco had fallen in love with Camilla, a courtesan who was being kept by a Spanish lord. Andrea feared that this new interest would interrupt his fleecing of Maco, but Maco was now all the more determined to become a courtier. He was still impatient about Camilla, however, and disguised himself as a groom in order to gain access to her house. To hinder him, Andrea and Maco's own groom cried out that the sheriff was after him for illegal entry into Rome. Afraid to appear in his own clothes, Maco ran off, still in his disguise as a servant.

Rosso and Alvigia were having their problems, too. Although Parabolano had agreed to allow Rosso to secure the services of the procuress for him, Livia proved unapproachable. The two then devised the following plan: Rosso was to tell Parabolano that Livia was willing to meet him, but that, being proper and shy, she would do so only in the profoundest dark; he must promise not to embarrass her with any light whatsoever. Once assured that Parabolano would not be able to see his mistress, Alvigia would substitute the baker's young wife, Togna, for the virtuous Livia. Parabolano, his lust now almost consuming him, was willing to agree to any stipulations. He was willing, even, to believe the calumnies of his groom and put his chamberlain, Valerio, in disgrace.

Maco, hiding in Parabolano's house from the supposed sheriff, finally mustered enough courage to emerge for the final courtier-making process. He was placed in a vat which, according to Andrea, was a courtier-mold. There he was thoroughly steamed. Once recovered, he headed for Camilla's house as a full-fledged courtier. Andrea and Maco's groom pretended to be Spaniards storm-ing the house. Maco leaped from the window, terrified, and fled in his underwear.

His embarrassment was followed by Parabolano's. Togna had planned to steal away to her assignation in her husband's clothes. Suspicious of her design, the old baker feigned drunken sleep while he watched her put on his garments and steal away. He then dressed in her clothes and followed her to the house of the procuress.

Parabolano discovered the ruse, however, once he was alone with Togna. At first he was enraged, but Valerio, embittered and determined to leave Rome and the fickleness of courtiers, arrived in time to calm him down. Admitting that, blinded by lust, he had allowed himself to be led around like a fool, Parabolano restored Valerio to favor and begged his forgiveness. Valerio advised him to admit the whole escapade openly and to treat it as a joke so that, by owning up to his own folly, he would be safe from having his enemies use it against him.

As Parabolano was beginning to see the humor in the situation, the baker Arcolano added to it by appearing, dressed in his wife's clothes. He too was enraged, but Parabolano convinced him that he had no designs on his wife. The two, Togna and Arcolano, were forced to kiss and make up. Then, in keeping with the comic ending that Parabolano insisted upon, everyone was forgiven—even the conniving Rosso, after he had returned a diamond which Parabolano had given him to help seduce Livia. He was a Greek, Parabolano observed, and was only acting according to his nature.

Finally Maco appeared, seeking help from the "Spaniards." When their true identity was revealed, Maco was shown what a fool he really was. He, in turn, was forced to forgive Andrea.

THE COURTSHIP OF MILES STANDISH

Type of work: Poem
Author: Henry Wadsworth Longfellow (1807-1882)
Type of plot: Sentimental romance
Time of plot: 1621
Locale: Massachusetts
First published: 1858

Prinicpal characters:
MILES STANDISH, a soldier
JOHN ALDEN, Miles Standish's friend
PRISCILLA, a girl loved by Standish and Alden

Critique:

The ironic situation which results when Miles Standish sent John Alden to plead his lover's case before Priscilla is tempered by the genial, placid tone of this poem. Simply and gracefully written, it has long been a favorite among American romantic poems.

The Story:

In the Pilgrim colony Miles Standish and John Alden shared a cabin. The latter was a young scholar; the former was a gruff captain of the soldiers, whose wife had died after the landing of the Mayflower the previous fall.

One night Standish dropped his copy of *Caesar's Commentaries* and turned to John, who was writing a letter filled with praise for Priscilla, one of the young girls of the colony. Standish spoke of the loneliness and weariness of his own life, and of the fact that Priscilla, too, was living alone, her parents having died during the winter. Since he himself was no scholar but only a blunt soldier, he asked John to take to Priscilla his proposal of marriage.

Taken aback by the request, John could only stammer that it would be wiser for Standish to plead his own case. When the captain asked the favor in the name of friendship, the youth could not refuse.

Priscilla was singing the Hundredth Psalm as John approached her cabin, and as he opened the door he saw her industriously spinning. Filled with woe at what he must do, he nevertheless stepped resolutely inside. Seizing what

seemed the opportune moment, John blurted out the captain's proposal. Priscilla flatly refused, for she felt that Standish himself should have come if she were worth the wooing. And she further confused the young man by asking him why he did not speak for himself.

Caught between his own love for Priscilla and his respect for Standish, John decided to go back to England when the Mayflower sailed next day.

Miles Standish was enraged when he heard the outcome of John's wooing, but the captain's tirade was interrupted by news of Indians on the warpath. He strode into the colony's council room and there saw a snakeskin full of arrows, the challenge to battle. Pulling out the arrows, he filled the skin with bullets and powder, and defiantly handed it back to the Indian. The savage quickly disappeared into the forest. Captain Standish, his eight men and their Indian guide left the village next morning before anyone else was awake.

Alden did not sail that day. Among the people on the beach he saw Priscilla, who looked so dejected and appealing that he decided to stay and protect her They walked back to the village to gether, and John described the reaction of Miles Standish to Priscilla's question. He also confided that he had planned to leave the colony, but had remained in order to look after her.

Miles Standish, marching northward along the coast, brooded over his defeat, but finally concluded that he should confine himself to soldiering and forget wooing. When he returned to the village from his attack on the Indian camp, he brought with him the head of one of the savages and hung it on the roof of the fort. Priscilla was glad then that she had not accepted Miles Standish.

That autumn the village was at peace with the Indians. Captain Standish was out scouring the countryside. John Alden had built his own house, and often walked through the forest to see Priscilla. One afternoon he sat holding a skein of thread as she wound it. As they sat talking, a messenger burst in with the news that Miles Standish had been killed by a poisoned arrow and his men cut off in ambush.

At last John felt free to make his own declaration. He and Priscilla were married in the village church, before all the congregation. The magistrate had read the service and the elder had finished the blessing when an unexpected guest appeared at the door. It was Miles Standish—recovered from his wound—and he came striding in like a ghost from the grave.

Before everyone, the gruff soldier and the bridegroom made up their differences. Then, tenderly, Standish wished John and Priscilla joy, and merrily the wedding procession set off through the forest to Priscilla's new home.

COUSIN BETTE

Type of work: Novel
Author: Honoré de Balzac (1799-1850)
Type of plot: Social criticism
Time of plot: Early nineteenth century
Locale: Paris, France
First published: 1847-1848

Principal characters:
BARON HULOT
ADELINE, his wife
HORTENSE, their daughter
VICTORIN, their son
LISBETH, Adeline's Cousin Bette
M. CREVEL, Baron Hulot's enemy
CÉLESTINE, Victorin's wife and daughter of M. Crevel
COLONEL HULOT, the baron's older brother
MADAME MARNEFFE, Baron Hulot's mistress
M. MARNEFFE, Madame Marneffe's husband
COUNT STEINBOCK, Hortense's husband
BARON MONTÈS, Mme. Marneffe's lover

Critique:

The plot of this book is involved; many of the incidents seem contrived, like the death of the newly-wed Crevels and the rescue of Baron Hulot from the slums. Yet the forces at work upon the characters give the book a unity. The characters, more than anything else, make the story what it is. Balzac is a master at depicting human nature; he knows what motive force lies behind good and evil actions. Cousin Bette, the author's attempt to present a person consumed by hate, will remain in the reader's mind long after he has forgotten the rest of the book.

The Story:

One day in the summer of 1838, M. Crevel called upon Adeline, the Baroness Hulot, with an offer to make her his mistress, but she refused his offer. M. Crevel swore that he would be revenged upon Baron Hulot, who had stolen his former mistress. Her price had been the baron's fortune. Now he was unable to give his daughter Hortense a satisfactory dowry. Hortense was able to forget her sorrow over her own marriage prospects by teasing Lisbeth, Adeline's cousin, about her lover. Lisbeth—Cousin Bette—was the old maid of the family; her lover was Count Steinbock, a

sculptor and a Polish refugee. The attachment was that of mother and son, but Cousin Bette was insanely jealous.

That evening the baron's older brother, Colonel Hulot, and his son and daughter-in-law, Victorin and Célestine, came for dinner. Célestine, the daughter of M. Crevel, did not share her father's dislike of Baron Hulot. After dinner Baron Hulot escorted Cousin Bette home and then went to see his mistress. He found that she had deserted him for a rich duke.

The next morning Baron Hulot laid plans to seduce Madame Marneffe, the wife of a clerk who worked for him. In the meantime, Hortense had managed to speak to Count Steinbock by buying one of his pieces of sculpture. He called shortly afterward. The Hulots felt that the penniless young nobleman might be a good match for Hortense, but the plan was kept secret from Cousin Bette.

Baron Hulot arranged to meet Madame Marneffe in Cousin Bette's rooms. Later he moved the Marneffes into a more lavish establishment in the Rue Varennes, and Cousin Bette went there to live. Through her new friend, Cousin Bette learned of the coming marriage between Hortense and Count Steinbock,

718

for Baron Hulot had no secrets from Madame Marneffe. Cousin Bette had always been treated in the family as the eccentric old maid and the ugly duckling; this stealing of her lover was the final humiliation. She swore vengeance upon the whole Hulot family, and Madame Marneffe agreed to aid her.

As her first step, Cousin Bette introduced M. Crevel to Madame Marneffe. As her second step, she had Count Steinbock imprisoned for debt. Then she told Hortense that he had returned to Poland. When he obtained his release through some friends, the wedding plans went ahead. No one suspected that Cousin Bette had put him in prison. Meanwhile, Baron Hulot managed to raise a dowry for Hortense and planned to keep himself solvent by sending Adeline's uncle to Algiers. There Baron Hulot had arranged to steal money from the government through dealings with the Army commissary; the uncle was to be an innocent dupe.

As soon as Hortense was married, Baron Hulot moved Adeline to a more modest house so that he could spend more money upon Madame Marneffe. She and the baron conducted their affair quietly so as to attract little notice. At the same time she was also intimate with M. Crevel. M. Marneffe gave little trouble to either of these gentlemen as long as they kept him supplied with money and a good position at the war office.

The appearance one evening of Baron Montès, an old lover of Madame Marneffe, worried Baron Hulot and M. Crevel. That same night Madame Marneffe denied Baron Hulot access to her apartment. M. Crevel revealed to Baron Hulot how he also had been the lover of Madame Marneffe. Reconciled, the two old rivals went next day to Madame Marneffe's house. She agreed to consider M. Crevel's offer to marry her after her husband died, but she told Baron Hulot that he need not hope to be her lover again. After the two old men had left,

she asked Cousin Bette to try to get Count Steinbock to come to her. She had always wanted to make a conquest of him; his downfall would also be Cousin Bette's revenge upon Hortense.

Count Steinbock was in need of money, and Cousin Bette slyly suggested borrowing from Madame Marneffe. The count went to see her secretly. Madame Marneffe's conquest was complete.

When Madame Marneffe found herself pregnant, she told each lover separately that he was the father. Hortense believed that Count Steinbock was the father and deserted him to return to her mother. Baron Hulot found it necessary to visit Adeline in order to see Hortense and ask her to return to her husband. Hortense refused and made a violent scene. Cousin Bette arrived to take the side of Hortense. She said that she could no longer stay with Madame Marneffe; she would keep house for old Colonel Hulot. It was her plan to marry the old man and gain control of the only money left in the family.

The baron's affairs were growing desperate. Adeline's uncle in Algiers wrote that the plot to steal from the government was discovered; money was needed to stop an investigation. Madame Marneffe was insisting upon money for her child and a better position for her husband. One night M. Marneffe brought the police to the lovers' room and said that he would prosecute unless he were promoted at the war office. Madame Marneffe had led Baron Hulot into a trap; her husband got his appointment.

At last, the Algerian scandal broke and the uncle killed himself. When Colonel Hulot learned of his brother's deed, he was crushed by this blow to the family honor. He paid the necessary money from his own savings and died only a few days later from wounded pride. Cousin Bette had her revenge. Baron Hulot was a ruined man.

In disgrace, he sought shelter with the mistress who had deserted him for the duke. She provided him with some capital and a pretty seamstress to keep him company. He lived in the slums under an assumed name. Through the efforts of Victorin, now a successful lawyer, the family slowly regained its wealth. Meanwhile Madame Marneffe's child was stillborn, and her husband died. Victorin was determined to keep his father-in-law from throwing himself away on the wretched woman. He hired an underworld character to inform Baron Montès that Madame Marneffe was having an affair with Count Steinbock and was to marry M. Crevel. Baron Montès took his revenge upon Madame Marneffe and M. Crevel by infecting them with a fatal tropical disease; they both died soon after their marriage.

Adeline began to do charity work in the slums. On one of her visits she discovered her husband and brought him back to live with his family. Cousin Bette meanwhile had taken to her bed with consumption; she died soon after Baron Hulot's return.

Baron Hulot became the model husband. Then one day his wife hired Agathe, a peasant girl, as a cook. A few evenings later Adeline discovered her husband in the servants' quarters. Three days later Adeline died. Shortly after his wife's funeral Baron Hulot left Paris, and as soon as possible he and Agathe were married. This impropriety caused Victorin to remark that parents can hinder the marriages of their children; but children can do nothing about the actions of their parents in their second childhood.

COUSIN PONS

Type of work: Novel
Author: Honoré de Balzac (1799-1850)
Type of plot: Naturalism
Time of plot: The 1840's
Locale: Paris
First published: 1847

Principal characters:

SYLVAIN PONS, an elderly musician and amateur art collector
SCHMUCKE, Pons' friend and fellow-musician
MADAME CIBOT, portress at Pons' residence
MONSIEUR DE MARVILLE, Pons' cousin
MADAME DE MARVILLE, M. de Marville's wife and enemy of Pons
FRAISIER, a rascally attorney
REMONENCQ, a friend and accomplice of Mme. Cibot

Critique:

Cousin Pons, like other of Balzac's novels, is a study of Parisian society in the mid-nineteenth century. Like Balzac's other work, also, it is a study of human nature in that vein of naturalism more common to writers of a half-century and more later, writers like Zola, Dreiser, and Frank Norris. There are no terms with squeamishness for Balzac. Indeed, he makes the reader often feel as if there can be no such aggregation of people anywhere but between the covers of a book. The hatred of mankind for one another, the grubbing after unearned inheritances, and the inhumanity of man to man all stand out in the most glaring colors in Balzac's work. Balzac himself said that only in Paris could one find the characters that he needed for his fiction. The reader is inclined to hope that such a race of men, if it ever did exist, exists no more.

The Story:

Sylvain Pons was an ugly man who had no family at all except one cousin, Monsieur de Marville, a rich and influential government official. Through his relative, Cousin Pons, as the de Marvilles called him, was able to dine out at a rich man's home at least once a week. Those opportunities satisfied one of Pons' two pleasures in life, a delight in good food well served. Pons' job as conductor of the orchestra at a ballet theater and his series of private music pupils gave him the money to live and to satisfy his other delight in life, collecting works of art.

By the time he was in his sixties, Pons had built up a collection worth over a million francs, though neither he nor anyone else realized that it was so valuable. Pons' only friend was a musician in his orchestra, an old German named Schmucke. The two men lived together in an apartment filled with Pons' art treasures. Their lives were extremely simple; the portress at the house, Madame Cibot, cooked for them and cleaned the apartment, and their work kept them busy most of the time. The only flaw in their existence, as Schmucke saw it, was the fact that Pons went out to dinner once a week and sometimes twice.

Even that flaw was remedied when Madame de Marville, the wife of Pons' cousin, grew tired of having the old man in her home and made her attitude obvious to him. He then began taking all his meals at home with Schmucke. But Pons was too fond of dining out on rich food to be happy with the arrangement, and he missed the company that he had enjoyed for over forty years. So, with Schmucke's help, he determined to try to make peace with Madame de Marville by securing a rich husband for Cécile, the de Marvilles' daughter. The attempt ended in failure, and as a result their house and the homes of all the de Marvilles' friends were closed to Pons, who was regarded as

721

vicious and hateful.

The shock of finding that his cousin and all his cousin's connections would no longer speak to him, much less have him in their homes, was too much for Pons. He fell ill, and nothing the doctor could do helped him. His friend Schmucke tried to keep their small establishment going with the aid of Madame Cibot, who acted as a nurse while Schmucke worked at the theater or gave music lessons.

Unfortunately for the two old men, Madame Cibot learned that the art treasures lying about the apartment were extremely valuable. At first she thought only of having Pons set up an annuity for her at his death, in return for her nursing care, but her avarice finally caused her to conceive the idea of getting the entire fortune into her own hands. She took into her confidence a small dealer in bric-a-brac named Remonencq, who in turn enlisted the aid of Elie Magus, a Jew with a passion for art. The Jew, with the help of the other two, gained admittance to Pons' apartment and made an estimate of the collection's value. At the same time he made an agreement to pay Madame Cibot over forty thousand francs if she would get Schmucke, who knew nothing of art, to sell four of his friend's pictures for money to pay Pons' doctor bills.

Poor Schmucke, who thought only of saving his friend's life, readily agreed to sell four masterpieces, whose value he did not know, for a fraction of their true value. After they had been sold, thinking that Pons would never notice, he simply hung four other pictures in their places. Madame Cibot, delighted at her success in fleecing the old men, decided to try to get all of the collection and enlisted the aid of the doctor, who was a poor man, and a rascally attorney named Fraisier. Fraisier, who knew of Pons' influential relatives, pointed out to Madame Cibot that the relatives would fight any attempt by the portress to get the old man's estate. He also convinced her that they were powerful enough to send her to the guil-

lotine if they could prove her guilt. Feeling that her only chance of success lay with him, Madame Cibot agreed to do what the attorney told her to do.

The attorney went to Madame de Marville, who was also avaricious, and told her of Pons' wealth and Pons' determination to leave it to Schmucke. Madame de Marville immediately agreed to do anything she could to gain the fortune for herself, for all the family's wealth had gone into her daughter's dowry. She promised to have her husband get good appointments for Fraisier and the doctor, and she consented to set up an annuity for Madame Cibot. Her husband, when she told him, agreed.

Fraisier and Madame Cibot then began to lay plans to find a way into Pons' confidence. Unfortunately for their designs, Pons became suspicious of Madame Cibot. His suspicions were confirmed when he awoke one afternoon to find Elie Magus, his rival collector, examining the art objects on the walls and tables. Summoning what strength he had left, Pons left his sickbed and staggered to the other rooms, where he discovered that his paintings were gone. He realized immediately that someone had been attempting to fleece him at poor Schmucke's expense. That night, after Schmucke had confessed to selling the paintings, he and Schmucke discussed what they could do. Pons forgave Schmucke, for he well knew that the German had no idea of the cash values of the paintings or the more personal value they had for Pons himself.

Pons drew up a will naming Madame Cibot as one of his heirs, in an attempt to deceive her as to his real intentions. He even left the will where she would see it. The portress was pleased, although the will did not provide for as much as she wanted. Fraisier, who also saw the document, was pleased because it was a will that could easily be broken in court for the benefit of the de Marville family. Pons had hoped that they would react in that way, and the following day he secretly made a new will which left his fortune to the crown, with the stipulation that in return the government should give Schmucke a lifetime annuity.

When Pons died shortly afterward, his death left poor Schmucke in a dreadful state. The German musician knew little of the world, and his friend's death left him without judgment or willpower. All he cared about was dying quickly in order to meet his friend in heaven. Because of his state of mind, the plotters felt that they would have little trouble in taking the estate away from him.

The de Marvilles, bringing a suit to break the will, hoped that Schmucke, to avoid trouble, would accept a small annuity and let them have the bulk of the estate. They were right in their belief, but just as the papers were about to be signed a messenger brought Schmucke a copy of the charges made in court against the old man, charges that he had influenced his friend in an attempt to get the estate. The shock to Schmucke was so great that he died within a few days, allowing the estate to go unchallenged to the de Marvilles, who had denied their cousin and despised him during his last years.

Many people gained by the deaths of Pons and Schmucke. The de Marvilles recouped their fortune; Fraisier, the rascally attorney, received an office of trust for his part in the affair; the doctor who had tended Pons received a sinecure; Elie Magus, the Jew, had his coveted pictures, and Madame Cibot had her annuity. She also had a new husband, for Remonencq, her fellow conspirator, poisoned her husband and then married her. Everyone, except Schmucke, the man Pons had wanted most to help, had benefited from Pons' fortune.

THE COXCOMB

Type of work: Drama
Authors: Francis Beaumont (1585?-1616) and John Fletcher (1579-1625)
Type of plot: Romantic comedy
Time of plot: Early seventeenth century
Locale: England and France
First presented: 1608-1610

Principal characters:
ANTONIO, a foolish gentleman
MERCURY, his former traveling companion
RICARDO, a young gentleman, Viola's sweetheart
VALERIO, a country gentleman
MARIA, Antonio's wife
VIOLA, a young lady in distress

Critique:

This play is a rather trivial compound of Jacobean comic commonplaces; it is perhaps one of the least happy of the Beaumont and Fletcher collaborations. The main plot and the subplot explore different aspects of love, but they are so tenuously related that neither reinforces the other, and a virtual act of violence is required to bring them together at the end. Not only is the plotting slovenly, but also the characters are so imperfectly drawn as to be almost completely unbelievable. Antonio, the coxcomb, is so poorly developed that his cuckolding seems more of a shabby trick played upon him than a just punishment for his foolishness, and Mercury appears more the betrayer of a genuine, though ridiculous, friendship than one who takes legitimate advantage of a fool. In spite of the dramatists' attempt to pass Maria off as a woman of wit and sophistication, her actions are little more than sordid. The young lovers of the subplot fare little better. Ricardo is fairly successful as the contrite youth who has lost his sweetheart through his own weakness, but Viola forgives him in the end not so much because she loves him as to extricate herself from an impossible situation. The minor characters are drawn directly out of the Elizabethan comic tradition, and nothing more is done with them than the tradition demanded. Nevertheless, the play seems to have been successful in its own time, perhaps because skilled actors were able to carry off the comic situations with farcical effect.

The Story:

Although carefully guarded by her father, Viola, a beautiful maid of sixteen, met and fell in love with handsome young Ricardo. Deciding to elope, they agreed to meet on a convenient street corner after Viola had provided herself with gold and jewels from her father's house. They had just reached this decision when Mercury and Antonio, two travelers home from an extended journey, appeared on the scene. Mercury, thoroughly sick of Antonio, tried to take his leave as graciously as he could so that he could proceed to his own home. Antonio, however, held him with protests: two travelers who had endured so much together could not part so casually—Mercury must visit for a few days. Overwhelmed by Antonio's extravagant courtesy, Mercury reluctantly accompanied him. At Antonio's house they found Maria, his handsome wife, entertaining at a dance a group of fashionable young people whom Ricardo and Viola had just joined. Before she was made known to him, Mercury was captivated by Maria's beauty; when he spoke with her he was further inflamed by her grace and wit. As the guests left and he prepared to go to his rooms, Mercury tried to still an irresistible desire to cuckold his ridiculous friend.

It now lacked only an hour until Ricardo's meeting with Viola. To pass the time, the young gallant went with a party of his friends to a nearby tavern, where one toast led to another so quickly that Ricardo became thoroughly intoxicated. About the time Viola fearfully left her father's house, throwing the key back through the window as a final gesture of farewell, Ricardo began to talk of seeking out wenches and perhaps beating up the watch as a culmination to the evening's sport. Leaving the tavern, Ricardo and his party reeled along the street; when they passed Viola, her lover in his blind drunkenness thought her to be a strumpet and attempted to throw her down in the gutter. Viola barely escaped as the watch came to take the revelers in tow.

Meanwhile, Mercury realized that the only way for him to overcome his desire for Maria was to separate himself from her. When he tried to leave secretly, Antonio discovered him and would not hear of his going. Pressed to desperation, Mercury revealed the truth, thinking that reason would cause Antonio to encourage him to leave. But to Antonio a wife was nothing in comparison with a friend; if Mercury wanted his wife, Antonio would woo her for him and thus gain immortality as the truest friend in history. Dumbfounded, Mercury got rid of his host only on the condition that he would seduce Maria with Antonio's approval.

Shocked, frightened, and too ashamed to return home, Viola by this time had fled to the outskirts of the city. There she fell in with a rude tinker and his trull, who robbed her and left her tied to a tree. She was discovered by Valerio, a country gentleman, who released her and agreed to help her by giving her a position as a maid. As they rode off together, he began to alter the terms of his proposal; she was not to be a maid after all, but his mistress. When Viola indignantly declined, Valerio left her and rode on.

It was now morning. In the city Ricardo, awaking, remembered the events of the night before and was overwhelmed with remorse for his actions. With the encouragement of Viola's father, he enlisted his friends to help him find her again.

Antonio, meanwhile, had attempted to further Mercury's suit by writing a letter reviling himself, signing Mercury's name, and delivering it to Maria in the disguise of an Irish footman. Maria, penetrating the disguise, decided to answer trick with trick. She had Antonio beaten and locked up; then she visited Mercury. To him she reported that Antonio was missing and doubtless murdered, and, pretending great grief, she requested that he take her to some place of retirement. Mercury suggested his mother's house in the country and the two departed, Maria still vowing secretly that she would be revenged on her husband for his foolishness. Learning that they had left the city, Antonio revealed himself to the servants who had kept him prisoner and declared that he would leave the two uninterrupted for a time so that Mercury could win his suit.

Having been abandoned by Valerio, Viola had fallen in with two sympathetic milkmaids employed by Mercury's mother; they took her to their mistress to seek work as a domestic servant. That honest but acerbic woman took Viola into the household, but her position grew more and more uncertain as she revealed her ineptitude for domestic tasks. Attention was diverted from her, however, by the arrival of Mercury and Maria. While Mercury told his mother of his travels, Maria retired to her chamber. There Antonio soon appeared, this time transparently disguised as a post-rider. Had he commanded his wife to return home, she would have done so; instead, he presented her with another ridiculously awkward letter in which he again advised her to favor Mercury. Maria, feeling that if he insisted on being such an utter ass she had little choice but to do as he wished, sent him to bring Mercury to her.

Ricardo's search had by this time led him to Valerio, who, after hearing the unhappy lover's story, allowed himself to be persuaded to help look for Viola. As the two rode through the countryside near the place where Valerio had left the maiden, they came upon her as she was going out to milk. When Ricardo abjectly threw himself upon his knees, confessed his faults, and begged forgiveness, Viola, who still loved him, yielded to his pleas. Meanwhile, Antonio's cousin, believing his kinsman murdered and Maria and Mercury probably guilty because of what seemed their precipitate flight from the city, arrived at the house of Mercury's mother with a warrant and a justice of the peace. As Mercury and Maria were about to be arrested, Antonio revealed himself, rather to the discomfiture of the justice, who had eagerly anticipated a hanging. Maria and Mercury, whose ardor for each other had cooled after their night together, pretended great joy at seeing Antonio alive. All celebrated at a banquet which Ricardo and Viola also attended.

THE CRADLE SONG

Type of work: Drama
Author: Gregorio Martínez Sierra (1881-1947)
Type of plot: Tragi-comedy
Time of plot: Early twentieth century
Locale: Spain
First presented: 1911

Principal characters:

SISTER JOANNA OF THE CROSS, eighteen years of age
TERESA, aged eighteen
THE PRIORESS, aged forty
THE VICARESS, aged forty
THE MISTRESS OF NOVICES, aged thirty-six
SISTER MARCELLA, aged nineteen
SISTER MARÍA JESÚS, aged nineteen
SISTER SAGRARIO, aged eighteen
SISTER INEZ, aged fifty
SISTER TORNERA, aged thirty
THE DOCTOR, aged sixty
ANTONIO, aged twenty-five

Critique:

G. Martínez Sierra served an apprenticeship in the theater as an actor under Jacinto Benavente, a prominent Spanish playwright, ten years before he wrote any plays of his own. Though not his first written play, *The Cradle Song, Canción de Cuna* in the original, was his first definite success in Madrid in 1911, in New York in 1921, in London in 1926, and again in New York in 1927, when Eva Le Gallienne brought it to her Civic Repertory Theater. Since that time it has been considered a success wherever it has been presented. Martínez Sierra's wife, usually his collaborator, had more than her usual interest in this play because it was reminiscent of her home town, where her father was the convent doctor and where his sister, Sister Joanna of the Cross in the play, became a nun. The two acts of the play are divided by a poem covering a lapse of eighteen years. This is a play of laughter and tears, in which the stifling of the mother instinct is the theme before which the characters pale.

The Story:

When the Prioress, the Mistress of Novices, the Vicaress and the other nuns begged her, Sister Joanna of the Cross consented to read the poem she had composed in celebration of the birthday of the Prioress. The Vicaress was sure that praise for the poem would lead to pride, a sin, but Sister Joanna of the Cross disclaimed all but a small part of the birthday present. She had composed the lines, it was true, but Sister María Jesús had copied the verses, Sister Sagrario painted the border, Sister Marcella tied the ribbons, and the Mistress of Novices made the gift possible by giving them the parchment and the ribbon.

The mayor's wife sent the Prioress a canary in a cage. The bird so delighted the novices that they begged permission to talk among themselves until time for prayers. The doctor interrupted them on his daily round. He looked at a felon Sister Sagrario had on her finger, and turned to prescribe for Sister María Jesús, who was melancholy. He asked her age and, when she said eighteen, he asked to see her face. It was a pretty one and he commented that the Lord had not bad taste. But, for a prescription? One of two things for a girl of that age: the Prioress could write the child's mother to take her home and provide a good husband, or Sister María Jesús would have to take cold baths every morning and say five Pater Nosters with each.

While the doctor and the Prioress went to see a bedridden sister, the novices stayed to guard the front grille. As they were talking, a bell rang by the grille, and a basket was placed on the revolving box by which gifts were brought into the cloister. The novices could not resist looking in the basket. Sister Marcella's cry when she saw a baby lying there brought all the other nuns back to determine the trouble. The Prioress read a letter, which had come in the basket, asking that the nuns bring up the baby because her mother could not keep her properly. The Vicaress was horrified that the sisters would even consider keeping the little girl. The doctor, remarking that legally the nuns had no right to maternity, proposed that he adopt the baby and leave her to be brought up in the convent. There were still other problems to be faced—the matters of feeding and clothing and tending the child—but Sister Joanna of the Cross had an answer for each. The gardener's wife, who had a baby of her own at the time, could help on all counts. The Prioress, thinking that the baby was the best of all birthday presents, appointed Sister Joanna of the Cross the child's guardian.

In the eighteen years that passed, the nuns spent all their pent-up love on the girl Teresa. She was a gay child, loving the gardens of the cloister and the adoring sisters; but it was easy to see that she would not spend her life as a hermit, though she was utterly devout. In time she met a man, Antonio, whom she promised to marry.

The nuns made for her an elaborate trousseau, hand-embroidered and trimmed with lace and blue ribbons. While they worked on fancy chemises, petticoats, and dressing jackets, one of their number would read aloud meditations of various sorts. As they tried to meditate, they were interrupted continually by Teresa's happy singing in the garden where she was picking flowers for the altar.

Sister Marcella had temptations to melancholy which the Prioress offered to alleviate by sending her out in the garden for a little sunshine, but Sister Marcella said that the flowers, the blue sky, and the sun tempted her to deeper melancholy. The other nuns sighed in accord. The Vicaress, on a round of inspection, had found a mirror hidden under Sister Marcella's mattress. Mirrors being definitely forbidden to the nuns, Sister Marcella was under deep suspicion of the sins of pride and vainglory. In confusion, she explained that when her melancholy became too deep, she used the mirror to catch a sunbeam and make it dance among the leaves, while pretending it was a bird or a butterfly that could go wherever it pleased. When Teresa came in to tell how she had had to climb the acacia trees to get enough white flowers for the altar, Sister Marcella's eyes grew wide with envy.

Teresa was bubbling over when she came to gather up her things before leaving the cloister for good. The nuns counseled a more subdued manner for the occasion. But Teresa could not be restrained, though she was grateful for all the love and care they had given her who would otherwise have been an outcast and a beggar. The nuns wanted no thanks; the convent had been her home as well as theirs, even if she could not feel the desire to join them by entering their order.

While they gathered together the pieces of the trousseau to put into Teresa's trunk, the Vicaress grumbled about the Devil's hand on the fashion sheets the sisters had used as patterns; but even she relented enough to tell Teresa that she deserved all the nuns had done for her because she had always worked for them inside the convent and out. Then the Vicaress gave Teresa an itemized account of the money the doctor, as foster father, had given for the materials in her trousseau.

When the packing was finished, Teresa and Sister Joanna of the Cross were left together to await the coming of Antonio, the groom-to-be, and the doctor, who was to drive Teresa to the train. Teresa admitted that she had always considered Sister Joanna of the Cross her own mother, and asked her blessing. Sister Joanna of the Cross admitted that Teresa had been her whole happiness all the years they had been together, that Teresa's coming into the cloister had dissipated the melancholy which had followed her own separation from the family she loved.

When Antonio came to the curtained grille, he assured Sister Joanna of the Cross that he would take care of Teresa because he loved her dearly, but that he knew she would never forget the peace and calm of the convent. As the sister went for the others to meet Antonio, he told Teresa that he had found honor, self-respect, and sympathy for his fellowman in loving her.

Hating to see Teresa go, the nuns tried to give Antonio instructions in her care. The Vicaress asked for and received his pledge that he would always respect the fear of God that Teresa would carry out of the cloister with her.

Antonio told them that he was taking Teresa to America. He begged the favor of being allowed to see the sisters before he left, and the Prioress allowed the curtains to be drawn.

Then the doctor came for Teresa and hurried her through her leave-taking. She begged him never to forsake the sisters and, with a final passionate embrace of Sister Joanna of the Cross, left the cloister with him.

CRANFORD

Type of work: Novel
Author: Mrs. Elizabeth Gaskell (1810-1865)
Type of plot: Comedy of manners
Time of plot: Early nineteenth century
Locale: England
First published: 1853

Principal characters:
MARY SMITH, the narrator
MISS DEBORAH JENKYNS, a genteel spinster
MISS MATILDA JENKYNS (MATTY), her sister
PETER JENKYNS, their long-lost brother
MRS. JAMIESON, leader of society
LADY GLENMIRE, Mrs. Jamieson's sister-in-law
MARTHA, Miss Matilda's faithful servant

Critique:

For a whimsical and kind, yet humorous account of the habits and customs of genteel spinsters of nineteenth-century England, *Cranford* is unsurpassed. Only a very warm and gentle woman could have portrayed the little peculiarities of her sex with affection and sly humor, as did Mrs. Gaskell. There is something of Charles Lamb in her finely drawn characters, her humorous accounts of even the most trivial events. The writer shows great understanding and sympathy for the everyday problems of poor but genteel ladies. All in all, *Cranford* is a book to please even the most sober realist.

The Story:

Cranford was a small English village inhabited mostly by ladies. Few gentlemen took up residence there, and most of those who did seemed to disappear on various and mysterious errands. The doctor, the shopkeepers, and a few male servants were all of their sex who crossed the ladies' vision with any regularity.

Most of the ladies lived in "elegant economy," and the spending of money was considered vulgar and showy. There was no mention of anyone's being poor unless in privacy with one's dearest friend. Thus when semi-retired Captain Brown moved to Cranford and talked openly about being poor, it was quite an affront to the ladies. But the captain was so kind and considerate to everyone, whether more

or less fortunate than he, that the ladies could not long resent his vulgar behavior and talk. He had two daughters. The elder, dying of an incurable illness, had a tongue sharpened by pain, but the kind women joined her younger sister in trying to make her last days pleasant and comfortable. Many a cup of tea and small delicacy found their way from the ladies' already poor stores to the suffering girl.

Their sorrow was great when the kind captain was killed while rescuing a small child from in front of a train. When his elder daughter soon followed him, all of the ladies were hard pressed to make suitable arrangements for the younger daughter, left alone. One day a former suitor appeared and took her for his wife. The village ladies rested happily in the knowledge that Captain Brown would be pleased with his daughter's security.

Until her death Miss Deborah Jenkyns was one of the more dominant spinsters in the town. She made all decisions for her younger sister, Miss Matilda, age fifty-five. Miss Matilda, affectionately called Miss Matty by all but her sister, knew that Deborah had the better mind and did not resent her sister's dominance. After Miss Deborah's death Miss Matty had almost to learn again how to live. Her particular friends were Miss Pole, Mrs. Forrester, and Mrs. Jamieson, who became the social leader of Cranford after Miss Deborah's death. Miss Mary Smith often visited Miss Matty and brought her the good advice of Mr. Smith, Mary's father and Miss Matty's financial adviser. Mary was surprised to learn that Miss Matty had long ago had a suitor whom she rejected in order to stay with her mother. Not long after Miss Deborah's death that gentleman returned to Cranford for a visit. Mary was disappointed that he did not renew his courtship of Miss Matty. Miss Matty grieved too, in secret, for she would never have admitted openly such vulgar sentiments.

Mary learned also that Miss Deborah and Miss Matty had once had a brother who had disappeared many years before, after being severely punished by their father for playing a practical joke on Miss Deborah. Peter Jenkyns was believed dead, although Miss Matty had heard rumors that he was living in India.

The genteel ladies were suddenly thrown into a flurry of excitement when they heard that Mrs. Jamieson's sister-in-law, Lady Glenmire, was to settle in Cranford. They spent long hours discussing how they should address her, for she was the first noblewoman they had encountered. Their worries were in vain, however, for Mrs. Jamieson subtly but firmly informed them that they would not be included in her guest list. At first the ladies were greatly hurt. Later Mrs. Jamieson was forced to relent and invite them to call, for most of the county gentility were away or otherwise occupied. Miss Matty, Miss Pole, and Mrs. Forrester first thought they would be engaged elsewhere for the fateful night, but their innate kindness, or perhaps their curiosity, prevailed, and they accepted the invitation. They found Lady Glenmire delightful and no more refined nor genteel than they themselves—a fact they, if not Mrs. Jamieson, considered not surprising.

Mrs. Jamieson departed Cranford for a time, leaving Lady Glenmire in charge of her home. And in that genteel lady's absence Lady Glenmire became engaged to the doctor of the town, a man not even recognized by the ladies except when his services were needed for bleeding. Thus, he was no higher socially than a shopkeeper. Even more exciting was the fact that the ladies at last knew someone who was to be married. They awaited Mrs. Jamieson's return with fear and anticipation. They were not disappointed. Mrs. Jamieson, deciding to cut Lady Glenmire, stated that she had always known her to be of low taste.

The engaged couple were married before Mrs. Jamieson returned. By that time a great tragedy had befallen Miss Matty. The bank in which her estate was deposited had to close its doors, and she was left with but thirteen pounds a year. She made no complaint; her biggest worry was whether Mrs. Jamieson would allow the ladies to continue their friendship with her. Mary Smith sent for her father to see what he could plan for Miss Matty. Miss Pole, Mrs. Forrester, and another friend, careful that she should not know of their gift, gave up some of their own small incomes so that they could help their friend. Mary and Mr. Smith persuaded Miss Matty to sell tea, but it took a good deal of convincing to assure her that this would be a genteel way for a lady to supplement her income. Miss Matty's faithful maid, Martha, forced her young man to marry her sooner than he had anticipated so that they could rent Miss Matty's house and have her for a lodger. In that way Martha could continue to look after her old mistress without injuring Miss Matty's pride. Everyone was happy when Mrs. Jamieson returned and said that the ladies could continue to call on Miss Matty because her father had been a rector and his daughter, who had never married, was entitled to the position he had left her.

More good fortune followed. Mary Smith wrote to Miss Matty's brother in India. When he received the letter, Peter Jenkyns sold his property and returned to Cranford to keep his sister in comfort and in some prosperity. Peter also brought about a reconciliation between Mrs. Jamie-

731

son and Lady Glenmire, who now called
herself a vulgar Mrs. instead of Lady.

Once more there was peace in Cranford.

THE CREAM OF THE JEST

Type of work: Novel
Author: James Branch Cabell (1879-1958)
Type of plot: Satiric fantasy
Time of plot: Twentieth century
Locale: Virginia
First published: 1917

Principal characters:

FELIX KENNASTON, an author
KATHLEEN KENNASTON, his wife
RICHARD HARROWBY, his neighbor
ETTARRE, a woman in his novel and his dreams

Critique:

The Cream of the Jest is fiction compounded of philosophic speculation, a fragile plot, and much literary allusion, often somewhat obscure. The novel is typical of that period of Cabell's career when his books maintained a skeptical tone and presented over and over again the values of chivalric love. The story represents Cabell's effort to escape the realities of naturalism through the speculations of romanticism.

The Story:

Felix Kennaston told his neighbor, Richard Harrowby, about his dreams. In writing his novels, Kennaston had created a world much different from the ordinary world of the Virginia countryside, and his dreams contained similar elements of the romantic and the marvelous. To Harrowby the whole thing seemed indecent, for Harrowby was a conventional, unimaginative gentleman farmer, who had made his money in soaps and beauty aids.

Kennaston was writing a novel called *The Audit at Storisende,* and in his dreams he identified himself with a character named Horvendile, who was looking for the elusive and highly improbable creature, the ideal woman. In Ettarre, his heroine, Kennaston felt he had found her. Much of his plot centered about a broken round medallion bearing mysterious symbols, a medallion he called the sigil of Scoteia.

One afternoon Kennaston, walking in his garden, stooped to pick up a little piece of shining metal, apparently a broken half of a small disc, and casually dropped it into his pocket. Later, while looking over some books in his library, he thought of the little piece of metal in his pocket. He brought it out and laid it where the light of the lamp fell upon it. At once he seemed to be talking with Ettarre, who explained that he had picked up half the broken sigil of Scoteia and that it had brought him back to her imagined world of romance and dream. As he reached out to touch her, she disappeared, and Kennaston found himself sitting again in his library.

Kennaston's novel was published as *The Men Who Loved Alison,* a title which his publisher assured him would bring better sales. When several readers, shocked by what they called indecency in the novel, wrote indignant letters to the newspapers, the book became a best seller. Mrs. Kennaston, who made it a point never to read her husband's books, enjoyed his success. She treated Kennaston with polite boredom.

Strange things happened to Kennaston. One day at a luncheon a famous man took him aside and asked him whether he bred white pigeons. This question puzzled Kennaston, as did the little mirror the man held in his hand. At another time he saw an ugly old woman who told him that there was no price of admission to her world but that one paid on leaving. Several times he talked to Ettarre in his dreams.

One day Kennaston received an invitation to call on a prelate who had come to Linchfield to attend the bishop's funeral. The prelate praised Kennaston's book. He spoke of pigeons, too, and mentioned how useful he found his little mirror. Kennaston was frankly puzzled. He returned to his dreamland, where, as Horvendile, he experienced almost every passion and emotion known to man. And always, as he reached out to touch Ettarre, the dream would come to an end.

Kennaston read widely in philosophy and the classics, and he began to question the reason for his own existence. He came to the conclusion that the present moment was all that was real—that the past and future had no part in the reality of today. As a man of letters, he became interested in the artistry of creation and decided that God must have been happy over his creation of the character of Christ. Probably because of his interest in God as an artist, Kennaston was confirmed in the country church nearby. This act on his part increased his stature among the people of the neighborhood. They even elected him to the vestry.

One day Kennaston went to the station to meet his wife's train. While he was waiting, a woman with whom he had once been in love came up to him and started to talk. She was about to go back to her home in St. Louis. They recalled the past and, as she left him to get on her train, he had a moment in which he identified her with Ettarre.

But his remark to his wife about her was that she was not keeping her good looks as she grew older. What haunted him, however, was that the woman had drawn from her purse a medallion resembling the sigil of Scoteia.

Kennaston—as Horvendile—dreamed of being in many parts of the world in many eras; and one of the mysteries was that he was always a young man of about twenty-five. He was at Queen Elizabeth's court; he was at Whitehall with Cromwell; he was at the French court of Louis Quartorze; he was among the aristocrats about to be beheaded during the French Revolution. And always beside him was Ettarre, whose contact would bring his dreams to an end.

One afternoon he found, quite by accident, the missing piece of the sigil of Scoteia in his wife's bathroom. After securing the other piece, he put them together on his wife's dressing table and began speculating about the relation of his wife to Ettarre. He hoped that her discovery of the entire sigil would express to her what he had never been able to convey. But she paid no attention to it and their life continued its banal rounds. Eleven months later Mrs. Kennaston died in her sleep without ever having discussed the sigil or its significance with her husband. After her death he showed Harrowby the two halves of the sigil, by which he had almost made his dreams come true. Far from being a magic emblem, the pieces proved to be merely the broken top of a cold cream jar. It was the final disillusionment for Kennaston, compelled at last to give up romantic youthful dreaming for the realities of middle age.

CRIME AND PUNISHMENT

Type of work: Novel
Author: Fyodor Mikhailovich Dostoevski (1821-1881)
Type of plot: Psychological realism
Time of plot: Mid-nineteenth century
Locale: Russia
First published: 1866

Principal characters:
RASKOLNIKOV, a Russian student
DOUNIA, his sister
SONIA, a prostitute
PORFIRY, inspector of police
RAZUMIHIN, Raskolnikov's ·friend

Critique:

The theme of this novel is that man pays by suffering for his crimes against men. Dostoevski's Raskolnikov is a tremendous study of a sensitive intellectual driven by poverty to believe that he was exempt from moral law. Other features of *Crime and Punishment* are the use of psychology in police investigation, the author's sympathy for the downtrodden as expressed in the person of Sonia, a young prostitute, and realistic descriptions of slum life in a large Russian city of the nineteenth century.

The Story:

Rodion Raskolnikov, an impoverished student in St. Petersburg, dreamed of committing the perfect crime. With an ax he murdered an old widowed pawnbroker and her stepsister, and stole some jewelry from their flat.

Back in his room, Raskolnikov received a summons from the police. Weak from hunger and illness, he prepared to make a full confession. But the police had called merely to ask him to pay a debt his landlady had reported to them. When he discovered what they wanted, he collapsed from relief. Upon being revived, he was questioned; his answers provoked suspicion.

Raskolnikov hid the jewelry under a rock in a courtyard. He returned to his room, where he remained for four days in a high fever. When he recovered, he learned that the authorities had visited him while he was delirious and that he had said things during his fever which tended to cast further suspicion on him.

Luzhin, betrothed to Raskolnikov's sister Dounia, came to St. Petersburg from the provinces to prepare for the wedding. Raskolnikov resented Luzhin because he knew his sister was marrying to provide money for her destitute brother. Luzhin visited the convalescent and left in a rage when the young man made no attempt to hide his dislike for him.

A sudden calm came upon the young murderer; he went out and read the accounts of the murders in the papers. While he was reading, a detective joined him. The student, in a high pitch of excitement caused by his crime and by his sickness, talked too much, revealing to the detective that he might well be the murderer. However, no evidence could be found that would throw direct suspicion on him.

Later, witnessing a suicide attempt in the slums of St. Petersburg, Raskolnikov decided to turn himself over to the police; but he was deterred when his friend, an ex-clerk named Marmeladov, was struck by a carriage and killed. Raskolnikov gave the widow a small amount of money he had received from his mother. Later he attended a party given by some of his friends and discovered that they, too, suspected him of complicity in the murder of the two women.

Back in his room. Raskolnikov found

his mother and his sister, who were awaiting his return. Unnerved at their appearance and not wanting them to be near him, he placed them in the care of his friend, Razumihin, who, upon meeting Dounia, was immediately attracted to her.

In an interview with Porfiry, the chief of the murder investigation, Raskolnikov was mentally tortured by questions and ironic statements until he was ready to believe that he had been all but apprehended for the double crime. Partly in his own defense, he expounded his theory that any means justified the ends of a man of genius, and that sometimes he believed himself a man of genius.

Raskolnikov proved to his mother and Dounia that Luzhin was a pompous fool, and the angry suitor was dismissed. Razumihin had by that time replaced Luzhin in the girl's affections.

Meanwhile Svidrigailov, who had caused Dounia great suffering while she had been in his employ as a governess, arrived in St. Petersburg. His wife had died and he had followed Dounia, as he explained, to atone for his sins against her by settling upon her a large amount of money.

Razumihin received money from a rich uncle and went into the publishing business with Dounia. They asked Raskolnikov to join them in the venture, but the student, whose mind and heart were full of turmoil, declined; he said goodbye to his friend and to his mother and sister and asked them not to try to see him again.

He went to Sonia, the prostitute daughter of the dead Marmeladov. They read Sonia's Bible together, Raskolnikov deeply impressed by the wretched girl's faith. He felt a great sympathy for Sonia and promised to tell her who had committed the murders of the old pawnbroker and stepsister. Svidrigailov, who rented the room next to Sonia's, overheard the conversation; he anticipated Raskolnikov's disclosure with interest.

Tortured in his own mind, Raskolnikov went to the police station, where Porfiry played another game of cat-and-mouse with him. His conscience and his imagined insecurity had resulted in immense suffering and torment of mind for Raskolnikov.

At a banquet given by Marmeladov's widow for the friends of her late husband, Luzhin accused Sonia of stealing money from his room. He had observed Raskolnikov's interest in Sonia and he wished to hurt the student for having spoken against him to Dounia. The girl was saved by the report of a neighbor who had seen Luzhin slipping money into Sonia's pocket. Later, in Sonia's room, Raskolnikov confessed his crime and admitted that in killing the two women he had actually destroyed himself.

Svidrigailov, having overheard the confession, disclosed his knowledge to Raskolnikov. Believing that Porfiry suspected him of the murder and realizing that Svidrigailov knew the truth, Raskolnikov found life unbearable. Then Porfiry told Raskolnikov outright that he was the murderer, at the same time promising Raskolnikov that a plea of temporary insanity would be placed in his behalf and his sentence would be mitigated if he confessed. Raskolnikov delayed his confession.

Svidrigailov, having informed Dounia of the truth concerning her brother, offered to save the student if Dounia would consent to be his wife. He made this offer to her in his room, which he had locked after tricking her into the meeting. He released her when she attempted unsuccessfully to shoot him with a pistol she had brought with her. Convinced at last that Dounia would have none of him, Svidrigailov gave her a large sum of money and ended his life with a pistol.

Raskolnikov, after being reassured by his mother and his sister of their love for him, and by Sonia of her undying devotion, turned himself over to the police. He was tried and sentenced to serve eight years in Siberia. Dounia and Razumihin, now successful publishers, were married. Sonia followed Raskolnikov to Siberia, where she stayed in a village near the prison camp. In her goodness to Raskolnikov and to the other prisoners, she came to be known as Little Mother Sonia. With her help, Raskolnikov began his regeneration.

THE CRIME OF SYLVESTRE BONNARD

Type of work: Novel
Author: Anatole France (Jacques Anatole Thibault, 1844-1924)
Type of plot: Domestic romance
Time of plot: Nineteenth century
Locale: France
First published: 1881

Principal characters:
SYLVESTRE BONNARD, a bibliophile
JEANNE, his ward
MME. COCCOZ, later the Princess Trépof, his benefactress
MLLE. PRÉFÈRE, a schoolteacher
HENRI GÉLIS, a student

Critique:

This gentle novel is the best known of France's work, and in many ways the most typical. In it we find the characteristic style—precise, elegant, gently ironic, and learnedly humorous. The old bibliophile becomes a real friend of the reader and Jeanne is a charming foil. The plot is tenuous. The chief pleasure in reading the book derives from the author's droll comments, the asides, the quips, and the keen observations. Parts of the novel have been widely quoted, especially France's remark that children learn only when they truly enjoy themselves.

The Story:

Bonnard was a retiring philologist, a Member of the Institute, and a bachelor. Thérèse, his maid, looked after him firmly; she was the real mistress of his domestic arrangements. Bonnard, his mind stuffed with antiquarian lore about the old abbeys of Paris, lived mostly in the past.

One day a sickly bookseller called and unsuccessfully showed him some cheap editions. Although he bought no books, Bonnard was moved by the thin, intense man. When he inquired of Thérèse she told him that the bookseller, M. Coccoz, lived up in the attic under a leaky roof with seldom even a fire, and his wife had just had a baby. Moved to pity, Bonnard sent up some logs for the indigent couple to burn.

Shortly afterward he heard that the husband had died. Thérèse sniffed virtuously at the gay widow who had far too many admirers. Bonnard saw the beautiful Mme. Coccoz only once on the stairs. She showed him her healthy baby and remarked on his kindness in sending firewood.

Ten years later Bonnard read in a catalogue of a manuscript of the *Golden Legend,* a work he wished very much to own. Finally he tracked it down, discovering that it was owned by one Signor Polizzi, who lived in Sicily. The Italian refused to lend the manuscript, but he invited Bonnard to come to Sicily to read it at his leisure. Although it was a long, hard trip for a shy man of letters, Bonnard set out for Sicily.

On the island he met Prince Trépof, a Russian, and his beautiful wife whom Bonnard never associated with the young widow he had met once on the stairs years before. They were rich travelers who had nothing to do but to look for match boxes for the prince's collection. The princess gently decried her nomadic existence, but she adored her husband.

Signor Polizzi's house was difficult to reach. Bonnard had to make the last part of the trip by mule litter. When he at last arrived, he found that Polizzi, a slippery jack-of-all-trades, had given the *Golden Legend* to his son, who had opened a shop in Paris. While Bonnard was making the long trip to Sicily, the manuscript had all the time been in a bookshop not far from his apartment. Furious at the unkindness done him,

Bonnard poured out his bitter story to the sympathetic princess.

Back in Paris, Bonnard went to the son's shop; there was the manuscript. The son refused to quote a price on it because he was putting it up at auction. When the sale took place, Bonnard hopefully bid up to six thousand francs, but some one always outbid him. To his consternation he found that it was Polizzi who had successfully bid on the manuscript. The dealer was acting as agent for a client who had instructed him to buy back the manuscript at any cost.

Back in his apartment, while Bonnard was gloomily thinking of his troubles, a young boy was shown in. The youngster gave him a package from his mother and disappeared, but not before Thérèse had seen the carriage. The package contained a make-believe log. Inside was a card from the Princess Trépof and a profusion of violets. Under the flowers Bonnard found the manuscript. Just then Thérèse lumbered in to ask what Mme. Coccoz was doing in such a rich carriage and why she had stopped at their door.

M. de Gabry invited Bonnard to come to his country estate to catalogue the library he had inherited. Bonnard found the estate in run-down condition, but the library was extensive. He happily settled down to his long task.

In front of him on the desk was a tiny fairy who scolded him for his dry preoccupations and threw ink at him. Bonnard awoke with a start and found that a sudden wind had upset his ink bottle. Mme. de Gabry listened to the story of his dream with much interest. A few days later Bonnard came back from a walk to find his dream fairy perched on a console in the hall. As he stared in astonishment, Mme. de Gabry came up to introduce Jeanne Alexandre.

Jeanne was a shy girl with red hands. After Mme. de Gabry had described the fairy to her, she made a like statuette to surprise Bonnard. The old man was much pleased by the gift, and when he heard something of Jeanne's story he was moved to emotions he had not felt for years. Jeanne was the granddaughter of Clémentine, a girl whom he had loved long ago. Now Jeanne's relatives were dead and she was staying a few days with Mme. de Gabry. Bonnard resolved to look after the girl for the sake of his dead Clémentine.

In Paris Mme. de Gabry went with him to Clémentine's grave and there listened to his nostalgic tale. When Bonnard, a young man, had loved her, Clémentine's mother was dead, and she lived with her choleric father, who was a map maker. They were renting rooms temporarily from Bonnard's father. Bonnard was afraid to disclose his love for Clémentine, but she seemed to know how he felt. One evening a great quarrel arose between Clémentine's father, a royalist, and Bonnard's uncle, who was a Bonapartist. After the quarrel Clémentine was taken away and Bonnard never saw her again.

After telling his story, Bonnard asked Mme. de Gabry how he could best help the orphan Jeanne. She reminded him that Jeanne had a guardian, Maître Mouche the notary, who would have to be consulted.

The honest bibliophile cared little for Maître Mouche's shifty ways, but the notary gave him permission to visit Jeanne each Thursday afternoon. Jeanne was in Mlle. Préfère's select school, where at first Bonnard was received with suspicion. As soon as Mlle. Préfère learned, however, that Bonnard was a Member of the Institute, she was effusive. Immediately Jeanne began to receive better treatment than she had as a charity student.

During the vacation period Mlle. Préfère frequently brought Jeanne to Bonnard's apartment. The schoolmistress quickly made herself at home and soon had her favorite rocker and her shelf for her knitting. One afternoon, while Jeanne was in the kitchen, Mlle. Préfère proposed marriage to Bonnard, who was thunderstruck at the idea.

The next time he went to the school to see Jeanne, Mlle. Préfère received him coldly and forbade him to have anything to do with the girl. Bonnard complained to Maître Mouche, who upheld Mlle. Préfère. Then on a rainy day Bonnard waited outside the school wall until he saw Jeanne and passed her through the gate by a ruse. Amazed at his own daring in kidnaping a minor, he took her to the de Gabry house.

M. de Gabry undertook to settle the affair with Maître Mouche, but that worthy had disappeared after embezzling his clients' funds. Bonnard was legally appointed Jeanne's guardian and took her home with him.

A young student, Henri Gélis, called on Bonnard for help with his thesis. He soon had eyes only for Jeanne and eventually he proposed to marry her, even though she had no dowry. Bonnard made arrangements to sell his library so that his ward could have a respectable financial start in her married life. One evening, just before the books were sold, he guiltily took a book and hid it. He would have one volume left, at any rate.

After Jeanne and Gélis were married, Bonnard went to live in Brolles, a small village. There Jeanne and her husband visited him twice each year, and there also he kept the cradle of little Sylvestre, their child who had died. Bonnard often reflected that the parents were young and healthy. There would be more family.

THE CRISIS

Type of work: Novel
Author: Winston Churchill (1871-1947)
Type of plot: Historical romance
Time of plot: Civil War period
Locale: Missouri and Virginia
First published: 1901

Principal characters:
STEPHEN BRICE, a young lawyer from Boston
VIRGINIA CARVEL, his sweetheart
CLARENCE COLFAX, Brice's rival for Virginia Carvel
JUDGE WHIPPLE, Brice's employer and friend
COLONEL CARVEL, Virginia's father
ABRAHAM LINCOLN

Critique:

The American-born Winston Churchill had several reasons for choosing St. Louis as the setting for this novel. First, it was his aim to show the remarkable contrasts in the lives of Sherman, Grant, and Lincoln, all of whom came from St. Louis and the neighboring state of Illinois. Secondly, two streams of emigration, from the North and from the South, met at St. Louis, with the result that Northern and Southern culture could be brought into focus and examined in detail. *The Crisis* remains one of the best novels of its type. The author brought in the historical characters, including the almost legendary Lincoln, in a natural way not found in many later efforts.

The Story:

In 1858 Stephen Brice emigrated from Boston to St. Louis with his widowed mother. He went to accept the offer of Judge Whipple, his father's friend, who had promised Stephen an opportunity to enter his law firm. Being a personable young man, Stephen Brice found favor among the people of St. Louis, including Colonel Carvel, and the colonel's daughter, Virginia. Stephen promptly fell in love with Virginia Carvel. He was not encouraged by the girl at first because he was a New Englander.

One day Judge Whipple sent Stephen to Springfield, Illinois, with a message for the man who was running for sena-tor against Stephen A. Douglas. When Stephen Brice finally found his man, Abraham Lincoln, he was in time to hear the famous Freeport debate between Lincoln and Douglas. Lincoln made a deep impression on Stephen, who went back to St. Louis a confirmed Republican, as Judge Whipple had hoped. Feeling that Stephen would some day be a great politician, the judge had sent him to Lincoln to catch some of Lincoln's idealism and practical politics.

Convinced by Lincoln that no country could exist half-slave and half-free, Stephen Brice became active in Missouri politics on behalf of the Republicans; a dangerous course to take in St. Louis because of the many Southerners living in the city. His anti-slavery views soon alienated Stephen from the girl he wanted to marry, who then promised to marry Stephen's rival, her cousin and fellow Southerner, Clarence Colfax.

Lincoln lost the election for the senate, but in doing so won for himself the presidency of the United States in 1860. During both campaigns, Stephen Brice worked for the Republican party. An able orator, he became known as a rising young lawyer of exceptional abilities.

The guns at Fort Sumter reverberated loudly in St. Louis in 1861. The city was divided into two factions, pro-slavery Southerners and anti-slavery Northerners. Friends of long standing no longer spoke to each other and members of the same family found themselves at odds over the question of which side Missouri should favor, the Union or the Confederacy. It was a trying time for Stephen Brice. Because of his widowed mother and his political activities, he was unable to join the army. Judge Whipple convinced him that, for the time being, he could do more for his country as a civilian. It was hard for the young man to believe the judge when all of Stephen's friends and acquaintances were going about the city in uniform.

When war was declared, Missouri had a little campaign of its own, for the state militia under the direction of the governor attempted to seize the state. This action was defeated by the prompt action of Federal forces in capturing the militia training camp without firing a shot. A spectator at that minor engagement, Stephen made the acquaintance of an ex-army officer named Sherman and of another shambling man who claimed he should be given a regiment. The young officers laughed at him; his name was Ulysses S. Grant.

Among those captured when Federal troops overcame the Missouri militia was Clarence Colfax, Stephen's rival. Clarence refused to give his oath and go on parole, and he soon escaped from prison and disappeared into the South. Virginia Carvel thought him more of a hero than ever.

Because communications with the South and the Southwest had been cut by the Union armies, Colonel Carvel went bankrupt. He and his daughter aided Southern sympathizers attempting to join the Confederate Army. At last the colonel himself felt that it was his duty to leave St. Louis and take an active part in the hostilities.

The war continued, putting the lie to those optimists who had prophesied that hostilities would end in a few months. By the time of the battle at Vicksburg, Stephen had become a lieutenant in the Union Army. He distinguished himself

in that battle and came once more to the attention of Sherman. When the city fell, Stephen found Clarence Colfax, now a lieutenant-colonel in the Confederate Army. The Southerner had received a severe wound. To save Clarence's life, Stephen arranged for him to be sent to St. Louis on a hospital ship. Stephen knew that he was probably sending his rival back to marry Virginia Carvel. Young Colfax realized what Stephen had done, and told Virginia as much while he was convalescing in St. Louis. The girl vowed that she would never marry a Yankee, even if Colfax were killed.

Judge Whipple had fallen ill, and he was nursed by Virginia and by Stephen's mother. While the judge was sinking fast, Colonel Carvel appeared. At the risk of his life, he had come through the lines in civilian clothes to see his daughter and his old friend. There was a strange meeting at Judge Whipple's deathbed. Clarence Colfax, Colonel Carvel, and Stephen Brice were all there. They all risked their lives, for the Confederates could have been arrested as spies, and Stephen, because he was with them, could have been convicted of treason. That night Virginia realized that she was in love with Stephen.

After the judge's death Stephen returned to the army. Ordered to General Sherman's staff, he accompanied the general on the march through Georgia. At the battle of Bentonville, Stephen again met Clarence Colfax, who had been captured by Union soldiers while in civilian clothes and brought to Sherman's headquarters as a spy. Once again Stephen interceded with Sherman and saved the Southerner's life. Soon afterward Stephen, promoted to the rank of major, was sent by Sherman with some dispatches to General Grant at City Point, in Virginia. Stephen recognized Grant as the man he had seen at the engagement of the militia camp back in St. Louis.

During the conference with the general an officer appeared to summon Stephen to meet another old acquaintance, Abraham Lincoln. The president, like Grant, wished to hear Stephen's first-hand account of the march through Georgia to the sea. When Stephen asked for a pardon for Clarence Colfax, Lincoln said he would consider the matter. Stephen went with Lincoln to Richmond for an inspection of that city after it had fallen to Grant's armies.

Virginia Carvel, not knowing of Stephen's intercession on behalf of Clarence Colfax, traveled to Washington to ask Lincoln for a pardon. She gained an audience with the president, during which she met Stephen once again. Lincoln granted them the pardon, saying that with the war soon to end the time to show clemency had come. He left Virginia and Stephen alone when he hurried to keep another appointment. The young people had realized during their talk with Lincoln that there was much to be forgiven and forgotten by both sides in the struggle which was drawing to a close. The emotion of the moment overcame their reticence at last, and they declared their love for each other. They were married the following day.

After the wedding they went to visit Virginia's ancestral home in Annapolis. A few days later word came to them that Lincoln had died from an assassin's bullet.

THE CRISIS

Type of work: Political essays
Author: Thomas Paine (1737-1809)
First published: 1776-1783

In the series of sixteen essays now known as *The Crisis*, Thomas Paine, called by Benjamin Franklin "an ingenious worthy young man," emerged as the ablest propagandist of the cause of liberty during the American Revolution. The first *Crisis* essay appeared during the darkest days of December, 1776, after Washington's forces had retreated from Fort Lee down through New Jersey and into Pennsylvania. Not only the army but the Continental Congress had been forced to flee before the advancing forces of General Howe. Many people believed that conditions had become so bad that Washington's army could be liquidated and the revolt suppressed before the end of 1776.

Paine, who had attached himself to the Continental Army as a civilian aide, was free to mix among the officers and enlisted men during the retreat, and he was well aware of the dire situation in which the new nation found itself. In the midst of those troubled times the military situation received another blow by the plotting of the Conway Cabal, which threatened to remove Washington from the post of commander-in-chief and place the army under the direction of General Gates. It was under these conditions that Thomas Paine, America's first great propagandist, entered the struggle as a writer to defend the honor of Washington and to advance the cause of the Revolution among the people. The first and best-known of the sixteen pamphlets appeared on December 19, 1776; it was signed "Common Sense."

The characteristics and style of Paine's writings may well be compared to those of Rousseau and Marx, for like them, he could electrify his audience with the written word. Also, he possessed the gift of using key words and phrases which had a magnetic effect upon those who read him. Nor have the words of Thomas Paine been forgotten. When the United States faced the great crisis of World War II, Franklin D. Roosevelt constantly turned to the words of Paine to express his thoughts. The two opening sentences of *The Crisis* offer excellent examples of Paine's ability to use key phrases and catch words:

> These are times that try men's souls. The summer soldier and the sunshine patriot will in this crisis, shrink from the service of his country; but he that stands it NOW, deserves the love and thanks of men and women.

Paine in an effort to bolster the sagging morale of the Americans made light of British successes, declaring that Howe was ravaging the countryside as a brigand and not as a successful invader making a lasting conquest. The withdrawal of Washington was considered by Paine to be a strategic retreat and the promise of victory, not disaster, was imminent. He was positive that final victory could be achieved, but he declared that a greater effort was needed, that "those who expect to reap the blessings of freedom, must, like men, undergo the fatigues of supporting it." In his opinion, a regular army was essential since the militia was unequal to the task at hand. He added to the hatred for the Tories by describing them in the most uncomplimentary manner in an effort to effect an irreconcilable breach between this group and the patriots. He defined Tories as being cowards with "servile, slavish, self-interested fear" and added that

> the Tories have endeavored to insure their property with the enemy, by forfeiting their reputation with us; from which may be justly inferred, that their governing passion is avarice.

Some students of the American Revolution are of the opinion that catch phrases

744

such as "summer soldier" and "sunshine patriot" were important in igniting the spark which enabled Washington to cross the Delaware River and fall upon the British forces in a limited offensive at Trenton and Princeton before going into winter quarters.

As conditions began to improve, Paine pointed out the hopeless position of the British by stating that General Howe's

> condition and ours are very different. He has everybody to fight, we have only his *one* army to cope with, and which wastes away at every engagement: we can not only reinforce, but can redouble our numbers; he is cut off from all suppliers, and must sooner or later inevitably fall into our hands.

Continuing his argument, Paine wrote that "if Britain cannot conquer us, it proves that she is neither able to govern nor protect us. . . ." Any victories for the British were interpreted as defeats because "it is distressing to see an enemy advancing into a country but it is the only place in which we can beat them, and in which we have always beaten them, whenever they have made the attempt." The losses of Philadelphia and Charleston were considered unimportant; those cities could be liberated in a matter of hours should the inhabitants decide to rise up against the enemy.

With the British armies growing weaker, in his opinion, Paine constantly urged the people to make sacrifices and to become active in their support of the movement for liberty: "The nearer any disease approaches a crisis, the nearer it is to a cure. Danger and deliverance make their advances together, and it is only the last push, in which one or the other takes the lead." The essays, since they were intended for propaganda purposes, by necessity had to be written in a simple, clear, and forceful style which could be completely understood by all who read them or heard them read. They were read to the pitifully small army; they were posted on trees and in taverns in the hope that they would inspire all who read them to a more strenuous effort for the cause of liberty. An example of the simple and direct approach utilized by Paine is shown in the following passage:

> Our support and success depend on such a variety of men and circumstances, that every one who does but wish well, is of some use: there are men who have a strange aversion to arms, yet have hearts to risk every shilling in the cause, or in support of those who have better talents for defending it. Nature, in the arrangement of mankind, has fitted some for every service in life: were all soldiers, all would starve and go naked, and were none soldiers, all would be slaves. As *disaffection* to independence is the badge of a Tory, so *affection* to it is the mark of a Whig; and the different services of the Whigs, down from those who nobly contribute every thing, to those who have nothing to render but their wishes, tend all to the same centre, though with different degrees of merit and ability. The larger we make the circle, the more we shall harmonize, and the stronger we shall be. All we want to shut out is disaffection, and, *that excluded*, we must accept from each other such duties as we are best fitted to bestow. A narrow system of politics, like a narrow system of religion, is calculated only to sour the temper, and be at variance with mankind. All we want to know in America is simply this, who is for independence, and who is not? Those who are for it, will support it, and the remainder will undoubtedly see the reasonableness of paying the charges; while those who oppose or seek to betray it, must expect the more rigid fate of the jail and the gibbet.

The true value of the essays to the reader of the present generation is to clear up the misconception of earlier historians who were of the belief that the Revolution had the almost universal support of the population. Also, the essays serve as a chief chronicle of events as they were occurring. It must be remembered, however, that Paine wrote favorably toward the American cause and that the true picture may not have been presented in every case.

Paine saw much of the actual fighting and perhaps understood the war more clearly than anyone else who wrote as the events occurred. He was a master at summing up the situation and then interpreting it as he would have liked it to have been. As an interpreter of changing events, he must be ranked among the outstanding interpreters of any period of history.

During the years of the Revolution, Thomas Paine was a widely read and highly influential propagandist. It was after the French Revolution, in which he participated, that he came to be considered a radical and a dangerous revolutionary. For a more complete understanding of the American Revolution one should read *The Crisis* pamphlets in their entirety.

THE CRITIC

Type of work: Drama
Author: Richard Brinsley Sheridan (1751-1816)
Type of plot: Literary satire
Time of plot: Eighteenth century
Locale: London
First presented: 1779

Principal characters:
MR. DANGLE, a wealthy, stage-struck Londoner
MRS. DANGLE, his wife
MR. SNEER, Dangle's friend
SIR FRETFUL PLAGIARY, a dramatist
MR. PUFF, dramatist and journalist

Critique:

In Sheridan's time *The Critic, Or, A Tragedy Rehearsed* was probably best known for its bitingly satirical portrait of Sheridan's fellow dramatist, Richard Cumberland, who was the prototype of Sir Fretful Plagiary. Today the play is most important for the light it sheds on what Sheridan thought of the drama prevalent in his own time. By showing the reader the insipidity of the tragedy rehearsed within the play, the laughable defense of trite dramatic devices by its author, and the comments by the actors themselves, Sheridan lets the reader see what he thought of the state of drama during his age. Nor should it be overlooked that Sheridan's *The Critic* is one of a line of English plays which use plays within plays to satirize the times and the drama. Sheridan's play can be compared with such similar plays as Buckingham's *The Rehearsal,* Henry Fielding's *Tom Thumb,* David Garrick's *Peep Behind the Curtain,* and Shaw's *Fanny's First Play.*

The Story:

Mr. Dangle, a well-to-do gentleman of London, sat one morning with his wife at breakfast. While he read the newspapers, Mrs. Dangle complained that her husband's hobby, the theater, was making her house unlivable, with disappointed authors, would-be actors, musicians, and critics making it their meeting place. Dangle protested vigorously, but as he did so a stream of callers arrived to prove her point.

The first caller was Mr. Sneer. He and Mrs. Dangle got into a discussion on the morality of the stage and the proper material for comedies. Then Sir Fretful Plagiary, a dramatist, was announced. Before he entered, Dangle reported that he was a close friend but that he could not accept criticism of his work. Sir Fretful told how his new play had been sent to the Covent Garden theater, rather than to Drury Lane, because of the envy he had uncovered there.

Sneer, Dangle, and Sir Fretful Plagiary began to discuss the latter's new play. In the discussion all criticism of his drama was brushed aside in one way or another by the author, who ended up with a diatribe against all who would say anything against his work, including the newspapers. At the end of their talk, a group of musicians entered looking for Dangle's assistance in securing work with the theaters. They were led by an Italian who knew no English and a Frenchman who knew little English, but was to act as interpreter.

The Frenchman and the Italian tried to make Dangle understand what they wanted, but with little success. After a trilingual conversation, in which not one of the participants could understand the others, Mrs. Dangle took the musicians into another room for refreshment and so relieved her husband of their troublesome presence.

As the musicians left Dangle and Sneer alone in the room, Mr. Puff, another dramatist who had a play in rehearsal at the theater, entered. Puff was introduced to Sneer by Dangle as a puffing writer for the newspapers, whose job it was to praise anyone or anything for a price; he was, in short, an eighteenth-century press agent. He explained for the benefit of Mr. Sneer the various kinds of "puffs" he wrote: the direct, the preliminary, the collateral, the collusive, and the oblique. At the end of the conversation, the three agreed to meet at the theater to watch a rehearsal of Puff's new play.

Later the three met, and Puff informed his two friends, Dangle and Sneer, that the time of his play was the days following defeat of the Spanish Armada during the reign of Elizabeth. The under-prompter, appearing to notify the author that the rehearsal was ready to begin, said that the play had been somewhat shortened. The actors, informed that anything they found unnecessary in the tragedy could be cut, had taken full liberties with Mr. Puff's script.

When the curtain rose, two watchmen were found asleep at four in the morning. Sir Christopher Hatton and Sir Walter Raleigh appeared on the stage and began the exposition of the plot. They were interrupted at intervals by protestations and explanations by the author, who spoke to the actors on the stage and to his two friends observing the rehearsal.

In the second act of the play a love story between the daughter of the fort commander and a captured Spanish prince was introduced, again with continued interruptions by the dramatist, who was enraged at the liberties taken by the actors in cutting his lines and parts of scenes. He and his friends, Sneer and Dangle, continued to discuss dramatic art as the rehearsal continued and found various aspects of the play to point up their discussion. Puff was particularly proud of the second sight credited to the heroine, a device by which he was able to describe the defeat of the Spanish Armada without showing the sea fight on the stage.

He was also quite proud of a verbal fencing match between the heroine and the Spanish prince. When Sneer and Dangle found the repartee ambiguous, Puff explained that he had written the dialogue completely in fencing terms, an explanation which his friends found scarcely more intelligible.

Puff irritated the actors by directing them as the rehearsal progressed, and they, in turn, continued to irritate him by cutting out more lines. At their protestations that they could not act because of his interruptions, he replied heatedly that he had feelings, too, and did not like to see his play shredded by the players.

At the end of the love scene in the play, Puff began an argument with the under-prompter, who informed him that it was impossible to rehearse the park scene because the carpenters had not built the scenery. Puff angrily announced that they could cut his play as they would; he intended to print it in its entirety.

The next scene in the rehearsal of Puff's play was a sentimental discovery scene not connected with the main story. In reply to his friends' comments, Puff explained that there was no need to have a logical connection between the main plot and the subplot. Then came what·Puff called the most perfect scene in the play. An actor entered, sat down, shook his head, arose, and went off the stage. The shaking of the head, according to Puff, said more than all the words he could have written.

In the last scene of the play the Spanish prince was killed in a duel, and his English sweetheart went mad. After her exit from the stage, a masque procession of all the British rivers and their tributaries passed over the stage, while an orchestra played Handel's water music.

Following the procession, Puff announced to his friends that the rehearsal was good, but that the actors were not yet perfect. To the actors he announced that another rehearsal would be held the next day.

748

CRITIQUE OF PURE REASON

Type of work: Philosophical treatise
Author: Immanuel Kant (1724-1804)
First published: 1781

Kant's *Critique of Pure Reason* is a masterpiece in metaphysics designed to answer the question, "How are synthetic *a priori* judgments possible?" Since a synthetic judgment is one whose predicate is not contained in the subject, and an *a priori* judgment is one whose truth can be known independently of experience, Kant's question meant, in effect, "How can there be statements such that the idea of the subject does not involve the idea of the predicate and which, nevertheless, *must* be true and can be known to be true without recourse to experience?"

To make the question clearer, Kant offered examples of *analytic* and *synthetic* judgments. The statement that "All bodies are extended" is offered as an analytic judgment, since it would be impossible to think of a body—that is, of a physical object—that was not spread out in space; and the statement "All bodies are heavy" is offered as a synthetic judgment, since Kant believed that it is possible to conceive of something as a body without supposing that it has weight.

Perhaps even clearer examples are possible. The judgment that "All red apples are apples" is surely analytic, since it would be impossible to conceive of something as being red and as being an apple without supposing it to be an apple; the predicate is, in this sense, included in the subject. But the judgment "All apples are red" is surely synthetic, since it is possible to think of something as being an apple without supposing it to be red; in fact, some apples are green. Synthetic judgments can be false, but analytic judgments are never false.

A priori knowledge is knowledge "absolutely independent of all experience," and *a posteriori* knowledge is empirical knowledge, that is, knowledge possible only through experience. We can know *a priori* that all red apples are apples (and that they are red), but to know that a particular apple has a worm in it is something that must be known *a posteriori*.

The question of how synthetic *a priori* judgments are possible is, then, a question concerning judgments that must be true—since they are *a priori* and can be known to be true without reference to experience—even though, as synthetic, their predicates are not conceived in thinking of their subjects.

As an example of a synthetic *a priori* judgment Kant offers, "Everything which happens has its cause." He argues that he can think of something as happening without considering whether it has a cause; the judgment is, therefore, not analytic. Yet he supposes that it is necessarily the case that everything that happens has a cause, even though his experience is not sufficient to support his claim. The judgment must be *a priori*. How are such synthetic *a priori* judgments possible?

One difficulty arises at this point. Critics of Kant have argued that Kant's examples are not satisfactory. The judgment that everything that happens has a cause is regarded as being either an *analytic*, not synthetic, *a priori* judgment (every event being a cause relative to an immediately subsequent event, and an effect relative to an immediately precedent event), or as being a synthetic *a posteriori*, not *a priori*, judgment (leaving open the possibility that some events may be uncaused). A great many critics have maintained that Kant's examples are bound to be unsatisfactory for the obvious reason that no synthetic *a priori* judgments are possible. (The argument is that unless the predicate is involved in the subject, the truth of the judgment is a matter of fact, to be determined only by reference to experience).

Kant's answer to the problem concerning the possibility of synthetic *a priori* judgments was that pure reason—that is, the faculty of arriving at *a priori* knowledge—is possible because the human way of knowing determines, to a considerable extent, the character of what is known. Whenever human beings perceive physical objects, they perceive them in time and space; time and space are what Kant calls "modes of intuition," that is, ways of apprehending the objects of sensation. Since human beings must perceive objects in time and space, the judgment that an object is in time must be *a priori* but, provided the element of time is no part of the conception of the object, the judgment is also synthetic. It is somewhat as if we were considering a world in which all human beings are compelled to wear green glasses. The judgment that everything seen is somewhat green would be *a priori* (since nothing could be seen except by means of the green glasses), but it would also be synthetic (since being green is no part of the conception of object).

In Kant's terminology, a *transcendental* philosophy is one concerned not so much with objects as with the mode of *a priori* knowledge, and a critique of pure reason is the science of the sources and limits of that which contains the principles by which we know *a priori*. Space and time are the forms of pure intuition, that is, modes of sensing objects. The science of all principles of *a priori* sensibility, that is, of those principles that make *a priori* intuitions (sensations) possible, Kant calls the *transcendental aesthetic*.

But human beings do more than merely sense or perceive objects; they also think about them. The study of how *a priori* concepts, as distinguished from intuitions, are possible is called *transcendental logic*. Transcendental logic is divided into *transcendental analytic*, dealing with the principles of the understanding without which no object can be thought, and *transcendental dialectic*, showing the error of applying the principles of pure thought to objects considered in themselves.

Using Aristotle's term, Kant calls the pure concepts of the understanding *categories*. The categories are of *quantity* (unity, plurality, totality), of *quality* (reality, negation, limitation), of *relation* (substance and accident, cause and effect, reciprocity between agent and patient), and of *modality* (possibility-impossibility, existence-nonexistence, necessity-contingency. According to Kant, everything which is thought is considered according to these categories. It is not a truth about things in themselves that they are one or many, positive or negative, but that all things fall into these categories because the understanding is so constituted that it can think in no other way.

Kant maintained that there are three subjective sources of the knowledge of objects: sense, imagination, and apperception. By its categories the mind imposes a unity on the manifold of intuition; what would be a mere sequence of appearances, were the mind not involved, makes sense as the appearance of objects.

The principles of pure understanding fall into four classes: axioms of intuition, anticipations of perception, analogies of experience, and postulates of empirical thought in general.

The principle of the axioms of intuition is that "All intuitions are extensive magnitudes," proved by reference to the claim that all intuitions are conditioned by the spatial and temporal mode of intuition.

The principle by which all perception is anticipated is that "the real that is an object of sensation has intensive magnitude, that is, a degree." It would not be possible for an object to influence the senses to *no* degree; hence various objects have different degrees of influence on the senses.

The principle of the analogies of experience is that "Experience is possible only through the representation of a necessary connection of perceptions." Our experience would be meaningless to us were it not ordered by the supposition that perceptions are of causally related substances which are mutually interacting.

Kant's postulates of empirical thought in general relate the *possibility* of things to their satisfying the formal conditions of intuition and of concepts, the *actuality* of things to their satisfying the material conditions of sensation, and the *necessity* of things to their being determined "in accordance with universal conditions of experience" in their connection with the actual.

A distinction which is central in Kant's philosophy is the distinction between the *phenomenal* and the *noumenal*. The phenomenal world is the world of appearances, the manifold of sensation as formed spatially and temporally and understood by use of the categories. The noumenal world is the world beyond appearance, the unknown and unknowable, the world of "things-in-themselves."

In the attempt to unify experience, the reason constructs certain ideas—of a soul, of the world, of God. But these ideas are transcendental in that they are illegitimately derived from a consideration of the conditions of reason, and to rely on them leads to difficulties which Kant's "Transcendental Dialectic" was designed to expose. The "Paralogisms of Pure Reason" are fallacious syllogisms for which the reason has transcendental grounds; that is, the reason makes sense out of its operations by supposing what, on logical grounds, cannot be admitted. The "Antinomies of Pure Reason" are pairs of contradictory propositions, all capable of proof provided the arguments involve illegitimate applications of the forms and concepts of experience to matters beyond experience.

Kant concludes the *Critique of Pure Reason* with the suggestion that the ideas of God, freedom, and immortality arise in the attempt to make moral obligation intelligible. This point was developed at greater length in his *Metaphysics of Morals* (1785) and his *Critique of Practical Reason* (1788).

THE CROCK OF GOLD

Type of work: Novel
Author: James Stephens (1882-1950)
Type of plot: Fantasy
Time of plot: Any time
Locale: Irish countryside
First published: 1912

Principal characters:
THE PHILOSOPHER
THE THIN WOMAN, his wife
SEUMAS AND BRIGID, two children
ANGUS OG, an early Irish god
CAITILIN, his mortal wife

Critique:

This tale of adventure and philosophical discussions is a modern classic in its field. Stephens is most successful in his attempt to bring old Irish legends to life in the pages of a delightful book. The philosophic discussions abound with a delightful humor, and the seriousness of some of the observations in no way lessens the magic quality of the story. The tale is a wandering one, containing many elements and telling many stories. All of them are entertaining to read, and most of them are perfect in execution.

The Story:

In the center of a very dark pine wood lived the two old Philosophers and their wives, the Grey Woman of Dun Gortin and the Thin Woman of Inis Magrath. One couple had a little boy named Seumas, the other a little girl named Brigid. Both were born on the same day.

When the children were ten years old, one of the old Philosophers decided that he had now learned all he was capable of learning. This conclusion depressed him so much that he decided to die. It was unfortunate, as he pointed out, that at the time he was in the best of health. However, if the time had come for him to die, then die he must. He took off his shoes and spun around in the center of the room for fifteen minutes until he fell over dead. So grieved was the Grey Woman that she, too, killed herself, but as she was much tougher than her husband she spun for forty-five minutes before she died. The Thin Woman calmly buried the two bodies under the hearthstone.

The people who lived on the edge of the pine wood often came to see the Thin Woman's husband when they needed advice. One day Meehawl Mac-Murrachu came to the Philosopher to learn who had stolen his wife's scrubbing board. The Philosopher, after much questioning, finally decided that the fairies had taken it. He advised Meehawl to go to a certain spot and steal the Crock of Gold that the Leprecauns of Gort na Gloca Mora had buried there. For years the Leprecauns had been filling their Crock of Gold by clipping the edges of gold coins that they found in men's houses at night. They needed the gold to ransom any of the little people caught by human beings.

Losing their gold to Meehawl made the Leprecauns angry, and they tried to make Meehawl bring it back by giving him and his wife all kinds of aches and pains. Next they came stealthily and lured Brigid and Seumas down into a little house in the roots of a tree, but fear of the Thin Woman was on them and they set the children free. Then they sent the Great God Pan, the god of the beast which is in every man, to lure away Caitilin, Meehawl's daughter, with the music of his pipes.

When Meehawl came with his tale of sorrow, the Philosopher sent Brigid and Seumas to tell Pan to let the girl go. But Pan refused to answer their questions. When they told the Philosopher, he became so angry that he ordered his wife to bake him some cakes to eat on the way, and he started off by himself to visit Pan. But none of the Philosopher's arguments could persuade Pan to free Caitilin, and the Philosopher went off to get the help of Angus Og of the old gods.

Angus Og himself went to see Pan and the girl in their cave and forced the girl to choose between them. Caitilin, who had learned the true meaning of hunger and pain with Pan, did not know how to choose. Angus Og explained to her that he was Divine Inspiration, and that if she would come and live with him and be his wife, he would show her peace and happiness. By several signs he proved that he was the favorite of the gods of the earth and had more power than Pan. Caitilin sensed that true happiness, which she had never known, would be found with Angus Og, and that only hunger could be found with Pan. So she chose to leave Pan and go with Angus Og. Thus she was saved from the beast in man.

The Philosopher, on his way back home, delivered several messages from the god. One message he gave to a young boy, a promise from Angus Og that in time the old gods would return, and that before they did the boy would write a beautiful poem in their praise. Cheered by the news that the gods would soon come back, the Philosopher finally arrived home, where he greeted his wife with such affection that she decided always to be kind to him and never again to say a cross word.

Unknown to them, the Leprecauns had informed the police in the village that there were two bodies buried under the hearthstone in the Philosopher's house. One day the police broke into the house, found the bodies, and accused the Philosopher of murder. Meanwhile Brigid and Seumas were playing in the woods, and quite by chance they happened to dig a hole and find the Crock of Gold where Meehawl had buried it. They gave it back to the Leprecauns, but the return of the gold was not enough to set matters right. The police kept the Philosopher in jail. Then the Thin Woman baked some cakes and set out to find Angus Og, dragging the children behind her and saying the worst curses there were against the police. The first gods she met were the Three Absolutes, the Most Beautiful Man, the Strongest Man, and the Ugliest Man. By her wisdom the Thin Woman was able to answer their questions and save herself and the children from their frightful powers. When they had passed these gods, they found the house of Angus Og. He was waiting for someone to come and ask him to aid the Philosopher, for it is impossible for the gods to help any· one unasked.

Calling all the old gods together, Angus Og and his wife led a great dance across the fields, and then they went down into the town with all the gods following. In the town their merry laughter brought happiness to all who saw them except the most evil of men. The charges against the Philosopher were forgotten and he was free to go back to his house in the pine woods and dispense wisdom once more. Then the gods returned singing to their own country to await the birth of Caitilin's and Angus Og's child and the day when the old Irish gods could again leave their hidden caves and hollows and rule over the land with laughter and song.

CROME YELLOW

Type of work: Novel
Author: Aldous Huxley (1894-1963)
Type of plot: Social satire
Time of plot: 1920's
Locale: England
First published: 1922

Principal characters:
HENRY WIMBUSH, owner of Crome
ANNE WIMBUSH, his niece
DENIS STONE, a young poet
MR. SCROGAN, a man of reason
GOMBAULD, an artist
MARY BRACEGIRDLE, a victim of repressions
JENNY MULLION, a keen-eyed observer

Critique:

Aldous Huxley has written an amusing satire on the ill-fated love affair of a sensitive young poet. Using the plot as an excuse for bringing together all sorts of interesting and unusual facts and stories, he holds the reader's interest by an almost continual shift of emphasis. We learn of each of the guests at the house party, their faults, interests, and virtues. As in all of Huxley's novels, there is much philosophical discussion. No particular ideas are set forth as correct, but a precise picture of the early twenties as Huxley saw them is presented to the reader with wit and dexterity.

The Story:

Denis Stone, a shy young poet, went to a house party at Crome, the country home of Henry Wimbush and his wife. He went because he was in love with Wimbush's niece, Anne. Anne looked down on Denis because he was four years younger than she, and treated him with scorn when he attempted to speak of love.

Mr. Wimbush was interested in little except Crome and the histories of the people who had lived in the old house. Mrs. Wimbush was a woman with red hair, probably false, and an interest in astrology, especially since she had recently won a bet on a horse with her star-given information. Other guests at the party included Gombauld, an artist who had been invited to paint Anne's picture; the diabolically reasonable Mr. Scrogan; deaf Jenny Mullion; and Mary Bracegirdle, who was worried about her Freudian dreams. Denis and Anne quarreled, this time over their philosophies of life. Denis tried to carry all the cares of the world on his back, but Anne thought that things should be taken for granted as they came. The quarrel cost Denis his first opportunity to tell Anne that he loved her.

Mary Bracegirdle discussed with Anne her dreams and repressions. Having decided to secure either Gombauld or Denis for a husband, she chose the wrong times to talk with both men. Gombauld was busy painting when Mary came up to him. Denis was smarting with jealousy over the time Anne and Gombauld spent together.

Ivor Lombard arrived for the party. Ivor, a painter of ghosts and spirits, turned his attentions toward repressed Mary, and secretly visited her one night in the tower. He went away without seeing her again.

From time to time Mr. Wimbush called the party together while he read stories of the early history of Crome. These stories were from a history at which Mr. Wimbush had worked for thirty years. Denis often wondered if he would ever get a chance to tell Anne that he loved her. Walking in the garden after a talk with Mr. Scrogan, whose cold-blooded ideas about a rationalized world annoyed him, he found a red notebook in which Jenny had been writing for the past week. In it he found a collection of sharply satirical cartoons of all the people at the house party. Jenny had drawn him in seven attitudes which showed up his absurd jealousy, incompetence, and shyness. The cartoons deeply wounded his vanity and shattered his conception of himself.

He was further discouraged by the fact that there was nothing for him to do at a charity fair held in the park outside Crome a few days later. Mr. Scrogan made a terrifying and successful fortune-teller; Jenny played the drums; Mr. Wimbush ran the various races; and Denis was left to walk aimlessly through the fair as an official with nothing to do. Gombauld made sketches of the people in the crowd, and Anne stayed by his side.

The night after the fair Denis overheard part of a conversation between Gombauld and Anne. Without knowing that Anne had repulsed Gombauld, for she had made up her mind to accept Denis if he ever got around to asking her, Denis spent hours of torture thinking of the uselessness of his life. At last he decided to commit suicide by jumping from the tower. There he found Mary grieving because she had received only a brisk postcard from Ivor. She convinced Denis that both their lives were ruined, and advised him to flee from Anne. Convinced, Denis arranged a fake telegram calling him back to London on urgent business. When it arrived, Denis realized with dismay that Anne was miserable to see him go. The telegram was the one decisive action of his life. Ironically, it separated him from Anne.

CROTCHET CASTLE

Type of work: Novel
Author: Thomas Love Peacock (1785-1866)
Type of plot: Comedy of manners
Time of plot: Nineteenth century
Locale: England
First published: 1831

Principal characters:
> EBENEZER MAC CROTCHET, a country squire
> YOUNG CROTCHET, his son
> LEMMA CROTCHET, his daughter
> SUSANNAH TOUCHANDGO, loved by young Crotchet
> MR. CHAINMAIL, an antiquarian
> CAPTAIN FITZCHROME, a young army officer
> LADY CLARINDA BOSSNOWL, loved by Fitzchrome

Critique:

In *Crotchet Castle,* as in his other novels, Peacock ridicules the excesses and exaggerations in human behavior. His satire is never unkind; rather, it is the product of a mind that is tolerant of weaknesses but vexed by an overabundance of those weaknesses in an imperfect world. The plot is almost non-existent, and the people are caricatures; but in spite of these apparent defects the book gives a fairly accurate picture of nineteenth-century English country life.

The Story:

The squire of Crotchet Castle had descended from Scotch and Jewish ancestors, but he tried to hide this ancestry under the guise of an English country squire. His background having given him the ability to make money readily, he used his wealth to buy a manor and a coat of arms. His wife was dead, his son in London, leaving the squire alone with a daughter. Young Crotchet, who had inherited his father's love for money, had taken his father's gift of a large sum and turned it into enormous profits. His business dealings were shady, and many thought his day of reckoning would come. For the present, however, he was riding on a crest of success. He had been engaged to Miss Susannah Touchandgo, the daughter of a great banker, but when that gentleman had absconded with the bank's funds, leaving his daughter almost penniless, young Crotchet had deserted his love without a backward glance. Susannah had retreated into Wales, where in simple surroundings she taught a farmer's children for her livelihood.

Squire Crotchet's daughter Lemma had assumed some of the facial characteristics of her ancestors, a fact which was compensated for in the eyes of local swains by the size of her father's fortune. A suitor had not yet been selected for her, but there would be no problem in choosing one from the many who sought her hand and her purse.

Crotchet Castle was a gathering place for philosophers and dilettantes picked at random by Squire Crotchet. These would-be intellectuals engaged in long and tiresome disputes on all branches of philosophy and science. One of them, a Mr. Chainmail, longed for a return to the customs and morals of the Middle Ages, for he believed that the present was decidedly inferior to the past. He was violently opposed by others of the group who worshipped mammon. No one of the philosophers ever changed his views; each found much pleasure in expounding his own pet theory.

While strolling through the grounds one day, some of the gentlemen came upon a young army officer, Captain Fitzchrome. The captain, invited to join the group, accepted readily, for he was in love with one of the guests, Lady Clarinda Bossnowl. Lady Clarinda obviously loved the captain, but she had been promised to young Crotchet. The match was purely a business arrangement; he would exchange his money for her title. The captain pleaded with her at every opportunity, but she silenced him and her own heart by ridiculing his lack of funds. Lemma Crotchet, in the meantime, was pledged to Lady Clarinda's brother. The four young people spent many hours together, much to Captain Fitzchrome's sorrow.

One day the squire took his guests on a river voyage down the Thames. They visited places of learning and culture, but saw little of either except the buildings supposed to house those virtues. During the trip the captain finally gave up his hopes of winning Lady Clarinda, and he left the party without notifying anyone. He settled in a village inn, where he was later joined by Chainmail, the antiquarian, who had left the party in order to study a ruined castle in the neighborhood. Since the captain knew the way to the castle, he offered to guide Chainmail, but he was called back to London on business before they could undertake their expedition. Chainmail went on alone.

During his researches Chainmail caught a glimpse of a nymph-like creature who fascinated him so much that he could not rest until he had made her acquaintance. After many false attempts, he met her and learned that she was Susannah Touchandgo, the lady betrayed by young Crotchet. Chainmail found her perfect in every way but one. He knew she would share the simple, old-fashioned life he loved, but he had determined to marry a lady of gentle birth. Susannah, ashamed of her father's theft, would tell him nothing of her family background. In spite of her reluctance in this respect, Chainmail loved her and spent many happy hours at the farmhouse in which she lived.

Captain Fitzchrome returned. Learning of his friend's plight, he encouraged Chainmail to ask for the lady's hand, but the antiquarian could not change his views on his need for a wife of gentle birth. The situation was brought to a climax when they saw in the paper an announcement of the approaching marriage of Lady Clarinda and young Crotchet. Susannah was temporarily overwrought by the news, and in trying to comfort her Chainmail inadvertently proposed. Then Susannah told him of her father's crime. Chainmail could overlook that fact in his joy over the discovery that Susannah was of good blood. In a few days the two were married.

The following Christmas most of the friends gathered again at Crotchet Castle. Lemma Crotchet had married Lord Bossnowl, but Lady Clarinda Bossnowl had not yet married young Crotchet. The young man was a little dismayed at seeing Susannah married to Chainmail, for he still held her in affection. Lady Clarinda cast longing glances at the captain, even to the point of singing a song that was obviously intended for him. There was no sorrow in her heart, consequently, when young Crotchet disappeared. His firm had failed and he was penniless. It was assumed that he had crossed the Atlantic to join forces with Susannah's father, who had set up business there; the two rogues would make good partners.

Lady Clarinda would not again be put up for sale. She gladly accepted Captain Fitzchrome and his smaller but more stable fortune.

THE CRUISE OF THE CACHALOT

Type of work: Pseudo-factual account
Author: Frank T. Bullen (1857-1915)
Type of plot: Adventure romance
Time of plot: Late nineteenth century
Locale: At sea
First published: 1898

Principal characters:
FRANK T. BULLEN, the narrator
MR. JONES, fourth mate
ABNER CUSHING, a sailor
MR. COUNT, first mate
CAPTAIN SLOCUM, of the *Cachalot*

Critique:

The Cruise of the Cachalot was for some years a favorite with boys, because of its dramatic picture of life aboard an American whaler during the last century. There is no plot and almost no character analysis; indeed the author made no pretense at writing a literary work. The chief value of the book lies in its full descriptions of whale hunting. As natural history the book must seem inexact to a modern reader; and the author's unquestioning acquiescence in the many needless hardships of the common sailor is indicative of an uncritical approach.

The Story:

By a strange combination of circumstances, Frank Bullen found himself in New Bedford, Massachusetts, looking for a ship. He was only eighteen at the time, but already he had spent six years at sea.

He was strolling down a street in New Bedford, intent on a possible berth aboard any ship, for his pockets were empty, when he was hailed by a scraggy Yankee with the inevitable tobacco juice dribbling down his whiskers. Asked if he wanted to ship out, he accepted eagerly without knowing the type of craft or any of the conditions of employment. He accompanied the sharp-featured Yankee to a small, dirty hall where he joined a group of men all bound for the same ship. When he saw the motley crowd of green-horns, he felt doubts about joining the ship, but there was little chance to back out. After hastily signing the ship's articles, he went with his mates to the docks.

All of the crew were carefully kept together until they were safe in the small boat. On the trip out into the harbor Bullen saw with many misgivings the *Cachalot*, which would be his home for three years. He deeply regretted signing on, for the *Cachalot* was a whaler and whalers were notoriously the worst ships afloat. The *Cachalot* did not compare favorably with the trim English whalers with which he was more familiar. She was small, a three hundred and fifty tonner, dirty and unpainted, and quite dumpy-looking because she had no raised bow or poop.

Once on board, Bullen's worst fears were realized. The officers were hard and mean; they carried lashes with them and a clumsy or slow sailor often felt the sting of a lash on his back. The men needed a great deal of discipline, however, to do a halfway decent job. Of the twelve white crew members, Bullen was the only one who had been to sea before. The hands were beaten and cursed, and they were not even allowed to rest while they were seasick.

Along with the white greenhorns, there were a score of Portuguese, all experienced whaling men. There were also

THE CRUISE OF THE CACHALOT by Frank T. Bullen. By permission of the publishers, Appleton-Century-Crofts, Inc.

four mates and Captain Slocum. The captain was a hard driver and a foul talker. The first mate, Mr. Count, was an older man, the only decent officer aboard. The fourth mate, Mr. Jones, was a giant Negro.

Because of his past experience, Bullen escaped most of the abuse meted out to his fellows. After the ship had been scrubbed and polished, and the men had been licked into shape, he became almost fond of the ship. That feeling was heightened when he learned the *Cachalot* was, in spite of her lines, seaworthy.

The ship was heading toward the Azores, to the delight of the Portuguese. At last the first whale was sighted. Bullen was put into the boat of the first mate and told to mind the sail. The boat came up almost on top of the whale before Louis, the harpooner, threw his great hook. When the whale sounded, the hands paid out over two hundred fathoms of line. Then the whale began to rush away at full speed, towing the boat in his wake. When he slowed down, the boat was brought close enough for the harpooner to use his lance. After a final flurry, the whale died and was towed alongside.

After some months at sea, Bullen had an unpleasant picture of ship's discipline. Abner Cushing, a Yankee sailor, tried to make some beer in the forecastle. Needing some potatoes for his brew, he stole a few from the officers' galley. One of the Portuguese reported the theft to the captain and, as punishment, Abner was strung up by the thumbs and lashed vigorously by one of the harpooners until he fainted. When his punishment was over, he was not allowed to go below, but was forced to turn to immediately.

The cruise was an ill-fated one for Abner. He was in a small boat when a whale unexpectedly turned and bore down on the frail craft. The line was hurriedly pulled in. Then the whale sounded, and as the line was paid out Abner's neck caught in a loop. The weight of the descending whale severed his head neatly.

Mr. Jones, after the *Cachalot* had been at sea over a year, became greatly depressed. He recalled a fortune-teller's prediction that he would die in a fight with a white man and finally decided that Captain Slocum was destined to cause his death. Deranged, he went on the bridge, wrapped his huge arms around the captain, and jumped with him into the sea. When Mr. Count assumed command, he promoted Bullen to Mr. Jones' vacant post.

Once Bullen nearly met his end when a harpooned cachalot suddenly turned sidewise and with his mighty tail smashed a boat to bits. His foot tangled in the wreckage, Bullen went under. When he came up, nearly exhausted, he caught blindly at a rope and hauled himself along until he came to the inert whale. He clambered aboard and clung to the harpoon in the side of the dead whale. But the whale suddenly came to life. When the other boats came alongside after the whale had finally died, Bullen had a dislocated thigh and severe rope burns on each arm.

At last, after three years, the *Cachalot's* barrels were full, and the ship headed home around Cape Horn. In good time the lookout sighted Cape Navesink. With every flag flying, she came into New Bedford. The cruise of the *Cachalot* was ended.

CRY, THE BELOVED COUNTRY

Type of work: Novel
Author: Alan Paton (1903-
Type of plot: Social criticism
Time of plot: Mid-twentieth century
Locale: South Africa
First published: 1948

Principal characters:
THE REVEREND STEPHEN KUMALO, a Zulu clergyman
GERTRUDE, his sister
ABSALOM, his son
MSIMANGU, his friend
MR. JARVIS, his white benefactor

Critique:

In South Africa today there is racial unrest more bitter than any now known in our own country. *Cry, The Beloved Country* is a beautiful and tragic story of that unrest, told with poetic loveliness. It is a story of personal tragedy, as well as a story of a national tragedy. This distinguished novel by a South African minister has quickly, and rightly, found a permanent place in twentieth-century literature. Dramatized, the story has been equally compelling as a play.

The Story:

The letter brought fear to the hearts of the Reverend Stephen Kumalo and his wife. To a Zulu, letters were rare and frightening. Once opened, they could never be closed again, their contents forgotten. Kumalo waited until he could control his fear before he opened the letter from Johannesburg telling him that his sister was a sick woman and needed his help. The trip would be costly for a poor Zulu clergyman, but he must go. Perhaps there he could also find their son Absalom, who had never been heard from since he left the village. They knew in their hearts that in Johannesburg Absalom had succumbed to the evil resulting from the white man's success at breaking up the tribes and compelling black men to work in the mines.

Taking their small savings, Kumalo journeyed to the city. He went first to the mission and met Msimangu, who had written the letter. Msimangu was a clergyman also, working for his people in the city as Kumalo worked in the country. He sorrowfully told Kumalo that his sister Gertrude was a prostitute and a dealer in illegal liquor. She and her child were in want, even though she had once made much money from her trade. Kumalo located Gertrude, with the help of Msimangu, and found her willing to go with him to the temporary rooms he had found with a good woman. When his business was finished, she and the child would go with him to his home, away from temptation.

Before looking for his son, Kumalo visited his brother John, a successful merchant and a politician who was under surveillance by the police for his ability to stir up the blacks. But John was discreet; he took no chance of being arrested and losing his business. Many of the black leaders sacrificed everything to help their people, but not John. Expediency was his only thought. He had left the church · and turned a deaf ear to his brother's pleas that he return to the good life.

Kumalo began his search for Absalom. With Msimangu, he searched everywhere, each place visited adding to his fear, for it was obvious that the boy had been engaged in stealing, drinking, and worse. Often they walked for miles, for the black leaders were urging their people to boycott the buses in order to get the fares reduced. Kumalo learned that Absalom had been in the company of his brother John's son, both of them in and out of trouble. The trail led to a reformatory, but the boy had been dismissed shortly before because of his good behavior. The white teacher of the reformatory joined Kumalo in his search because the boy's behavior reflected on his training. Kumalo found next the girl who, soon to bear Absalom's child, waited to marry him. The old man knew at once that should Absalom not be found, the girl must return to the hills with him and make her home there.

At last he found Absalom in prison. In company with John's son and another boy, Absalom had robbed and killed Arthur Jarvis, a white man who had befriended the blacks. Broken-hearted, the old man talked with his son. He could tell that the son did not truly repent but only said the right things out of fear. His one ray of goodness was his desire to marry the girl in order to give his unborn child a name. Kumalo wept for his son. But he wept also for the wife and children, for the father and mother of the slain man.

At the trial Absalom was defended by a lawyer found by Kumalo's friends. The plea was that the murder was not planned, that the boy had shot in fear. The judge, a good man, weighed all the evidence and pronounced a verdict of guilty; the punishment, death by hanging. John's son and the other boy were acquitted for lack of evidence. The verdict was a gross miscarriage of justice, but John was more powerful than Kumalo.

Before Kumalo left Johannesburg, he arranged for the marriage between his son and the girl. Then he started home, taking the girl and Gertrude's child with him. Gertrude had disappeared the night before they were to leave, no one knew where. She had talked to him of becoming a nun, but Kumalo feared that she had gone back to her old life; Gertrude liked the laughter and fun.

At home, the people welcomed their minister, showering love and blessings upon him. The crops were poor that season and people were starving. Kumalo prayed for his people and worked for them. Knowing that they must learn to use the land wisely, ne was helpless to guide them. He went to their chief to ask for coöperation, but the chief was concerned only for himself and his family.

Hope came to the people in the form of a child. He was the grandchild of Mr. Jarvis, father of the man Absalom had murdered. Mr. Jarvis had always helped the black people, and after his son's death he gave all his time to the work started by the murdered man. He sent milk for the children and brought to the people an agricultural demonstrator who would help them restore fertility to the soil. Mr. Jarvis built a dam and sent for good seed. His grandchild became Kumalo's friend, and through him the white man learned of the needs of the people. Kumalo, whose son had killed his benefactor's son, was at first ashamed to face Mr. Jarvis. When they met, few words were exchanged, but each read the heart of the other and understood the sorrow and grief there.

The bishop came and told Kumalo that it would be best for him to leave the hills and the valley, to go where his son's crime was unknown. Kumalo grieved and stood silent. Before the bishop left there came a letter from Mr. Jarvis, thanking Kumalo for his friendship and offering to build his people a new church. The bishop felt ashamed. How little he understood this man and his people.

When the day came for Absalom's execution, Kumalo went into the mountains. There he had gone before when struggling with fear. Mr. Jarvis, knowing the torment that was in his soul, bade him go in peace. When the dawn came, Kumalo cried out for his son. He cried too for his land and his people. When would dawn come for them?

CUDJO'S CAVE

Type of work: Novel
Author: John Townsend Trowbridge (1827-1916)
Type of plot: Historical romance
Time of plot: 1861
Locale: Tennessee
First published: 1863

Principal characters:
PENN HAPGOOD, a Quaker schoolmaster
MR. VILLARS, a blind clergyman
VIRGINIA, and
SALINA, his daughters
LYSANDER SPROWL, Salina's estranged husband
AUGUSTUS BLYTHEWOOD, a planter
MR. STACKRIDGE, a Unionist farmer
CARL, a German boy, friend of Penn
OLD TOBY, a freed slave
CUDJO, and
POMP, runaway slaves
SILAS ROPES, a bully

Critique:

Written during the Civil War, *Cudjo's Cave* mingles elements of propaganda with its historical setting and romantic theme. Because the novel displays deep sincerity, however, and a considerable degree of literary skill, it has enjoyed a popularity outlasting by many years the political issues which gave it birth. The book presents clearly and forcefully the problem of the rural population in Tennessee during that difficult time of decision at the beginning of the Civil War period. In that particular time and place the problem was peculiarly acute because Tennessee was a border state and its citizens had many reasons for indecision when faced by the realities of conflict between North and South. The writer, working close to actual history, dramatized effectively the guerrilla warfare fought among the people of Tennessee and Kentucky.

The Story:

In 1861, Penn Hapgood, a young Quaker, was the schoolmaster in the small Tennessee town of Curryville. Because he made no effort to conceal his anti-slavery convictions, he was unpopular among the hot-headed Secessionists of the community. The Unionists, on the other hand, had offered him a commission in the militia unit they were secretly organizing. Penn refused the commission offered him on the grounds of his religious faith.

His unpopularity grew after he aided Dan Pepperill, a poor white flogged and ridden on a rail because he had befriended a whipped slave. Penn's friend, a kindly young German named Carl, offered him a pistol to use in self-defense if he were attacked, but the schoolmaster saw no need to arm himself. A short time later a party of ruffians seized Penn and tarred and feathered him. Carl, unable to save his friend, searched for some Union sympathizers to defend Penn, but by the time the rescue party arrived at the schoolhouse the young teacher was not to be found. It was learned, however, that he had gone to his boarding-house, where his landlady, Mrs. Sprowl, had refused to let him in. She had acted on the orders of Silas Ropes, the leader of the mob.

Penn had found shelter in the home of a blind clergyman, Mr. Villars. The minister's household was made up of his two daughters, Virginia and Salina, old

Toby, a freed slave, and Carl, the young German. Old Toby and Farmer Stackridge, a stanch Unionist, tended to Penn and put him to bed in the clergyman's home. While he was still resting, Augustus Blythewood, a planter in love with Virginia, appeared at the house. Although she was little attracted to her suitor, Virginia entertained him graciously in order to conceal the fact that the fugitive was hidden nearby. Another caller was Lysander Sprowl, the son of Penn's landlady. Salina, the older sister, and young Sprowl were married, but they had separated some time before.

Sprowl, having learned Penn's whereabouts, promised to lead the villagers to the schoolmaster's hiding place. The aroused townspeople accused Mr. Villars of hiding an Abolitionist. While they were threatening the old man, Penn disappeared from the house under mysterious circumstances.

A mob, aroused by Blythewood, seized old Toby and prepared to flog him in an effort to learn Penn's whereabouts. Carl managed to cut the Negro's bonds before the mob could carry out its threat. Toby, escaping, ran into Blythewood and recognized him. The planter then called off the mob and went to the minister's house, where he pretended great indignation at what had happened.

Penn, meanwhile, was safe in Cudjo's Cave, a hide-out known only to runaway slaves. Having heard the angry townspeople threatening Mr. Villars, he had in his half-delirious condition fled into an adjoining field before he fainted. When he came to, he found himself beside a fire in a cavern, with Cudjo and Pomp, two escaped slaves, ministering to his wants. They had befriended Penn because of the help he had given Pepperill several weeks before. Pomp, in particular, was a magnificent old fellow, almost heroic in his dignity and spirit. Both slaves had suffered at the hands of Blythewood and Ropes, the town bully. Through the two Negroes Penn sent word to Mr. Villars that he was safe. The clergyman

sent Penn's clothes and food to the hiders.

When he was able to travel, Penn decided to set out for the North. Near Curryville he fell into the hands of a small detachment of Confederate soldiers. Convicted at a drumhead trial, he was sentenced to be hanged unless he joined the army. He refused. Carl, who had helped his friend before, volunteered to enlist in Penn's place. Set free, Penn was again in danger from a group of townspeople led by Ropes and Sprowl, but with the aid of Farmer Stackridge he managed to elude his pursuers. Blythewood, hearing of his escape, was furious that Penn had slipped through his fingers.

Penn did not go far, however, for he was unwilling to leave the Villars family without protection. His fears were justified. When he returned secretly to the minister's home, he learned that Mr. Villars had been seized and carried off to prison. Penn himself was captured a short time later, and among his fellow prisoners he found the blind clergyman. Because Carl was one of the soldiers detailed to guard them, he and the minister were able to make their escape. Stackridge was guiding them to a place of safety in the mountains when they were again captured. As the soldiers were about to run Penn through with their bayonets, one of their number dropped dead. The others ran away. Pomp and Cudjo appeared and led the fugitives to Cudjo's Cave.

Augustus Blythewood proposed to Virginia Villars, but she, realizing his dislike for Penn, would have nothing to do with the young planter. Meanwhile Stackridge and a party of his Unionist friends were skirmishing with the Confederate soldiers in the woods nearby. Virginia, while searching for Penn, was captured by a Confederate soldier, but she was relieved when she discovered that her captor was Carl. Before the young German could lead her out of the forest, set afire by the skirmishers, he himself was captured by Ropes' men. After she had climbed to a rocky ledge, the fire having cut off her escape on both sides, she was rescued from her predicament by Penn and Cudjo, who conducted her to the cave. That night rain put out the forest fire. In the morning old Toby appeared at the cave. He was overjoyed to discover that his mistress and her father were both safe.

Lysander Sprowl, in the meantime, had taken possession of Mr. Villars' house and forced Salina to serve him there. When Toby returned with a note to tell Salina that her sister and her father were safe, the Negro tried to deceive Sprowl as to the fate of the fugitives, but Salina, who still loved her worthless husband, incautiously showed him Virginia's note. Sprowl brutally ordered Toby flogged in order to learn where Mr. Villars and Penn were hidden. Angered by Sprowl's cruelty, Salina set fire to her father's house and under cover of the confusion helped old Toby to make his escape.

Sprowl, encountering Carl, demanded that the young German lead him to the cave. Carl pretended to agree, but along the way he managed to hit the bully over the head with a stone. While Sprowl was still unconscious, Carl dragged him to the cave, where he was securely bound. Meanwhile old Toby and Salina made their way to the cave, and they arrived about the time Carl appeared with the wounded Sprowl. Pomp had also conducted to the cave the band of Unionists led by Stackridge. They prepared to turn their quarters into an underground fortress.

Before long a party led by Silas Ropes discovered the location of the cave. He and his men guarded the entrance in the hope of starving the occupants into submission.

Salina, ever changeable, loosened Sprowl's bonds so that he was able to escape. He went at once to the troops under Blythewood and arranged to have a squad of men sent to attack the cave. When Sprowl, at the head of the attacking force, reached the entrance of the cave, he found it defended by his wife. She fired at her husband, wounding him fatally, and was herself bayoneted by one of the Confederate soldiers. Virginia and her father were captured and taken before Blythewood.

The planter again pleaded his suit with Virginia, but she received his offers with contempt. While they argued, apart from the camp, Pomp suddenly appeared and told his former master that any sudden move would mean his death. Carl and Penn were covering Blythewood with their guns, and he was taken a prisoner to the cave. There Pomp compelled his former master to sign a safe conduct pass for the defenders and an order for the attackers to cease the fight.

Under safe conduct, the defenders left the cave. Mr. Villars, Virginia, Penn, and Pomp set out for Ohio. They left behind them in the cave the body of Salina, as well as those of Cudjo and Ropes, who had killed each other during an earlier attack. Pomp returned long enough to free Blythewood before joining his friends on their way to safety.

Penn and Carl went from Ohio to Pennsylvania, where they enlisted in the same regiment. Pomp served the Union as a colored scout. In many battles of the war Penn did heroic service, earning for himself the nickname of "The Fighting Quaker."

CUPID AND PSYCHE

Type of work: Classical myth
Source: Folk tradition
Type of plot: Allegory of love
Time of plot: The Golden Age
Locale: Ancient Greece
First transcribed: Unknown

Principal characters:
  PSYCHE, daughter of a Greek king
  CUPID, the god of love
  VENUS, the goddess of beauty

Critique:

Cupid and Psyche is the simple but moving story of the union of a mortal, Psyche, and the god Cupid. In this ancient mythological tale a beautiful maiden achieved immortality because her love and faith triumphed over mistrust.

The Story:

Psyche, daughter of a Greek king, was as beautiful as Venus and sought after by many princes. Her father, seeking to know what fate the gods might have in store for her, sent some of his men to Apollo's oracle to learn the answer.

To the king's horror, the oracle replied that Psyche was to become the mate of a hideous monster, and the king was ordered to leave his daughter to her fate upon a mountaintop, to prevent the destruction of his people. Psyche was led, clad in bridal dress, to a rocky summit and left there alone. The weary girl soon fell into a swoon.

Venus, jealous of Psyche's beauty, called her son Cupid and ordered him to use his arrows to turn Psyche's heart toward a creature so hideous that mortals would be filled with loathing at the sight of Psyche's mate. But when Cupid saw his victim asleep he fell in love with her and decided that she should be his forever. While Psyche slept, Zephyrus came at Cupid's bidding and carried her to the valley in which Love's house stood. There she awoke in a grove of trees in which stood a magnificent golden palace. She entered the building and wandered through the sumptuously furnished rooms.

At noon Psyche found a table lavishly spread. A voice invited her to eat, assured her that the house was hers, and told her that the being who was to be her lover would come that night.

As she lay in bed that night a voice close beside her told her not to be afraid. The voice spoke so tenderly that the girl welcomed her unseen suitor and held out her arms to him. When Psyche awoke the next morning, her lover had gone, but he had left behind a gold ring and had placed a circlet on her head.

For a time Psyche lived happily in the golden palace, visited each night by the lover whose face she had not seen. But at last she became homesick for her two sisters and her father. One night she asked her lover to permit her sisters to visit her the next day. He gave his consent, but he warned that she was not to tell them about him.

Zephyrus carried the sisters to the valley. Overjoyed to see them, Psyche showed them the beauties of the palace and loaded them with gifts. Jealous of her good fortune, they tried to make her suspicious of her unseen lover. They suggested that her lover was a serpent who changed into the form of a youth at night, a monster who would at last devour her. To save herself, they advised her to hide a lamp and a knife by her bed so that she might see him and slay him as he slept.

Psyche did as they had suggested. That night, as her love 'lay asleep, she lit the lamp and brought it close so that she might look at him. When she saw

766

the handsome young man by her side, she was powerless to use her knife. As she turned, sobbing, to extinguish the flame, a drop of burning oil fell on Cupid's shoulder. Awaking with a cry, he looked at her reproachfully. With the warning that love cannot live with suspicion, he left the palace. Psyche tried to follow, but fell in a swoon at the threshold.

When she awoke, the palace had vanished. Determined to seek her lover, she wandered alone across the countryside and through cities hunting the god. Meanwhile Cupid took his vengeance on her sisters. To each he sent a dream that she would become his bride if she were to throw herself from the mountaintop. Both sisters, obeying the summons, found only the arms of Death to welcome them.

No god would give the wandering Psyche shelter or comfort, or protect her from the wrath of Venus. At the temples of Ceres and Juno she was turned away. At last she came to the court of Venus herself. Warned by her heart to flee, she was nevertheless drawn before the throne of the goddess. Venus decided that Psyche should be kept as a slave. She was to be given a new task to do each day and was to live until she once more began to hope.

Psyche's first task was to sort a huge pile of mixed seeds and grain into separate heaps, with the warning that if there were so much as one seed in the wrong pile she would be punished. But by dusk she had separated only small heaps of grain. Cupid so pitied her that he commanded myriads of ants to complete the task for her.

Next day Psyche was ordered to gather the golden fleece of Venus' sheep. Obeying the advice of a reed at the edge of the river, she waited until the animals had lain down to sleep and then collected the wool which had been left clinging to the bushes.

Psyche's third task was to fill a jug with the black water which flowed down a steep mountain into the rivers Styx and Cocytus. This task she was able to complete with the aid of a bird who carried the jug to the stream, collected the water, and brought it back to her.

On the fourth day Psyche was given her most difficult task; she was to go to the land of the dead and there collect some of the beauty of the goddess Proserpine in a golden box. If she succeeded, Venus promised, she would treat Psyche kindly thereafter. But to visit Proserpine and to return was an almost impossible achievement. In despair, Psyche determined to cast herself from a tower, but as she was about to kill herself a voice called to her and told her how she might fulfill her mission.

Following instructions, Psyche traveled to Proserpine's realm. There she might have stayed on forever if she had not thought suddenly of her love. On her way back, she had almost reached the daylight when envy seized her. She opened the box, thinking she would have whatever it contained for herself, but no sooner had she lifted the lid than she fell into a deep sleep filled with nightmares.

She might have lain that way forever if Cupid, going in search of her, had not found her. He awoke her with one of his arrows and sent her on to his mother with the box. Then he flew off and presented himself before Jove with his petition that Psyche be made immortal. Jove, after hearing his pleas, sent Mercury to conduct Psyche into the presence of the gods. There she drank from the golden cup of ambrosia Jove handed her and became immortal. So she and Cupid were at last united for all time.

THE CUSTOM OF THE COUNTRY

Type of work: Novel
Author: Edith Wharton (1862-1937)
Type of plot: Social criticism
Time of plot: Late nineteenth century
Locale: New York, Paris
First published: 1913

Principal characters:
UNDINE SPRAGG, a predatory woman
ELMER MOFFATT, her first husband
RALPH MARVELL, Undine's second husband
PAUL, son of Undine and Ralph Marvell
RAYMOND DE CHELLES, her third husband
PETER VAN DEGEN, her lover
ABNER E. SPRAGG, her father

Critique:

This novel traces the development and refinement of a woman's ambition. Undine Spragg is a heartless creature whose striking beauty has led her to believe that the sole aim of society is to provide diversion and security for its women. However deeply Edith Wharton may incriminate the heroine, there is an even greater incrimination of the ·society that produced her, for Undine is the purest exponent of a world motivated by the desire for power and status. The well-constructed story is carried along by a direct, unornamented prose style.

The Story:

Undine Spragg, who came from Apex City with her parents, had been in New York for two years without being accepted in society. Her opportunity came at last when she was invited to the dinner given by Laura Fairford, whose brother, Ralph Marvell, took an interest in Undine.

Ralph, although his family was prominently established in social circles, had little money. Moreover, he was an independent thinker who disliked the superficiality of important New York figures like Peter Van Degen, the wealthy husband of Ralph's cousin, Clare Dagonet, with whom Ralph had once been in love.

About two months after their meeting Undine became engaged to Ralph. One night they went to see a play. Undine was shocked to find herself sitting next to Elmer Moffatt, a figure in her past whom she did not want to recognize in public. She promised to meet him privately in Central Park the next day. When they met, Moffatt, a bluntly spoken vulgarian, told Undine that she must help him in his business deals after she married Ralph.

Moffatt also went to see Undine's father and asked him to join in a business deal. Moffatt threatened to make Undine's past public if Mr. Spragg refused.

Ralph and Undine were married and Ralph was happy until he realized that Undine cared less for his company than for the social world. Mr. Spragg, having made the business deal with Moffatt, had thus been able to give Undine a big wedding. Ralph soon began to realize the ruthlessness of Undine's desire for money. Her unhappiness and resentment were increased when she learned that she was pregnant.

In the next several years Moffatt became a significant financial figure in New York. Ralph, in an attempt to support

Undine's extravagance, went to work in a business to which he was ill-suited. Undine, meanwhile, kept up a busy schedule of social engagements. She had also accepted some expensive gifts from Peter Van Degen, who was romantically interested in her, before Peter left to spend the season in Europe.

One day Undine saw Moffatt, who wanted to meet Ralph in order to make a disreputable business deal. The business deal succeeded and Undine went to Paris to meet Peter. Before long she had spent all her money. She then met the Comte Raymond de Chelles, a French aristocrat whom she thought of marrying. In the face of this competition Peter frankly told Undine of his desire for her and said that if she would stay with him he could give her everything she wanted. At this point Undine received a telegram announcing that Ralph was critically ill with pneumonia and asking her to return to New York immediately. Undine decided to stay in Paris.

Ralph recovered and, after four years of marriage to Undine, returned to the Dagonet household with his son Paul. He began to work hard at the office for Paul's sake and on a novel which he had begun.

Undine, after an uncontested divorce from Ralph, lived with Peter Van Degen for two months. Peter, however, was disillusioned when he learned that Undine had not gone to see Ralph when he was critically ill; he left her without getting the promised divorce from his wife Clare.

Ralph, meanwhile, was concerned only with his son and his book. Then he learned that Undine was engaged to Comte Raymond de Chelles and badly needed money to have her marriage to Ralph annulled by the Church. Undine agreed to waive her rights to the boy if Ralph would send her one hundred thousand dollars to pay for her annulment. Ralph borrowed half of the needed sum and went to Moffatt to make another business deal. As Undine's deadline approached, with the deal not yet concluded, Ralph went to see Moffatt, who told him that the matter was going more slowly than expected and that it would take a year to go through. Moffatt told Ralph that he himself was once married to Undine, back in Apex City, but that Undine's parents had forced the young couple to get a divorce. After hearing this story Ralph went home and committed suicide.

Undine, now in possession of her son, married Raymond de Chelles. She was very happy in Paris, even though Raymond was strict about her social life. After three months they moved to the family estate at Saint Désert to live quietly and modestly. When Raymond began to ignore her, Undine became bored and angry at her husband's family for not making allowances for her customary extravagance.

One day she invited a dealer from Paris to appraise some of the priceless Chelles tapestries. When the dealer arrived, the prospective American buyer with him turned out to be Moffatt, now one of the richest men in New York. Over the next several weeks Undine saw a great deal of her former husband. When the time came for Moffatt to return to New York, Undine invited him to have an affair with her. Moffatt told her that he wanted marriage or nothing.

Undine went to Reno, where she divorced Raymond and married Moffatt on the same day. Moffatt gave Undine everything she wanted, but she realized that in many personal ways he compared unfavorably with her other husbands. The Moffatts settled in a mansion in Paris to satisfy Undine's social ambitions and her husband's taste for worldly display. When Undine learned that an old society acquaintance, Jim Driscoll, had been appointed ambassador to England, she decided that she would like to be the wife of an ambassador. Moffatt told her bluntly that that was the one thing she could never have because she was a divorced woman. Still dissatisfied, Undine was certain that the one thing she was really meant for was to be an am- bassador's wife.

THE CYCLOPS

Type of work: Drama
Author: Euripides (c. 485-c. 406 B.C.)
Type of plot: Satyr play
Time of plot: Remote antiquity
Locale: Mt. Aetna in Sicily
First presented: Fifth century B.C.

Principal characters:
ODYSSEUS, King of Ithaca
THE CYCLOPS
SILENUS, aged captive of the Cyclops
CHORUS OF SATYRS
COMPANIONS OF ODYSSEUS

Critique:

By purely aesthetic standards, the *Cyclops* cannot be considered a valuable or important play, but it otherwise has a twofold interest as the only complete satyr play preserved from ancient Greece and as a dramatization of an episode from Homer's *Odyssey.* Euripides has kept the main line of Homer's tale, but for the sake of enhanced humor has added the character of old Silenus and, of course, the Chorus of Satyrs. Furthermore, the exigencies of stage presentation have made it necessary for him to change Homer's ingenious escape device to a mere slipping through the rocks past the blind Cyclops. The light tone of the play must have been a welcome relief to the Greek audience, for it followed three somber tragedies presented in succession.

The Story:

As he raked the ground before the cave of his master, the Cyclops, old Silenus lamented the day he was shipwrecked on the rock of Aetna and taken into captivity by the monstrous, one-eyed offspring of Poseidon, god of the sea. About Silenus gamboled his children, the Chorus of Satyrs, who prayed with their father to Bacchus for deliverance. Suddenly Silenus spied a ship and the approach of a group of sailors obviously seeking supplies. Odysseus and his companions approached, introduced themselves as the conquerors of Troy, driven from their homeward journey by tempestuous winds

and desperately in need of food and water. Silenus warned them of the cannibalistic Cyclops' impending return, urged them to make haste and then began to bargain with them over the supplies. Spying a skin of wine, the precious liquid of Bacchus which he had not tasted for years, Silenus begged for a drink. After one sip he felt his feet urging him to dance. He offered them all the lambs and cheese they needed in exchange for one skin of wine.

As the exchange was taking place, the giant Cyclops suddenly returned, ravenously hungry. The wretched Silenus made himself appear to have been terribly beaten and accused Odysseus and his men of plundering the Cyclops' property. Odysseus denied the false charge, but although he was supported by the leader of the Chorus of Satyrs, the Cyclops seized two of the sailors, took them into his cave, and made a meal of them. Horrified Odysseus was then urged by the satyrs to employ his famed cleverness, so effective at Troy, in finding some means of escape.

After some discussion, Odysseus hit upon a subtle plan: first they would make the Cyclops drunk with wine; then, while he lay in a stupor, they would cut down an olive tree, sharpen it, set it afire, and plunge it into the Cyclops' eye. After that escape would be easy.

When the Cyclops emerged from his cave, Odysseus offered him the wine, and

771

the giant and Silenus proceeded to get hilariously drunk. So pleased was the monster with the effects of the Bacchic fluid that Silenus without much trouble persuaded him not to share it with his fellow giants but to drink it all up by himself. The grateful Cyclops asked Odysseus his name (to which the clever warrior replied "No man") and promised that he would be the last to be eaten. Soon the Cyclops found the earth and sky whirling together and his lusts mounting. He seized the unhappy Silenus and dragged him into the cave to have his pleasure with him.

As the Cyclops lay in a stupor, Odysseus urged the satyrs to help him fulfill the plan they had agreed upon, but the cowardly satyrs refused and Odysseus was forced to take his own men for the task. Soon the agonized Cyclops, shouting that "no man" had blinded him, came bellowing out of the cave. The chorus mocked and jeered him for this ridiculous charge and gave him false directions for capturing the escaping Greeks. The berserk giant thrashed about and cracked his skull against the rocks. When the escaping Odysseus taunted him with his true name, the Cyclops groaned that an oracle had predicted that Odysseus would blind him on his way home from Troy, but he told also that the clever one would pay for his deed by tossing about on Poseidon's seas for many years. The satyrs hastened to join the escape so that they could once more become the proper servants of Bacchus in a land where grapes grew.

CYMBELINE

Type of work: Drama
Author: William Shakespeare (1564-1616)
Type of plot: Tragi-comedy
Time of plot: First century B.C.
Locale: Britain, Italy, and Wales
First presented: c. 1609

Principal characters:
CYMBELINE, King of Britain
THE QUEEN, Cymbeline's wife
CLOTEN, the queen's son by a former husband
IMOGEN, Cymbeline's daughter by a former marriage
POSTHUMUS LEONATUS, Imogen's husband
PISANIO, servant of Posthumus
IACHIMO, an Italian braggart
BELARIUS, a banished lord
GUIDERIUS, and
ARVIRAGUS, Cymbeline's sons, reared by Belarius
CAIUS LUCIUS, a Roman ambassador

Critique:

Shakespeare apparently drew upon a number of sources for the plot of *The Tragedy of Cymbeline.* All historical accuracy of the play is debatable and actually unimportant. Cymbeline himself was a mythical character of tribal legend. The details of relationship among the characters are to be found in other romantic writings which appeared prior to Shakespeare's time and which were apparently adopted to clothe the skeletal international aspects of the story. *Cymbeline* presents a plot of political intrigue—both domestic and international—and personal emotional involvement. That the personal well-being of the characters takes precedence over military and political details gives the play its human-interest appeal. The apparition of Posthumus has the richness of detail found in similar scenes in *Macbeth.*

The Story:

Gullible Cymbeline and his conniving queen planned to have Imogen, his daughter, marry his stepson Cloten. Instead, Imogen chose the gentle Posthumus as a husband and secretly married him. Banished by the king in a fit of anger, Posthumus fled to Italy after promising that his loyalty and fidelity to his bride

would always be above reproach. As a token of their vows Imogen gave Posthumus a diamond ring that had belonged to her mother, and Posthumus placed a bracelet of rare design upon Imogen's arm.

In Rome Posthumus met Iachimo, a vain braggart who tried to tempt Posthumus by appealing to his sensuality. Posthumus, not to be tempted into adultery, told Iachimo of his pact with Imogen and of the ring and bracelet they had exchanged. Iachimo scoffingly wagered ten thousand ducats against Posthumus' ring that he could seduce Imogen.

Iachimo went to Britain with letters to which he had forged the name of Posthumus. Because of these letters Imogen received him. Then Iachimo, by ambiguities and innuendo, played upon her curiosity regarding the faithfulness of her husband. Failing to win her favor in that way, he gained access to her bedroom in a trunk which, he had told her, contained a valuable gift, bought in France, intended for the Roman emperor; he had asked that the trunk be placed in her chamber for safekeeping. While Imogen slept, he noted the details of the furnishings in the room, took the bracelet from her arm, and observed a cinque-spotted mole on her left breast.

Back in Italy, Iachimo described Imogen's room to Posthumus and produced the bracelet, which he said Imogen had given him. Incredulous, Posthumus asked Iachimo to describe some aspect of Imogen's body as better proof of his successful seduction. Iachimo's claim that he had kissed the mole on Imogen's breast enraged Posthumus, who swore that he would kill Imogen. He sent a letter to Pisanio, commanding that the servant kill Imogen. He also sent a letter to Imogen asking her to meet him in Milford Haven. Pisanio was to kill Imogen as they traveled through the Welsh hills.

On the journey Pisanio divulged the real purpose of their trip when he showed Imogen the letter ordering her death. Unable to harm his master's wife, Pisanio instructed her to dress as a boy and join the party of Caius Lucius, who was in Britain to collect tribute to the Emperor Augustus and who was soon to return to Rome. Then Imogen would be near Posthumus and could ultimately disprove Iachimo's accusations against her. Pisanio also gave Imogen a box containing a restorative, entrusted to him by the queen in case Imogen became ill during her trip. The contents, presumed by the queen to be a slow-acting poison, had been procured from her physician, who, suspecting chicanery, had reduced the drug content. The medicine would only induce long sleep. Taking leave of his mistress, Pisanio returned home.

Dressed in boy's clothing, Imogen, hungry and weary, came to the mountain cave of Belarius, who, banished from Cymbeline's court twenty years before, had kidnaped Guiderius and Arviragus, Cymbeline's infant sons. In Wales the two boys had been brought up to look upon Belarius as their father. Calling herself Fidele, Imogen won the affection of the three men when she asked shelter of them. Left alone when the men went out to hunt food, Imogen, emotionally spent and physically ill, swallowed some of the medicine which Pisanio had given her.

Cymbeline, meanwhile, had refused to pay the tribute demanded by Rome, and the two nations prepared for war. Cloten, infuriated by Imogen's coldness to his attentions, tried to learn her whereabouts. Pisanio, thinking to trick her pursuer, showed him the letter in which Posthumus asked Imogen to meet him at Milford Haven. Disguised as Posthumus, Cloten set out to avenge his injured vanity.

In Wales he came upon Belarius, Arviragus, and Guiderius as they hunted. Recognizing him as the queen's son, Belarius assumed that Cloten had come to arrest them as outlaws. He and Arviragus went in search of Cloten's followers while Guiderius fought with Cloten. Guiderius cut off Cloten's head and threw it into the river. Returning from their search, Arviragus found Imogen in a deathlike stupor. Thinking her dead, the three men prepared for her burial. Benevolent Belarius, remembering that Cloten was of royal birth, brought his headless body for burial and laid it near Imogen.

Imogen, awakening from her drugged sleep, was grief-stricken when she saw close by a body dressed in Posthumus' clothing. Still sorrowing, she joined the forces of Caius Lucius as the Roman army marched by to engage the soldiers of Cymbeline.

Remorseful Posthumus, a recruit in the Roman army, regretted his order for Imogen's death. Throwing away his uniform, he dressed himself as a British peasant. Although he could not restore Imogen's life, he would not take any more British lives. In a battle between the Romans and Britons, Posthumus vanquished and disarmed Iachimo. Cymbeline, taken prisoner, was rescued by Belarius and his two foster sons. These three had built a fort and, aided by Posthumus, had so spurred the morale of the fleeing British soldiers that Cymbeline's army was victorious.

Failing to die in battle, Posthumus identified himself as a Roman after Lucius had been taken, and was sent to prison by Cymbeline. In prison he had a vision in which Jove assured him that he would yet be the lord of the Lady Imogen. Jove ordered a tablet placed on Posthumus' chest. When Posthumus awoke and found the tablet, he read that a lion's whelp would be embraced by a piece of tender air and that branches lopped from a stately cedar would revive. Shortly before the time set for his execution, he was summoned to appear before Cymbeline.

In Cymbeline's tent, the king conferred honors upon Belarius, Guiderius, and Arviragus and bemoaned the fact that the fourth valiant soldier, so poorly dressed, was not present to receive his reward. Cornelius, the physician, told Cymbeline that the queen had died after her villainies. Lucius pleaded for the life of Imogen, still dressed as a boy, because of the page's youth. Pardoned, Imogen asked Iachimo to explain his possession of the ring he wore. As Iachimo confessed his dastardly cunning and lying to win the ring from Posthumus, Posthumus entered and identified himself as the murderer of Imogen. When Imogen protested against his confession, Posthumus struck her. Pisanio then identified Imogen to keep Posthumus from striking her again.

The truth disclosed, Belarius understood his foster sons' affinity for Imogen. Posthumus and Imogen, reunited, professed lifelong devotion to each other.

After Guiderius had confessed the murder of Cloten, Cymbeline ordered him bound, but he stayed the sentence when Belarius identified himself and the two young men. Cymbeline then blessed his three children who stood before him. A soothsayer interpreted Jove's message on the tablet left on Posthumus' chest. The lion's whelp was Posthumus, the son of Leonatus, and the piece of tender air was Imogen. The lopped branches from the stately cedar were Arviragus and Guiderius, long thought dead, now restored in the king's love. Overjoyed, Cymbeline made peace with Rome.

CYRANO DE BERGERAC

Type of work: Drama
Author: Edmond Rostand (1868-1918)
Type of plot: Tragi-comedy
Time of plot: Seventeenth century
Locale: France
First presented: 1897

Principal characters:
 CYRANO DE BERGERAC, poet and soldier
 ROXANE, with whom Cyrano is in love
 CHRISTIAN DE NEUVILLETTE, a clumsy young soldier

Critique:

Considered by many the most popular play of the modern French theater, *Cyrano de Bergerac* is also a perennial favorite with American audiences. Cyrano is more than a hot-tempered swordsman who gets into trouble because he resents people who make fun of his nose, and his name is more than a symbol for physical ugliness. Cyrano de Bergerac symbolizes magnanimity, unselfishness, beauty of soul.

The Story:

In the theater hall of the Hôtel de Burgundy, a young soldier named Christian de Neuvillette anxiously waited for the beautiful Roxane to appear in her box. Christian had fallen passionately in love with this girl whom he had never met. While he was waiting for her arrival, Christian became increasingly upset because he feared that he would never be able to summon sufficient courage to address her, for he believed she was as brilliant and as graceful as he was doltish and clumsy.

Also in the audience, waiting for the curtain to go up, was one Ragueneau, a romantic tavern-keeper and toss-pot poet, whose friends praised his verses to his face while behind his back they helped themselves to the pastries that he made. Ragueneau inquired of another poet concerning the whereabouts of Cyrano de Bergerac. The actor Montfleury, Cyrano's enemy and one of Roxane's suitors, was to star in the play, and Cyrano had threat-

ened him with bodily injury if he appeared for the performance. Cyrano, however, had not yet arrived.

At last Roxane appeared. The play began, and Montfleury came out on the stage to recite his lines. Suddenly a powerful voice ordered him to leave the stage. After the voice came the man, Cyrano de Bergerac, one of the best swordsmen in France. The performance was halted abruptly.

Another of Roxane's suitors tried to provoke a fight with Cyrano by ridiculing de Bergerac's uncommonly big nose. Cyrano, sensitive about his disfiguring nose, became the insulter instead of the insulted. Words led to a duel. To show his contempt for his adversary, Cyrano composed a poem while he was sparring with his opponent, and when he had finished the last word of the last line, Cyrano staggered his man. Le Bret, Cyrano's close friend, cautioned the gallant swordsman against making too many enemies by his insults.

Cyrano confessed that he was exceptionally moody lately because he was in love with his lovely cousin Roxane, despite the fact he could never hope to win her because of his ugliness. While Le Bret tried to give Cyrano confidence in himself, Roxane's chaperone appeared to give Cyrano a note from his cousin, who wanted to see him. Cyrano was overcome with joy.

The place selected for the meeting between Cyrano and Roxane was Ragueneau's tavern. Cyrano arrived early, and, while he waited for his beautiful cousin, he composed a love letter which he left unsigned because he intended to deliver it in person. When Roxane appeared, she confessed to Cyrano that she was in love. Cyrano thought for a moment that she was in love with him. But he soon realized that the lucky fellow was not Cyrano himself, but Christian. Roxane asked Cyrano to take the young soldier under his wing, to protect him in battle. Cyrano sadly consented to do her bidding.

Later, when Christian dared jest with Cyrano concerning the latter's nose, Cyrano restrained himself for Roxane's sake. When he learned that Cyrano was Roxane's cousin, Christian confessed his love for Roxane and begged Cyrano's help in winning her. Christian was a warrior, not a lover; he needed Cyrano's ability to compose pretty speeches and to write tender, graceful messages. Although his heart was broken, Cyrano gave the young man the letter he had written in Ragueneau's tavern.

Cyrano visited Roxane to inquire about her love affair with Christian. Roxane, who had recently received a letter from Christian, was delighted by his wit. Cyrano did not tell her that he was the writer of the letter.

Shortly afterward Christian told Cyrano that he now wanted to speak for himself in his wooing of Roxane. Under her balcony one evening Christian did try to speak for himself, but he became so tongue-tied that he had to ask the aid of Cyrano, who was lurking in the shadows. Cyrano, hidden, told Christian what to say, and Roxane was so delighted by these dictated protestations that she bestowed a kiss on Christian.

A friar appeared with a letter from the Count de Guiche, commander of Cyrano's regiment, to Roxane. The count wrote that he was coming to see her that night, even though by so doing he was deserting his post. Roxane deliberately misread the letter, which, she said, ordered the friar to marry her to Christian. Roxane asked Cyrano to delay de Guiche until after the ceremony, a request which de Bergerac effectively carried out by making the count think that Cyrano was mad. After learning that Roxane and Christian were already married, the duped de Guiche ordered Christian to report immediately to his regiment.

In a battle which followed, Cyrano and the other cadets were engaged against the Spanish. During the conflict Cyrano risked his life to send letters to Roxane through the enemy's lines, and Roxane never suspected that the author of these messages was not Christian. Later Roxane joined her husband, and to him she confessed that his masterful letters had brought her to his side.

Realizing that Roxane was really in love with the nobility and tenderness of Cyrano's letters, Christian begged Cyrano to tell Roxane the truth. But Christian was killed in battle shortly afterward, and Cyrano swore never to reveal Christian's secret. Rallying the cadets, Cyrano charged bravely into the fight, and under his leadership the Spanish were defeated.

Fifteen years passed. Roxane, grieving for Christian, had retired to a convent. Each week Cyrano was accustomed to visit Roxane. But one day he came late. When he arrived, he concealed under his hat a mortal wound which one of his enemies had inflicted by dropping an object from a building on Cyrano's head. While talking about her dead husband, Roxane recited to Cyrano Christian's last letter, which she kept next to her heart. With Roxane's permission, Cyrano read the letter which he himself had written, even though it had grown so dark that neither he nor Roxane could see the words.

Suddenly Roxane realized that Cyrano knew the contents of the letter by heart, that he must have written it. With this realization came her conviction that for fifteen years she had unknowingly loved the soul of Cyrano, not Christian. Roxane confessed her love for Cyrano, who died knowing that at last Roxane was aware of his love and that she shared it with him.

DAISY MILLER

Type of work: Novelette
Author: Henry James (1843-1916)
Type of plot: Psychological realism
Time of plot: Mid-nineteenth century
Locale: Vevey, Switzerland, and Rome
First published: 1878

Principal characters:
DAISY MILLER, an American tourist
WINTERBOURNE, an American expatriate
GIOVANELLI, Daisy's Italian suitor

Critique:

As in most of James' work, there is practically no plot in *Daisy Miller*. Rather, James is interested in a conflict between European and American customs and ideals. The crudities and touching innocence of Daisy Miller are revealed against a background of European manners and morals, and both are shown from the point of view of an expatriate American who has lived abroad too long. The special point of view makes *Daisy Miller* an ironic study of contrasts.

The Story:

Winterbourne was a young American who had lived in Europe for quite a while. He spent a great deal of time at Vevey, which was a favorite spot of his aunt, Mrs. Costello. One day, while he was loitering outside the hotel, he was attracted by a young woman who appeared to be related to Randolph Miller, a young American boy with whom he had been talking. After a while the young woman exchanged a few words with him. Her name was Daisy Miller. The boy was her brother, and they were in Vevey with their mother. They came from Schenectady, Winterbourne learned, and they intended to go next to Italy. Randolph insisted that he wanted to go back home. Winterbourne learned that Daisy hoped to visit the Castle of Chillon. He promised to take her there, for he was quite familiar with the old castle.

Winterbourne asked his aunt, Mrs. Costello, to meet Daisy. Mrs. Costello, however, would not agree because she thought the Millers were common. That evening Daisy and Winterbourne planned to go out on the lake, much to the horror of Eugenio, the Millers' traveling companion, who was more like a member of the family than a courier. At the last moment Daisy changed her mind about the night excursion. A few days later Winterbourne and Daisy visited the Castle of Chillon. The outing confirmed Mrs. Costello's opinion that Daisy was uncultured and unsophisticated.

Winterbourne made plans to go to Italy. When he arrived, he went directly to the home of Mrs. Walker, an American whom he had met in Geneva. There he met Daisy and Randolph. Daisy reproved him for not having called to see her. Winterbourne replied that she was unkind, as he had just arrived on the train. Daisy asked Mrs. Walker's permission to bring an Italian friend, Mr. Giovanelli, to a party Mrs. Walker was about to give. Mrs. Walker agreed. Then Daisy said that she and the Italian were going for a walk. Mrs. Walker was shocked, as young unmarried women did not walk the streets of Rome with Italians. Daisy suggested that there would be no objection if Winterbourne would go with her to the spot where she was to meet the Italian and then walk with them.

Winterbourne and Daisy set out and eventually found Giovanelli. They walked together for a while. Then Mrs. Walker's carriage drew alongside the strollers. She beckoned to Winterbourne and implored him to persuade Daisy to enter her carriage. She told him that Daisy had been ruining her reputation by such behavior; she had become familiar with Italians and was quite heedless of the scandal she was causing. Mrs. Walker said she would never speak to Winterbourne again if he did not ask Daisy to get into the carriage at once. But Daisy, refusing the requests of Mrs. Walker and Winterbourne, continued her walk with the Italian.

Mrs. Walker determined to snub Daisy at the party. When Winterbourne arrived, Daisy had not made her appearance. Mrs. Miller arrived more than an hour before Daisy appeared with Giovanelli. Mrs. Walker had a moment of weakness and greeted them politely. But as Daisy came to say goodnight, Mrs. Walker turned her back upon her. From that time on Daisy and Giovanelli found all doors shut to them. Winterbourne saw her occasionally, but she was always with the Italian. Everyone thought they were carrying on an intrigue. When Winterbourne asked her if she were engaged, Daisy said that she was not.

One night, despite the danger from malarial fever, Giovanelli took Daisy to the Colosseum. Winterbourne, encountering them in the ancient arena, reproached the Italian for his thoughtlessness. Giovanelli said that Daisy had insisted upon viewing the ruins by moonlight. Within a few days Daisy was dangerously ill. During her illness she sent word to Winterbourne that she had never been engaged to Giovanelli. A week later she was dead.

As they stood beside Daisy's grave in the Protestant cemetery in Rome, Giovanelli told Winterbourne that Daisy would never have married her Italian suitor, even if she had lived. Then Winterbourne realized that he himself had loved Daisy without knowing his own feelings, that he could have married her had he acted differently. He reasoned, too late, that he had lived in Europe too long, that he had forgotten the freedom of American manners and the complexity of the American character.

DAME CARE

Type of work: Novel
Author: Hermann Sudermann (1857-1928)
Type of plot: Domestic romance
Time of plot: Nineteenth century
Locale: Germany
First published: 1887

Principal characters:
PAUL MEYERHOFER, a simple farmer
MAX MEYERHOFER, his father
FRAU ELSBETH, his mother
ELSBETH DOUGLAS, a neighbor girl

Critique:

This novel, which has enjoyed wide-spread critical acclaim, is frequently read in language classes. It is an outstanding example of German romanticism. The three hallmarks of its epoch are the style colored by a kind of world-sadness, its completely rural setting, and its sentimental tone. *Dame Care—Frau Sorge* in the original—covers a wide span of years in its action, but it is gracefully concise without being abrupt. Sudermann exhibits a paternal sympathy for his characters; perhaps his greatest gift is his understanding of all classes of people.

The Story:

About the time their third son, Paul, was born, the Meyerhofers lost through forced sale their country estate, Helenenthal. Meyerhofer tried to keep his wife, Frau Elsbeth, in ignorance of what was going on, but she was so uneasy in her bed that at last he told her that a family named Douglas had bought his property.

Meyerhofer was a violent man, given to grandiose schemes to make wealth and endowed with a martyr complex. It suited him to move his family to a humble farm, within sight of Helenenthal, where they would be constantly reminded of their lost prosperity. Frau Elsbeth, who was a docile woman, shuddered at the prospect.

Mrs. Douglas, a kind-hearted woman, came to see the mother and her baby. She assured Frau Elsbeth that she could stay on at Helenenthal as long as the family wished. The two women became good friends. Mrs. Douglas acted as godmother for Paul, and Frau Elsbeth was godmother for Elsbeth, a daughter born to the Douglases a short time later. In spite of their friendship, however, Meyerhofer took offense at a fancied slight and moved his family in bleak November to their farm on the moor.

In those poor surroundings Paul led a secluded childhood. His mother, sensing his retiring disposition, was kind to him; his father was brutal. He continually ridiculed his son by comparing him unfavorably with his two lively older brothers. Paul was frequently beaten by his heavy-handed father, and after the beatings his mother would comfort him. She often told him stories; the one he remembered best was a frightening tale. It was about Dame Care, a gray woman who laid great burdens on poor people. Some years after they moved, Frau Elsbeth had twin daughters, Katie and Greta.

About the time Paul was learning to whistle, bad times came to the farm. The mortgage was due and there was no money to pay it. Day after day Meyerhofer drove into town and came back very late, usually drunk. In spite of the awe she felt for her husband, Frau Elsbeth determined to seek help. She took Paul with her to Helenenthal on a memorable visit. There she explained her husband's dislike for the Douglas family and asked for their help. The amiable Mr. Douglas gave her the money to pay the mortgage. Paul played with Elsbeth while the grownups visited.

At school Paul did not succeed easily. He had to study a long time to get his work done and he had to memorize all the answers to problems. But his handwriting was very good. The Erdmann brothers, wild-eyed and saucy, made his life miserable for years. They often beat him, stole his lunch, and threw his clothes into the river.

The Meyerhofer property was surrounded by a peat bog. Always too busy to pay attention to his farm, Meyerhofer bought a used steam engine to harvest peat. He gave half his harvest as down payment to Levy, a sharp trader, and hired an engineer whom Levy had recommended. But the old engine would never run, and Meyerhofer learned that the supposed engineer was only a tramp hired by Levy for a few days' imposture. That winter, when Levy came to collect the other half of the harvest, the duped Meyerhofer drove him off with a whip. Levy, a shrewd man of business, went to a lawyer. Meyerhofer was compelled to give up his harvest and, in addition, pay a heavy fine.

After the older brothers had been sent away to school there was no money to educate Paul, who was sent to confirmation classes. He saw Elsbeth there, even sat near her. She was kind to the boy and went out of her way to speak to him. The Erdmann brothers teased them about the friendship and said that Paul was sweethearting. Hating ridicule, Paul seldom spoke to Elsbeth.

For five years Paul, toiling on the farm, got little help from his father. Once when he was out seeding a distant field, Paul saw Elsbeth. Delighted to see him again, she gave him a book of Heine's poetry, and she was impressed with his ability to whistle whole symphonies. Once after she had been abroad for a long time, a party was given on her return and Paul and his family were invited. The rest of the Meyerhofers went early in the day, but Paul went after dark so that no one would see his shabby clothes. He watched his two sisters having a merry time, and saw his father talking grandly with Mr. Douglas.

Out of sympathy for Paul, Mr. Douglas agreed to go in with Meyerhofer on one of his schemes. On the strength of Douglas' endorsement, Meyerhofer borrowed money recklessly. When he heard what was going on, Mr. Douglas came to the farm and told Meyerhofer to stop. Meyerhofer set the dog on him, but Mr. Douglas, though bitten, choked the savage beast. While Paul was apologizing to his neighbor, Meyerhofer attacked a servant, Michel, who had watched the scene. Michel picked up an ax. Paul took it away from him and threw it down a well. Then he carried his struggling father into the house. From that day on Paul was master in the household.

While Paul was wandering late one night near Helenenthal, he saw brilliant flames shooting from his farm buildings. Michel had fired the barn. Paul was able to save the house, the livestock, and the old steam engine, but everything else was lost.

Beaten in spirit, Frau Elsbeth died a lingering death. At the funeral Paul saw Elsbeth again. Since her own mother was incurably ill, she felt a strong bond of sympathy for Paul. Later Paul, with the aid of books on mechanics sent by his remote brothers, began to rebuild the steam engine which had been his father's folly. He worked so hard that he had little time to look after his sisters. One night he overheard them in the meadow with the Erdmann boys and learned that his sisters' honor had been smirched by his old enemies. Waiting in a deserted road for them at night, he forced them at pistol point to swear they would marry Katie and Greta.

Finally getting the old steam engine to work, Paul began to cut and market peat. As his trade increased he became a man of substance and traveled about Germany. He heard of Elsbeth from time to time and knew she planned to marry her cousin.

One night, eight years after their barn burned, Paul suspected Meyerhofer's intention to burn the Douglas barn. To distract his father from his mad deed, he set fire to his own house and barn and was seriously burned in the flames.

Paul was taken to Helenenthal. The searchers had found Meyerhofer dead of a stroke near the Douglas barn, a broken pot of petroleum by his side. Although it was Elsbeth's wedding day, she insisted on staying by Paul's bed. The vicar was sent away, and her cousin left. For many weary days Elsbeth watched over Paul.

After his recovery Paul was tried for the deliberate burning of his own house. Admitting his guilt, he blamed himself for always having been so timid and withdrawn. Now that he had lost everything, he felt himself free at last. Dame Care, who had been his nemesis all his life, had been routed.

Paul was sentenced to two years in prison. On his release Elsbeth and Mr. Douglas met him to take him home. Both Helenenthal and Elsbeth would be his.

THE DAMNATION OF THERON WARE

Type of work: Novel
Author: Harold Frederic (1856-1898)
Type of plot: Social criticism
Time of plot: The 1890's
Locale: New York State
First published: 1896

Principal characters:
THERON WARE, a young Methodist minister
ALICE WARE, his wife
FATHER FORBES, a Catholic priest
CELIA MADDEN, a rich young Irish-Catholic girl
DR. LEDSMAR, Father Forbes' friend
MR. GORRINGE, a trustee of Theron's church

Critique:

The Damnation of Theron Ware was one of the first novels to deal with the problems of an American clergyman. While the book was in part an indictment of the hypocrisy of a particular denomination, it was not meant to be wholly so. The author intended to show that any individual was bound to fall who was not given a moral bulwark on which to lean in adversity. The novel condemns the minister's denomination only in so far as it did not prepare him to meet the beliefs of others and accept them, while still holding to the beliefs in which he had been trained. It is the training, not the denomination, which is taken to task.

The Story:

Theron Ware had gone to the annual statewide meeting of the Methodist Episcopal Church with great expectation of being appointed to the large church in Tecumseh. He was greatly disappointed, therefore, when he was sent to Octavius, a small rural community.

To the minister and his wife, the town and its citizens did not appear formidable at first, but a hint of what was to come occurred the first morning after their arrival. A boy who delivered milk to Mrs. Ware informed her that he could not deliver milk on Sunday because the trustees of the church would object. Shortly afterward the trustees told the new minister that his sermons were too dignified and that Mrs. Ware's Sunday bonnet was far too elaborate for a minister's wife. Theron and his wife were depressed. Unhappy in his new charge, Theron decided to write a book about Abraham.

One day Theron assisted an injured Irish-Catholic workman and went home with him to see what help he might give. At the man's deathbed Theron observed the parish priest and a pretty young red-haired girl, Celia Madden, who assisted him. Upon becoming acquainted with these two, the minister was surprised to find that his earlier hostility to Catholics and the Irish was foolish. These people were more cultured than he, as he learned a few evenings later when he went to the priest for some advice in connection with his proposed book.

At the priest's home he met Dr. Ledsmar, a retired physician interested in Biblical research. Both the priest and the doctor knew a great deal about the actual culture of Abraham and his people. They tried to be tactful, but the young minister quickly saw how wrong he had been to think himself ready to write a religious book on any topic; all he knew was the little he had been taught at his Methodist Seminary.

Upon leaving Father Forbes and the doctor, Theron walked past the Catholic church. Hearing music within, he entered to find Celia Madden at the organ. Later he walked home with her and discovered that she was interested in literature and art as well as music. Once again that evening Theron was made to realize how little he actually knew. He went home with the feeling that his own small world was not a very cultured one.

Three months later there was a revival at Theron's church. Mr. and Mrs. Soulsby, two professional exhorters, arrived to lead a week of meetings which were designed to pay off the church debt and put fervor into its members. The Wares, who entertained the Soulsbys, were surprised to find that the revival leaders were very much like insurance salesmen, employing very much the same tactics. During the revival week Theron was nonplussed to discover what he thought were the beginnings of an affair between his wife and one of the trustees of his church, Mr. Gorringe.

In a long talk with Mrs. Soulsby, Theron told her that he had almost decided to give up the Methodist ministry because of the shallowness he had discovered in his people and in his church. Mrs. Soulsby pointed out to him that Methodists were no worse than anyone else in the way of hypocrisy, and that all they lacked was an external discipline. She also reminded him that he was incapable of making a living because he lacked any worldly training.

Theron's life was further complicated when he realized that he was beginning to fall in love with Celia Madden. Because of her interest in music, he had asked her advice in buying a piano for his home, and she had, unknown to him, paid part of the bill for the instrument. He also found time to call on Dr. Ledsmar, whose peculiar views on the early church interested him. He disgusted the old doctor, however, with his insinuations of an affair between Father Forbes and Celia.

In September the Methodists of Octavius had a camp meeting. Its fervor did not appeal to Theron, after his more intellectual religious reading and his discussions with Celia and Father Forbes, and he went off quietly by himself. In the woods he came upon a picnic given by Father Forbes' church. At the picnic he met Celia and had a long talk with her, kissed her, and told her of his unhappiness in his double bondage to church and wife.

Soon afterward he alienated Celia by telling her that he was afraid of scandal if he were seen talking with her. He also offended Father Forbes by reports that Dr. Ledsmar had spoken slightingly of Celia. The priest told his housekeeper that he was no longer at home to Theron Ware.

One day Theron openly confronted his wife with his suspicions about her and Mr. Gorringe. She denied the charges, but her very denial seemed to speak against her in her husband's mind. In his unhappiness he went to see Celia. She was not at home, but her brother, who was dying slowly of tuberculosis, saw him. With the license of the dying he said that when Theron arrived in Octavius he had the face of an angel, full of innocence, but that in the eight months the minister had spent in the little town his face had taken on a look of deceit and cunning. Celia's brother continued by warning the minister that he should stay among his own people, that it was bad for him to tear himself from the support which Methodism had given him.

Leaving the Madden home, Theron learned that Celia was going to New York City. It occurred to him that Father Forbes was also going to the city that evening and perhaps they were traveling together. He went home and told his wife that urgent business called him to Albany; then he went to the station and boarded the train unseen. In New York he saw the priest and Celia meet, and he followed them to a hotel. After the priest had left the hotel, he went upstairs and knocked at Celia's door. She told him that she was busy and did not wish to see him, adding that she had noticed him following her earlier in the journey. While he pleaded with her, Father

Forbes came in with some other gentlemen and informed Theron that they had come to New York to get another brother of Celia's out of a bad scrape.

Dismissed, Theron stumbled down the stairs. A few days later he arrived at the Soulsby house at dawn. He told an incoherent story of having tried to commit suicide, of stealing money from the church at Octavius, and of wandering alone about the city for hours while he tried to drink himself to death.

The Soulsbys took him in and sent for his wife. He was ill for months. After his recovery both he and his wife realized that he was never meant for the ministry. Through the Soulsbys, Theron was finally able to make a new start in a real estate office in Seattle. Theron knew he would make a successful real estate agent. Or if that failed, he could try politics. There was still time enough for him to be in Congress before he was forty.

THE DANCE OF DEATH

Type of work: Drama
Author: August Strindberg (1849-1912)
Type of plot: Psychological realism
Time of plot: Late nineteenth century
Locale: Sweden
First presented: 1901

Principal characters:
  EDGAR, a captain in the Swedish coast artillery
  ALICE, his wife
  JUDITH, their daughter
  CURT, Alice's cousin
  ALLAN, Curt's son, in love with Judith

Critique:

The dramatic works of Strindberg have seldom been translated or produced in English-speaking countries, although his plays are known throughout Europe. Strindberg was especially interested in establishing a Swedish dramatic literature comparable to that of Ibsen in Norway. This particular play was written in two parts, in the way that Shakespeare wrote *Henry IV* in two parts; it is, in essence, a double play, the first part dealing with the mature adults and the second with their children. European critics have often referred to *The Dance of Death* as Strindberg's greatest dramatic achievement. The characters are real to the reader, shockingly so. And yet, beyond the intense realism, there is a fabric of symbolism, the meaning of which is nothing less than the vast sum of human relationships.

The Story:

For twenty-five years Edgar, a captain in the Swedish coast artillery, and his wife Alice had lived an unhappy existence. Their unhappiness was caused by Edgar's contempt for everyone else in the world; he thought of himself as a better being than others, even his wife, and he had made their marriage a tyranny. They lived on an island off the coast, where Edgar was the commanding officer of the artillery detachment. Living in an old prison, they avoided the other people of the island as well as officers of the post and their wives. Indeed, Alice was virtually a prisoner in her home. The only means of communication she had with the mainland was through a telegraph key, which she had taught herself to operate. Her skill she kept a secret, for her husband did not want her to have any means of communication with the outside world.

Alice's only hope of release from her husband's tyranny lay in the fact that he was ill and might die at any time. On their silver wedding anniversary Curt, Alice's cousin, arrived on the island to officiate as the quarantine officer. On his first visit to Edgar and Alice he learned about the life which they led, when Edgar suffered an attack and Alice gloated over her husband's illness. Curt, who had been divorced by his wife, also learned that Edgar had caused the divorce and persuaded the court to award the custody of the children to Curt's wife.

During the two days that Edgar lay ill, grave changes took place in the three people. Alice turned gray-haired; feeling that the time had come when she should admit her age, she had stopped tinting her hair. She also became an object of distrust to Curt, for she tried

THE DANCE OF DEATH by August Strindberg, from PLAYS BY AUGUST STRINDBERG. Translated by Edwin Björkman. By permission of the publishers, Charles Scribner's Sons. Copyright, 1912, by Charles Scribner's Sons. Renewed, 1940, by Edwin Björkman.

to make love to her cousin while her husband lay ill. Curt, unable to understand her actions, could not fully realize how much she hated her husband and how much she had suffered during the past twenty-five years. Edgar himself resembled a corpse after his illness; but he immediately tried, upon his recovery, to dominate the others.

On the third day after his attack the captain told his wife he was going to divorce her. In retaliation, she tried to have him convicted of the embezzlement of government funds, of which he was innocent. She also embraced her cousin Curt in her husband's presence, at which time Edgar tried to kill her with his saber. After that incident, both husband and wife subsided emotionally, admitting they had tortured each other enough. They both said they hoped that they could get along with each other peaceably, if not happily.

A few months later Curt's son Allan, a cadet stationed with Edgar's artillery company, fell in love with Judith, the daughter of Alice and Edgar. The parents, failing to realize the youngsters were serious in their affair, thought that Judith was making game of Allan at her father's request, for Edgar hated Allan because he was Curt's son. At the time Edgar was trying to arrange a marriage for Judith with a major in the regiment, a man older than Edgar. The lovers' quarrels of the two young people only served to heighten the illusion under which the three grownups labored.

Edgar, meanwhile, was also busy undermining Curt's position as quarantine officer. After gleaning information from Curt, he then published articles about quarantine management in periodicals and thus gained a reputation for himself in a field in which he was actually ignorant. After his retirement, the result of his illness, he planned to run for the national legislature, in opposition to Curt, who had expected to try for an office. Edgar completely discredited Curt with the voters by taking up a subscription for his rival, who, acting on Edgar's advice, had lost a great deal of money in an unwise investment. With deliberate malice, Edgar did everything he could to discredit Curt in the eyes of the world and to reduce him to abject poverty and dependence.

After Curt had lost his money, Edgar bought his house and its furnishings and then left the house exactly as it was, in order to make the loss more poignant to Curt. Then Edgar was made an inspector of quarantine stations, an appointment which made him Curt's superior in employment. Curt, accepting his reverses calmly and stoically, refused to lose his head, even though Alice tried to make him seek revenge. Alice still hoped that her ailing husband might die quickly, before he could completely ruin the lives of Curt, his son Allan, Judith, and Alice herself.

In the meantime the captain continued his plan to marry Judith to a man who could help to fulfill Edgar's ambitions. Instead of marrying her to the major, he arranged a marriage to the colonel of his old regiment, notwithstanding the fact that the colonel was more than forty years older than the girl. So far as anyone could suppose, the marriage was to take place; Judith herself seemed to be agreeable to the match. Alice made one last attempt to spoil the plan, but a letter she had written was intercepted by Edgar and returned by him to his wife.

Judith herself ruined Edgar's scheme by revealing her true love to Allan. To prevent the marriage, she called the colonel on the telephone, insulted him, and broke off the engagement. Then, with her mother's aid, she arranged to go to Allan at the military post to which Edgar had sent him. The failure of his plan was too much for Edgar. He suffered an apoplectic stroke, much to the delight of his wife, who saw revenge at last for all that she and the other members of the family had suffered at the sick man's hands. Unable to control her delight at

Edgar's approaching death, she taunted him on his deathbed with the fact that he was hated and that his evil plans were finally going awry. His only answer, since he had lost the power of speech, was to spit in her face.

After Edgar's death, which occurred within a few hours, both his wife and her cousin admitted that death had changed their attitudes toward the dead man. Alice said she must have loved him as well as hated him, and she hoped that peace would rest with his soul.

DANGEROUS ACQUAINTANCES

Type of work: Novel
Author: Pierre Choderlos de Laclos (1741-1803)
Type of plot: Psychological realism
Time of plot: Mid-eighteenth century
Locale: Paris and environs
First published: 1782

Principal characters:
CÉCILE DE VOLANGES, a young girl of good family
MADAME DE VOLANGES, her mother
THE COMTE DE GERCOURT, betrothed to Cécile
THE CHEVALIER DANCENY, Cécile's admirer
THE MARQUISE DE MERTEUIL, a fashionable matron, Gercourt's former
  mistress
THE VICOMTE DE VALMONT, a libertine
MADAME DE TOURVEL, the wife of a judge
SOPHIE CARNAY, Cécile's confidante
MADAME DE ROSEMONDE, Valmont's aunt

Critique:

Dangerous Acquaintances (*Les Liaisons Dangereuses*) is the only novel of a French artillery officer turned writer. It is a slow-paced but fascinating story in which Laclos proved himself a master of the epistolary form popularized by Samuel Richardson and other novelists of the eighteenth century. The letters are so skillfully interplayed and the characterizations so scrupulously presented that the reader willingly accepts the letters as real and the characters as people rather than as tools for telling a story. The illusion is furthered by Laclos' use of frequent footnotes explaining details in the letters. On its publication the novel achieved a *succès de scandale* which has caused the book to be stigmatized as a pornographic work. In actuality, the writer employed a theme of sexual intrigue in order to dissect the decadent society of his age and to lay bare its underlying tensions and antagonisms, so that it stands in sharp contrast to contemporary erotic romances which threw an atmosphere of glamor about a subject Laclos revealed in all its starkness. Interestingly, examples of the Freudian concepts of sex appear throughout the novel.

The Story:

When Cécile de Volanges was fifteen years old, her mother removed her from a convent in preparation for the girl's marriage to the Comte de Gercourt, a match already arranged by Madame de Volanges but without her daughter's knowledge. Shortly after her departure from the convent Cécile began an exchange of letters with Sophie Carnay, her close friend. Except for trips to shops for the purchase of an elaborate wardrobe, Cécile had few contacts with her fashionable mother. The little she knew about the plans for her future she learned from her maid.

Knowing of the match, the Marquise de Merteuil, an unscrupulous woman, saw in the proposed marriage an opportunity to be revenged on Gercourt, who some time before had deserted her for a woman of greater virtue. In her wounded vanity she schemed to have the Vicomte de Valmont, a libertine as unscrupulous as she, effect a liaison between Cécile and the Chevalier Danceny. Such an affair, circulated by court gossip after Cécile and Gercourt were married, would make the husband a laughing stock of the fashionable world. To complete her plan for revenge, the marquise also wanted Valmont to seduce Madame de Tourvel, the wife of a judge. Madame de Tourvel was the woman for whom Gercourt had aban-

789

doned the Marquise de Merteuil. As a reward for carrying out these malicious designs she promised to reinstate Valmont as her own lover.

Valmont was able to arrange a meeting between Cécile and Danceny. Although she was attracted to the young man, Cécile hesitated at first to reply to his letters. Her final consent to write to him, even to speak of love, was concealed from Madame de Volanges.

Valmont, meanwhile, had turned his attention to Madame de Tourvel. A woman of virtue, she tried to reject the vicomte's suit because she was aware of his sinister reputation. In spite of her decision she nevertheless found herself attracted to him, and in time she agreed to write to him but not to see him. She stipulated also that Valmont was not to mention the subject of love or to suggest intimacy. Eventually Valmont and Madame de Tourvel became friends. Aware of her indiscretion even in friendship, she finally told Valmont that he must go away, and he accepted her decision.

In the meantime, although she wrote him letters in which she passionately declared her love, Cécile was steadfast in her refusal to see Danceny. With love Cécile had grown more mature. She still wrote to Sophie Carnay, but not as frankly as before. Instead, she turned to the Marquise de Merteuil, whom she saw as a more experienced woman, for advice. In turn the marquise, impatient with the slow progress of the affair between Cécile and Danceny, informed Madame de Volanges of the matter, with the result that the mother, in an angry interview with her daughter, demanded that Cécile forfeit Danceny's letters. The marquise' plan produced the effect she had anticipated; Cécile and Danceny declared themselves more in love than ever.

Hoping to end her daughter's attachment to Danceny, Madame de Volanges took Cécile to the country to visit Madame de Rosemonde, Valmont's ailing aunt. Valmont soon followed, on the Marquise de Merteuil's instructions, to keep alive the affair between Cécile and the young chevalier and to arrange for Danceny's secret arrival. Then Valmont, bored with rustic life, decided to take Cécile for himself. Under the pretext of making it safer for him to deliver Danceny's letters, he persuaded her to give him the key to her room. At the first opportunity that arose Valmont seduced her. At first the girl was angered and shocked by his passion, but before long she was surrendering herself to him willingly. At the same time Valmont was still continuing his attentions to Madame de Tourvel. Deciding that persistence accomplished nothing, he began to ignore her. Madame de Tourvel then wrote offering her friendship.

Cécile, deep in her affair with Valmont, wrote asking the Marquise de Merteuil's advice on how to treat Danceny. Madame de Volanges, not knowing the true situation, also wrote the marquise and said that she had considered breaking off the match with Gercourt; her daughter's happiness, she declared, was perhaps worth more than an advantageous marriage. In reply, the marquise earnestly cautioned Madame de Volanges on a mother's duty to guide a daughter and to provide for her future.

Madame de Tourvel, also a guest of Valmont's aunt, gave that gallant the opportunity to seduce her. Although tempted, he took greater pleasure in seeing her virtue humbled. After his refusal and Madame de Tourvel's own moral scruples had forced her to flee in shame, she wrote Madame de Rosemonde a letter in which she apologized for her abrupt departure and explained fully her her emotional straits. Madame de Rosemonde's reply was filled with noble sentiments and encouragement for her friend.

Valmont was surprised to find himself deflated by Madame de Tourvel's departure. His ego suffered another blow when Cécile locked him out of her room.

The marquise, more impatient than

ever with Valmont's slow progress, decided to work her revenge through Danceny. Her first step was to captivate the young chevalier. An easy prey, he nevertheless continued to write impassioned letters to Cécile.

Valmont then decided to possess Madame de Tourvel. Her initial hesitation, surrender, and complete abandon he described in a triumphant letter to the Marquise de Merteuil. His account closed with the announcement that he was coming at once to claim the reward she had promised him. But the marquise managed to put off his importunate claim by reproving him about his handling of his affair with Madame de Tourvel. The difference between this and his other affairs, she said, was that he had become emotionally involved; his previous conquests had been smoothly and successfully accomplished because he had regarded them only as arrangements of convenience, not relationships of feeling. The irony of her attitude was that she was still in love with Valmont and had not counted on losing him, even for a short time. She had lost control of the strings by which she had dangled Valmont to satisfy her desire for vengeance.

Valmont, meanwhile, was trying to free himself of emotional involvements with Cécile and Danceny. Cécile had miscarried his child; Danceny's devotion no longer amused him. Although he made every effort to win the favor of the marquise, she held herself aloof, and after a quarrel she capriciously turned from him to Danceny and made that young man a slave to her charms and will.

Both Valmont and the marquise were eventually defeated in this duel of egotistic and sexual rivalry. Danceny, having learned of Valmont's dealings with Cécile, challenged the vicomte to a duel and mortally wounded him. As he was dying, Valmont gave the chevalier his entire correspondence with the marquise. Her malice exposed, she faced social ruin. After an attack of smallpox which left her disfigured for life, she fled to Holland. Madame de Tourvel, already mentally upset because of the treatment she had received from Valmont, died of grief at his death. Cécile entered a convent. Danceny gave the incriminating letters to Madame de Rosemonde and, vowing celibacy, entered the order of the Knights of Malta. Madame de Rosemonde sealed the letters which had brought disaster or death to all who had been involved with so dangerous an acquaintance as the Marquise de Merteuil.

DANIEL DERONDA

Type of work: Novel
Author: George Eliot (Mary Ann Evans, 1819-1880)
Type of plot: Social realism
Time of plot: Mid-nineteenth century
Locale: Rural England, London, the Continent
First published: 1876

Principal characters:
DANIEL DERONDA
MIRAH LAPIDOTH, a girl he saves from drowning
SIR HUGO MALLINGER, Daniel's guardian
LADY MALLINGER, his wife
GWENDOLEN HARLETH, a beautiful young lady
MRS. DAVILOW, her mother
MRS. GASCOIGNE, Gwendolen's sister
MR. GASCOIGNE, her husband
REX GASCOIGNE, their son
ANNA GASCOIGNE, their daughter
MALLINGER GRANDCOURT, Gwendolen's husband, Sir Hugo's heir
LUSH, his follower
HERR KLESMER, a musician
CATHERINE ARROWPOINT, his wife, an heiress
HANS MEYRICK, one of Deronda's friends
MRS. MEYRICK, his mother
EZRA COHEN, a shopkeeper in the East End
MORDECAI, a boarder with the Cohens, Mirah's brother
MRS. LYDIA GLASHER, Grandcourt's former mistress

Critique:

Daniel Deronda shifts from a novel depicting the difficulties and romances of a group of people in English society to a treatment of anti-Semitism in Victorian England. The character Daniel Deronda, the ward of Sir Hugo Mallinger, provides a bridge between the two portions of the book. With all its heavy evidence against the evil of anti-Semitism, the novel does not become an essay, for throughout the work George Eliot maintains sharp observation of the follies and delusions of Victorian life, as well as a keen sense of moral discrimination between her characters. Like *Middlemarch,* this novel is distinguished by realistic appraisals of people in all levels of society from the august and benevolent Sir Hugo Mallinger to Ezra Cohen, the crafty yet generous shopkeeper in the East End. If the novel does not show the consistency of theme or careful construction of George Eliot at her best, it still propagandizes skillfully for worthy causes and creates a vivid, clear, and varied scheme of life.

The Story:

Gwendolen Harleth, a strikingly beautiful young woman, was gambling at Leubronn. Playing with a cold, emotionless style, she had been winning consistently. Her attention was suddenly caught by the stare of a dark, handsome gentleman whom she did not know and who seemed to be reproving her. When her luck changed, and she lost all her money, she returned to her room to find a letter from her mother requesting her immediate return to England. Before she left, Gwendolen decided that she would have one more fling at the gaming tables. She sold her turquoise necklace for the money to play roulette, but before she could get to the tables the necklace was repurchased and returned to her with an anonymous note. Certain that the unknown man was her benefactor, she felt that she could not very well return to the roulette table. She went back to England as soon as she could. Her mother had recalled her because the family had lost all their money through unwise business speculations.

Gwendolen a high-spirited, willful, accomplished, and intelligent girl, was Mrs. Davilow's only child by her first marriage, and her favorite. By her second marriage —Mr. Davilow was also dead—she had four colorless, spiritless daughters. About a year before, she had moved to Offendene to be near her sister and brother-in-law, the prosperous, socially acceptable Gascoignes and to see what she could do about arranging a profitable marriage for her oldest daughter. Gwendolen's beauty and manner had impressed all the surrounding gentry, but her first victim was her cousin, affable Rex Gascoigne. Although he had been willing to give up his career at Oxford for Gwendolen, his family refused to countenance so unwise a move. Rex, broken in spirit, was sent away temporarily, but Gwendolen remained unmoved by the whole affair.

Soon afterward the county became excited over the visit of Mallinger Grandcourt, the somewhat aloof, unmarried heir to Diplow and several other large properties owned by Sir Hugo Mallinger. All the young ladies were eager to get Grandcourt to notice them, but it was Gwendolen, apparently indifferent and coy in conversation with the well-mannered but monosyllabic Grandcourt, who had most success. For several weeks, Grandcourt courted Gwendolen, yet neither forced to any crisis the issue of possible marriage. Gwendolen's mother, uncle, and aunt urged her to try to capture Grandcourt. Just when it seemed that Grandcourt would propose and Gwendolen would accept, Mrs. Lydia Glasher appeared, brought to the scene by the scheming of Grandcourt's companion, Lush, to tell Gwendolen that she was the mother of four of Grandcourt's illegitimate children and that she had left her husband to live

with Grandcourt. She begged Gwendolen not to accept Grandcourt so that she might have the chance to secure him as the rightful father of her children. Gwendolen, promising not to stand in Mrs. Glasher's way, had gone immediately to join friends at Leubronn.

Before he came to Leubronn, Daniel Deronda, the man whom Gwendolen had encountered in the gambling casino, had been Sir Hugo Mallinger's ward. He did not know his parents, but Sir Hugo had always treated him well. Sir Hugo, who had married late in life, had only daughters. Although he lavished a great deal of expense and affection on Deronda, his property was to go to his nephew, Mallinger Grandcourt. At Cambridge, Deronda had been extremely popular. There, too, he had earned the undying gratitude of a poor student named Hans Meyrick, whom Deronda helped to win a scholarship at the expense of his own studies. One day, after leaving Cambridge, while in a boat on the river, Deronda saved a pale and frightened young woman, Mirah Lapidoth, from committing suicide. She told him that she was a Jewess, returned after years of wandering with a brutal and blasphemous father, to look for her lost and fondly remembered mother and brother in London. Deronda took her to Mrs. Meyrick's home. There Mrs. Meyrick and her daughters nursed the penniless Mirah back to health.

When Gwendolen returned to Offendene, she learned that her family would be forced to move to a small cottage and that she would have to become a governess. The idea oppressed her so strongly that when she saw Grandcourt, who had been pursuing her on the Continent, she agreed at once to marry him, in spite of her promise to Mrs. Glasher. Her mother, aunt, and uncle knew nothing of Mrs. Glasher; Grandcourt knew only that she had spoken to Gwendolen, knowledge that he kept to himself.

After their marriage, Grandcourt soon turned out to be a mean, domineering, demanding man. He had set out to break

Gwendolen's spirit, and he did. In the meantime, at several house parties, Gwendolen had met Daniel Deronda and found herself much attracted to him. At a New Year's party at Sir Hugo Mallinger's, Gwendolen, despite her husband's disapproval and biting reprisals, had spoken to Deronda frequently. When she told Deronda her whole story and confessed her guilt in breaking her promise to Mrs. Glasher, Deronda suggested that she show her repentance by living a less selfish life, caring for and helping others less fortunate than she. Gwendolen, realizing the folly of her marriage to Grandcourt, and wishing to find some measure of happiness and peace, decided to follow the course Deronda had proposed.

Meanwhile, Deronda was attempting to secure Mirah's future and, if possible, to find her family. Mirah had been an actress and had some talent for singing. Deronda arranged an interview for her with Herr Klesmer, a German-Jewish musician with many connections, who could get Mirah started on a career. Herr Klesmer was very much impressed with Mirah's singing. He had known Gwendolen at Offendene and, in his honesty, had refused to help her when she also asked for singing engagements; he had thought her without sufficient talent and had given her ego its first blow. Herr Klesmer had also married Miss Arrowpoint, the most talented and attractive girl, save Gwendolen, in the vicinity of Offendene.

Still trying to find Mirah's family, Deronda went wandering in the London East End. There he became friendly with the family of Ezra Cohen, a shopkeeper of craft and generosity. For a time, on the basis of some slight evidence, Deronda believed that the man might be Mirah's brother. There also, through Ezra's family, he met Mordecai, a feeble and learned man who immediately felt a great kinship with Deronda. Mordecai took Deronda to a meeting of his club, a group of men who discussed scholarly, political, and theological topics far removed from the commercial interests of Ezra.

Deronda was delighted when he finally learned that Mordecai was really Mirah's brother. This discovery helped Deronda himself to acknowledge and accept his own spiritual and literal kinship with the Jews. The boy of unknown origin, able to move successfully in the high society of England, had found his real home in London's East End.

DAPHNIS AND CHLOË

Type of work: Tale
Author: Attributed to Longus (third century)
Type of plot: Pastoral romance
Time of plot: Indefinite
Locale: Island of Lesbos
First transcribed: Third century manuscript

Principal characters:
DAPHNIS, a young shepherd
CHLOË, a shepherdess

Critique:

A product of decadent Greek literature, *Daphnis and Chloë* is one of the most popular of the early predecessors of the modern novel. Highly romantic in both characterization and incident, it centers about the innocent though passionate love of two children of nature amid idyllic scenes of natural beauty. We forgive the many extravagant improbabilities of the story because of the charming portrayal of the refreshing, often amusing, naïveté of two children unspoiled by contact with city manners.

The Story:

On ·the Greek island of Lesbos a goatherd named Lamo one day found a richly dressed infant boy being suckled by one of his goats. Lamo and his wife, Myrtale, hid the purple cloak and ivory dagger the boy had worn and pretended he was their own son. They named him Daphnis. Two years later a shepherd named Dryas discovered in a cave of the Nymphs an infant girl being nursed by one of his sheep. This child also was richly dressed. Dryas and his wife Nape kept the girl as their own, giving her the name Chloë.

When the two children were fifteen and thirteen respectively, they were given flocks to tend. Daphnis and Chloë played happily together, amusing themselves in many ways. One day, while chasing a goat, Daphnis fell into a wolf-pit, from which he was rescued unharmed by Chloë and a herdsman she had summoned to help her. Daphnis began to experience delightful but disturbing feelings about Chloë. Dorco, a herdsman, asked permission to marry Chloë but was refused by Dryas. Disguising himself in a wolfskin, Dorco shortly afterward attempted to seize Chloë. Attacked by the flock dogs, he was rescued by Daphnis and Chloë, who innocently thought he had merely been playing a prank. Love, little understood by either, grew between Daphnis and Chloë.

In the autumn some Tyrian pirates wounded Dorco, stole some of his oxen and cows, and took Daphnis away with them. Chloë, who heard Daphnis calling to her from the pirate ship, ran to aid the mortally wounded Dorco. Dorco gave her his herdsman's pipe, telling her to blow upon it. When she blew, the cattle jumped into the sea and overturned the ship. The pirates drowned, but Daphnis, catching on to the horns of two swimming cows, came safely to shore.

After the celebration of the autumn vintage Daphnis and Chloë returned to their flocks. They attempted in their innocence to practice the art of love, but they were not successful. Some young men of Methymne came to the fields of Mitylene to hunt. When a goat gnawed in two a withe used as a cable to hold their small ship, the Methymneans blamed Daphnis and set upon him. In a trial over the affair Daphnis was judged innocent. The angry Methymneans later carried away Chloë. The god Pan warned the Methymnean captain in a dream that he should bring back Chloë, and she was returned. Daphnis and Chloë joyfully celebrated holidays in honor of Pan.

The two lovers were sad at being parted by winter weather, which kept the flocks in their folds. In the spring the lovers happily drove their flocks again to the fields. When a woman named Lycaenium became enamored of the boy, Daphnis finally learned how to ease the pains he had felt for Chloë; but Lycaenium warned him that Chloë would be hurt the first time she experienced the ecstasy of love. Through fear of doing physical harm to his sweetheart the tender Daphnis would not deflower his Chloë. Meanwhile many suitors, Lampis among them, asked for the hand of Chloë, and Dryas came near consenting. Daphnis bewailed his inability to compete successfully with the suitors because of his poverty. Then with the aid of the Nymphs he found a purse of silver, which he gave Dryas in order to become contracted to Chloë. In return Dryas asked Lamo to consent to the marriage of his son, but Lamo answered that first he must consult his master, Dionysophanes.

Lamo, Daphnis, and Chloë prepared to entertain Dionysophanes; but Lampis ravaged the garden they had prepared because he had been denied Chloë's hand.

Fearing the wrath of his master, Lamo lamented his ill fortune. Eudromus, a page, helped to explain the trouble to Lamo's young master Astylus, who promised to intercede with his father and blame the wanton destruction on some horses in the neighborhood. Astylus' parasite, Gnatho, fell in love with Daphnis but was repulsed. Finally the depraved Gnatho received Astylus' permission to take Daphnis with him to the city. Just in time Lamo revealed the story of the finding of Daphnis, who was discovered to be Dionysophanes' son. Meanwhile Lampis stole Chloë, who was later rescued by Gnatho. After Dryas told how Chloë had been found as a child, it was learned that she was the daughter of Megacles of Mitylene. Thus the supposed son and daughter of Lamo and Dryas were revealed as the children of wealthy parents who were happy to consent to their marriage. The wedding was celebrated amid the rural scenes dear to both bride and groom. Daphnis became Philopoemen and Chloë was named Agéle. On her wedding night Chloë at last learned from Daphnis how might be obtained the delights of love.

THE DARK JOURNEY

Type of work: Novel
Author: Julian Green (1900-   )
Type of plot: Psychological realism
Time of plot: Early twentieth century
Locale: France
First published: 1929

Principal characters:
PAUL GUÉRET, a neurotic tutor
ANGÈLE, a young laundress
MADAME LONDE, a restaurant proprietress
MONSIEUR GROSGEORGE, Guéret's employer
MADAME GROSGEORGE, his wife
FERNANDE, a young girl

Critique:

Like all of Julian Green's work, *The Dark Journey* is a bleak and somber book, impressive both in its realistic evocation of French provincial life and in its metaphysical overtones of human destiny. Shadows of disaster and doom brood over his pages; his characters, as in the case of Paul Guéret and Madame Grosgeorge, have premonitions of their fates, but they are powerless to help themselves. This novel, published in France under the title *Léviathan*, deals with the twin themes of violence and lust. Nothing is trivial, however, and little is vulgar. Instead, with impersonal detachment and classic gravity of style, the writer tells a story of disturbing but compelling vigor, in which violence and melodrama are only incidental to his vastly greater effects of cumulative passion and tragic finality.

The Story:

Paul Guéret was an incompetent, prematurely-aged tutor hired to instruct the sickly, backward son of a prosperous provincial family named Grosgeorge. Knowing himself a failure and tired of the wife whom he no longer loved, he had hoped that life would be better in Chanteilles; but within a month he was just as wretched there as he had been in Paris, where his feelings of self-pity and frustration had often driven him into sordid love affairs. In Chanteilles, bored by his dreary surroundings, he soon found himself infatuated with Angèle, a young girl who worked in a laundry. Hoping to become her lover, he began to write letters asking her to meet him. Sometimes he followed her at a distance when she delivered washing to her customers.

One night he accosted her at a footbridge on the outskirts of the town. Hating himself for his shabby clothes and stammering speech, he offered her a cheap ring stolen from his wife. Although she accepted the ring, the girl did not encourage his attentions. His abrupt yet furtive ardor both attracted and repelled her.

That same night Guéret went by chance to the Restaurant Londe in nearby Lorges. There Madame Londe, the proprietress, presided majestically behind her cashier's desk. A sly woman whose days were given over to spying and gossip, she delighted in alternately cajoling and bullying her patrons, who seemed to hold her resentfully in awe. When Guéret entered, she was disturbed because he was a stranger and she knew nothing about him. Refusing to let him pay for his dinner, she had him write his name in her account book. Her desire was to add him to her regular clientele.

Madame Londe's hold over her patrons

was a sinister one, maintained through her niece, Angèle. Because the girl was indebted to her for food and a room, she forced Angèle to sell her favors to the habitués of the restaurant. With knowledge thus gained of the guilt and secret vices of her patrons, she was able to dictate to them as she pleased. Her own position as a procuress gave her no worry; her only concern was her lust for power over others.

Upset by his desire for Angèle, Guéret paid little attention to his duties as a tutor. André Grosgeorge was a poor student, but his mother shrewdly blamed Guéret for her son's slow progress. Madame Grosgeorge was a woman in whom the starved passions of her girlhood had turned to a tortured kind of love which found its outlet in cruelty and treachery. Because the husband whom she despised ignored her nagging tirades, she took special pleasure in beating her son and in humiliating Guéret.

Monsieur Grosgeorge felt sorry for the browbeaten tutor. Having guessed that Guéret was unhappily married, he bluntly advised him to find a mistress before he wasted his years in moping dullness. That, said Grosgeorge, was the course he himself had followed. One day he boastingly produced a note in which the writer asked Grosgeorge to meet her the next night. Guéret, staring at the letter, shook with suppressed rage. He recognized the scrawl as Angèle's handwriting.

Angèle, after several meetings with Guéret, became more independent in her attitude toward Madame Londe. Because his conduct was quite different from that of other men who sought her favors, she no longer wished to sell herself in order to act as her aunt's informant. During a quarrel Angèle, who refused to keep an assignation the old woman had arranged, threatened to run away. Madame Londe was worried. Afraid that she would lose her hold over her patrons, she began to train Fernande, a twelve-year-old girl, to take Angèle's place.

Guéret returned to the Restaurant Londe. During the meal he learned from the talk of the other diners that Angèle was Madame Londe's niece and that she had given herself to most of the men there. That night, driven to desperation by his knowledge, he broke into her bedroom. It was empty. When Madame Londe, aroused by his entry, screamed for help, he ran away and hid in a wood. On his way back to Chanteilles he met Angèle. In sudden, brutal fury he picked up a branch and struck at her until blood covered her face and head.

All that day he skulked beside the river. While he was sneaking back into town after dark, he met a feeble old man. Fearing capture, he seized the old man's stick and beat him to death. Filled with blind terror, he fled across the yards of unknown houses and through back streets of the town.

The neighborhood was shocked by the brutality of Guéret's crime, and for weeks the townspeople refused to venture into the streets at night. Angèle, disfigured for life, refused to give the name of her assailant and remained shut up in her room above the restaurant. Only Madame Grosgeorge scoffed at those who bolted their doors at dusk. Indeed, she seemed to relish the fact that the shabby, blundering tutor had scarred the face of her husband's mistress and violently disrupted the monotony of her own existence.

At last the hue and cry died down. Guéret, unable to stay away from Angèle, returned to the district. Madame Grosgeorge, out walking, saw him near the footbridge and called after him that she would meet him there the next evening. Guéret did not appear, although she waited impatiently for more than an hour. Later he came to her villa, and she, unknown to her husband, hid the fugitive in her private sitting-room. She promised that she would give him money and some of her husband's clothing before she sent him away in the morning.

But his presence in the house gave her such strange satisfaction that she refused to let him go as she had promised. The next morning she went to her sitting-room and tried to talk to him about his crimes. When his answers showed only that he was still in love with Angèle, Madame Grosgeorge felt cheated. She had admired him for his violence; now she despised him for his foolish passion. Again she locked him in the room while she tried to decide what to do. Little Fernande came to deliver some laundry. On impulse Madame Grosgeorge wrote a note telling Angèle that Guéret was in her house and asking that the police be called.

Madame Londe, always on the alert, intercepted the message and hurried to give the alarm. Angèle, learning what had happened, sent Fernande to warn the fugitive that he must escape at once. Madame Grosgeorge, meanwhile, had returned to Guéret. When he insisted that she let him go, she locked the door and threw the key out of the window. Then she told him that Angèle knew his whereabouts and that if he were betrayed the laundress would be to blame. Taking a revolver from her desk, she put it in her belt and calmly prepared to write a letter. Fernande ran into the garden. Guéret, leaning out of the window, asked her to pick up the key and unlock the door. A report sounded behind him. Madame Grosgeorge had shot herself.

DARK LAUGHTER

Type of work: Novel
Author: Sherwood Anderson (1876-1941)
Type of plot: Psychological realism
Time of plot: 1920's
Locale: Old Harbor, Indiana
First published: 1925

          Principal characters:
              BRUCE DUDLEY, formerly John Stockton, a Chicago reporter
              SPONGE MARTIN, a workman close to the grass roots
              FRED GREY, owner of an automobile wheel factory
              ALINE, his wife

Critique:

Dark Laughter, Sherwood Anderson's most popular novel, is a book of moods rather than of plot. Its simple story is that of two individuals in revolt against the restrictions of modern life and seeking happiness together. Anderson seems to say that Bruce Dudley and Aline Grey were unhappy because they were repressed; they gave themselves over to the secret desires within them and therefore they became happy. One may question whether Bruce and Aline were not merely restless and somewhat adolescent emotionally, rather than strong and brave in their attempt to live by amoral standards.

The Story:

Bruce Dudley's name was not Bruce Dudley at all. It was John Stockton. But he had grown tired of being John Stockton, reporter on a Chicago paper, married to Bernice who worked on the same paper and who wrote magazine stories on the side. She thought him flighty and he admitted it. He wanted adventure. He wanted to go down the Mississippi as Huckleberry Finn had done. He wanted to go back to Old Harbor, the river town in Indiana where he had spent his childhood. And so, with less than three hundred dollars, he left Chicago, Bernice, and his job on the paper. He picked up the name Bruce Dudley from two store signs in an

Illinois town. After his trip to New Orleans he went to Old Harbor and got a job varnishing automobile wheels in the Grey Wheel Company.

Sponge Martin worked in the same room with Bruce. Sponge, a wiry old fellow with a black mustache, lived a simple, elemental life. That was the reason, perhaps, why Bruce liked him so much. Sometimes when the nights were fair and the fish were biting, Sponge and his wife took sandwiches and some moonshine whiskey and went down to the river. They fished for a while and got drunk, and then Sponge's wife made him feel like a young man again. Bruce wished he could be as happy and carefree as Sponge.

When Bruce was making his way down the Mississippi and when he stayed for five months in an old house in New Orleans—that was before he came to Old Harbor—he watched the Negroes and listened to their songs and laughter. It seemed to him that they lived as simply as children and were happy, laughing their dark laughter.

Aline, the wife of Fred Grey, who owned the Grey Wheel Company, saw Bruce Dudley walking out the factory door one evening as she sat in her car waiting for Fred. Who he was she did not know, but she remembered another man to whom she had felt attracted in the same way. It happened in Paris after the war. She had seen the man at Rose Frank's apartment and she had wanted him. Then she had married Fred, who was recovering from the shock of the war. He was not what she wished for, but, somehow, she had married him.

One evening Bruce Dudley passed by the Grey home as Aline stood in the yard. He stopped and looked first at the house and then at Aline. Neither spoke but something passed between them. They had found each other.

Aline, who had advertised for a gardener, hired Bruce after turning down several applicants. Bruce had quit his job at the factory shortly before he saw her advertisement. When Bruce began to work for her, the two maintained some reserve, but each was determined to have the other. Bruce and Aline carried on many imaginary conversations. Fred apparently resented Bruce's presence about the grounds, but he said nothing to the man. When he questioned his wife, he learned that she knew nothing of Bruce except that he was a good worker.

As Aline watched her husband leave for the factory each morning she wondered how much he knew. She thought a great deal about her own life and about life in general. Her husband was no lover. Few women nowadays had true lovers. Modern civilization told one what he could not have. One belittled what he could not possess. Because one did not have love, one made fun of it, was skeptical of it, and besmirched it. The little play of the two men and the woman went on silently. Two Negro women who worked in Aline's house watched the proceedings. From time to time they laughed, and their dark laughter seemed mocking. White folks were queer. They made life so involved. Negroes took what they wanted—simply, openly, happily.

One day in June, after Fred had gone to march in a veterans' parade and the Negro servants had gone to watch the parade, Aline and Bruce were left alone. She sat and watched him working in the garden. Finally he looked at her, and he followed her into the house through a door she purposely left open. Before Fred returned, Bruce had left the house. He disappeared from Old Harbor. Two months later Aline told Fred she was going to have a child.

As Fred came home one evening in the early fall, he saw his wife and Bruce together in the garden. Aline calmly called to him and announced that the child she was expecting was not his. She and Bruce had waited, she went on, so that she might let him know they were leaving. Fred pleaded with her to stay, knowing she was hurting herself, but they walked away, Bruce carrying two heavy bags.

Fred told himself, as he stood with his revolver in his hand a few minutes later, that he could not dispassionately let another man walk away with his wife. His mind was filled with confused anger. For a moment he thought of killing himself. Then he followed the pair along the river road. He was determined to kill Bruce. But he lost them in the darkness. In a blind fury he shot at the river. On the way back to his house he stopped to sit on a log. The revolver fell to the ground and he sat crying like a child for a long time.

After Fred had returned to his home and gone to bed, he tried to laugh at what had happened. He could not. But outside in the road he heard a sudden burst of laughter. It was the younger of the two Negresses who worked in the Grey home. She cried out loudly that she had known it all the time, and again there came a burst of laughter—dark laughter.

DARKNESS AT NOON

Type of work: Novel
Author: Arthur Koestler (1905-   )
Type of plot: Social criticism
Time of plot: 1930's
Locale: Russia
First published: 1941

Principal characters:

NICHOLAS RUBASHOV, a political prisoner
IVANOV, a prison official
GLETKIN, another official
MICHAEL BOGRAV, another prisoner
KIEFFER (HARE-LIP), an informer

Critique:

This remarkable modern novel by Arthur Koestler is a highly analytical piece of writing which transports the reader into a Russian prison and into the very consciousness of a political prisoner, accused of crimes he never committed. *Darkness at Noon* represents an ironic and scathing criticism of the Moscow trials. At the same time, it presents a careful analysis of the Soviet principles. Reference to Russia is made only in the foreword, however, and the party leader is known only as No. 1 in this powerful but highly restrained social document.

The Story:

Nicholas Rubashov, ex-Commissar of the People and once a power in the party, was in prison. Arrested at his lodgings in the middle of the night, he had been taken secretly to cell 404, which bore his name on a card just above the spy-hole. He knew that he was located in an isolation cell for condemned political suspects.

At seven o'clock in the morning Rubashov was awakened by a bugle, but he did not get up. Soon he heard sounds in the corridor. He imagined that someone was to be tortured, and he dreaded hearing the first screams of pain from the victim. When the footsteps reached his own section, he saw through the judas-eye that guards were serving breakfast.

Rubashov did not receive any breakfast because he had reported himself ill. He began to pace up and down the cell, six and a half steps to the window, six and a half steps back.

Soon he heard a quiet knocking from the wall of adjoining cell 402. In communicating with each other prisoners used the "quadratic alphabet," a square of twenty-five letters, five horizontal rows of five letters each. The first series of taps represented the number of the row; the second series the number of the letter in the row. From the tappings Rubashov pictured his neighbor as a military man, one not in sympathy with the methods of the great leader or with the views of Rubashov himself. From his window he saw prisoners walking in the courtyard for exercise. One of these, a man with a hare-lip, looked repeatedly up at Rubashov's window. From his neighbor in cell 402, Rubashov learned that Hare-lip was a political prisoner who had been tortured by a steam bath the day before. A little later Hare-lip, in cell 400, sent Rubashov his greetings, through the inmate of 402, but he would not give his name.

Three days later Rubashov was brought up for his first examination. The examiner was Ivanov, Rubashov's old college friend and former battalion commander. During the interview the

DARKNESS AT NOON by Arthur Koestler. By permission of the author and the publishers, The Macmillan Co. Copyright, 1941, by The Macmillan Co.

prisoner learned that he was accused of belonging to the opposition to the party and that he was suspected of an attempt on the party leader's life. Ivanov promised a twenty-year prison term instead of the death penalty if Rubashov confessed. The prisoner was given a fortnight to arrive at a decision.

After the hearing Rubashov was allowed to have paper, pencil, soap, towels, and tobacco. He started writing in his journal and recasting his ideas about the party and the movement. He recalled a young man named Richard arrested in Germany while Rubashov was at the head of the party Intelligence and Control Department. He could not forget an incident which had happened in Belgium two years later. There Rubashov had been tortured and beaten. In Belgium he expelled from the party a hunchbacked, eager worker who later hanged himself in his room. Rubashov also thought constantly of Arlova who had been his mistress and who had met her death because of him.

The night before the time set by Ivanov had expired, Rubashov felt a tenseness in the atmosphere. His friend in 402 communicated to him that one of the prisoners was to be shot. This prisoner was Michael Bograv, who had always been Rubashov's close friend. As the condemned man was brought through the corridors, the prisoners tapped his progress from one cell to another and drummed on the doors of their cells as he passed. The beaten, whimpering figure of Bograv came by Rubashov's cell. Rubashov believed that his friend shouted to him as he was dragged down the stairs.

Rubashov's second hearing took place late at night. Ivanov came to Rubashov's cell with a bottle of brandy and convinced him that to keep faith with the living was better than betrayal of the dead. Accordingly, Rubashov wrote a letter to the Public Prosecutor renouncing his own oppositional attitude and acknowledging his errors. The third night after delivering the letter to the warder, Rubashov was awakened and taken to the office of Gletkin, another official of the prison. Under blinding lights in Gletkin's office, he was questioned day and night for an interminable period of time. Ivanov, he learned, had been liquidated for conducting Rubashov's case negligently. Gletkin called in Hare-lip as a witness against Rubashov. It was only with great difficulty that Rubashov recognized in that broken, cringing man the son of his former friend and associate, Keiffer. The bright spotlight, the lack of sleep, the constant questionings—these factors combined to make Rubashov sign a trumped-up charge that he had plotted to take the life of the party leader.

Rubashov had committed none of these crimes. He was merely the victim of a change in party policy. One night he heard the sound of drumming along the corridor. The guards were taking Hare-lip to be executed. When the drumming started again, Rubashov knew that his time had come. He was led into the cellar. An officer struck him twice on the head with a revolver. Another party incident was closed.

DAVID COPPERFIELD

Type of work: Novel
Author: Charles Dickens (1812-1870)
Type of plot: Sentimental romance
Time of plot: Early nineteenth century
Locale: England
First published: 1849-1850

Principal characters:
DAVID COPPERFIELD, the narrator
CLARA COPPERFIELD, his mother
MISS BETSY TROTWOOD, David's great-aunt
PEGGOTTY, a nurse
MR. PEGGOTTY, her brother
LITTLE EM'LY, his orphan niece
HAM, his orphan nephew
MR. MURDSTONE, David's stepfather
MISS JANE MURDSTONE, his sister
MR. CREAKLE, master of Salem House
JAMES STEERFORTH, David's schoolmate
TOMMY TRADDLES, a student at Salem House
MR. WILKINS MICAWBER, a man of pecuniary difficulties
MR. WICKFIELD, Miss Trotwood's solicitor
AGNES WICKFIELD, his daughter
URIAH HEEP, a clerk
MR. SPENLOW, under whom David studied law
DORA SPENLOW, his daughter, later David's wife
MR. DICK, Miss Betsy's protégé

Critique:

One of the many qualities that distinguish *David Copperfield* from more modern and more sophisticated novels is its eternal freshness. It is, in short, a work of art which can be read and re-read, chiefly for the gallery of characters Dickens has immortalized. The novel has its flaws. These faults seem insignificant, however, when the virtues of the novel as a whole are considered. The first-person point of view adds much to realistic effects and sympathetic treatment of character and helps to explain, in part, why *David Copperfield* is the most loved piece of fiction in the English language.

The Story:

David Copperfield was born at Blunderstone, in Suffolk, six months after his father's death. Miss Betsy Trotwood, an eccentric great-aunt was present on the night of his birth, but she left the house abruptly and indignantly when she learned that the child was a boy who could never bear her name. David spent his early years with his pretty young mother, Clara Copperfield, and a devoted servant named Peggotty. Peggotty was plain and plump; when she bustled about the house her buttons popped off her dress.

The youthful widow was soon courted by Mr. Murdstone, who proved, after marriage, to be stingy and cruel. When his mother married a second time, David was packed off with Peggotty to visit her relatives at Yarmouth. There her brother had converted an old boat into a seaside cottage, where he lived with his niece, Little Em'ly, and his sturdy young nephew, Ham. Little Em'ly and Ham were David's first real playmates, and his visit to Yarmouth remained a happy memory of his lonely and unhappy childhood. After Miss Jane Murdstone arrived to take charge of her brother's household, David and his mother were never to feel free again from the dark atmosphere of suspicion and gloom the Murdstones brought with them.

One day in a fit of childish terror

David bit his stepfather on the hand. He was immediately sent off to Salem House, a wretched school near London. There his life was more miserable than ever under a brutal headmaster named Creakle. But in spite of the harsh system of the school and the bullyings of Mr. Creakle, his life was endurable because of his friendship with two boys whom he was to meet again under much different circumstances in later life— lovable Tommy Traddles and handsome, lordly James Steerforth.

His school days ended suddenly with the death of his mother and her infant child. When he returned home, he discovered that Mr. Murdstone had dismissed Peggotty. Barkis, the stage driver, whose courtship had been meager but earnest, had taken Peggotty away to become Mrs. Barkis and David was left friendless in the home of his cruel stepfather.

David was put to work in an export warehouse in which Murdstone had an interest. As a ten-year-old worker in the dilapidated establishment of Murdstone and Grinby, wine merchants, David was overworked and half-starved. He loathed his job and associates such as young Mick Walker and Mealy Potatoes. The youngster, however, met still another person with whom he was to associate in later life. That was Wilkins Micawber, a pompous ne'er-do-well in whose house David lodged. The impecunious Mr. Micawber found himself in debtor's prison shortly afterward. On his release he decided to move with his brood to Plymouth. Having lost these good friends, David decided to run away from the environment he detested.

When David decided to leave Murdstone and Grinby, he knew he could not return to his stepfather. The only other relative he could think of was his father's aunt, Miss Betsy Trotwood, who had flounced indignantly out of the house on the night of David's birth. Hopefully he set out for Dover, where Miss Betsy lived, but not before he had been robbed of all his possessions. Consequently, he arrived at Miss Betsy's home physically and mentally wretched.

David's reception was at first not cordial. Miss Betsy had never forgotten the injustice done her when David was born instead of a girl. However, upon the advice of Mr. Dick, a feeble-minded distant kinsman who was staying with her, she decided to take David in, at least until he had been washed thoroughly. While she was deliberating further about what to do with her bedraggled nephew, she wrote to Mr. Murdstone, who came with his sister to Dover to claim his stepson. Miss Betsy decided she disliked both Murdstones intensely. Mr. Dick solved her problem by suggesting that she keep David.

Much to David's joy and satisfaction, Miss Betsy planned to let the boy continue his education, and almost immediately sent him to a school in Canterbury, run by a Mr. Strong, a headmaster quite different from Mr. Creakle. During his stay at school David lodged with Miss Betsy's lawyer, Mr. Wickfield, who had a daughter, Agnes. David became very fond of her. At Wickfield's he also met Uriah Heep, Mr. Wickfield's cringing clerk, whose hypocritical humility and clammy handclasp filled David with disgust.

David finished school when he was seventeen. Miss Betsy suggested he travel for a time before deciding on a profession. On his way to visit his old nurse, Peggotty, David met James Steerforth and went home with his former schoolmate. There he met Steerforth's mother and Rosa Dartle, a girl passionately in love with Steerforth. Years before, the quick-tempered Steerforth had struck Rosa, who carried a scar as a reminder of Steerforth's brutality.

After a brief visit, David persuaded Steerforth to go with him to see Peggotty and her family. At Yarmouth, Steerforth met Little Em'ly. In spite of the fact that she was engaged to Ham, she and Steerforth were immediately attracted to each other.

At length David told his aunt he wished to study law. Accordingly, he was articled to the law firm of Spenlow and Jorkins. At this time David saw Agnes Wickfield, who told him she feared Steerforth and asked David to stay away from him. Agnes also expressed a fear of Uriah Heep, who was on the point of entering into partnership with her senile father. Shortly after these revelations, by Agnes, David encountered Uriah himself, who confessed he wanted to marry Agnes. David was properly disgusted.

On a visit to the Spenlow home, David met Dora Spenlow, his employer's pretty but childish daughter, with whom he fell instantly in love. Soon they became secretly engaged. Before this happy event, however, David heard some startling news—Steerforth had run away with Little Em'ly.

Nor was this elopement the only blow to David's happiness. Shortly after his engagement to Dora, David learned from his aunt that she had lost all her money, and from Agnes that Uriah Heep had become Mr. Wickfield's partner. David tried unsuccessfully to be released from his contract with Spenlow and Jorkins. Determined to show his aunt he could repay her, even in a small way, for her past sacrifices, he took a part-time job as secretary to Mr. Strong, his former headmaster.

But the job with Mr. Strong paid very little; therefore David undertook to study for a position as a reporter of parliamentary debates. Even poor simple Mr. Dick came to Miss Betsy's rescue, for Traddles, now a lawyer, gave him a job as a clerk.

The sudden death of Mr. Spenlow dissolved the partnership of Spenlow and Jorkins, and David learned to his dismay that his former employer had died almost penniless. With much study on his part, David became a reporter. At twenty-one he married Dora, who, however, never seemed capable of growing up. During these events, David had kept in touch with Mr. Micawber, now Uriah Heep's confidential secretary. Though something had finally turned up for Mr. Micawber, his relations with David, and even with his own family, were mysteriously strange, as though he were hiding something.

David soon learned what the trouble was, for Mr. Micawber's conscience got the better of him. At a meeting arranged by him at Mr. Wickfield's, he revealed in Uriah's presence and to an assembled company, including Agnes, Miss Betsy, David, and Traddles, the criminal perfidy of Uriah Heep, who for years had robbed and cheated Mr. Wickfield. Miss Betsy discovered that Uriah was also responsible for her own financial losses. With the exposure of the villainous Uriah, partial restitution both for her and for Mr. Wickfield was not long in coming.

His conscience cleared by his exposure of Uriah Heep's villainy, Mr. Micawber proposed to take his family to Australia. There, he was sure something would again turn up. To Australia, too, went Mr. Peggotty and Little Em'ly; she had turned to her uncle in sorrow and shame after Steerforth had deserted her. David watched as their ship put out to sea. It seemed to him the sunset was a bright promise for them as they sailed away to a new life in the new land. The darkness fell about him as he watched.

The great cloud now in David's life was his wife's delicate health. Day after day she failed, and in spite of his tenderest care he was forced to see her grow more feeble and wan. Agnes Wickfield, like the true friend she had always been, was with him on the night of Dora's death. As in his earlier troubles, he turned to Agnes in the days that followed and found comfort in her sympathy and understanding.

Upon her advice he decided to go abroad for a while. But first he went to Yarmouth to put into Ham's hands a last letter from Little Em'ly. There he witnessed the final act of her betrayal. During a storm the heavy seas battered a ship in distress off the coast. Ham went to his death in a stout-hearted attempt to rescue a survivor clinging to a broken mast. The bodies washed ashore by the rolling waves were those of loyal Ham and the false Steerforth.

David lived in Europe for three years. On his return he discovered again his need for Agnes Wickfield's quiet friendship. One day Miss Betsy Trotwood slyly suggested that Agnes might soon be married. Heavy in heart, David went off to offer her his good wishes. When she burst into tears, he realized that what he had hoped was true—her heart was already his. They were married, to matchmaking Miss Betsy's great delight, and David settled down to begin his career as a successful novelist.

DAVID HARUM

Type of work: Novel
Author: Edward Noyes Westcott (1846-1898)
Type of plot: Regional romance
Time of plot: Late nineteenth century
Locale: Upstate New York
First published: 1898

Principal characters:
DAVID HARUM, a banker and horse trader
JOHN LENOX, Harum's assistant
MARY BLAKE, John's sweetheart
POLLY BIXBEE, Harum's widowed sister

Critique:

Westcott, who himself had been a banker in upper New York State, wrote *David Harum* to give the country at large a picture of his region and its people. The greatness of the book lies in the characterization of David Harum, that original and delightfully humorous horse trader who has fascinated two generations of readers. Harum was a dry, quaint, semi-literate countryman with a shrewd knowledge of human nature. Unfortunately, the horse-trading banker does not dominate the story completely. The novel is threaded together by a love story involving Harum's banking assistant and a young heiress. The best chapters, by far, are those in which David Harum tells stories in dialect, swaps horses, or indulges in reminiscences of other days.

The Story:

John Lenox was the son of a well-to-do businessman in New York. After college he lived for several years in Europe at his father's expense. He was twenty-six years old when he returned to America, without having done anything which fitted him to earn a living.

John returned to find 'that his father's business was failing rapidly and that he would soon have to make a living for himself. His father found a place for him with a New York law firm, but reading law proved uncongenial. When

his father died, John left the firm. Then, through an old friend of his father's, John became assistant to the owner of a small bank in Homeville, New York.

David Harum, the owner of the bank, was a crusty old man who enjoyed his reputation as a skinflint. What most of the townspeople did not know was that he was quite a philanthropist in his own way, but preferred to cover up his charity and good deeds with gruff words. Harum's one vice was horse trading. His sister, who kept house for him, firmly believed that he would rather trade horses than eat or sleep. Moreover, he usually came out ahead in any swapping deal.

David Harum was well pleased with the appearance of his new assistant, John Lenox. And when John took hold of his duties better than any other clerk in the bank had ever done, David Harum began to think seriously of looking after the young man's future. Harum felt that John should have an opportunity to better himself, but he wanted first to be certain that he was not mistaken in judging the young man's character. He set out to discover what he wanted to know in a peculiar way. He let John live uncomfortably in a broken-down hotel for several months to ascertain his fortitude. He also gave John several chances to be dishonest by practices which a sharp trader like Harum might be expected to approve. John's straight-forward dealings won Harum's respect and approval. He casually gave John five ten-dollar gold pieces and asked him to move into a room in Harum's own large house with him and his sister, Polly.

John had begun to discover that Harum was not the selfish and crusty old man he appeared. He knew that Harum had called in a widow whose mortgage was overdue and had torn up the paper because the woman's husband had at one time taken Harum to the circus when the banker was a little boy without a cent to his name. Even Harum's horse trading was different when one came to know him. As John Lenox discovered, Harum only let people cheat themselves. If someone professed to know all about horses, Harum used the trade to teach him a lesson, but if a tyro professed his ignorance of the animals Harum was sure to give him a fair exchange. He was a living example of the proverb which propounds shrewdly that it is impossible to cheat an honest man, and the corollary, that it is almost impossible not to cheat a dishonest one.

John Lenox's life in Homeville was restricted, and he was thrown much on his own resources. He secured a piano for himself and played in the evenings or read from a small collection of books which he had saved from his father's library. His only real friends were David Harum and Harum's sister, Polly, both old enough to be John's parents. He spent many pleasant hours in Harum's company. They would often take Harum's horses out for a drive, during which the loquacious banker would regale the young man with stories of horse trading, of the foibles of the people in the community, or of Harum's early life when he had run away from home to work along the Erie Canal. On one of these rides Harum learned that John was in love with an heiress he had met in Europe. John felt that he could not ask her to marry him until he had proved himself a success.

Soon afterward Harum gave John an opportunity to make a large amount of money. Harum had a tip on a corner in pork on the Chicago market. Harum and John bought several thousand barrels of pork and sold them at a considerable profit. This deal was the first step Harum took to make John financially independent.

John's second year in Homeville was more eventful. By that time he had been accepted as a member of the community and had made friends both in the town and among the wealthy people who came to Homeville during the summer months. Meanwhile Harum revealed to his sister his plan to retire from active work in the bank and to make John his partner. He also revealed to her that John had a tract of land in Pennsylvania which everyone had considered worthless, but which was likely to produce oil. Harum, in his younger days, had spent some time in the Pennsylvania oil fields, and like most small-town bankers of the time, he knew something about a great many financial activities. What he did not reveal to his sister was that he also planned to leave his estate to John, for, excepting Polly, he had no relatives.

By the end of his third year in Harum's bank, John had made enough money through market operations to make himself independent, and he could have left the bank and the town for New York City if he had cared to do so. When the banker broached the subject to him, John admitted that two years before the prospect of returning to the city would have been welcome. Now he had come to like Homeville and had no desire to leave the home of David Harum and his sister. That was exactly what Harum wanted to hear. He told John that he was to become a partner in the bank. Harum also told him that a company wanted to lease his Pennsylvania land for the purpose of drilling for oil.

Then John fell ill, and his doctor sent

him on a Mediterranean cruise. While aboard ship, John met Mary Blake, the young heiress with whom he had fallen in love several years before. At first John thought, because of an error in the ship's passenger list, that Mary Blake was already married. One moonlight night, on a mountain overlooking the bay at Naples, Mary informed John of his mistake and promised to marry him, and a few days later Harum was over- joyed to receive a cable announcing John's marriage. Harum wired back the good news that drilling had begun on the property in Pennsylvania.

When John and Mary Lenox returned to the United States several months later, they settled in Homeville and John took over the bank. Then David Harum was free to spend the rest of his days driving about the countryside and swap' ping horses.

DE RERUM NATURA

Type of work: Didactic epic
Author: Lucretius (Titus Lucretius Carus, c. 98 B.C.-55 B.C.)
First transcribed: First century B.C.

The *De rerum natura* (*On the Nature of Things*) is justly renowned as the greatest poetic monument of Epicurean philosophy. It is outstanding both as a scientific explanation of the poet's atomic theory and as a fine poem. Vergil himself was much influenced by Lucretius' dactylic hexameter verse, and echoes passages of the *De rerum natura* in the *Georgics,* a didactic epic modeled on Lucretius' poem, and in the *Aeneid.*

Lucretius, following his master Epicurus' doctrine, believed that fear of the gods and fear of death were the greatest obstacles to peace of mind, the object of Epicurean philosophy. He felt that he could dispel these unfounded terrors by explaining the workings of the universe and showing that phenomena interpreted as signs from the deities were simply natural happenings. His scientific speculations were based on Democritus' atomic theory and Epicurus' interpretation of it. Lucretius outlined the fundamental laws of this system in the first book of his poem.

According to Lucretius, everything is composed of small "first bodies," tiny particles made up of a few "minima" or "least parts" which cannot be separated. These "first bodies," atoms, are solid, indestructible, and of infinite number. They are mixed with void to make objects of greater hardness or softness, strength or weakness.

Lucretius "proves" these assertions by calling upon the reader's reason and his observation of nature, pointing out absurdities that might come about if his point were not true. For example, he substantiates his statement that nothing can be created from nothing by saying, "For if things came to being from nothing, every kind might be born from all things, nought would need a seed. First men might arise from the sea, and from the land the race of scaly creatures, and birds burst forth from the sky." These proofs, which may fill fifty or one hundred lines of poetry, are often unconvincing, but they reveal the author's knowledge of nature and his imaginative gifts.

The universe is infinite in the Epicurean system. Lucretius would ask a man who believed it finite, "If one were to run on to the end . . . and throw a flying dart, would you have it that that dart . . . goes on whither it is sped and flies afar, or do you think that something can check and bar its way?" He ridicules the Stoic theory that all things press toward a center, for the universe, being infinite, can have no center. Lucretius is, of course, denying the law of gravity. He often contradicts what science has since proved true, but he is remarkably accurate for his time.

Book II opens with a poetic description of the pleasure of standing apart from the confusion and conflicts of life: "Nothing is more gladdening than to dwell in the calm high places, firmly embattled on the heights by the teaching of the wise, whence you can look down on others, and see them wandering hither and thither." Lucretius is providing this teaching by continuing his discussion of atoms, which he says move continuously downward like dust particles in a sunbeam. They have a form of free will and can swerve to unite with each other to form objects. Lucretius adds that if the atoms could not will motion for themselves, there would be no explanation for the ability of animals to move voluntarily.

The poet outlines other properties of atoms in the latter part of the second book: they are colorless, insensible, and of a variety of shapes which determine properties of the objects the atoms compose. Sweet honey contains round, smooth particles; bitter wormwood, hooked atoms.

While Lucretius scorns superstitious fear of the gods, he worships the creative force of nature, personified as Venus in the invocation to Book I. Nature controls the unending cycle of creation and destruction. There are gods, but they dwell in their tranquil homes in space, unconcerned for the fate of men.

A passage in praise of Epicurus precedes Book III, the book of the soul. Lucretius says that fear of death arises from superstitions about the soul's afterlife in Hades. This fear is foolish, for the soul is, like the body, mortal. The poet describes the soul as the life force in the body, composed of very fine particles which disperse into the air when the body dies. Since man will neither know nor feel anything when his soul has dissolved, fear of death is unnecessary.

A man should not regret leaving life, even if it has been full and rich. He should die as "a guest sated with the banquet of life and with calm mind embrace . . . a rest that knows no care." If existence has been painful, then an end to it should be welcome.

The introductory lines of Book IV express Lucretius' desire to make philosophy more palatable to his readers by presenting it in poetry. His task is a new one: "I traverse the distant haunts of the Pierides (the Muses), never trodden before by the foot of man."

The poet begins this book on sensation with an explanation of idols, the films of atoms which float from the surfaces of objects and make sense perception possible. Men see because idols touch their eyes, taste the bitter salt air because idols of hooked atoms reach their tongues. Idols become blunted when they travel a long distance, causing men to see far-off square towers as round.

Lucretius blames the misconceptions arising from visual phenomena like re-fraction and perspective on men's reason, not their senses, for accuracy of sense perception is an important part of his theory: "Unless they are true, all reason, too, becomes false."

A second eulogy of Epicurus introduces the fifth book, for some readers the most interesting of all. In it Lucretius discusses the creation of the world and the development of human civilization. Earth was created by a chance conjunction of atoms, which squeezed out sun, moon, and stars as they gathered together to form land. The world, which is constantly disintegrating and being rebuilt, is still young, for human history does not go back beyond the Theban and Trojan wars.

The poet gives several explanations for the motion of stars, the causes of night, and eclipses. Since proof can come only from the senses, any theory which does not contradict perception is possible.

Lucretius presents the curious idea that the first animals were born from wombs rooted in the earth. Monsters were created, but only strong animals and those useful to man could survive. A delightful picture of primitive man, a hardy creature living on nuts and berries and living in caves, follows. Lucretius describes the process of civilization as men united for protection, learned to talk, use metals, weave, and wage war. Problems arose for them with the discovery of wealth and property, breeding envy and discord. It was at this point that Epicurus taught men the highest good, to free them from their cares.

The sixth book continues the explanation of natural phenomena which inspired men to fear the gods: thunder, lightning, clouds, rain, earthquakes. Lucretius rambles over a great many subjects, giving several explanations for many of them. He concludes the poem with a vivid description of the plague of Athens, modeled on Thucydides' account.

812

DEAD FIRES

Type of work: Novel
Author: José Lins do Rêgo (1901-1957)
Time: 1848-1900
Locale: Paraíba, Brazil
First published: 1943

> *Principal characters:*
> JOSÉ AMARO, a crippled, embittered saddlemaker
> SINHA, his wife
> COLONEL JOSÉ PAULINO, owner of Santa Clara plantation
> COLONEL LULA, owner of Santa Fe plantation
> CAPTAIN VICTORINO CARNEIRO DA CUNHA, a humane lawyer
> LIEUTENANT MAURICIO, of the army
> SILVINO, a bandit

Dead Fires (Fogo morto), the tenth novel by Lins do Rêgo, marks his return to the themes of his original Sugar Cane Cycle, after four weak experiments in other fields. The author, descendant of an aristocratic planter family settled for years in Northeast Brazil, was educated for the law, but friendship with Brazil's great sociologist, Gilberto Freyre, showed him the rich literary inspiration in Brazil's *ingenhos,* or sugar centers, and turned him to fiction writing. Beginning with the novel *Plantation Lad,* Lins do Rêgo went on with *Daffy Boy, Black Boy Richard, Old Plantation,* and *The Sugar Refinery,* all dealing with the same characters. In 1943, after four lesser novels based on other themes, came *Dead Fires,* his masterpiece, in which some of the characters from the earlier novels reappear. The novel is marked by improved technique, a greater use of dialogue, less morbidity and better character portrayal.

Some critics see in Victorino, the penniless, abused lawyer, a Brazilian Don Quixote, sure of what is right, hating bandits, cruel soldiers, and haughty plantation owners alike, and fighting all injustice, regardless of the cost to him. Like the Spanish don, Victorino was an aristocrat, related by blood to many of the important families of the region, but censuring their use of power because of his feeling for the common man. There is also a parallel with Don Quixote in the way Victorino was first ridiculed and then admired.

The main character, the crippled and ugly saddlemaker José Amaro, was a failure who tried to hide his sense of inferiority and cowardice behind a biting tongue and a scornful attitude toward everybody. He insisted that nobody owned him, or, as he expressed it more vividly, that nobody could scream at him. His only friends were the kindly Negro hunter Leandro, who occasionally left part of his bag at José's door, and white Victorino, sunk so low that even the *moleques,* the black boys, mocked him in the streets, calling aften him "Papa Rabo."

José's attitude toward the bandit, Captain António Silvino, arose from the admiration of a coward for a man daring enough to brave the power of the plantation owners. The imagination of the saddlemaker built Silvino into a kind of Robin Hood, siding with the poor against the grasping landlords, especially at the moment when the bandit attacked the town of Pilar and sacked the strongbox of the prefect, Quinca Napoleon. Afterward he invited the villagers to pillage the house. José was grateful because the bandit came to his defense when he was ordered evicted from the house his father and he had occupied for half a century. However, Silvino's threats of interference stiffened the determination of José's landlord.

Not until the end was José disillusioned and the bandit's self-interest revealed. Attracted by rumors that Colonel

Lula still possessed the gold inherited from his father-in-law, Silvino came after it, threatening torture unless the hiding place was revealed. In reality, the wealth was not at the plantation. Lula, vanquished by circumstances and about to abandon his estate for the big city, had sent the money ahead. An attack of convulsions momentarily saved the landowner from torture; the protests of Victorino brought him further respite; but it was the arrival of Colonel Paulino that drove off the bandit. Until he realized Silvino's cruelty, José Amaro made sandals for him and his men, spied on his pursuers for him, and even got food and provisions to him when Lieutenant Mauricio and his soldiers were on his trail.

José's feelings toward the wealthy plantation owners were determined by their attitude toward him. The novelist introduces two of them as representative of the landed gentry of the nineteenth century in Northeastern Brazil, men who derived their titles from their social and political positions.

With Colonel José Paulino, whose family had long owned the Santa Clara plantation, José Amaro was continually at odds because, as the wealthy man rode past the saddlemaker's house in his family carriage, he would only nod condescendingly. At the beginning of the novel, when Laurentino, the house painter, paused to talk on a May afternoon, while on his way to help the colonel beautify his manor house for the wedding of his daughter, José from his doorway said angrily that he would never work for a man he hated as much as he hated Colonel Paulino.

His attitude toward the other big sugar planter, Colonel Lula César de Holanda Chacón, supposedly modeled on a cousin of the author's grandfather, was less bitter. He finally agreed to go to the Santa Fe plantation to repair the family carriage, whose history is related in the second part of the novel.

During the Revolution of 1848, Captain Tomás Cabral de Malo arrived with his cattle, his slaves, and his family in Parahyba (or Paraíba). He took possession of the Santa Fe plantation, adjoining Santa Clara, bought additional land from the Indians, and planted cotton. About then a penniless cousin, Lula, turned up and began courting the plantation owner's daughter.

Having won the captain's permission, Lula took her away on a honeymoon from which they returned with a pretentious carriage, practically useless in that roadless region. The rest of Lula's progress, as told in Dead Fires, makes him anything but admirable. At Captain Tomás' death, he fought the widow for control until her death. Then, in complete possession of the plantation and sugar refinery, he revealed his avaricious and cruel nature. José overlooked the past of his landlord, however, because Lula occasionally exchanged a word with him.

José's family is introduced early in the story. When Laurentino stopped to talk, the saddlemaker invited him for supper with his wife and their thirty-year-old daughter. The girl had never married because she insisted that she did not want to, but she nearly drove the old man frantic because she spent her days weeping. Eventually, in his exasperation, he beat her until he dropped unconscious; from that time on his wife thought only of ways to get herself and her daughter safely away. José had no other children. Lacking a son to carry on at his death, he had no incentive to enlarge his leather business or attract new customers.

Lins do Rêgo is continually making thrifty use of minor episodes, not only to carry forward the story, but to reveal character. For example, while working at Colonel Lula's plantation, José revealed his trait of showing contempt for those he tries to impress; and by his actions he so roused the enmity of the Negro Florîpes, the Santa Fe overseer, that from then on he worked against José and hastened his tragedy. It was Floripes' lie, the report that José had promised aid to Victorino's candidate against the politician backed by Lula, that persuaded the landowner that his tenant was ungrateful, and so José was ordered to leave the cabin occupied by his family for many years.

The kindness of the hunter in leaving a rabbit at José's door revealed the old man's nausea at the sight of blood, while the blood started a rumor that José was a werewolf. This rumor was crystallized into belief when he was found unconscious beside the river, where, in reality, he had collapsed trying to warn the bandits of the coming of soldiers.

In telling the story, Lins do Rêgo divides his narrative into three parts, with the second one, "The Santa Fe Plantation," a flashback of half a century, covering the rise to power of Lula.

When Isabel, daughter of Emperor Pedro, freed Brazil's last slaves in 1888, Lula was left without anyone to run the plantation or the refinery, for his Negroes were quick to get away from a master who used to beat them until he fell down in convulsions. In contrast, Colonel Paulino's field hands, who had been treated kindly, stayed on even after the liberation, and so he was able to lend his cousin by marriage enough laborers to help with the work. But still the hearth fires of Santa Fe burned lower and the plantation was doomed. Neighbors brought suits against Lula that were settled only because Colonel Paulino intervened. And Lula could find no one willing to marry his daughter.

José's fortunes also declined. Disillusioned about the outlaws, he found the soldiers of Lieutenant Mauricio even more cruel. Coming to protect the villagers, Lieutenant Mauricio beat blind Torcuato as a spy, arrested José, and mistreated Victorino, who had won the admiration of his fellow citizens by facing the domineering officer with a writ of habeas corpus in order to free the saddlemaker.

Freedom was meaningless now to old José. His family had left him, and he had no friends. He committed suicide in his empty house, where his Negro friend, Pajarito, found his body. Two cycles had ended. When Pajarito looked out the window, smoke was billowing from the chimneys of the Santa Clara sugar refinery, but he saw no activity at Santa Fe —where the fires were dead.

DEAD SOULS

Type of work: Novel
Author: Nikolai V. Gogol (1809-1852)
Type of plot: Social satire
Time of plot: Early nineteenth century
Locale: Russia
First published: 1842

Principal characters:
PAVEL IVANOVITCH TCHITCHIKOFF, an adventurer
MANILOFF, from whom he bought souls
TENTETNIKOFF, whom he tried to marry off
PLATON PLATONOFF, with whom he later traveled
KLOBUEFF, whose estate he bought
KOSTANZHOGLO, who lent him money
ALEXEI IVANOVITCH LYENITZEN, who threw him into jail

Critique:

This novel is written in high good humor. Its portraits of various Russian types—peasant, landhólder, prince—are delightful. The plot itself is not complex. The length of the novel is accounted for by the author's numerous digressions, which add up to a rich picture of provincial Russian life in the early nineteenth century. The satire ranks with the best the world has produced.

The Story:

Pavel Ivanovitch Tchitchikoff had arrived in the town accompanied by his coachman, Selifan, and his valet, Petrushka. He had been entertained gloriously and had met many interesting people, who insisted on his visiting them in their own homes. Nothing could have suited Tchitchikoff better. After several days of celebration in the town, he took his coachman and began a round of visits to the various estates in the surrounding country.

His first host was Maniloff, a genial man who wined him and dined him in a manner fit for a prince. When the time was ripe, Tchitchikoff began to question his host about his estate and learned, to his satisfaction, that many of Maniloff's souls, as the serfs were called, had died since the last census and that Maniloff was still paying taxes on them and would continue to do so until the next census. Tchitchikoff offered to buy these dead souls from Maniloff and so relieve him of his extra tax burden. The contract signed, Tchitchikoff set out for the next estate.

Selifan got lost and in the middle of the night drew up to a house which belonged to Madame Korobotchkina, from whom Tchitchikoff also bought dead souls. When he left his hostess, he found his way to an inn in the neighborhood. There he met Nozdreff, a notorious gambler and liar. Nozdreff had recently lost a great deal of money at gambling, and Tchitchikoff thought he would be a likely seller of dead souls. But when he broached the subject, Nozdreff asked him the reason for his interest in dead souls. For every reason Tchitchikoff gave, Nozdreff called him a liar. Then Nozdreff wanted to play at cards for the souls, but Tchitchikoff refused. They were arguing when a police captain came in and arrested Nozdreff for assault on a man while drunk. Tchitchikoff thought himself well rid of the annoying Nozdreff.

His next host was Sobakevitch, who at first demanded the unreasonable sum of one hundred roubles for each name of a dead soul. Tchitchikoff finally argued him into accepting two and a half roubles apiece, a higher price than he had planned to pay.

Pliushkin, with whom he negotiated next, was a miser. He bought one hundred and twenty dead souls and seventy-eight fugitives after considerable haggling. Pliushkin gave him a letter to Ivan Grigorievitch, the town president.

Back in town, Tchitchikoff persuaded the town president to make his recent purchases legal. Since the law required that souls when purchased be transferred to another estate, Tchitchikoff told the officials that he had land in the Kherson province. He had no trouble in making himself sound plausible. Some bribes to minor officials helped.

Tchitchikoff proved to be such a delightful guest that the people of the town insisted that he stay on and on. He was the center of attraction at many social functions, including a ball at which he was especially interested in the governor's daughter. Soon, however, rumors spread that Tchitchikoff was using the dead souls as a screen, that he was really planning to elope with the governor's daughter. The men, in consultation at the police master's house, speculated variously. Some said he was a forger; others thought he might be an officer in the governor-general's office; one man put forth the fantastic suggestion that he was really the legendary Captain Kopeykin in disguise. They questioned Nozdreff, who had been the first to report the story of the purchase of dead souls. At their interrogation Nozdreff confirmed their opinions that Tchitchikoff was a spy and a forger who was trying to elope with the governor's daughter.

Meanwhile Tchitchikoff had caught a cold and was confined to his bed. When at last he had recovered sufficiently to go out, he found himself no longer welcome at the houses of his former friends. He was, in fact, turned away by servants at the door. Tchitchikoff realized it would be best for him to leave town.

The truth of the matter was that Tchitchikoff had begun his career as a humble clerk. His father had died leaving no legacy for his son, who served in various capacities, passing from customs officer to smuggler to pauper to legal agent. When he learned that the Trustee Committee would mortgage souls, he hit upon the scheme of acquiring funds by mortgaging dead souls that were still on the census lists. It was this purpose which had sent him on his current tour.

He turned up next on the estate of Andrei Ivanovitch Tentetnikoff, a thirty-three-year-old bachelor who had retired from public life to vegetate in the country. Learning that Tentetnikoff was in love with the daughter of his neighbor, General Betrishtcheff, Tchitchikoff went to see the general and won his consent to Tentetnikoff's suit. He brought the conversation around to a point where he could offer to buy dead souls from the general. He gave as his reason the story that his old uncle would not leave him an estate unless he himself already owned some property. The scheme so delighted the general that he gladly made the transaction.

Tchitchikoff's next stop was with Pyetukh, a generous glutton whose table Tchitchikoff enjoyed. There he met a young man named Platonoff, whom Tchitchikoff persuaded to travel with him and see Russia. The two stopped to see Platonoff's sister and brother-in-law, Konstantin Kostanzhoglo, a prosperous landholder. Tchitchikoff so impressed his host that Kostanzhoglo agreed to lend him ten thousand roubles to buy the estate of a neighboring spendthrift named Klobueff. Klobueff said he had a rich old aunt who would give great gifts to churches and monasteries but would not help her destitute relatives. Tchitchikoff proceeded to the town where the old woman resided and forged a will to his own advantage. But he forgot to insert a clause canceling all previous wills. On her death he went to interview His Excellency, Alexei Ivanovitch Lyenitzen, who told him that two wills had been discovered, each contradicting the other. Tchitchikoff was accused of forging the second will and was thrown into prison. In the interpretation of this mix-up,

Tchitchikoff learned a valuable lesson in deception from the crafty lawyer he consulted. The lawyer managed to confuse the affair with every public and private scandal in the province, so that the officials were soon willing to drop the whole matter if Tchitchikoff would leave town immediately. The ruined adventurer was only too glad to comply.

DEAR BRUTUS

Type of work: Drama
Author: James M. Barrie (1860-1937)
Type of plot: Romantic fantasy
Time of plot: Midsummer Eve
Locale: England
First presented: 1917

Principal characters:
LOB, the ancient Puck
MATEY, his butler
GUESTS AT LOB'S HOUSE PARTY

Critique:

Barrie's thesis—that the exigencies of human life are the fault of the individual, not of so-called Fate—is fancifully developed in *Dear Brutus* by means of a folk superstition concerning Midsummer Eve. The play is fantastic and realistic at the same time, fantastic in that its characters are transported into the realm of the unreal, realistic in the perfectly candid way in which the various relationships among the characters are set forth.

The Story:

Dinner was over, and the ladies of Lob's house party returned to the drawing-room after leaving the gentlemen to their cigars and wine. Matey, the butler, had stolen jewelry from one of the guests. The women called him in to tell him they knew he was the thief. When Matey returned the jewelry, the women stated that they would not report him if he told them why they were guests at the house. Matey either could not or would not give them a direct answer. In the course of the conversation it was learned that their host was mysteriously ageless and that Lob was another name for the legendary Puck. Matey admitted that Lob always asked a different party of guests to his house for Midsummer Week. He warned the women not to venture outside the garden on this Midsummer Eve. When he left them with the warning not to go into the wood, the women were puzzled because there

was no wood within miles of the house.

Host Lob entered thoughtfully. He was followed by old Mr. Coade, who was collecting notes for a projected work on the Feudal System, and Mr. Purdie, an intellectual young barrister. Coade and Purdie suggested that the group take a walk to discover a mysterious wood. Lob said slyly that the villagers believed that a wood appeared in a different part of the neighborhood each Midsummer Eve. He pretended skepticism to sharpen the curiosity of his guests, who went to prepare for the adventure.

Among Lob's guests was Lady Caroline Laney, unmarried and of disdainful poise, and Joanna Trout, single and in love with love. Joanna and Mr. Purdie were caught kissing in the living room by Mabel Purdie, who saw them from the garden. She came in. Joanna, surprised, asked Mabel what she was doing in the garden. Mabel answered that she was looking for her lost love. Her calm candor caught Jack Purdie and Joanna completely off guard. Jack admitted his love for Joanna. Mabel left the lovers grieving that fate had not brought them together earlier. Alice Dearth entered. Cattishly, Joanna revealed that Mrs. Dearth had at one time been an artist's model. Dearth, an artist now broken by drink, entered. Alice Dearth had grown to despise him for his sottishness. Dearth regretted not having a child; Alice Dearth

819

regretted not having married a former suitor.

When the party reassembled, Lob revealed that to go into the forest gave one another chance, something nearly everyone in the group was seeking. Dearth drew aside the curtain to reveal a forest in the place of the garden. He entered the wood and disappeared. Mabel Purdie followed him. Next went Jack Purdie and Joanna, followed by Alice Dearth, Lady Caroline, and old Mr. Coade. Lob enticed Matey to the edge of the wood and pushed him into it.

In the moonlight of Midsummer Eve, in the fanciful realm of the second chance, Matey and Lady Caroline discovered that they were vulgar husband and wife. Joanna was in search of her husband. When Mr. Coade, now a woodlander, appeared dancing and blowing a whistle, Joanna said that she was Mrs. Purdie; she suspected her husband of being in the forest with another woman. They saw Purdie in the company of Mabel, whom he chased among the trees. In the forest, Mabel and Joanna had changed places. Purdie and Mabel mourned that they had met too late.

In another part of the forest, Will Dearth and his young daughter Margaret raced to the spot where the artist's easel was set up, for Dearth was painting a moonlit landscape. Margaret was worried over her excess of happiness; she expressed her fear that her father would be taken from her. The pair agreed that artists, especially, needed daughters and that fame was not everything.

Alice, a vagrant searching for scraps to eat, passed the happy pair. She told them that she was the Honorable Mrs. Finch-Fallowe, the wife of the suitor that she had recalled in Lob's house, and that she had seen good times. Dearth approached a nearby house to get food for the vagrant woman. Margaret, somehow afraid, tried to restrain him.

Back in the house, Lob was waiting for the return of his guests. There was a tapping on the window and Jack Purdie and Mabel, still charmed, entered. They noticed but did not recognize the sleeping Lob. Still under the influence of Midsummer magic, Purdie spoke words of love to Mabel. He was interrupted by the entrance of Joanna, his Midsummer Eve wife. Lob seemed to leer in his sleep. Suddenly the enchantment disappeared; the trio recognized the room and Lob. After the complete return to reality, Purdie realized that fate was not to blame for human destiny. Ashamed but honest, he admitted that he was a philanderer and asked Mabel to forgive him.

Matey returned, still the vulgarian in speech and dress. He stated, to the surprise of those present, that his wife was with him and he introduced Lady Caroline Matey. The charm was broken, to the horror of the fastidious Caroline Laney and to the embarrassment of Matey.

Still piping on his whistle, Mr. Coade returned. Although he did not recognize Mrs. Coade, he expressed his admiration for her lovable face. The old man returned to reality after making his wife proud that he had chosen her again in the world of the second chance.

Alice Dearth, hungry, entered and looked ravenously at the refreshments. Between mouthfuls of cake she bragged of her former affluence as Mrs. Finch-Fallowe; she mystified the other guests with talk of a painter and his daughter in the forest. Dearth, the happy painter of the forest, came in. In their disenchantment, Alice knew that she would have been unhappy with the former suitor, and that Will Dearth would have been happier without her. Dearth was momentarily crushed by the loss of Margaret, but he recovered to thank Lob for providing that night's experience.

Lob, who had been curled up in a chair in a trance-like sleep during the adventures, and who had leered and smiled in his sleep as his guests came back to the actual world, returned to the care of his beloved flowers. Midsummer

Eve was past; the world of might-have- been had ended.

DEATH COMES FOR THE ARCHBISHOP

Type of work: Novel
Author: Willa Cather (1876-1947)
Type of plot: Historical chronicle
Time of plot: Last half of the nineteenth century
Locale: New Mexico and Arizona
First published: 1927

Principal characters:
> FATHER JEAN MARIE LATOUR, Vicar Apostalic of New Mexico
> FATHER JOSEPH VAILLANT, his friend, a missionary priest
> KIT CARSON, frontier scout
> JACINTO, an Indian guide

Critique:

Death Comes for the Archbishop is a novel reaffirming the greatness of the American past. This chronicle of the Catholic Southwest is a story, beautifully told, which re-creates in the lives of Bishop Latour and Father Vaillant, his vicar, the historical careers of Bishop Lamy and Father Macheboeuf, two devout and noble missionary priests in the Vicarate of New Mexico during the second half of the nineteenth century. Bishop Latour is scholarly and urbane; Father Vaillant, energetic and passionately the man of feeling. A novel of these dedicated lives, the book presents also a picture of a region and a culture. There are many strands of interest here —the bleak desert country of sand and gaunt red mountains, colorful adobe towns and Mexican customs, conflicts with a stubborn and sometimes corrupt native clergy, missionary journeys in all weathers, the rituals and legends of the Indian pueblos, frontier heroes like Kit Carson and desperadoes like Buck Scales, relics of the conquistadores who brought the sword and the Cross into the New World. The novel lives in its bright glimpses of the past, stories that cut backward into time so that the action is not always upon the same level. Tales and legends that go beyond the period of American occupation into three centuries of Spanish colonial history and back to the primitive tribal life of the Hopi, the Navajo, and the vanished cliff-dwellers break this chronicle at many points and give the effect of density and variety to a work which recaptures so completely the spirit and movement of the pioneer West.

The Story:

In 1851 Father Jean Marie Latour reached Santa Fé, where he was to become Vicar Apostolic of New Mexico. His journey from the shores of Lake Ontario had been long and arduous. He had lost his belongings in a shipwreck at Galveston and had suffered painful injury in a wagon accident at San Antonio.

Upon Father Latour's arrival, in company with his good friend, Father Joseph Vaillant, the Mexican priests refused to recognize his authority. He had no choice but to ride three thousand miles into Mexico to secure the necessary papers from the Bishop of Durango.

On the road he lost his way in an arid landscape of red hills and gaunt junipers. His thirst became a vertigo of mind and senses, and he could blot out his own agony only by repeating the cry of the Saviour on the Cross. As he was about to give up all hope, he saw a tree growing in the shape of a cross. A short time later he arrived in the Mexican settlement called *Agua Secreta*, Hidden Water. Stopping at the home of Benito, Bishop Latour first performed the marriage ceremonies and then baptized all the children.

At Durango he received the necessary documents and started the long trip back to Santa Fé. Meanwhile Father Vaillant had won over the inhabitants from enmity to amity and had set up the Episcopal residence in an old adobe house. On the first morning after his return to Santa Fé the bishop heard the unexpected sound of a bell ringing the Angelus. Father Vaillant told him that he had found the bell, bearing the date 1356, in the basement of old San Miguel Church.

On a missionary journey to Albuquerque in March, Father Vaillant acquired as a gift a handsome cream-colored mule and another just like it for his bishop. These mules, Contento and Angelica, served the men in good stead for many years.

On another such trip the two priests were riding together on their mules. Caught in a sleet storm, they stopped at the rude shack of an American, Buck Scales. His Mexican wife warned the travelers by gestures that their lives were in danger, and they rode on to Mora without spending the night. The next morning the Mexican woman appeared in town. She told them that her husband had already murdered and robbed four travelers, and that he had killed her four babies. The result was that Scales was brought to justice, and his wife, Magdalena, was sent to the home of Kit Carson, the famous frontier scout. From that time on Kit Carson was a valuable friend of the bishop and his vicar. Magdalena later became the housekeeper and manager for the kitchens of the Sisters of Loretto.

During his first year at Santa Fé, the bishop was called to a meeting of the Plenary Council at Baltimore. On the return journey he brought back with him five nuns sent to establish the school of Our Lady of Light. Next, Bishop Latour, attended by the Indian Jacinto as his guide, spent some time visiting his own vicarate. Padre Gallegos, whom he visited at Albuquerque, acted more like a professional gambler than a priest, but because he was very popular with the natives Bishop Latour did not remove him at that time. At last he arrived at his destination, the top of the mesa at Ácoma, the end of his long journey. On that trip he heard the legend of Fray Baltazar, killed during an uprising of the Ácoma Indians.

A month after the bishop's visit, he suspended Padre Gallegos and put Father Vaillant in charge of the parish at Albuquerque. On a trip to the Pecos Mountains the vicar fell ill with an attack of the black measles. The bishop, hearing of his illness, set out to nurse his friend. Jacinto again served as guide on the cold, snowy trip. When Bishop Latour reached his friend's bedside, he found that Kit Carson had arrived before him. As soon as the sick man could sit in the saddle, Carson and the bishop took him back to Santa Fé.

Bishop Latour decided to investigate the parish of Taos, where the powerful old priest, Antonio José Martinez, was the ruler of both spiritual and temporal matters. The following year the bishop was called to Rome. When he returned, he brought with him four young priests from the Seminary of Montferrand and a Spanish priest to replace Padre Martinez at Taos.

Bishop Latour had one great ambition; he wanted to build a cathedral in Santa Fé. In that project he was assisted by the rich Mexican *rancheros,* but to the greatest extent by his good friend, Don Antonio Olivares. When Don Antonio died, his will stated that his estate was left to his wife and daughter during their lives, and after their decease to the Church. Don Antonio's brothers contested the will on the grounds that the daughter, Señorita Inez, was too old to be Doña Isabella's daughter, and the bishop and his vicar had to persuade the vain, coquettish widow to swear to her true age of fifty-three, rather than the forty-two years she claimed. Thus the money was saved for Don Antonio's family and, eventually, the Church.

Father Vaillant was sent to Tucson, but after several years Bishop Latour decided to recall him to Santa Fé. When he arrived, the bishop showed him the stone for building the cathedral. About that time Bishop Latour received a letter from the Bishop of Leavenworth. Because of the discovery of gold near Pike's Peak, he asked to have a priest sent there from Father Latour's diocese. Father Vaillant was the obvious choice.

Father Vaillant spent the rest of his life doing good works in Colorado, though he did return to Santa Fé with the Papal Emissary when Bishop Latour was made an archbishop. Father Vaillant became the first Bishop of Colorado. He died there after years of service, and Archbishop Latour attended his impressive funeral services.

After the death of his friend, Father Latour retired to a modest country estate near Santa Fé. He had dreamed during all his missionary years of the time when he could retire to his own fertile green Auvergne in France, but in the end he decided that he could not leave the land of his labors for his faith. Memories of the journeys he and Father Vaillant had made over thousands of miles of desert country became the meaning of his later years. Bernard Ducrot, a young Seminarian from France, became like a son to him.

When Father Latour knew that his time had come to die, he asked to be taken into town to spend his last days near the cathedral. On the last day of his life the church was filled with people who came to pray for him, as word that he was dying spread through the town. He died in the still twilight, and the cathedral bell, tolling in the early darkness, carried to the waiting countryside the news that at last death had come for Father Latour.